# Building a Multiethnic Military in Post-Yugoslav Bosnia and Herzegovina

# Building a Multiethnic Military in Post-Yugoslav Bosnia and Herzegovina

Elliot Short

BLOOMSBURY ACADEMIC
LONDON • NEW YORK • OXFORD • NEW DELHI • SYDNEY

BLOOMSBURY ACADEMIC
Bloomsbury Publishing Plc
50 Bedford Square, London, WC1B 3DP, UK
1385 Broadway, New York, NY 10018, USA
29 Earlsfort Terrace, Dublin 2, Ireland

BLOOMSBURY, BLOOMSBURY ACADEMIC and the Diana logo are
trademarks of Bloomsbury Publishing Plc

First published in Great Britain 2022

Cover image: Bosnian soldiers board a US airforce plane 01 June 2005, at Sarajevo
airport. The 36-men unit, trained in unexploded ordnance removal will join the
US-led forces in Iraq. © Elvis Barukcic/Afp Via Getty Images.

A catalogue record for this book is available from the British Library.

A catalog record for this book is available from the Library of Congress.

ISBN: HB: 978-1-3501-9093-1
ePDF: 978-1-3501-9094-8
eBook: 978-1-3501-9095-5

Typeset by Newgen KnowledgeWorks Pvt. Ltd., Chennai, India

To find out more about our authors and books visit www.bloomsbury.com
and sign up for our newsletters.

# Contents

# Figures

# Maps

# Foreword

When Elliot interviewed me a few years ago, I did not imagine that I would one day be writing the foreword to his book. I am pleased to be doing so: the development of Armed Forces of Bosnia and Herzegovina is worth examination, both in its own right as a piece of history and as a source of broadly applicable lessons. Elliot has captured both elements effectively, bringing fresh perspective and extracting lessons of interest to defence and security sector reform practitioners.

My involvement with the Armed Forces of Bosnia and Herzegovina began one morning early in 2003. I was in my office at 5 Combat Engineer Regiment in Valcartier, Quebec, when the telephone rang. A voice from National Defence Headquarters in Ottawa asked whether I would be interested in a one-year secondment to the Office of the High Representative in Sarajevo. I had no idea what a High Representative was, so I temporised and promised to ring back the following day with my response.

The Canadian Army in those days had not yet seen fit to provide internet access on all of its workstations, so I rang my wife, Maggie, who conducted some expedited research. When I got home she informed me that the High Representative was responsible for the implementation of civilian aspects of the Dayton Peace Accords, and that the Office of the High Representative included a Military Advisor, supported by several staff officers, one of whom was Canadian. I happened to know him, and the next day I sent a brief email: what exactly was he doing, and would I like it? His response was equally brief: he was helping to build an army, and yes, I would like it. I rang Ottawa and said 'Yes'.

On a sunny Sunday afternoon six months later, newly arrived in Sarajevo, I installed myself in a sidewalk café on the street known to many as 'Sniper Alley', and opened the dark blue cover of a thick report. 'The Path to Partnership for Peace' was a detailed proposal for placing the entity armies under a single chain of command.

As I sipped my coffee, I could see the Holiday Inn a short distance to the west across a patch of waste ground, diagonally opposite the parliament building. When war came to Sarajevo in April 1992, two of the anti-war protestors around parliament were killed by shots fired from the Holiday Inn. There was a plaque to their memory, affixed to a bridge a short distance to the south, down the street to my left. Shortly after they died, that section of the river became part of the front line between the two armies that the authors of the report proposed to unite. It was an ambitious undertaking: less than eight years earlier, those armies had made the intersection where I was sitting one of the most dangerous places in the world. It would be an interesting way to spend a year.

As it turned out, by the time Maggie and I left Sarajevo, it had been our home for roughly the same amount of time that the Armed Forces of Bosnia and Herzegovina had been in existence: sixteen years. My first major task, in the autumn of 2003, had been to conduct a week-long workshop during which the structure of the new Ministry of Defence, Joint Staff, and Operational Command were drafted. My last major task, in the summer of 2019, had been to produce a comprehensive political and security analysis of BiH, encompassing the Armed Forces of Bosnia and Herzegovina among other factors.

During the intervening years I had somehow become a person whom diligent researchers sought to interview. Many of them asked what I had learned. I typically listed the standard lessons: buy-in from all parties, grudging or otherwise; facilitation, support, and if required pressure from a united and consistent international community; cultural awareness and understanding; a suitably comprised and adequately resourced staff to keep the wheels turning; and so on.

Elliot, wisely, asked me instead to write about things that often 'get lost in the scholarship'. So here are the things that I learned during my long relationship with the Armed Forces of Bosnia and Herzegovina, its Ministry of Defence, a constellation of BiH political and institutional actors, and an alphabet soup of international community organisations.

*Strategy is an abused word.* Large organisations engaged in defence and security sector reform are as vulnerable to management imperatives as any other. They must have their strategies and plans, and they must assess results against criteria of some sort. As practitioner one must participate in these time-consuming processes in order to keep the interest, influence, support, and resources flowing. They can also be useful tools with which to educate upwards. However, the actual work of defence and security sector reform is improvised jazz, not symphonic music.

In the case of the Armed Forces of Bosnia and Herzegovina, the strategic work was done by the Defence Reform Commission in its two reports: 2003, 'The Path to Partnership for Peace'; 2005, 'The AFBiH: A Single Military Force for the 21st Century'. Everything else was, and is, implementation. In that context it is critical to remember the strategic objective, but to remain flexible on how to get there.

Practitioners should be agile, responsive, and persistent. They should be able to identify and exploit opportunities to make progress even when it means making radical changes to best-laid plans. In an ideal world, organisations would provide the tools and leave it to the practitioners on the ground to decide when and how to use them. In the real world the conditions imposed by organisational structures and processes are often more of a hindrance to progress than so-called 'spoilers'.

*Expertise matters less than one might think.* I arrived in Sarajevo with a fresh MA in War Studies that was peripherally relevant to my new job, a long-distant BSc that was not, and no experience at ministry or national military headquarters level. This proved far less problematic than I had anticipated. There is certainly a role for technical expertise, for example, in designing the nuts and bolts of personnel management or procurement systems, and for specialists such as lawyers. However, the overarching need is for generalists who have a reasonable amount of civilian or uniformed experience in the defence and security sector, and who can work with local and international experts to break the big tasks into smaller bites, to synchronise diverse work-streams, to identify and exploit opportunities, and to keep the show on the road.

*Relationships are the fruit of years, not months.* This, at least, was something I had learned before arriving in BiH. I had spent a year as an embedded advisor in a demining unit of the Cambodian Mine Action Centre. It had taken most of that year to get to the point where my Khmer counterparts would tell me what was really on their minds. In many cases they simply did not see the point of getting to know yet another one-year visitor. With this in mind I worked hard to get to know the people with whom I would be working, both from BiH and from the international community. I soon learned to distinguish between work that could be handled by short-term visitors, such as technical training or data analysis, and work that could not really begin until a few years had been invested in learning the environment and building relationships.

As my sojourn in BiH extended, first by one year, then another year, and then indefinitely, I too became relatively disinterested in new experts who would be gone in a year or less. Conversely, as my BiH counterparts saw me year after year, they became increasingly more willing to tell me what was really going on, trusting my discretion because I had proved to be discreet. Seeing that I was not going anywhere, and knowing that Maggie and I had made our home in BiH, they took the time to educate me, to listen to me, to assess my ideas frankly, and to bring their ideas to me. My effectiveness grew exponentially as the years passed, as did my confidence that I had penetrated at least a few layers below the surface.

It is unlikely that many practitioners will have the opportunity or desire to spend sixteen years in one place, or indeed a spouse who is interested in moving semi-permanently to such a place, but anything less than a few years is insufficient.

*Your way is not the best way*. It is tempting to fall back upon what one knows, and there is no harm in starting from there. However, copying and pasting from a given national system is both lazy and futile. External ideas are useful only insofar as they guide the development of sustainable local solutions. If a practitioner holds up their national system as the exemplar, in effect claiming innate superiority, they are unlikely to gain meaningful support from the other side of the table.

*Do not preach*. The people on the other side of the table live in the national system. They are not insulated from it; they do not have the scope to depart radically from it; and they are in many cases under real pressure to conform. This can begin with attempted bribery and extend to career damage, consequences to family members, and physical harm. When faced with resistance from counterparts, remember that they are the people who actually have something precious to lose or gain. Rather than preaching at them, one should seek to understand their situation and genuinely seek ways to gain their cooperation by addressing their concerns.

The real lesson that I learned in BiH is that there are real lives behind the dry term 'defence and security sector reform', and real people involved in the process – some for, some against. I hope that the reader will keep these human considerations in mind while reaping the benefits of Elliot's well-researched and well-presented analysis of an institution close to my heart: the Armed Forces of Bosnia and Herzegovina.

Rohan Maxwell

# Acknowledgements

This book is the product of a journey which began in September 2014, when I left the UK for Sarajevo. I spent over two years living in a house, still scarred with damage from the siege, in the old Bistrik neighbourhood of the city. I became fast friends with my neighbours, who welcomed me into their lives with curiosity and heartfelt kindness. My time there was split between learning the local language, conducting fieldwork, interning with a Bosnian security think tank, and travelling around the wider region. Converting that work into this book represents the final chapter of the journey.

First, I must thank the scholars and students who have helped to shape this manuscript and my understanding of the Western Balkans. These include Richard Mills, Cathie Carmichael, Chris Jones, James Gow, Catherine Baker, John Paul Newman, as well as my good friends Andrew Seaton, Matt Webber, and Charles Beacroft. The insights and support you have all offered over the years are much appreciated! One of the great strengths of this book is the material I gained from interviews. I would like to thank Bojan Dimitrijević, Raffi Gregorian, Denis Hadžović, and Trevor Minter for offering me their wisdom and time. The insights they have given me have proven invaluable. I am also indebted to the late Paddy Ashdown. When I asked to discuss his time in Bosnia and Herzegovina, he generously invited me to his London home and enthusiastically spoke of his time as High Representative. When he discovered that I lived in Sarajevo and enjoyed walking the same mountains that he had walked, the delight on his face made it evident how deeply he cared for Bosnia and Herzegovina. Paddy sadly died just weeks before I could send him my completed dissertation, but I will always appreciate the time he spared for my work. Rohan Maxwell has an unrivalled depth of knowledge and understanding of many of the topics I explore in the book. He was kind enough to invite me to NATO Headquarters Sarajevo to discuss the subject and helped to provide an extra layer of depth that would have simply been unavailable to most researchers. I am thankful and very proud that he agreed to write the foreword to this book.

My heartfelt thanks go to the people who shared their lives with me during two years of fieldwork in the region: Miles Atkinson, Rik Bennendijk, Saša Buljević, Ben Cunningham, Dino Hakalović, Dakota Hall, Zlatan Halilović, Kate Llewellyn, Leni Mueller, Salih Palo, Dino Pečar, Amir Redžić, Ruth Rist, Katie Ryken, Maxim Sant'Orsala, Edin Sulejmanović, Hannah Wade, and Jonny Wrate. I am also incredibly grateful for the kindness and generosity of Jack Allen, Tim Bowers and family, Matthew Baseden Butt, Joe Currie, Alex Doak, Oliver Dunham, Rob and Charlotte Gow, Charlie Horne, Josh Keane, Axel Kohnen, Tom Livesey, Rob Moss, Beth Quinn, Patrick Sutton and Millie Pearce, Laura Swain, and Ben Thomas. Finally, I would like to express my gratitude to my partner, Chantelle Cohen, and my parents, Denise and

Galvin. Without their encouragement, patience, and support none of this would have been possible. There really are not enough words to describe how grateful I am. Last, but by no means least, I would never be forgiven if I did not mention my faithful canine companion, Jeka. We met on my first day in Sarajevo and years later I brought him back to the UK. *Hvala drug*!

# Abbreviations

| | |
|---|---|
| APC | Armoured Personnel Carrier |
| APZB | *Autonomna Pokrajina Zapadna Bosna* (Autonomous Province of Western Bosnia) |
| ARBiH | *Armija Republike Bosne i Hercegovine* (Army of the Republic of Bosnia and Herzegovina) |
| AVNOJ | *Antifašističko vijeće narodnog oslobođenja Jugoslavije* (Antifascist Council of the National Liberation of Yugoslavia) |
| BCMS | The Bosnian, Croatian, Montenegrin, and Serbian language |
| BiH | *Bosna i Hercegovina* (Bosnia and Herzegovina) |
| BIHCON-1 | Bosnia and Herzegovina Contribution One |
| BOV | *Borbeno oklopno vozilo* (Armoured Personnel Carrier) |
| CIA | Central Intelligence Agency |
| CSS | Centre for Security Studies, BiH |
| DAP | *Demokratska alijansa za promjene* (Democratic Alliance for Change) |
| DPA | Dayton Peace Agreement |
| DRC | Defence Reform Commission |
| EC | European Community |
| ECMM | European Community Monitoring Mission |
| EU | European Union |
| EUFOR | European Union Force |
| EUTM RCA | European Union Training Mission in the Central African Republic |
| FBiH | *Federacija Bosne i Hercegovine* (Federation of Bosnia and Herzegovina) |
| GDP | Gross Domestic Product |
| HB | Herceg-Bosna |
| HDZ | *Hrvatska demokratska zajednica* (Croat Democratic Union) |
| HOS | *Hrvatske obrambene snage* (Croat Defence Forces) |
| HSP | *Hrvatske stranke prava* (Croat Party of Rights) |
| HSS | *Hrvatska seljačka stranka* (Croat Peasants' Party) |
| HV | *Hrvatska vojska* (Croatian Army) |
| HVO | *Hrvatsko vijeće obrane* (Croat Defence Council) |
| ICTY | International Criminal Tribunal for the former Yugoslavia |
| IFOR | Implementation Force |
| IISS | International Institute for Strategic Studies |
| ISAF | International Security Assistance Force |
| JA | *Jugoslovenska armija* (Yugoslav Army) |
| JKV | *Jugoslovenska kraljevska vojska* (Yugoslav Royal Army) |
| JNA | *Jugoslovenska narodna armija* (Yugoslav People's Army) |
| KPJ | *Komunistička partija Jugoslavije* (Communist Party of Yugoslavia) |

| | |
|---|---|
| k.u.k. Army | *kaiserlich und königlich Armee* (Imperial and Royal Army) |
| MAP | Membership Action Plan |
| MDNG | Maryland National Guard |
| MONUC | *Mission de l'Organisation des Nations Unies en République démocratique du Congo* (United Nations Mission in the Democratic Republic of Congo) |
| MONUSCO | *Mission de l'Organisation des Nations Unies pour la stabilisation en République démocratique du Congo* (United Nations Organization Stabilization Mission in the Democratic Republic of the Congo) |
| MPRI | Military Professional Resources, Incorporated |
| MUP | *Ministarstvo unutrašnjih poslova* (Ministry of the Interior) |
| NATO | North Atlantic Treaty Organisation |
| NCO | Non-Commissioned Officer |
| NEL-1 | NATO Evaluation Level 1 |
| NGO | Non-governmental Organisation |
| NOP | *Narodnooslobodilački pokret* (National Liberation Movement) |
| NOVJ | *Narodnooslobodilačka vojska Jugoslavije* (National Liberation Army of Yugoslavia) |
| NPA | Norwegian People's Aid |
| OHR | Office of the High Representative |
| ONO | *Opštenarodna odbrana* (Total National Defence) |
| OSBiH | *Oružane snage Bosne i Hercegovine* (Armed Forces of Bosnia and Herzegovina) |
| OSCE | Organisation for Security and Cooperation in Europe |
| OSRBiH | *Oružane snage Republike Bosne i Herzegovine* (Armed Forces of the Republic of Bosnia and Herzegovina) |
| PfP | Partnership for Peace |
| PIC | Peace Implementation Council |
| PII | Partnership Interoperability Initiative |
| PL | *Patriotska liga* (Patriotic League) |
| PSOTC | Peace Support Operations Training Centre |
| RS | *Republika Srpska* (Serb Republic) |
| RSK | *Republika Srpska Krajina* (Serb Republic of Krajina) |
| SAO | *Srpska autonomna oblast* (Serb Autonomous Regions) |
| SCMM | Standing Committee on Military Matters |
| SDA | *Stranka demokratse akcije* (Party of Democratic Action) |
| SDB | *Služba državne bezbednosti* (State Security Service) |
| SDS | *Srpska demokratska stranka* (Serb Democratic Party) |
| SEL-1 | Self-Assessment Level 1 |
| SFOR | Stabilisation Force |
| SFRJ | *Socijalistička federativna Republika Jugoslavije* (Socialist Federal Republic of Yugoslavia) |
| SKJ | *Savez komunista Jugoslavije* (League of Communists of Yugoslavia) |
| SNSD | *Savez nezavisnih socijaldemokrata* (Alliance of Independent Social Democrats) |

| | |
|---|---|
| SPP | State Partnership Program |
| SRBiH | *Srpska Republika Bosna i Hercegovine* (Serb Republic of Bosnia and Herzegovina) |
| SRJ | *Savezna Republika Jugoslavija* (Federal Republic of Yugoslavia)SVK *Srpska vojska krajine* (Serb Army of Krajina) |
| TO | *Teritorijalna odbrana* (Territorial Defence) |
| TORBiH | *Teritorijalna odbrana Republike Bosne i Herzegovine* (Territorial Defence of the Republic of Bosnia and Herzegovina) |
| UN | United Nations |
| UNMEE | United Nations Mission in Ethiopia and Eritrea |
| UNMIBH | United Nations Mission in Bosnia and Herzegovina |
| USSR | Union of Soviet Socialist Republics |
| UXO | Unexploded Ordnance |
| VF | *Vojska federacije* (Army of the Federation) |
| VJ | *Vojska Jugoslavije* (Army of Yugoslavia) |
| VL | *Vojna linija* (Military Line) |
| VRS | *Vojska Republike Srpske* (Army of Republika Srpska) |
| ŽRS | *Žandarmerija Republike Srpske* (Gendarmerie of Republika Srpska) |

# Introduction

On 1 January 2006, the Armed Forces of Bosnia and Herzegovina (*Oružane snage Bosne i Hercegovine*, OSBiH) officially entered service. The emergence of this new, multiethnic military came just over a decade after a long and bloody war divided the majority of the Bosnian population along ethnic lines, both politically and geographically. Upon its formation, the OSBiH became the largest multiethnic institution in Bosnia and Herzegovina (*Bosna i Hercegovina*, BiH), and ever since its architects have held the military integration process as a model for the rest of Bosnian society to follow.[1] Much of BiH has remained divided since the Dayton Peace Agreement (DPA) ended the war in December 1995. State-level governance remains largely deadlocked, while economic stagnation and falling standards of living continue to drive population decline. It is in this challenging political climate that the Bosnian military has quietly been strengthening itself as an institution, and BiH as a state.

Since 2001, Bosnian troops have served on multilateral operations around the world alongside soldiers from a host of other armed forces, first as individual military observers in the United Nations Mission in Eritrea and Ethiopia (UNMEE). Then, in 2005, a thirty-six-person Unexploded Ordnance (UXO) Disposal Team was deployed alongside US forces in Iraq, representing the first entire OSBiH unit to serve in an active operational environment. Since then, Bosnian soldiers have worked with North Atlantic Treaty Organisation (NATO) forces in Afghanistan, European Union (EU) personnel in the Central African Republic, and United Nations (UN) peacekeepers in the Democratic Republic of Congo, Eritrea, Ethiopia, and Mali. The personnel who are sent on such missions reflect the diversity of the Bosnian population, with Bosnian Croat, Bosnian Serb, and Bosniak (Bosnian Muslims in the ethnic sense) soldiers being equally represented in deployed units. The UXO team deployed to Iraq, for example, was composed of twelve troops from each constituent people.[2] Serving alongside more experienced armed forces presents an excellent opportunity for Bosnian troops to develop their capabilities, while also contributing to the institutional identity and cohesion of the OSBiH. Since the OSBiH entered service, over 1,600 Bosnian troops have served on multilateral operations. Through its participation in such operations, the OSBiH has earned itself a good reputation, as this report from the independent Bosnian think tank Centre for Security Studies (CSS) makes clear:

> The participation of members from BiH in peace support operations has been rated positively and they can be seen as ambassadors of their country. Their

outstanding achievements attracted the attention of world media through various events on missions where they participated, and were rewarded with recognition by the UN, NATO, and local governments.[3]

Since its formation, the OSBiH has been a partner of the Maryland National Guard through the US Department of Defense State Partnership Program. In this time, thousands of soldiers from across BiH have deployed on training exercises together and participated in events with their counterparts from Maryland, further enhancing their professionalism.[4] Additional international assistance has been provided to the OSBiH from the British Embassy in Sarajevo, which since 2013 has sponsored an initiative to rejuvenate the 'ageing' OSBiH officer corps by 'identifying the best young leaders from the civilian post-graduate sector' and establishing the 'best possible model for selecting and training' the next generation of Bosnian military leaders.[5] The result of these activities is an increasingly capable and professional military which is viewed as a reliable partner by the officers and soldiers of other armed forces. The successful development of the OSBiH was recognised by the leadership of NATO in December 2018, when they formally invited BiH to take the final steps required for the fulfilment of its Membership Action Plan (MAP). Once the MAP is complete, BiH will be ready to join NATO as a full member state if the political consensus to do so can be found.[6]

The path to NATO membership has not been smooth, with progress towards accession stalling entirely for almost a decade prior to December 2018. Since NATO offered its invitation, the issue has dominated domestic politics in BiH, with parliamentary deadlock over how to respond to the invitation causing a fourteen-month delay in the formation of a national government following elections in October 2018.[7] An administration was finally formed in December 2019 after the relevant Bosnian parties agreed to send a document known as the 'Reform Programme' to NATO in place of the more controversial Annual National Plan required to complete the MAP. Given that the political parties in BiH that are most opposed to NATO membership remain committed to impeding accession and have a proven record of successfully doing so, there is no guarantee that the MAP of BiH will ever be completed.[8]

The debate surrounding BiH's accession to NATO is far from being the only matter keeping the military at the centre of Bosnian politics. In 2017, uniformed Bosnian Serb soldiers of the OSBiH attended a parade celebrating the formation of the Bosnian Serb entity in BiH, Republika Srpska (RS), in defiance of a Bosnian government declaration that such action was unconstitutional.[9] More recently, RS President Milorad Dodik (now the Bosnian Serb member of the state-level presidency) called for Bosnian Serb troops to wear their old wartime uniforms during ceremonies, rather than the standard-issue ones inspired by those worn in the US military.[10] Furthermore, current estimates suggest that the RS administration has built up an arsenal of weaponry, largely imported from Russia, including enough automatic rifles to arm 'roughly 75 percent of its [5,238-strong] police with Kalashnikov-type firearms', and is even rumoured to have procured Igla 1-V anti-aircraft missiles.[11] In 2019, an armed gendarmerie (replete with sniper rifles and armoured vehicles) was established within the framework of the RS police and, more recently, the entity purchased its fifth helicopter. In this climate, in which the very existence of BiH is regularly questioned, simple processes such as providing state-level institutions with the resources that they require remain contentious.

To properly illustrate how a multiethnic army was built in such an environment, this book explores the political-military history of BiH from its emergence as a political entity in the medieval period until the present day. It charts the history of the armed forces that operated in the region prior to the emergence of an independent Bosnian state in the 1990s, before providing detailed analysis of the armies which fought in BiH during the 1992–5 war. With the origins and development of these armies in place, the book culminates with an unprecedented account of the defence reform and military integration process that created the OSBiH and an assessment of its first fifteen years of existence.

## Scope

Although primarily a historical work, this book draws on a body of research that has much broader implications. Since the violent collapse of Yugoslavia in the 1990s, most wars that have taken place around the world have been complex intra-state conflicts with many characteristics similar to the war in BiH.[12] The global response to the armed conflicts in former Yugoslavia set a precedent for international intervention which prevails to this day. Much of our contemporary understanding of peacekeeping operations and diplomatic mediation initiatives are rooted in the successes and failures witnessed in the region during the 1990s.[13] Similarly, it was events in the Western Balkans that inspired the revival of aspects of international law and justice that had lain dormant since the aftermath of the Second World War, leading to the establishment of the International Criminal Tribunal for the former Yugoslavia (ICTY) in 1993.[14] Since then, institutions such as the International Criminal Court and the Special Court for Sierra Leone have become key instruments in global initiatives to limit armed conflict.[15]

The international state-building effort that took place in post-war BiH was an unprecedented endeavour, both in terms of ambition and the scale of resources committed to it.[16] Since the international community took responsibility for constructing the institutions and processes of the post-war Bosnian state in December 1995, similar approaches have been employed in post-conflict environments around the world, with varying degrees of success. Indeed, echoes of the international response to the War in BiH can be identified in almost every society which has experienced armed conflict since.[17] Like in BiH, the integration of former belligerents into unified armed forces and the development of a professional military is often seen as the most significant step towards consolidating peace. However, unlike BiH, an estimated 60 per cent of post-conflict states relapse into war within a few years, while many of those which remain at peace experience the rise of authoritarian regimes.[18] Thus, despite the political deadlock and economic hardships that have defined the post-war period for much of the population, the construction of a peaceful, semi-functional, and democratic state in BiH represents a relatively rare success story.

This book explains this success by focusing on the construction of the OSBiH. It argues that getting military integration right was the most important step in consolidating peace in post-war BiH and provides a comprehensive account of how this was achieved. As a result, the findings and insights presented in these pages resonate far beyond the Western Balkans and can help develop and inform our global understanding of armed conflict, international intervention, and post-war state-building initiatives.

## Sources

A meaningful investigation into the complex topics tackled in this book required identifying and analysing a broad base of source material, as well as developing a nuanced understanding of the society and history of the former Yugoslavia. Furthermore, although many sources (particularly those produced after the war) have been published in English, much of the material upon which this research is based only exists in the Bosnian/Croatian/Montenegrin/Serbian language and can only be found in the region.

The cornerstone of a diverse source base is the material that was gathered from 'elite interviews' with individuals who were directly involved in the construction of the OSBiH. These include the late Lord Ashdown, a British politician who served as the international community's High Representative in BiH from May 2002 until January 2006. In this time, he was responsible for overseeing the governance of BiH and ensuring that Bosnian politicians adhered to the terms of the DPA, making him the most politically powerful individual in the country. As this book demonstrates, his ambition and vision were the key forces which led to the construction of a unified Bosnian military just a decade after the war. The practical and technical aspects of the defence reform process were carried out by various intergovernmental organisations such as NATO and the Organisation for Security and Cooperation in Europe (OSCE), which worked alongside Bosnian politicians and military personnel to build the OSBiH. One of the most significant NATO figures involved in this process was Dr Raffi Gregorian, a US State Department official who co-chaired the Defence Reform Commission which designed the OSBiH and created the blueprint for its construction. Gregorian was supported in his work by Rohan Maxwell, a Canadian officer who advised the OSCE during the defence reform process in 2003–4 before serving as NATO's Senior Political-Military Advisor in BiH until 2019. Maxwell was initially responsible for developing a model of military organisation that was affordable, practical, and acceptable to Bosnian politicians of all parties. He then spent almost fifteen years monitoring and advising on the development of the OSBiH. These three men were integral to the construction of a multiethnic military in post-Yugoslav BiH. Indeed, few other individuals can be said to have had more access to the process, making their insights invaluable. The perspectives that have been gained by interviewing such figures are complemented by lengthy conversations with a range of Bosnian politicians, scholars, and officials who played important roles in the reform and unification process.

The National and University Library of Bosnia and Herzegovina holds the majority of the archival material that was used in this book, including the official journals of every armed force which fought in the war, the memoirs of a broad range of Bosnian military and political figures as well as extensive newspaper and media records covering some key events. The National Library of Serbia offers access to a considerable collection of specialist books and documents. Many are first-hand accounts written by former military personnel and politicians, while others represent the research of leading scholars from the region. The interview transcripts of the 1995 BBC documentary *The Death of Yugoslavia*, held at the Liddell Hart Centre for Military Archives at King's College London, proved to be another invaluable resource. The collection includes extensive interviews with almost every major diplomatic, military, and political figure involved in the conflict, to the extent that many were used as evidence by the ICTY. The US Army Center for Military History in Washington, DC, also provided some excellent material such as the After-Action Reports and transcribed oral history testimonies produced by US personnel serving in the Implementation Force (IFOR) and Stabilisation Force (SFOR) – the NATO peacekeeping forces deployed to BiH after Dayton.

In the aftermath of the war, an extensive range of intergovernmental and non-governmental organisations began working in BiH. The EU, NATO, OSCE, and UN all maintained substantial missions which focused on upholding peace and driving the recovery from conflict, while countless private organisations implemented humanitarian projects and conducted research on the post-war transition in BiH. The reports, publications, and other records produced by such organisations, particularly those that operated in the security sector, provide an additional layer of excellent source material. The most noteworthy are the assessments and analysis offered by peacekeepers who were deployed to BiH, as their military expertise and unique perspectives on the conflict are particularly insightful for a book of this nature. Documents such as these are supplemented by similar reports and publications produced by various institutions of the Bosnian state, including the Ministry of Defence and the OSBiH itself. Additional material was drawn from the trials of the ICTY. The witness testimonies, legal assessments, expert analysis, and verdicts of the tribunal provide a wealth of information and insights into the conflict in BiH and the armies which fought it. The efforts of prosecutors to prove the link between the Army of Republika Srpska and the administration of Slobodan Milošević in Belgrade, for example, are particularly useful, as the details of such ties may otherwise have been lost.

## Literature

A growing body of literature explores some of the subjects and themes covered in this book. In 2002, the US Central Intelligence Agency's (CIA's) Office of Russian and European Analysis published *Balkan Battlegrounds*, an unclassified treatise based on the Agency's tracking of the conflict.[19] It remains the most comprehensive strategic analysis of the conflicts that took place in the Western Balkans during the 1990s, and also provides useful analysis of key political developments that affected the military aspects of the conflict. A more refined evaluation of these developments is presented in James Gow's *The Serbian Project and Its Adversaries*. Based on research conducted for trials at the ICTY, Gow's work provides an authoritative account of the complex machinations and key events of the disintegration of Yugoslavia, illustrating the complex dynamics of power and influence which guided the conflicts.[20] Marko Attila Hoare's *How Bosnia Armed* offers a detailed study of how the Bosnian government, facing an international arms embargo and a much more powerful foe, managed to raise and equip an army during the war.[21] Kenneth Morrison explores the conflict from a range of unique perspectives, highlighting the significance of the Holiday Inn in Sarajevo throughout the war, for example, adding important detail to our understanding of this complex period.[22] A considerable number of volumes have been published by participants and witnesses of the war. Indeed, most leading political and military protagonists from all sides of the conflict have published diaries or memoirs from the period. Some of the most insightful contemporary accounts, however, come from observers rather than participants, such as war correspondent Anthony Loyd, who reported from BiH for most of the conflict. The reflections he offers in *My War Gone By, I Miss It So* portray many complexities of the conflict that are often overlooked, particularly the trials and tribulations of ordinary people.[23] The head of the European Community Monitoring Mission deployed to wartime BiH, Colm Doyle, provides a similarly insightful commentary on political developments in the first years of the conflict based on his observations from meetings and investigations as a peacekeeper.[24] Catherine Baker surveys much of the literature on the conflicts that took place in the region in *The Yugoslav Wars of the 1990s*, offering a wide range of valuable perspectives and revealing some of the key debates in the field.[25]

Considerable scholarship has focused on the DPA and its implementation. Many of the facilitators and signatories of the agreement produced publications which illustrate their perspectives, while the implementation of the agreement has been analysed by countless political scientists and NGOs.[26] Christopher Bennett's *Bosnia's Paralysed Peace* offers the most comprehensive analysis of the efforts to stabilise BiH in this period.[27] Post-war defence reform has been the subject of more focused studies, with *Destination NATO: Defence Reform in Bosnia and Herzegovina*, written by Rohan Maxwell and John Andreas Olsen, providing the most detailed account of this process.[28] An excellent overview is also offered in *Military Integration after Civil Wars*, in which Florence Gaub examines the case of BiH alongside other examples of post-conflict defence reform.[29]

This book navigates these established works, drawing on many key ideas and observations but ultimately providing something distinct. None of the existing literature assesses the military history of BiH as an integral whole, and very little research has considered the impact that armed forces had on the creation and development of states and identities as Yugoslavia collapsed. The findings presented in the final part also represent previously uncharted territory for historians, and thus offer unique and unprecedented insights into this complex period of Bosnian history.

## The Military

The military is a key component of a state. Indeed, according to sociologist Charles Tilly, the emergence and development of the military and the state are wholly intertwined, with the demands of maintaining standing armies directly driving the creation of the state: 'It did so both because an army became a significant organisation within the state and because its construction and maintenance brought complementary organisations – treasuries, supply services, mechanisms for conscription, tax bureaux, and much more – into life.'[30] Max Weber, who ruminated on the nature of the state long before Tilly, defines the state as a 'compulsory political association with continuous organisation' whose 'administrative staff successfully upholds a claim to the monopoly of the legitimate use of physical force.'[31] In other words, as Francis Fukuyama suggests, 'the essence of stateness is enforcement: the ability, ultimately, to send someone with a uniform and a gun to force people to comply with the state's laws.'[32] Thus, at its simplest, the military should be understood as the armed force of a state which serves to enforce its policies and laws.

The Roman satirist Juvenal asked, 'Quis custodiet ipsos custodes?' (Who will guard the guardians?) in the first century.[33] His question has been considered in the context of armed forces ever since, with many scholars puzzling over the dilemma of how to ensure that the military serves the state and does not simply seize power for itself. Samuel Finer suggests:

> Instead of asking why the military engage in politics, we ought surely to ask why they ever do otherwise. For at first sight the political advantages of the military vis-a-vis other civilian groupings are overwhelming. The military possess vastly superior organisation. And they possess arms.[34]

He proposes that the key to preventing military involvement in politics is to create a professional military class, over which objective military control is achieved by 'militarizing the military, making them the tool of the state.'[35] He views a professional officer as someone 'who pursues a "higher calling" in the service of society', defining their professionalism as being earned through expertise, responsibility and corporateness.[36] According to Samuel Huntington, the key task of an officer is limited to the 'management of violence', while the function of a professional military is simply achieving 'successful armed combat'.[37] This definition is expanded by Anthony Forster, Timothy Edmunds, and Andrew Cottey, who state that professional armed forces are those which

> accept that their role is to fulfil the demands of the civilian government of the state and are capable of undertaking military activities in an effective and efficient way, and whose organisation and internal structures reflect these assumptions.[38]

Huntington suggests that 'the inherent quality of a military body can only be evaluated in terms of independent military standards. The ends for which the military is employed, however, are outside its competence to judge.'[39] Such thinking clearly disabuses the military of any role or accountability in the social and political aspects of the society which it serves. This detachment is the result of one key assumption, summarised by Thomas-Durrell Young:

> There are key requisites, however, that legitimate the use of force and violence by a soldier in a democracy: force and violence are employed only in a rational way, for a public purpose and with public consent.[40]

This professional and militarised model of the military has prevailed, to varying degrees, in most NATO member states and many other developed democracies. For many other states, however, a 'political' (or 'praetorian') military is often not just tolerated but encouraged.[41]

Kees Koonings and Dirk Kruijt define 'political' militaries as 'those institutions that consider involvement in – or control over – domestic politics and the business of government to be a central part of their legitimate function'.[42] William Odom highlights, for example, the relationship between Soviet military leaders and the Communist Party, noting that the military was in fact an administrative arm of the party, most of the military elite were party members, and civil and military activities were interlinked in fields such as industry, education, and regional administration.[43] Odom also questions Huntington's definition of professionalism, arguing that much of the expertise needed for a modern military has civilian counterparts, such as technical and medical professionals, and that 'one seldom finds a military establishment that is effectively bound by a comprehensive professional ethic'.[44] Indeed, Odom takes issue with many assumptions regarding the military, stating, 'One finds that these establishments are highly politicised institutions as diverse as the polities to which they belong. They are no easier to fit into a global model than the polities themselves.'[45]

Florence Gaub argues that the military is 'intentionally or unintentionally, a part of the wider social system' and thus exerts an influence on society regardless of whether it is intended to be political or not.[46] In divided societies, the military can serve as an institutional source of cohesion and unity for an otherwise disparate population, thereby helping to maintain stability. Zoltan Barany highlights the example of Iraq, noting that

> while the Ba'ath regime was uniformly hated in Kurdistan and amongst the population in southern Iraq, the military – a conscript army with a large proportion of Shia Muslim draftees and Sunni officers – had enjoyed considerable sympathy and respect in the rest of the country.[47]

Following the 2003 invasion, the Coalition Provisional Authority issued Authority Order No. 2, disbanding the Iraqi military entirely. Barany argues that this decision left a 'security and public safety vacuum; produced a large pool of trained, armed, humiliated, and desperate men for whom joining the anti-American insurgency became a logical choice; and destroyed the only national institution in a deeply divided society'.[48] The ensuing chaos has been well documented, but after almost two decades of international efforts to rebuild a functioning state and military, the security situation has deteriorated to the point where the viability of Iraq is in question.

The case of Iraq highlights how the military is often the only state institution which spans a multiethnic society. Indeed, as Alon Peled points out: 'Throughout history, most military organisations have been multi-ethnic in nature, and this phenomenon is even more common in the post-soviet era.'[49] Recruitment into the armed forces of such states presents something of a quandary, commonly referred to as the 'Trojan Horse' dilemma, which can be summarised in one simple question: 'If recruited, trained, and armed, will ethnic soldiers become loyal soldiers or dangerous saboteurs?'[50] In this context, ethnicity must be understood as adaptable and fluid; however, Cynthia Enloe offers this concise definition of the term: 'An ethnic group is, at root, a collectivity whose members share a belief in a common heritage which is, in turn, legitimated and sustained through cultural expression.'[51]

Echoes of Enloe's words can be identified in the work of Benedict Anderson, who just a few years later offered his infamous definition of the nation. He states, 'It is an imagined political community – and imagined as both inherently limited and sovereign.'[52] He elaborates that 'it is *imagined* [emphasis in original] because the members of even the smallest nation will never know most of their fellow-members, meet them, or even hear of them, yet in the minds of each lives the image of their communion.'[53] Eric Hobsbawm contends that whilst modern nations claim to be 'natural human communities' which are 'rooted in the remotest antiquity', they are in fact composed of constructs such as 'fairly recent symbols' and 'suitably tailored discourse' such as national history, and therefore represent the 'invention of tradition'.[54] By such a definition, nationality, like ethnicity, becomes an extremely fluid concept, the boundaries of which can expand or contract, both spatially and temporally, based on how they are invented and imagined.

In the context of Yugoslavia and BiH, an official lexicon developed which continues to inform the discussion around national identity. The architects of the Socialist Federal Republic of Yugoslavia (*Socijalistička federativna Republika Jugoslavija*, SFRJ) utilised two designations for identity: *narodi*, which translates to nations or peoples, and *narodnosti*, which means nationalities. In the framework of the SFRJ, the nations (Croats, Macedonians, Montenegrins, Serbs, Slovenes, and, from 1971, Bosnian Muslims) were represented by one of the constituent republics of the federation (Bosnia and Herzegovina, Croatia, Macedonia, Montenegro, Serbia, and Slovenia) while the nationalities enjoyed no such associations with territory. The post-war Bosnian constitution established at Dayton shares much of its vocabulary with those of Yugoslavia, with Bosniaks, Croats, and Serbs referred to as constituent nations or peoples, and groups such as Jews and Roma being considered as other nationalities.

The puzzle of how best to organise an army composed of a range of social groups has been considered for millennia, with the ancient works of Herodotus and Sun Tzu providing some of the earliest analysis of the issue.[55] Although all armed forces are unique to the states they serve and the societies from which they are built, two contrasting methods of organising multiethnic armies have developed and remain in use within militaries across the world. Gaub highlights how the military can be employed as a 'school for the nation' in which conscripts or recruits are inculcated with a form of 'official nationalism' in order to forge a cohesive fighting force. This ideology serves as an overarching identity in place of the myriad regional, ethnic, religious, and other ties that the soldiers may have. In theory, this official nationalism then disseminates throughout wider society, fostering unity and stability.[56] For example, the contemporary Lebanese Army was built in the aftermath of a long civil war (1975–90) with the express intention of fostering unity among the eighteen different religious groups from which it drew conscripts. A key priority was ensuring that the composition of the army accurately reflected Lebanese society, establishing its legitimacy as an inclusive institution and allaying fears that it would remain dominated by Marionite Christians. Within the military, however, all ethnic and regional labels were removed from army units, recruits joined mixed units and were deployed away from their homes, and the military promoted publications and events celebrating the past glories achieved by a unified Lebanon.[57] In other words, the Lebanese Army served as the lead instrument in post-war efforts to rebuild the Lebanese nation. To borrow terminology from Sabrina Ramet's exemplary analysis of the approaches with which the administration attempted to resolve the national question in socialist Yugoslavia, this method can be understood as 'Integral Organisation'.[58]

Rather than attempting to use the military to forge an overarching national identity, nineteenth-century British policymakers entrenched Irish, Scottish, and Welsh identity in the framework of the British Army alongside the proportionally dominant English by establishing distinct units, known as regiments, such as the Royal Irish, Scots Guards, and Welch Fusiliers.[59] Military service was not necessarily defined by ethnicity, with many Irish soldiers joining English regiments and many English troops serving in Scottish regiments.[60] However, each regiment celebrates the traditions and heritage of its respective namesake, carrying the appropriate symbols into battle and representing those communities during ceremonies. The Highland regiments, for example, became iconic features of Scottish identity and 'proud symbols of Scotland's ancient nationhood and of her equal partnership with England in a British Empire'.[61] In his insightful book on the regimental system, David French highlights:

> Regiments were culturally defined organisations that were bound together by shared historical memories, customs, and a myth of descent, not by the common ethnic or local origins of their members … The idea of a 'regiment' was something that was artificially constructed by the Colonels of Regiments and their senior officers. In many cases their efforts were rewarded with success.[62]

The regimental system developed for the British Army has successfully preserved the integrity of the military and the legitimacy of the state in Great Britain for centuries and has since been employed as an institutional model by armed forces across the world. To borrow again from Ramet, this method reflects 'Organic Organisation'.[63]

Viewed through the lens of identity, the military becomes an even more complex feature of society. Rather than simply a professional organisation, the military also generates the founding myths and gallant heroes of the national narrative, serving as both the protagonist in the historic trials faced by the nation and the clergy tasked with performing the sacred rituals of remembrance. Anthony D. Smith defined the nation as 'a named community possessing an historic territory, shared myths and memories, a common public culture and common laws and customs'.[64] He later argued that myths of sacrifice and war 'are particularly effective in creating the consciousness and sentiments of mutual dependence and exclusiveness, which reinforce the shared culture, memories and myths of common ancestry'.[65] Discussing Smith's work, John Hutchinson notes that warfare creates heroes and epochal events which provide 'role models and reference points especially when taken up by poets, artists and writers who embed these in the collective consciousness'.[66] He argues that 'Smith conceives of the nation in Durkheimian terms as a sacred community that elicits mass sacrifice in its defence, although he observes that nationalism and its referent, the nation, combine both secular and "religious" qualities'.[67] Smith offers an example of this 'secular religion', noting the 'many rituals and ceremonies of national remembrance for soldiers fallen in war "for their country"'.[68] He argues that at the collective level such rituals and ceremonies serve as a 'grim and solemn reminder of communal fate, of the trauma and survival of the nation in the face of its enemies and of the repeated blood sacrifice of its youth to ensure the regeneration of the nation'.[69]

Roy Licklider observes that of the peace agreements negotiated since 1989, many 'have, as a central component, provisions to merge competing armed groups in a single national army'.[70] The desire for integration is succinctly explained by Ronald Krebs and Licklider:

> The intuition appears to be that a professional, communally representative force could allay vulnerable groups' security fears by serving as a credible signal of the governments' commitment to power sharing and by keeping communal or ideological compatriots under arms. Such a force could also provide a symbolic model for the political community, allowing all to identify with a larger national project.[71]

In their book, they discuss the military integration of formerly warring groups in Rwanda, the Philippines, South Africa, the Democratic Republic of Congo, Mozambique, Bosnia and Herzegovina, Sierra Leone, and Burundi. In all cases, it was reconciling the various identities that had become polarised by conflict that posed the greatest obstacle to efforts to military integration.[72] As they note, building a military is regularly placed at the centre of initiatives to support states recovering from war, not only to provide security and stability but also to serve in the vanguard of institutional reconciliation across society as a whole.

The military must be understood as far more than an organisation created for successful armed combat. It is a key component of the state, both as an instrument of power and an expression of legitimacy. Some militaries strive for an idealised professionalism, whereby they ostensibly exist as a monolithic institution separate from the rest of society, while others actively engage in domestic politics and economic activity. Regardless of their philosophical underpinnings, all armed forces remain part of their respective social system, influencing their personnel and becoming an object of political debate and cultural expression within the societies they serve. As most states contain a diversity of ethnic groups within their populations, the military often represents the only state-wide institution in an otherwise divided society. The failure to account for this diversity with the appropriate mechanisms for recruitment and organisation can undermine the legitimacy of the military in the eyes of the population it serves, with severe repercussions for the state. The military can be employed as an instrument of nation-building, either forging new identities or institutionalising old ones. In societies recovering from war, the military also constitutes a key feature of the peace process and a barometer for the overall progress of the post-conflict transition. Utilising this wide range of perspectives highlights the extent to which the recruitment practices, symbolism, degree of civilian oversight, and methods of organisation that are used by the military are just as important for maintaining the integrity of the state as martial prowess.

## Structure

This book is divided into three chronological sections: Precursors, Components, and Construction. Part 1, containing Chapters 1 and 2, explores the various armed forces which operated in the territory that subsequently became independent BiH in the 1990s. Chapter 1 begins by establishing the origins of BiH as a political entity, before charting the broad sweeps of the region's political-military history up until the outbreak of the Second World War and assessing several Bosnian armed forces that were created in this period. This survey highlights previous multiethnic armed forces that were built from the Bosnian population, introduces many of the political ideas and constituencies that played key roles during and after the war, and places the rest of the book in its proper historical context. Chapter 2 picks up the story amid the armed struggle against the Axis occupation, mapping the development of the Yugoslav People's Army (*Jugoslovenska narodna armija*, JNA) and the territorial defence formations that supported it throughout the socialist period. All the armies that fought each other during the war and were ultimately unified in 2006 emerged from the institutions of Yugoslavia, while the JNA played a major role in the earliest phases of the conflict. Furthermore, the entire military integration process and the public conversation surrounding it was framed by the legacy of Yugoslav efforts to forge a multiethnic military, making this period vital for understanding the decisions and compromises that were made after the war. Together, these two chapters cover every antecedent armed force built on the territory that became BiH and provide essential context for understanding not just the violent disintegration of Yugoslavia but also the post-conflict environment in which the OSBiH was built.

Chapters 3 and 4 make up Part 2 of the book, Components. They provide a detailed account of the origins and wartime development of the three armies which fought each other during the war and ultimately became the components with which the OSBiH was constructed. Chapter 3 focuses on the Army of Republika Srpska (*Vojska Republike Srpske*, VRS), illustrating how a significant portion of the once inclusive and multiethnic JNA was transformed into a force for the construction of a larger Serbian state by assessing how the VRS's military capabilities, methods of organisation, and institutional identity developed throughout the war. Chapter 4 charts the rise of the VRS's main opponents, the Army of the Republic of Bosnia and Herzegovina (*Armija Republike Bosne i Hercegovine*, ARBiH) and the Croat Defence Council (*Hrvatsko vijeće obrane*, HVO), exploring how these forces were built in extremely adverse circumstances and assessing their evolution as the conflict progressed. Like the VRS, they are assessed on structure, adherence to civilian command, institutional identity, and their capabilities on the battlefield. By revealing how these armies became the foci of the efforts of their respective political leaders to build states and forge nations during the war, these chapters not only map the size and strength of these armies as organisations but also illustrate the symbolic and political value that they held among the societies that they served.

The final part of the book, Construction, offers unprecedented insights into the process of building a multiethnic military in post-conflict BiH. Based on extensive archival material and interviews with some of the key architects of the OSBiH, this section navigates the complexities of domestic politics in the region and the shifting priorities of the international community to explain exactly how the OSBiH was built. Chapter 5 explores the immediate post-war challenges faced by the armed forces in BiH, covering the creation of the Army of the Federation (*Vojska federacije*, VF) of Bosnia and Herzegovina out of the ARBiH and HVO and examining the divergent development of the VF and VRS during this period. With its focus on the years 2002–6, Chapter 6 provides a detailed account of the events, decisions, and compromises that culminated with the formation of the OSBiH. In addition, it explains the rationale behind the structures and symbols that were adopted by the new force, unveiling many of the intricate processes that together resulted in the successful integration of formerly warring armies into a single professional military. Chapter 7 reflects on the development of the OSBiH since its creation, balancing ongoing institutional development and participation in multilateral operations abroad with the pervasive division and deadlock of the Bosnian political arena.

Part 1

# Precursors

1

# The region before the Second World War

BiH is a land of densely wooded mountains and valleys in the heart of the Dinaric Alps. Its contemporary borders rise north and northwest from a slither of land on the Adriatic coast to the Pannonian Steppe, ending on the Sava and Una rivers. The eastern frontier is marked by the River Drina, which also served as the demarcation line between the Eastern and Western Roman Empires upon the death of Emperor Theodosius in 395. In the centuries that followed this division, the territory was conquered by the Ostrogoths, reconquered by the Eastern Roman Empire, and settled by the migratory Avars and Slavs, who lived alongside its Romano-Illyrian population. The Bosnian state of today is very much a child of the socialist period (1943–91), inheriting both its borders and population from the SFRJ. However, charting the broad sweeps of the region's history prior to the formation of this polity provides vital context for understanding many of the decisions, perspectives, and processes that are the focus of this book.

A diverse and multiethnic population has inhabited the territory of contemporary BiH for centuries. Owing to their position on the frontier of rival empires, this population developed a long tradition of serving in distinctly Bosnian armed forces within the framework of powerful kingdoms and empires. Exploring the history of these 'precursors' to the OSBiH offers important context for understanding its construction; however, each obviously existed within its own unique historic circumstances and was subjected to its own pressures and challenges. While understanding the political and military structures of the SFRJ is vital for making sense of the war in BiH and the post-conflict military integration process, this longer sweep of history explains how the people, armed forces, and political entities of the region developed over the centuries. In an area as diverse, complex, and contested as the Western Balkans, this history continues to shape political decisions and influence the construction and development of institutions such as the OSBiH.

## The Kingdom of Bosnia, 1377–1463

The first documented mention of Bosnia can be found in a 958 historical account written by the Byzantine Emperor Constantine Porphyrogenitus, who referred to 'Bosona' as one of his domains. Constantinople's grip on the Balkans soon waned and the territory fell under the control of the medieval kingdoms of Croatia, Serbia, and Hungary for almost two centuries. During the period of Hungarian rule, the *Banate* of Bosnia was established as a largely autonomous administrative unit governed by a *Ban* (Lord). Following the Byzantine victory over the Hungarians at the Battle of Zemun in 1167, the Banate was once again ruled by Constantinople.[1] The Bans of Bosnia were able to greatly increase their holdings throughout the fourteenth century until, in 1377, Ban Tvrtko threw off Byzantine rule and established the independent Kingdom of Bosnia (encompassing much of contemporary BiH and Serbia), before adding Dalmatia, Croatia, and Primorje to his crown in 1390.[2] Centuries of autonomy and a fleeting period of independence during the medieval period served as an incubator for unique expressions of Bosnian culture, such as the *Bosančica* alphabet and *Stećci* tombstones, as well as the development of autonomous religious traditions among its population.[3]

Less than three decades after it was established, the Kingdom of Bosnia faced its first attacks from Ottoman forces. Having swept aside resistance in Serbia in 1389 and Bulgaria in 1396, the rising Ottoman tide began to have a major influence on politics in the kingdom, with rivals for the Bosnian throne vying for influence among the powerful Catholic kingdoms to the northwest or with the growing power in the south. It was in this context that the kingdom began to fracture, with conflicts over succession leading one influential aristocrat to model himself as the *herzog* (duke) of Hum, a predominantly Orthodox region on the Adriatic coast, and establish the independent Duchy of Saint Sava in 1435. In 1446, the herzog and the king of Bosnia reconciled their differences and restored the borders of the kingdom, returning the duchy to crown control.[4] Just a few years later, the Ottomans conquered Constantinople, heralding the beginning of their rapid expansion into Europe.

## The Ottoman period, 1463–1878

Following the capture of Constantinople, the Ottomans returned to the Balkans. Serbia was conquered in 1459, Greece fell in 1460, followed by Bosnia in 1463. The Kingdom of Hungary occupied territory in northern Bosnia during the conquest to build a military frontier against the Ottomans, while the herzog managed to preserve the independence of the Duchy of Saint Sava until 1481.[5] However, following the 1526 Ottoman victory over the Hungarians at the Battle of Mohács, all the territory comprising contemporary BiH fell under the rule of the Sultan. Just three years later, the Ottoman army was at the gates of Vienna, and by 1541, the Kingdom of Hungary had been conquered, leaving Bosnia in the provincial hinterland of a tri-continental empire.[6] The introduction of rule by the Porte (the traditional name for the imperial Ottoman government in Constantinople) brought with it sweeping changes to Bosnian society. The territory was administratively divided into three *sanjaks*: the land ruled by the herzog became the Sanjak of Herzegovina, while the rest of the kingdom was divided into the Sanjak of Bosnia and the Sanjak of Zvornik. From 1580, the *sanjaks* roughly comprising the territory of contemporary BiH were administratively unified as the *Eyalet* of Bosnia, establishing a Bosnian political entity that stood for almost three centuries.[7]

The Kingdom of Bosnia (1377–1463) was populated by a complex mix of communities that developed over centuries of conquest and migration, the majority of whom worshipped in the local Catholic tradition.[8] Disputes over religious practices within this tradition represented something of an existing confessional division in Bosnia; however, the introduction of Ottoman rule gave Bosnian society the complex, multifaceted character it has retained until the present day. Following the conquest, mosques and madrassas were built across the *Eyalet* and growing numbers of Bosnians converted to Islam, with new adherents being spared from certain taxes and rising to positions of power and influence among the ruling elite as the Ottoman *millet* system was established in Bosnia.[9] The system stratified the population into broad confessional groupings, or *millets*, with Muslim landowners being entitled to certain privileges, predominantly Muslim soldiers and civil servants enjoying a comfortable status in the middle of society, and peasants of all faiths at the bottom, but still enjoying certain rights, such as communal autonomy and freedom of worship.[10] Combined with the long-standing Ottoman policy of promoting tolerance and stability in the empire, the administrative and social framework built by the Porte allowed Bosnia to become home to an increasingly diverse and prosperous society.[11] At the end of the fifteenth century, thousands of Sephardic Jews fleeing the inquisitions on the Iberian Peninsula found sanctuary in the relatively peaceful mountains of Bosnia and chose to settle there.[12]

Although Christians of all denominations were free to worship under Ottoman rule, followers of the Orthodox Church enjoyed a relatively privileged position within the empire. This was partly due to the fact that the Patriarch had his seat in Constantinople, and thus represented an institution within the purview of the Porte, while the frequent wars between the Ottomans and the Catholic monarchies of Europe meant those within the empire who looked to Rome for spiritual guidance were rarely trusted to the same degree.[13] This unique position granted the Orthodox population access to the powerful institutions of the Porte. Beginning almost immediately after the conquest, the Ottomans introduced the *devşirme* system to incorporate new subjects into the mechanisms of state. This entailed taking young Orthodox boys to Constantinople, converting them to Islam, and training them as civil servants or elite janissary soldiers. The janissaries served across the empire, including their homelands, and as early as 1488 (twenty-five years after the conquest), the *Eyalet* of Bosnia was administered by a Bosnian governor trained in the capital.[14] Many Bosnians rose to the highest offices in the land; indeed, during the sixteenth and seventeenth centuries, nine grand viziers (the equivalent of prime minister) of the empire hailed from Bosnia, including the infamous Mehmed-paša Sokolović.[15] Such was the extent of Balkan influence among the janissaries and within the institutions of the Porte that 'Slavonic' was described as the third language of the empire, after Turkish and Arabic.[16]

Orthodox subjects could find a degree of standing and status defending the empire along its lengthy borders. The territory of northern and western Bosnia, for example, was demarcated as a military frontier by the Ottoman administration to serve as a buffer against hostile incursions by its European neighbours. This entailed providing land and subsidies for militarily capable Orthodox subjects to settle in the area, in return for which they were expected to guard the frontier from incursion, monitor the border, and mount raids against the enemies of the Porte. While much of the Ottoman armed forces were only mobilised every few decades for large campaigns, these frontier troops fought almost every year (largely against their fellow Orthodox frontiersmen in service to the Austrians), making them the 'most feared element in the Ottoman military machine'.[17]

For much of the seventeenth century, the *Eyalet* of Bosnia served as a staging ground for ongoing conflicts with Austria and Venice, absorbing not just the considerable financial and material costs of such endeavours, but also eventually becoming a battleground itself. The failed 1683 Ottoman attempt to capture Vienna marked the high-water mark of the empire in Europe. In the ensuing years, the Sultan's armies (in which many Bosnians served) were driven from Hungary and Croatia, bringing with them up to 130,000 predominantly Muslim refugees, many of whom settled in Bosnia.[18] The following year, an Austrian army struck deep into Ottoman territory, temporarily occupying Belgrade and the surrounding area, and, in 1697, a force led by Prince Eugene of Savoy plundered Sarajevo after defeating the Ottoman army at the Battle of Szenta in southern Hungary.[19] While such incursions were temporary, they inspired a complete re-evaluation of Bosnia's position and role in the Ottoman Empire.

With its European ambitions curtailed and the presence of an emboldened enemy across its northern border, the Porte transformed Bosnia into a proverbial fortress, constructing extensive fortifications along the frontier and developing a unique system of military organisation for the Bosnian population.[20] In contrast to much of the empire, the entire male population (including Christians) was made eligible for mobilisation in territorial units, serving in exchange for a reduced tax burden. Although this territorial force remained an integral part of the Ottoman military, it was 'structurally distinct and peculiarly Bosnian'.[21] In 1737, this multi-confessional force comprehensively defeated an invading Austrian army at the Battle of Banja Luka without assistance or leadership from the Porte, demonstrating both the autonomy and effectiveness of this Bosnian military institution.[22]

By the eighteenth century, the Porte's treasury was strained by the costs of ongoing military campaigns across the empire, leading to rising taxes for the Bosnian population. Beginning in 1727, Muslim and Orthodox subjects in Herzegovina repeatedly revolted in defiance of the increased levies. A particularly large rebellion in the town of Mostar in 1768 required the deployment of an Ottoman army to suppress it.[23] These events were, for the most part, limited to relatively localised uprisings. However, a package of imperial reforms known as the *Tanzimat* (Reorganisation) introduced to Bosnia by the Sultan in 1832 sparked the first province-wide revolt of the Ottoman period.[24] Many aspects of the *Tanzimat*, such as the reduction of the number of *sanjaks* in the *Eyalet* to two (Bosnia and Herzegovina), were not controversial to the Bosnian elite; however, the decision to transfer some territory along the Drina from the *Eyalet* of Bosnia to neighbouring Serbia and integrate the Bosnian territorial force into the regular military framework of the empire inspired much of the population to unite in rebellion.[25]

Led by the *Zmaj od Bosne* (Dragon of Bosnia), the richest landowner in the *Eyalet*, the rebellion was dominated by the Muslim elite but received considerable support from both Orthodox and Catholic communities.[26] The Dragon of Bosnia led an independent Bosnian state for about a year; however, the rebellion was crushed in 1834. In its aftermath, all institutions for self-rule in Bosnia were dismantled by the Porte and Herzegovina was established as a separate *Eyalet* from Bosnia.[27] In 1865, Bosnia and Herzegovina were reunified to form a single administrative *Vilayet* (a new designation created during the *Tanzimat*), only to be separated once again ten years later. The Ottomans faced a final rebellion in Bosnia and Herzegovina in 1875, when much of the Orthodox population rebelled in response to further tax rises and demanded union with Serbia or self-rule for Bosnia.[28] In 1877, in one of its last acts as the governing administration of the area, the Porte united Bosnia and Herzegovina as a single *Vilayet*.[29]

The 1875–8 rebellion, the impact of which was compounded by similar events in Bulgaria and Serbia, as well as the comprehensive defeat of the Ottoman army during the 1877–8 Russo-Turkish War, served as the death knell for the Porte's authority in Bosnia. Among its many other provisions, the 1878 Treaty of San Stefano between the Ottomans and Imperial Russia originally promised autonomy for the *Vilayet* of Bosnia within the Ottoman Empire. However, this decision was ultimately rescinded a few months later by the great powers gathered at the Congress of Berlin. The delegates of the Congress agreed that in compensation for Russian gains in the eastern Balkans, the Austro-Hungarians could occupy and administer BiH, with the caveat that the territory would formally remain under the (largely symbolic) suzerainty of the Porte for thirty years.[30] In a further demonstration of the diminishing power of the Ottomans in the Balkans, the Congress also formally recognised the sovereignty and independence of the Principality of Serbia.

## Bosnia and Herzegovina under the Double Eagle, 1878–1918

Austro-Hungarian leaders had watched the 1875–8 rebellion in BiH with a close eye. Although a policy of non-intervention was formally adopted, plans for the occupation of the territory had been developed in 1876 as BiH not only represented a potentially rich source of valuable raw materials but would also allow the southern boundary of the empire to be consolidated along a much shorter and more defensible frontier.[31] Following the Congress of Berlin (13 June–13 July 1878), roughly 75,000 troops of the Austro-Hungarian *kaiserlich und königlich Armee* (Imperial and Royal Army, k.u.k. Army), led by General Josip Filipović, a Croat with Serb ancestry, crossed into Bosnia, marking the beginning of the first war of the Dualist age.[32] Rather than finding a province stripped of Ottoman power and a population ready to welcome the new administration, the k.u.k. soldiers were faced with approximately 93,000 Ottoman and Bosnian troops, who bitterly resisted their advance.[33]

Over 154,000 Austro-Hungarian infantry, 4,500 cavalry, and almost 300 artillery pieces were eventually required to pacify BiH.[34] Gunther Rothenberg suggests that a total of 250,000 k.u.k. troops were mobilised during the invasion, representing 'nearly a third of her entire war strength'.[35] Faced with such insurmountable numbers, Ottoman troops were forced to withdraw and, after a bloody battle in which most of the city was destroyed, Sarajevo was eventually captured in August 1878 (see Figure 1.1). Considerable numbers of Bosnian Muslims left with the Ottomans, finding sanctuary in Albania, Macedonia, or in the empire's heartlands.[36] On 29 October 1878, an Imperial and Royal Commission, responsible to the Joint Ministerial Cabinet (and thus, both Austrian and Hungarian parts of the Dual Monarchy), was established to administer BiH, marking the formal beginning of Austro-Hungarian rule.[37] However, as the territory officially remained under the suzerainty of the Porte until 1908, BiH was governed as an occupied military zone by k.u.k. governors-general who 'held extraordinary authority throughout Bosnia-Herzegovina' until 1910.[38]

The Austro-Hungarian entry into Bosnia and Herzegovina was a costly affair, leaving the k.u.k. Army with over 3,300 dead, 7,000 wounded, and an additional 110,000 suffering from illnesses brought on by poor sanitation and the harsh terrain.[39] Neither side had taken prisoners during the fighting, and many strategic towns and cities lay in ruins. Once the fighting was over, however, BiH became a key strategic outpost of the empire. The military headquarters of one of the six Austro-Hungarian military districts was relocated to Sarajevo and provided with unprecedented resources for building railways and infrastructure and defending the empire's newest province.[40] The new administration greatly expanded educational access, introduced a framework for the emergence of political parties, promoted a territorial (and thus, inclusive)

**Figure 1.1** *Soldiers of the k.u.k. Army planting the imperial flag on Bosnian soil.* Engraving from *L'Illustrazione Italiana*, Year 5, No. 37 (15 September 1878). Courtesy of DEA/ Biblioteca Ambrosiana via Getty Images.

form of Bosnian nationalism known as *bošnjastvo*, and conducted the first reliable census of the Bosnian population.[41] The 1879 survey revealed that 42.88 per cent of the population was Orthodox, 38.75 was Muslim, 18.08 was Catholic, with the final 0.31 per cent being categorised as 'others'.[42] Although approximately 77 per cent of the total population that was governed by the Dual Monarchy was Catholic, the range of nationalities and faiths within the empire meant that although Bosnian Muslims represented the first significant Islamic community in the empire, the diversity of confessional outlooks among the Bosnian population was fairly unremarkable. In an effort to maintain stability and win over Bosnian Muslim landowners, the Ottoman *millet* system was maintained following the occupation, leaving the vast majority of the population (of all faiths) as illiterate and landless peasants.

Considerable numbers of Slovenes, Croats, and Serbs already lived under the Dual Monarchy and served in its military, often with distinction. Indeed, much like the Ottoman equivalent in Bosnia, the Austro-Hungarian *militärgrenze* (military frontier) had been populated and defended over the centuries by various South Slavic 'Grenzers' and their families in exchange for a degree of autonomy and the freedom to practice their religion. Gunther E. Rothenberg stresses that 'of outstanding importance during this period was dynastic allegiance of the Grenzer. At a time when serfdom and subservience were still the general rule, the Grenzer regarded themselves as free tenants of the emperor'.[43] During countless battles for the empire, these communities developed a distinguished military tradition.[44] Although the frontier itself was quickly dissolved because, as Rothenberg asserts, 'the imperial military … were too suspicious of a nationally conscious Slavic military institution', this legacy provided an established South Slavic military tradition within the empire into which Bosnian troops were quickly incorporated.[45] Indeed, such was the pace of integration that Bosnian military units were raised in 1879, just a year after the occupation and despite the protests of the Porte. The Bosnian troops were first recruited to an elite *jaeger* (rifle/ranger) battalion and were assessed to be of such quality that in 1881 universal male conscription into the k.u.k. Army was introduced across BiH.[46] Initial resistance against conscription inspired a revolt in 1882, requiring the k.u.k. to conduct a complex counter-insurgency campaign before restoring order.[47] Despite such setbacks, four full battalions of Bosnian infantry, composed of troops of all faiths and trained by elite Austrian regiments, were serving across the Austro-Hungarian empire by 1885.[48] In 1903, they were joined by the newly established Bosnian 'Field Jaeger' battalion, a specialised mountain warfare unit.

Dressed in blue uniforms modelled on traditional Balkan dress and sporting red fezzes on their heads, Bosnian k.u.k. soldiers were clearly identifiable compared with their counterparts from other parts of the empire. Jiří Hutečka argues that k.u.k. soldiers such as the Czech writer Josef Váchel projected the images of the 'noble savage' and 'warrior races' of West European imperialism onto the Bosnian soldiers, highlighting Váchel's statement that 'those sons of nature deeply revered anyone who had mastered the mystery of "letters" in a manner that is usually reserved for the most sacred deities'.[49] As the presence of Bosnians in the military became established, the Styrian composer Eduard Wagnes penned the marching song *Die Bosniaken Kommen* (The Bosnians Are Coming), which quickly became the *de facto* anthem of all Bosnian k.u.k. units.[50] Over 10,500 Bosnians served in the peacetime k.u.k. Army, of whom

39 per cent were Orthodox, 31 per cent were Muslim, and 25 per cent were Croat. The remainder were Jews, Greek Catholics, and Protestants.[51] Following a period of significant mobilisation in the year prior to the First World War, the number of Bosnians in the k.u.k. Army increased to roughly 39,000.[52]

South Slavic soldiers in the armed forces of the Dual Monarchy spoke their respective *Regimentsprache* (Regiment language, such as Slovenian or Croatian) within their units, but were required to learn eighty-eight words of command in German, the universal language of the k.u.k. officer corps. In addition to this requirement, South Slavic officers in Hungarian regiments had to also speak Hungarian.[53] The Austro-Hungarian military placed a great emphasis on the ritual and ceremony of Mass before battle, but ensured all faiths in the ranks had their spiritual needs accounted for by recruiting imams, rabbis, and Orthodox priests to serve as military chaplains alongside Catholic clergy.[54] Particular efforts were also made within the k.u.k. to ensure that the integration of Muslim troops went smoothly. Consultations were held with the British and French governments, both of which recruited considerable numbers of Muslims into their respective armies, leading to the construction of prayer rooms and separate kitchens, as well as the observance of Islamic holidays in Bosnian units.[55] Through provisions such as these, the Austro-Hungarians went to great lengths to go 'beyond nationalism' and develop a unifying military identity based on regimental pride and institutional loyalty to the k.u.k. Army.[56]

Bosnians lived in the empire and served in its armies largely without incident for decades, with most military duties being limited to maintaining law and order in the empire's heartlands. Gunther Rothenberg suggests these deployments were informed by two key factors: 'For one, these troops were considered reliable because their language, religion, and customs kept them apart from the populace, and secondly, it also removed these regiments from the continuing pan-Serb agitation in their home stations.'[57] This changed dramatically in 1903, when Peter Karađorđević became king of Serbia after his predecessor was assassinated by a group of Serbian Army officers.[58] The assassination represented just the latest act of political violence that had prevailed in Serbia during its rise from provincial obscurity to regional power in the nineteenth century. During this period, the Serbian administration imported constitutions and administrative structures from powerful European states, built a large army, and invested heavily in education and infrastructure. Siniša Malešević observes that 'there was no nationalism among the early nineteenth century Serbian elites', highlighting the complete lack of national institutions and the illiteracy of almost the entire the population as key factors. He argues that despite such efforts to bring Serbia and its population into modernity, there was not 'an automatic transition from peasants into Serbs. For this to happen an entire organisational and ideological apparatus had to be created.'[59] The consolidation of the region's confessional identities into their contemporary nations (*narodi*) was a slow and complicated process, but by the beginning of the twentieth century Catholics were increasingly identified as Croats and Orthodox Christians as Serbs. Bosnian Muslims were not recognised as a nation until 1971 but maintained a distinct political and cultural tradition throughout the period. Henceforth, the Bosnian population is discussed in terms of Bosnian Croats,

Muslims, and Serbs, while the moniker South Slavs is used to describe all the Slavic inhabitants of the region.

For Malešević, the 'vicious cycle of forced abdications and royal assassinations was a symptom of deep divisions at the top of the Serbian state'.[60] These divisions created an atmosphere in which 'the two dominant elite groupings had to, and were also willing to, demonstrate that they are more capable than their rival of achieving nationalist goals and bringing about the unification of all Serbs into one state'.[61] During King Peter's reign, formerly friendly relations between the Dual Monarchy and the Kingdom of Serbia 'declined precipitously' as the idea of unifying the Serb population of the Balkans (or indeed all South Slavs) under the Serbian crown gained traction within the Serbian elite.[62] Although South Slavic unity was not actively promoted by the Serbian administration, the large Serb population in BiH represented a major point of interest for those hoping to continue the kingdom's seemingly inexorable territorial expansion, particularly as the thirty-year occupation mandated in Berlin was coming to an end. As a result, the decision of the Austro-Hungarian administration to formally annexe BiH into the empire in 1908 sparked a major diplomatic crisis, bringing the Dual Monarchy and the Kingdom of Serbia (and with them, Europe) to the verge of war.

In December 1908, civilians in Serbia established the *Narodna odbrana* (National Defence) society with the goal of rallying support and volunteers for an armed struggle against Austro-Hungarian rule in BiH and ultimately unifying all Serbs in a single kingdom.[63] Three years later, the army officers responsible for the 1903 regicide formed *Ujedinjenje ili smrt* (Union or Death, more commonly known as the 'Black Hand') with the express intention of building a greater Serbia.[64] Although noteworthy signals of the emerging pan-Serb nationalism, the development of such organisations must be understood in the context of the time. 'Most Bosnian Serbs, who were still illiterate, impoverished and mostly landless peasants, largely remained indifferent towards the idea of national unification' and the principal conflicts in Austro-Hungarian BiH were 'much more vertical than horizontal: the peasant majority of all three groups was dissatisfied with the actions and inactions of the Habsburg regime'.[65]

In 1911, the Kingdom of Italy seized the Ottoman provinces of Tripolitania and Cyrenaica in North Africa and the Dodecanese islands in the Aegean, before shelling defences on the Dardanelles.[66] With the Porte on the strategic backfoot, the Balkan kingdoms of Bulgaria, Greece, Montenegro, and Serbia formed a loose alliance and declared war on the Ottomans the following year.[67] Many Serbs and other South Slavs from Austro-Hungarian lands volunteered for service in the Serbian Army, crossing the Drina following the declaration of war to fight for Serbian territorial gains.[68] Malešević highlights how 'the Serbian establishment put a great deal of effort into developing the ideological narratives that would legitimise territorial expansion throughout the Balkans' during these conflicts.[69] These ideological narratives later served as the conceptual foundation of the 'Greater Serbia' project of the 1990s. Following the Serb victories in the Balkan Wars (1912–13), the 'political, military, cultural and administrative elites of Belgrade were emboldened in their belief that unification [with Bosnian Serbs] was close and inevitable'.[70] These developments worsened relations between the Dual Monarchy and the Kingdom of Serbia even further, causing the Serb population of the empire to become increasingly viewed with suspicion.

By the time Archduke Franz Ferdinand and his wife were assassinated on the streets of Sarajevo on 28 June 1914, the loyalties of the Bosnian population were very much divided. The conspirators responsible for the attack were part of the *Mlada Bosna* (Young Bosnia) movement, which the Dual Monarchy judged to have been coordinated from Belgrade. In the ensuing month, much of the impoverished and landless Bosnian Serb population was subjected to atrocities, massacres, and mass internment by the Austro-Hungarian authorities and other communities in BiH.[71] On 28 July, the Dual Monarchy declared war on the Kingdom of Serbia, placing the embattled Serb subjects of the empire in an even more precarious position. Upon the outbreak of war, Serbs and many other South Slavs from Croatia-Slavonia, Dalmatia, BiH, and Hungary clandestinely crossed into Serbia to join the Serbian Army, bringing with them 200,000 predominantly Serb civilians fleeing persecution in the empire.[72] Up to 27,000 non-Serb South Slavs from Austro-Hungarian lands volunteered for service in the Serbian Army during the First World War, with 5,000 troops from Bosnia serving in the vaunted First Serbian Volunteer Division and additional contingents from Herzegovina joining the Montenegrin army.[73] Although some Serb k.u.k. soldiers were permitted to retain their positions if their commanding officers vouched for them, many of those who remained in service to the Dual Monarchy were disarmed and organised into labour battalions.[74]

For most Bosnian combatants, the First World War meant service in the k.u.k. Army (see Figure 1.2). The pressures of war on many fronts led to the expansion of the Bosnian contingent of the Dual Monarchy's armed forces, which rose to a peak of 36 battalions, representing over 43,000 men.[75] Indeed, while the k.u.k. officer corps remained largely dominated by ethnic Germans, 11.7 per cent of the rank and file were South Slavic by 1915.[76] Many Bosnian units were used in the initial offensives against the Kingdom of Serbia alongside troops from Croatia, creating k.u.k. Army Corps that were composed almost entirely of South Slavs.[77] Many of these troops remained in the Balkan theatre for much of the war, assisting with the Austro-Hungarian occupation of Serbia and Albania.[78] Additional Bosnian armed forces were raised outside the framework of the k.u.k. Army to serve as an auxiliary gendarme. These *Schutzkorps* (Defence Forces) could muster approximately 11,000 men and were mostly composed of Bosnian Muslims and Croats but included some Serbs. Ostensibly raised by the Dual Monarchy to maintain order in BiH, the Schutzkorps had little impact on the war, and instead embarked on a campaign of paramilitary violence against the Serb population in the province. Mitja Velikonja argues that this campaign represents the first time that a significant number of the inhabitants of BiH were 'persecuted and liquidated' for their national affiliation.[79]

Considerable numbers of Bosnian troops (of all faiths) served on the Italian or Eastern Fronts during the war, participating in some of the most significant battles fought by the k.u.k. Army. In August–September 1914, Bosnian units fought against the Russians at the Battle of Galicia, earning themselves a formidable reputation despite taking significant casualties.[80] From July 1915, a k.u.k. force led by the Croat General Svetozar Borević defended the Alpine frontier of the empire along the Izonzo River, facing repeated attacks by the Italian Army. In his analysis of the writings of Czech soldiers, Hutečka observes that 'sending the Bosnians in' 'is an oft-repeated phrase, usually mixed with horror and awe'.[81] He cites numerous examples of k.u.k.

**Figure 1.2** *A military brass band of the 1st Bosnian Infantry Regiment, 1915/1916.* Courtesy of Alamy Stock Photos.

soldiers writing about sending the leonine Bosnians in, drunk on rum and armed just with daggers, to take any Italian positions that other troops could not take.[82] While such views clearly evoke ideas of 'martial races' that are usually associated with the colonies of West European empires, they serve to highlight the unique and distinctive place of the Bosnian regiments of the k.u.k. Army. Of the Austro-Hungarian troops serving on the Italian Front, 42 per cent were South Slavic.[83] Among this force was the 'legendary' *Zweier Bosniaken* (Second Bosnian) Regiment, which had not only fought with distinction in Galicia before becoming the most feared unit on the Italian Front but ultimately became the most decorated unit of the entire Austro-Hungarian military during the war.[84] Richard Bassett highlights the role of Bosnians in the complex machinery of the wartime k.u.k. Army, noting that 'the army's most highly decorated regiments were made up of Bosnian Muslims and Alpine Catholics, not infrequently commanded by Jewish officers and led by a general whose father had been a stalwart of the Serbian Orthodox community'.[85] Approximately 150,000 South Slavic soldiers died in service to the Dual Monarchy during the First World War.[86]

## The interwar period, 1918–41

The ongoing pressures of war on multiple fronts, growing calls for national self-determination from within the empire, and a failed harvest sparked a sequence of events that culminated with the dissolution of the Dual Monarchy in October 1918.[87] Although the demise of the 700-year-old Habsburg dynasty marked the beginning of an uncertain period for much of central and eastern Europe, the fate of BiH had already been decided. On 20 July 1917, a group of exiled political representatives from the South Slavic population living under the Dual Monarchy met with officials from the Kingdom of Serbia at a conference held under the auspices of the British and French governments on the island of Corfu. The Yugoslav Committee, as the group was known, agreed to a framework for the creation of a unified South Slavic state, which they declared would be a parliamentary monarchy led by the Karađorđević dynasty in Belgrade.[88] By September 1918, most South Slavic political parties within the Austro-Hungarian empire were convinced that a South Slavic state needed to be established. At a national assembly held in Zagreb on 29 October 1918, representatives proclaimed the formation of the State of Slovenes, Croats, and Serbs from the South Slavic lands of the Austro-Hungarian empire, formed a National Council to administer the territory, and raised an ad hoc armed force of approximately 15,000 former k.u.k. troops.[89] A month later, representatives of this internationally unrecognised state travelled to Belgrade to invite Serbian leaders to formally proclaim the unification of the South Slavs into a single state: The Kingdom of Serbs, Croats, and Slovenes.[90]

The newly established kingdom faced myriad challenges upon its formation, the most pressing of which were ending armed insurrections in various parts of the country and consolidating the authority of the state. However, several obstacles stood in the way of achieving these goals. The Serbian Army had fought relentlessly during the war, first opposing Austro-Hungarian offensives into Serbia before evading encirclement by crossing over the inhospitable mountains of northern Albania and being redeployed by the French navy to the Salonika Front, from where it eventually reconquered Serbia. The cost of these endeavours was great, with somewhere in the region of 300,000 Serbian troops (approximately 40 per cent of those mobilised) and 450,000 civilians losing their lives during the conflict.[91] In contrast to the Western Front, where combat ended abruptly following the armistice, the beleaguered Serbian forces were required to continue fighting for years after the war. In the provinces of 'Old Serbia' and 'South Serbia' (contemporary Kosovo and North Macedonia, respectively), which had only been conquered from Bulgaria during the Second Balkan War (1913), the authority of the Kingdom of Serbs, Croats, and Slovenes faced an insurrection from Macedonian and ethnic Albanian rebels, while in Montenegro an armed conflict between advocates and opponents of union with Serbia continued until 1924. In BiH, Muslim landlords and peasants alike faced the wrath of the Serb population and returning volunteers from the Serbian Army, who killed approximately 2,000 Bosnian Muslims and persecuted many more between 1918 and 1920.[92] More pressingly, the collapse of the Dual Monarchy and the return of huge numbers of combatants and former prisoners of war (including many Bolshevik converts) to parts of Croatia created a situation of near lawlessness in the northern reaches of the kingdom, the danger of which was compounded by a series of violent border disputes with Austria, Hungary, Romania, and, most significantly, Italy.[93]

There were 145,225 soldiers in the Serbian military at the end of the First World War.[94] Following the creation of the Kingdom of Serbs, Croats, and Slovenes, these soldiers were supplemented by roughly 50,000 troops of the wartime Montenegrin army and the 15,000-strong force raised by the State of Slovenes, Croats, and Serbs. The ongoing security concerns of the administration in Belgrade led to the incremental mobilisation of even greater numbers of soldiers from across the kingdom in the post-war period until almost 450,000 troops were serving in July 1919.[95] The new military maintained the structures of the old Serbian military, making it 'less of a composite force' and more 'an enlargement of the Serbian Army'.[96] Furthermore, an offer from the 'Lion of Izonso' General Boroević to join the new military was rejected and none of the 172 post-war positions of general were filled by a Croatian or Slovenian, leaving the senior leadership of the army exclusively in Serbian hands.[97] However, where the Serbian Army had previously represented a vehicle for the advancement of the Serbian nation, the new institution was tasked (initially, at least) with bringing the 'tri-nominal people' of the kingdom together.

In his book on the period, John Paul Newman highlights an article published by the army's General Staff which called for the military to become 'a school for an education in the spirit of national oneness' and the officer corps to serve as 'the vanguard of national unity'.[98] To this end, during the period of mobilisation in 1919, 2,330 former k.u.k. officers were accepted into the military (although almost all were of junior ranks), making the officer corps roughly 40 per cent Slovenian, Croat, and Bosnian.[99] Furthermore, a concerted effort was made to recruit officers from Croatian and Slovenian communities in the initial post-war period. However, after some initial success recruiting a cadre of cadets composed of 60 per cent Serbs, 30 per cent Croats, and 9 per cent Slovenes in 1919, uptake to Yugoslav military academies increasingly became the preserve of the Serb community, with Serbs making up 84 per cent of the 1928 cadet class.[100] Similarly, the incorporation of former k.u.k. soldiers only lasted until 1923, when considerable numbers were retired.[101] Newman states that 'even allowing for the intake of former Habsburg officers and soldiers, it was to be remembered that the Yugoslav army, and indeed Yugoslavia itself, owed its existence to the victory of the Serbian Army during the war'.[102]

The kingdom initially maintained the existing administrative boundaries within its borders, preserving an internal Bosnian political entity. However, the June 1921 *Vidovdan* (St Vitus Day) Constitution which established the kingdom as a constitutional monarchy also established a new administrative framework, creating thirty-three new centrally governed *oblasts* (provinces) across crown territory and dividing BiH into the oblasts of Bihać, Vrbas, Tuzla, Travnik, Sarajevo, and Mostar. By 1924, BiH had lost all vestiges of regional autonomy.[103] In 1929, King Aleksander prorogued parliament and abolished the constitution, placing sole executive authority in the hands of the monarchy. As part of his efforts to forge a cohesive nation from his various subjects, he renamed his kingdom *Yugoslavia*, literally meaning the land of the South Slavs. In October 1929, he once again redrew the administrative borders of the kingdom, replacing the oblasts with nine new *banovine*, which were named after geographical features such as rivers. In this structure, the territory of contemporary BiH became parts of the three *banovine* of Littoral, Drina, and Vrbas.

Within this framework, Marko Attila Hoare argues, the Bosnian population was subjected to a 'political conquest' by 'foreign political parties based in Serbia and Croatia', resulting in an 'increasingly bitter struggle for power and possession; at once a struggle between Bosnians and a struggle between Serbia and Croatia over

Bosnia-Hercegovina'.[104] Dejan Djokić highlights how the idea of BiH remained a force in politics throughout the period, with political leaders from across the kingdom campaigning to restore the administrative borders of BiH as they searched for the 'elusive compromise' which would establish a functioning political settlement.[105] The Bosnian Muslim community, which represented just 6 per cent of the Yugoslav population, was politically sidelined by the centralisation of state power and the abolition of BiH as an administrative unit; however, Djokić observes that 'the sense of Bosnian identity and the memory of Bosnia's historic borders clearly remained strong among local Muslims'.[106] Although freedom of worship and communal autonomy were guaranteed in the kingdom, the proportion of Muslims holding power declined and agrarian reforms came at the expense of Muslim landowners.[107] Furthermore, while Bosnians who had volunteered for service in the Serbian Army were celebrated as heroes who had overcome the fault lines of war in the name of South Slavic unity, k.u.k. veterans faced institutionalised hostility and discrimination.[108] These many challenges inspired growing numbers of Bosnians to emigrate throughout the interwar period.[109]

As BiH ceased to exist as an administrative unit, it is impossible to calculate the number of Bosnian troops that served in the Yugoslav Royal Army (*Jugoslovenska kraljevska vojska*, JKV), as it was called from 1929. However, as the Yugoslav military remained a predominantly Serb institution throughout the interwar period, it is likely that military service was popular among Bosnian Serbs but taken up by relatively few Bosnian Croats and Muslims. Indeed, while a few Croats rose to the senior ranks of the army, there is no record of any Muslim officers holding senior positions in the military other than the Chief Military Imam, though the presence of this office suggests there was at least some uptake among the Muslim population of Yugoslavia.[110] The failure of the JKV leadership to properly integrate non-Serb soldiers and build an effective military proved terminal upon the Axis invasion of the kingdom in April 1941. Less than 30 per cent of reservists reported for duty when mobilised, and some military units composed of Slovenes and Croats refused to resist the advancing German troops.[111] Mile Bjelajac highlights that it was the 'predominantly local' and 'nationally heterogenous' Army Group I (which was tasked with defending Slovenia and Croatia) that failed to oppose the invasion, with some Croatian JKV troops openly requesting transfers to Axis units from Wehrmacht officers rather than fighting them.[112] Although not every Croatian unit in the JKV mutinied, some Croatian units from every division of Army Group I refused orders, arrested their Serb commanders (including the entire Army Group leadership), and joined the Axis forces. When the Wehrmacht entered Zagreb, its troops were greeted by cheering crowds. The main Axis thrust, however, came via a Wehrmacht offensive towards Skopje from Bulgaria, which cast aside the more homogenous Serb units of the JKV with little more difficulty than their counterparts in the north of the kingdom.[113]

The JKV surrendered twelve days after the initial invasion, having inflicted just 558 casualties (151 killed and 407 wounded) on the Wehrmacht.[114] The only meaningful resistance was offered by the Yugoslav air force, incidentally the most diverse institution in the military, which led a desperate defence of Belgrade during the Luftwaffe's 'Operation Punishment' bombing campaign of the city.[115] In addition to facilitating a resounding military defeat, the failure of the Yugoslav administration to develop a political settlement that its subjects were willing to defend undermined its own legitimacy to an extent from which it never recovered. Hoare observes that 'the neglect of Bosnia-Hercegovina's needs ... created a political void – of which some observers were aware and lamented – that could be filled by a political current that was not based solely on a single nationality, but on a genuinely all-Bosnian foundation'.[116] Chapter 2 charts how the Communist Party of Yugoslavia filled this political void, rising to lead the armed resistance against the Axis occupation from mountain fastnesses in Bosnia and Montenegro and ultimately building a new Yugoslavia in the aftermath of the war. Although the various political entities that existed prior to 1941 had a significant impact on the development of the region and its population, the independent Bosnian state that emerged in the 1990s was very much a product of the socialist period.

## Conclusion

Reflecting on the *longue durée* of Bosnian political-military history highlights three key observations. First, a distinct political entity stood on the approximate territory of BiH from the twelfth century until 1921 (roughly 800 years), either as an autonomous political unit within imperial administrations or, briefly, as an independent kingdom. Second, Bosnians of all faiths served alongside each other in distinctly Bosnian military units for well over 200 years, first under the Ottomans as a territorial defence force, and then in the Bosnian regiments of the k.u.k. Army. In both cases, Bosnians were reputed to be among the most effective troops in the imperial armies of their erstwhile conquerors, highlighting the enduring salience of this unique military heritage and demonstrating that there is a long tradition of capable multiethnic Bosnian armed forces. Third, every armed force that was raised from the Bosnian population prior to 1941 reflected, to some degree at least, the social complexity and confessional diversity of that population. Efforts to 'unmix' the Bosnian population and build armed forces based on a single confessional or ethnic identity throughout the Second World War and again during the collapse of Yugoslavia thus represent relatively brief aberrations in the long history of military organisation in BiH.

# 2

# The Yugoslav People's Army

The Yugoslav People's Army (*Jugoslovenska narodna armija*, JNA) was one of the largest military forces in Europe during the Cold War. Alongside a wide range of territorial defence forces that were established by each Yugoslav republic, it was credited with making the SFRJ 'an invincible bastion for every aggressor' an 'armed fortress' and a 'veritable hornets' nest for any enemy force'.[1] From its origins as a modest force of 12,000 communist agitators at the outset of the Second World War, the predecessor forces grew throughout the conflict to become the most power armed force in the region. After liberating Yugoslav territory with relatively little assistance, the military developed and expanded to become an integral part of Yugoslav society.[2] As the political leadership of the SFRJ developed their unique interpretation of socialism, so the role and structures of the JNA changed to reflect the evolving nature of the state it served. It succeeded in its task of deterring invasion from both east and west and remained a cohesive force through numerous political and economic crises. In the final years of its existence, however, this uniquely Yugoslav institution became a pawn in the machinations of various nationalist leaders as they vied for power during the collapse of the Yugoslav state. Ultimately, the soldiers of the JNA ended up fighting each other across the territory they had once defended.

The heroic wartime struggle of the Partisans became the founding myth of the post-war Yugoslav state, placing the military in a unique position within the culture and society of the SFRJ. The perennial threat of invasion demanded a large and well-equipped army, while the socialist ideology of the Yugoslav leadership provided a framework within which the military was employed in both the economic and political aspects of life in Yugoslavia. The JNA approached this broad range of challenges while attempting to build a cohesive fighting force from a diverse population that was, despite the protestations of party dogma, divided by the legacies of a brutal and recent armed conflict. The armies which fought each other in Croatia and BiH as the SFRJ collapsed all emerged from the institutions that were built in the socialist period, while considerable numbers of combatants who fought in the war had, through conscription, at least some experience of life in the JNA. Many of the weapons that were used in this period were either seized from Axis forces by the Partisans during the war or made in JNA factories, many of which were located in the mountains of Bosnia for strategic reasons. Furthermore, it was a somewhat transformed JNA that played a pivotal role in supporting the early efforts to establish exclusively Serb states in Croatia and

BiH, before being stripped of all vestiges of its multiethnic past and formally divided into three extremely well-equipped armies which then served Slobodan Milošević's attempt to carve a large Serb state out of the remnants of the SFRJ. Understanding the structures, capabilities, and principles of the JNA is therefore vital for understanding the conflicts that took place across the region during the 1990s. For the case of BiH, this understanding is exceptionally important. The officials and military personnel who later designed and built the OSBiH were all fully aware of the JNA and its efforts to forge a multiethnic military, none more so than the senior officers of the entity armies, almost all of whom spent many years in its ranks. The decisions these individuals made, the compromises they agreed to, and the vocabulary that they employed in their work were all informed by their experiences in the JNA. Thus, the OSBiH was not just built from components that had evolved from blueprints originally designed by the JNA, it was also created in an environment in which every decision was informed by the legacy of the JNA's efforts to forge a multiethnic military.

## Origins

In April 1941, the Kingdom of Yugoslavia was invaded and occupied by Axis forces, which effortlessly routed the JKV. The exiled King Peter II convened a government in London, while a former JKV officer, Dragoljub 'Draža' Mihailović, organised a resistance movement in occupied-Serbia centred around traditional Serbian irregular formations known as *Četnički pokret*, or Chetnik Detachments. This movement was widely known as the *četnici* (the Chetniks) and was characterised by its monarchist and Serb nationalist ideology. Although the Chetniks later established *modus vivendi* and collaborated with the occupying forces, they were initially recognised by the British as allies. The Communist Party of Yugoslavia (*Komunistička partija Jugoslavije*, KPJ) remained underground in the immediate aftermath of the invasion in April. However, when Axis forces launched Operation Barbarossa and attempted to invade the Soviet Union in June 1941, President of the KPJ Josip 'Tito' Broz issued a proclamation to the peoples of Yugoslavia to 'rise up against the German, Italian, Hungarian, and Bulgarian invaders.'[3] Meanwhile, the party began organising military units and formed the National Liberation Movement (*Narodnooslobodilački pokret*, NOP) to lead the uprising.

The *partizani* (Partisans), as the members of the NOP were called, employed guerrilla tactics and strategy to combat their more numerous, better armed, and more prepared opponents. Initially, the scope of their operations was limited due to the overwhelmingly disparity between their own forces and those of the Axis occupation, which were also supported by troops raised by local quisling governments. These early operations were executed by small groups, often simply carrying out ambushes and raids in their local area. Nikola Ljubičić, a Partisan who fought alongside Tito throughout the war and became secretary of defence in 1967, highlights the limited military capacity of the NOP at this stage:

> In the initial period of the National Liberation War … our military organisation featured a wide network of territorial units of different types, names and sizes.

But the basic form of military organisation was the National Liberation Partisan Detachment.[4]

The KPJ led the movement but were careful to garner support from as much of the Yugoslav population as possible. Retaining a broad base not only strengthened the legitimacy of the Partisans as the rightful defender of the Yugoslav people, but also allowed them to fill their ranks and increase the scale of their operations more rapidly. Vladimir Dedijer, another Partisan (who later fell out of favour with the regime), notes:

> Tito stressed that the Partisan detachments were called National Liberation Detachments because they were the fighting formations not of any political party or group ... but were the fighting forces of the people of Yugoslavia and should therefore include all patriots, whatever their views.[5]

On 22 December 1941, exactly six months after Tito proclaimed the beginning of the uprising, the first regular military formation of the NOP, the First Proletarian Brigade, was established. Dedijer records that after observing the high number of workers and miners in some units, Tito decided to bring them together into a larger force than the usual Partisan Detachments. The new units were elite, with service in them being considered the 'highest honour for every individual fighting man'.[6] They were 'characterised by their firm discipline and by their methods of warfare', were distinguished from other units by flying the hammer and sickle standard and wearing the red star on their *titovka* (adapted from the Russian *pilotka*) caps, and were not 'bound to regions where they had originated, but would fight in all parts of Yugoslavia'.[7] (See Figure 2.1.) While the National Liberation Detachments offered localised resistance to the occupiers, the Proletarian Brigades were intended to emulate the 'shock' units of the Red Army and serve as a foundation from which an army capable of liberating all Yugoslav territory could be built. The NOP leadership planned for the brigades to draw personnel from across Yugoslavia. They believed that by fighting shoulder-to-shoulder, the brigades would help to 'overcome the deep divisions in the Yugoslav society' and 'mould a "new man"'.[8] In practice, however, the First Brigade remained dominated by Serbs and Montenegrins, and contained 'only sprinklings of "fighters" from other nations'.[9]

In terms of doctrine, personnel, and ideology, the Proletarian Brigades were the genesis of the JNA. As the war developed, they increased both in size and number alongside regionally based units that were commanded principally by officers from the local area. These units answered to a regional command and used the local language.[10] In early 1942, the NOP was renamed, becoming the National Liberation Army of Yugoslavia (*Narodnooslobodilačka vojska Jugoslavije*, NOVJ), and by the end of that year, it consisted of 150,000 fighters. This figure doubled within a year.[11] Yugoslav communists who had fought in the International Brigades of the Republic during the Spanish Civil War (known as *Španjolski borci*, Spanish Warriors) were key in organising and leading the rapidly expanding army. Twenty-nine of them became Partisan generals, every Partisan army was led by a Spanish Warrior, and Tito's deputy, Ivan Gosnjak, had also fought in Spain.[12] Alongside ensuring its leaders retained

**Figure 2.1** *Josip Broz Tito and his entourage present a banner to battalions of the First Proletarian Division, 1942.* Courtesy of ITAR-TASS News Agency via Alamy.

direct military command of the NOP, the KPJ also consolidated its control of the army through commissars, who established 'Political Sections' within Partisan formations for 'the transmittal of political directives'.[13]

On 29 November 1943, the Antifascist Council of the National Liberation of Yugoslavia (*Antifašističko vijeće narodnog oslobođenja Jugoslavije*, AVNOJ) met in the town of Jajce, in Central Bosnia. The council had been formed a year before to administer territory liberated by the Partisans and represented the political leadership of the resistance movement. The dominance of the KPJ in the armed forces of the NOVJ was reflected in the composition of the AVNOJ. For all intents and purposes, the latter was simply the political arm of the Partisan movement, and the former was the military arm, as William Deakin, a British officer who served alongside the Partisans, notes: 'The political and military aspects of the direction of the Yugoslav National Liberation Movement were deliberately and inextricably intertwined.'[14] The meeting in Jajce culminated with the formal rejection of the authority of the exiled monarchy, the declaration that a new Yugoslav state based on 'democratic federal principles' had been formed, and the appointment of Tito as marshal of Yugoslavia and prime minister.[15] There was little that King Peter II and his government in London could offer in response, particularly as the Partisans' strength and reputation increased across Yugoslavia.

By the end of the war, the NOVJ had grown into a formidable force which incorporated between 700,000 and 800,000 fighters organised in forty-eight divisions and four armies.[16] This figure includes significant numbers of women who had joined the Partisans in a 'degree of female military participation unprecedented and unrepeated in the region' and survived the conflict.[17] Estimates vary, but between 50,000 and 100,000 female combatants (including 2,000 officers) served in the NOVJ, approximately 25,000 of whom were killed.[18] The NOVJ changed its name again in March 1945, this time to the Yugoslav Army (*Jugoslavenska armija*, JA). Over the course of the war, it had developed from a largely Serb and Montenegrin (75–80 per cent) force to an army which, in terms of nations and nationalities, broadly reflected the Yugoslav population. The Partisans claimed that in May 1944 the national composition of the NOVJ was 44 per cent Serb, 30 per cent Croat, 10 per cent Slovene, 5 per cent Montenegrin, 2.5 per cent Macedonian, and 2.5 per cent Muslim.[19] Such claims are supported by the observations of outsiders such as Deakin, who notes that 'the central conclusion of our observations was that the National Liberation Army, in marked and forceful contrast to the pan-Serb, anti-Croat, and anti-Moslem obsessions of the Mihailović Četniks, was a *Yugoslav* military organization'.[20] Although the NOVJ received limited supplies from the British, and Soviet forces provided considerable assistance in the Belgrade Offensive, the Partisans had liberated the majority of Yugoslav territory by themselves, making Yugoslavia (with the exception of Albania) the only country in Europe able to claim it had liberated itself.[21] In the process, they swept aside other armed groups such as the Chetniks and established themselves among the population as the primary and ultimately sole resistance movement in BiH and the wider region.[22] Central to the Partisans' effort to overcome the divisions of war and forge effective Yugoslav institutions such as the military was the mantra of 'brotherhood and unity', which A. Ross Johnson argues signified 'opposition both to the Serb hegemony of interwar Yugoslavia and the national fratricide of World War II'.[23] The inclusivity of brotherhood and unity, coupled with a respectful policy towards Yugoslav civilians during the war and the ultimate victory of the Partisans, laid a solid foundation upon which the nascent state could draw legitimacy across its territory and consolidate its position in the aftermath of war.

The cost of their victory was considerable. Yugoslav estimates placed wartime losses at approximately 1.7 million, causing Dedijer to lament: 'Every ninth Yugoslav gave his life in the war.'[24] These figures are likely to have been exaggerated, as James Gow notes, 'around 1 million Yugoslavs died, according to calculations broadly accepted by non-partisan experts'.[25] On Victory Day (9 May 1945), Tito gave a speech celebrating the triumph of the Partisans. He lauded the soldiers of the NOVJ:

> Your immortal deeds will live forever in the hearts of our peoples and their future generations. The arena of the glorious battles of the Sutjeska, of Zelengora, Kozara, and the Neretva, etc, will remain eternal monuments to your heroism and that of your fallen comrades. They will inspire future generations of our peoples and will teach them how to love their country and how to die for it. They will be monuments of our national pride in the struggle for freedom and independence. The new Yugoslav Army, an Army forged in the fires of the fiercest battles, an Army which is comprised of yourselves, a true people's army which has won such

glorious victories, must remain, and will remain, the unshakable defender of the achievements of our superhuman struggle.[26]

Through recognising the sacrifices and bravery of the Partisans, promising eternal monuments, and designating a role for the army following the war, Tito was outlining his vision for the SFRJ. The costly victory earned by the Partisans provided the founding myth and a common focus of memorialisation for the new state, whilst the JA would preserve what had been won – national liberation and social revolution. This narrative, emphasising the shared nature of the triumph, was embraced by the Yugoslav military leadership, as Branko Mamula, a Partisan and later minister of defence, illustrates:

> Each of our nations and each of our nationalities were the vehicles of the struggle for their own national emancipation and that all of them together, by their common struggle managed, despite adversity, to score a victory over a militarily far superior enemy.[27]

In March 1945, the JA was quickly reorganised from its irregular structure into a more conventional fighting force. Adam Roberts argues that this process took place because 'Soviet influence and Soviet-style administrative socialism were at their height in the country' and Yugoslavia's main challenge at this point was 'reasserting central authority in a fragmented country'.[28] The Soviets had sent their first military mission to Yugoslavia in February 1944, and following Victory Day their assistance rapidly increased: thousands of Yugoslav officers and soldiers were sent to military schools in the USSR, the JA was organised on the Red Army model, and Yugoslav troops were increasingly armed with Soviet weaponry. In the immediate post-war period, the JA received 125,446 rifles, 38,210 sub-machine guns, 14,296 machine guns, in addition to hundreds of tanks and aeroplanes, and thousands of artillery pieces and mortars.[29] Although the transformation of the JA into a conventional army may seem at odds with the Yugoslav experience of the Second World War, James Gow contends that this decision resulted from Yugoslav belief in Soviet institutions (particularly the effective and experienced Red Army), and was consistent with other efforts to emulate Soviet structures during Yugoslavia's 'statist' phase.[30]

Within a few years, the differing visions that Stalin and Tito had for the future of the Balkans proved to be irreconcilable. Jeronim Perović, in his analysis of Soviet documents relating to the period, challenges the 'version propagated in the official Yugoslav historiography' and argues that 'the main reason for the conflict was Stalin's dismay when Tito continued to pursue an expansionist foreign policy agenda'.[31] Robert Niebuhr concurs, noting that 'there was simply little room for a strong personality like Tito, whose rise to supremacy in Belgrade threatened to upset the global competition for power'.[32] As a result, in June 1948 Yugoslavia was condemned at a meeting of Cominform and expelled from the organisation.[33] The following year, the Soviets renounced the Soviet–Yugoslav friendship treaty and began a series of military manoeuvres in neighbouring countries.[34]

Fear of Soviet invasion led to a rapid reconsideration of Yugoslavia's defensive capabilities, resulting in the (re)formation of Partisan units and the establishment

**Map 2.1** *The Western Balkans, 1945–91*

of Partisan headquarters and arms caches throughout Yugoslav territory.[35] By 1949, 149 Partisan regiments and 20 independent brigades had been formed by the JNA to supplement their defensive capacity.[36] Yugoslavia's isolation in the communist world forced it to look westwards for assistance. While Tito continued to denounce imperialism publicly, economic aid was negotiated from Britain, France, and the United States in 1950, followed by American military aid in 1951. This continued until 1958, providing the Yugoslav military with an array of heavy weapons and aircraft.[37] On 22 December 1951 (celebrated in the SFRJ as the Day of the Army), the military was renamed the JNA in order to signal severance with the past and Soviet organisational methods, including the commissar system, were abolished.[38] The threat of invasion stimulated further military expansion, and by 1952 Yugoslavia boasted an army of 500,000 troops and a defence budget that was the biggest in the world as a percentage of the national economy.[39]

## Post-war consolidation and Integral Yugoslavism

The 1946 constitution of the SFRJ reveals a clear link between the legitimacy of the regime and its wartime credentials. Authority in the new Yugoslav order, the constitution explained, 'derives from the people and belongs to the people' who had 'exercised their authority through the people's committees ... which had originated and developed during the struggle for national liberation ... and are the fundamental achievement of that struggle'.[40] The constitution established Yugoslavia as a federation of six republics: Serbia, Croatia, Slovenia, Bosnia and Herzegovina, Macedonia, and Montenegro, along with the autonomous province of Vojvodina and the autonomous region of Kosovo-Metohija (see Map 2.1). In contrast to the interwar kingdom, the new Yugoslavia offered considerable respect to the national sensitivities, linguistic rights, and cultural needs of almost all of the Yugoslav population. Two broad categories were recognised: the *narodi* (nations), consisting of Serbs, Croats, Slovenes, Macedonians, Montenegrins, and (from 1971) Muslims; the *narodnosti* (nationalities), consisting of Albanians, Hungarians, Turks, Slovaks, Bulgarians, Romanians, Ruthenes/Ukrainians, Czechs, and Italians.[41] The constitution enshrined the sovereign rights, security, equality, and national freedom of the nations through the republics, and the right of the nationalities to 'their own cultural development and the free use of their own language'.[42] However, not all groups within Yugoslav territory were included in the constitutional provisions. Romani people were guaranteed 'individual rights' but were only afforded equal status with other national groups in the Republic of Macedonia, whilst ethnic Germans (half a million of whom had lived in Yugoslavia prior to 1939) who survived the war and ensuing reprisals had their property confiscated and were interned in work camps until March 1948. Many left when they could, and those who remained after 1948 were employed in state industry and even conscripted into the JA.[43]

The JA was quick to begin adapting its own structures to reflect Yugoslav society because, as Gow argues, 'the armed services' legitimacy is dependent, to some considerable extent, on their congruence with the society that spawns them ... the armed forces' composition must be generally representative of social and ethnic cleavages within society'.[44] Universal male conscription meant that a significant cohort of the JA/JNA was proportionally representative of the male Yugoslav population. However, approximately half of the personnel in the JNA were career soldiers. Throughout the socialist period, the Yugoslav leadership was unable to achieve genuine proportional representation among these professional troops, with Serbs and Montenegrins consistently making up between 60 and 68 per cent of the office corps despite only constituting roughly 42 per cent of the population. However, although a predominantly Serb institution, the JNA was composed of soldiers and officers from every *narodi* and *narodnosti* who served alongside each other across the territory of the SFRJ.[45] Such diversity was (and remains) unprecedented in armed forces from the region. Florian Bieber argues that the multiethnic nature of the military was 'not only key in the general effort to structure Yugoslavia as an inclusive state but was also based on the experience of the Royal Yugoslav Army, which lacked legitimacy because it was viewed by non-Serbs as being dominated by Serb officers'.[46] Mile Bjelajac notes that following the war 'one of the most important preoccupations of the state and military management was to adapt the nationality structure [of the army] to the nationality structure of the population', and contends that the KPJ 'hoped that the problem of legitimacy in a multi-ethnic society would be overcome by appropriate representation of non-Serbs among Generals and the officer corps in general'.[47]

The initial efforts to create a more representative military, coupled with the federal structure and constitutional provisions of the state, were intended to establish the legitimacy of the new Yugoslavia. However, such policies were not necessarily intended to be permanent, as Sabrina Ramet argues:

The federal system was presumed to be largely an ephemeral formality and relinquished little authority to the republics. The national heterogeneity was the sole raison d'être for the establishment of federalism, with each republic except Bosnia-Herzegovina named after and consecrated as the official political embodiment of a discrete national group. The anticipated process of homogenization would, therefore, erode the basis for the federal system.[48]

This argument is strengthened if the changes in the structure and role of the JA in the aftermath of the Second World War are considered. From the AVNOJ declaration in 1943 until the Eight Congress of the League of Communists of Yugoslavia (the successor of the KPJ; *Savez komunista Jugoslavije*, SKJ) in December 1964, the dominant school of thought within the Yugoslav leadership was that the nations and nationalities of Yugoslavia would homogenise into a new socialist nation.[49] It was during this period that the term 'Yugoslav' was first considered as a national category, and the idea of 'Yugoslav Culture' was endorsed, signifying party recognition of 'Yugoslavism' (*Jugoslovenstvo*).[50] Yugoslavism developed alongside the state that espoused it, undergoing transformations and reinterpretations when it was deemed necessary. Initially, at least, it represented what Ramet describes as 'Integral Yugoslavism': the belief that a new Yugoslav nation was in the process of forming, and that 'national specificity and affective attachment to Yugoslavia were ... antagonistic'.[51] One of the leading proponents of this thinking was Aleksandar Ranković, an ardent centralist who was widely viewed as having 'Stalinist' tendencies. As head of all public and secret police forces (and organisation secretary of the SKJ), he was the third most powerful man in socialist Yugoslavia and carried a great deal of influence.[52]

The JA/JNA was a conscript force in which all able males served. The period of service changed several times, but in 1972 was set at fifteen months for Ground and Air Forces, and eighteen months for the Navy, with a reduction to twelve months for people 'of a high education'.[53] The conscripts, as a matter of policy, underwent training in republics other than their own, and would serve in units of mixed nationality.[54] Such a model can be explained by two key factors. Primarily, mixing conscripts and career soldiers from across Yugoslav territory clearly indicates an intention to utilise the military as a 'School of the Nation' in which men of different trades, ethnicity, and geographical origin are forged into the vanguard of the Yugoslav nation-building project. However, as the SFRJ leadership believed that 'every nationalism is dangerous' a more palatable rationale was offered.[55] Mitja Ribičič, as president of the Federal Executive Council, provides this explanation:

> Our point of departure is the working man and self-manager as the basic factor ... the dilemma over the creation of armies belonging to each nationality has no real basis in our society, as the peoples and nationalities already have their army, created in revolution and through joint efforts and sacrifices.[56]

The JNA was the army of the Yugoslav working class, a revolutionary army, in which there was no place for reactionary tendencies such as nationalism and, by extension, military organisation on the basis of nationality. Tito emphasised as much following the Croatian Crisis in 1971, when he said that by calling for a 'Croatian Army', Croatian separatists had wanted

> little by little, to take the army in their own, Croatian hands … they will have to wait a long time for this. I believe that the Sava will first have to start running upstream toward the Triglav before that happens.[57]

With conscripts from various nations deployed and trained away from their homes, language came to pose a challenge to integration efforts. Serbo-Croat was spoken across Croatia, Bosnia-Herzegovina, Serbia, and Montenegro, but was spoken in a variety of regional dialects, the most dominant of which are *ekavica* and *ijekavica*. Slovenian and Macedonian are distinct languages, and an additional complication to the linguistic composition of Yugoslavia can be found in the use of two alphabets. Generally, the Latin script is used in Slovenia and Croatia, Macedonian is written Cyrillic, and both are used to varying degrees in BiH, Serbia, and Montenegro. The JNA found a balance between functionality and national equality by employing the *ekavica* (largely spoken in Serbia) variation of Serbo-Croat written in the Latin script as the language of command.[58] This language represented an effort to inculcate Yugoslav soldiers and officers with a shared language, and with it a shared identity.

For multiple national groups to unite in an area as venerated and symbolically powerful as the military, a shared focus of loyalty that can transcend national differences must be present. For Yugoslavia, this was Tito. Revolutionary, Partisan leader, heroic liberator, field marshal, supreme commander, secretary of defence, prime minister, and president, Tito was inextricably intertwined with the Yugoslav state and its military. His wartime credentials earned him unparalleled prestige across Yugoslav society, while his half Croat, half Slovene heritage helped to allay fears of a return to Serb hegemony. Partisans who had fought alongside him dominated the institutions of Yugoslavia. Bjelajac suggests that in 1954, 86.7 per cent of JNA officers were former Partisans; in 1959, 80 per cent; in 1963, 73.8 per cent; and in 1969, 43.9 per cent.[59] Robin Alison Remington describes this 'generational cohort bonded to the military' as 'the "club of 1941"'.[60] Ljubičić, one of the members of the Club of '41, expresses his veneration clearly. He notes 'Tito's greatness as a revolutionary, as the inspirer and strategist of the revolution on Yugoslav soil', and argues that his wartime strategy was 'the equivalent of a scientific discovery' which 'opened a new epoch in the history of war'.[61] Edvard Kardelj, another Club of '41 member and a prominent architect of the Yugoslav state, declared:

> It is at this point that Tito's great role in the history of the working class and peoples of Yugoslavia begins. For Tito is the leading creative personality of our revolutionary workers' movement, armed by the Communist Party of Yugoslavia with the highest perceptions and means, which assured its success and victory.[62]

Ann Lane notes that during the early 1950s 'Tito, as founding father of the Yugoslav state was elevated, or perhaps elevated himself, into the role of cult figure'.[63] Tamara Pavasović Trošt argues that 'one can quickly conclude that Josip Broz Tito possessed – and indeed succeeded in building the perception of – the qualities of genuine charismatic authority' and further stipulates that he was 'particularly successful in maintaining his public image and using it as an anchor for a united Yugoslavia.'[64] (See Figure 2.2.) Even following his death in 1980, Tito remained a powerful figure in the JNA. Miroslav

**Figure 2.2** *President of Yugoslavia Josip Broz Tito (1892–1980) in the library of his villa in the Dedinje suburb of Belgrade, Yugoslavia, February 1953.* Courtesy of Westwood/Popperfoto via Getty Images.

Hadžić observes that he came to be used as 'a model, a theoretical and methodological standard, as legitimacy, supreme evidence, an ideological and political whip, and also a totem'.[65]

Along with Tito, socialism provided a key pillar of unity in Yugoslavia. For the military, it served as a powerful integrative agent and provided an inclusive, supranational ideology which could offer the most direct solution to the problems arising from creating a multiethnic military. If soldiers and officers could be convinced to subscribe to socialism and identify as socialists, they would come to share an ideology which emphasised their equality and class (rather than national) identity. The army, therefore, was not only responsible for defending the state and forging a Yugoslav identity, but also became the custodian of the achievements of the revolution and the torchbearer for its continuation, a duty made clear by Tito in 1971: 'The task of our army is not merely to defend the territorial integrity of our country, but also to defend our socialism when we see that it is in danger and that it cannot be defended by other means.'[66] In order to diffuse and promote Yugoslav socialism within the military and out into society, the army was utilised as 'a key instrument by which conscript youths were socialised into the values of the Yugoslav Communist system'.[67] Soldiers were given obligatory reading from the party and the military's own press, had to attend political and ideological lectures, and were encouraged to participate in recommended political and social activities in civilian society.[68] Furthermore, they received political education and training (*političko obrazovanje i vaspitanje*) which provided them with 'Marxist-based scientific knowledge about society and man, the working class as the mainstay of revolutionary changes, the War of National Liberation and the socialistic revolution, [and] about building a self-managed society as a community of equal nations and nationalities'.[69] Gow notes that 'the result of this education, other political work within the army and, presumably, peer-group pressure, was the nurturing of a "brotherhood and unity" spirit and the "Yugoslav" idea'.[70]

During the Second World War, the Yugoslav communists had been careful to portray the NOP as an open organisation largely free from strict ideological tenets. However, as the war progressed, the KPJ element of the Liberation Movement became increasingly pronounced, and by Victory Day the JA was undoubtedly a socialist army. As an organisation, the KPJ grew tremendously during the war from an interwar figure of 12,000 to a 1945 membership of 140,000, the vast majority of whom had joined via the military.[71] Dean observes that 'the institutional roots of party and army are the same: they grew together out of the Partisan struggle and in that formative period were highly integrated organisationally and ideologically', whilst Vašić argues that the army was simply the military arm of the KPJ.[72] The only political organisations that JNA soldiers could associate with was the party itself and its youth wing, and any vestige of religious representation that remained from the NOVJ was repressed.[73] The open and enforced politicisation of the military was a notable success. The JNA itself proudly stated that the SKJ 'exists in every military collective, unit and establishment and more than 90 per cent of the leading cadres belong to it', continuing that the purpose was to ensure the 'highest level of ideo-political consciousness possible'.[74] Marko Milivojević reports that in 1978, 100,000 of the JNA's 240,000 men were in the

SKJ, with all commanding officers and nearly all senior enlisted men being members as 'membership of the [SKJ] is a condition that has to be met by anyone who wishes to be considered for officer status'.[75] Such was the presence of the party in the military that the JNA developed its own communist party, the SKJ-JNA, which accounted for 5–6 per cent of the total SKJ membership.[76] Ljubičič describes the SKJ-JNA as having 'concerned themselves ... with everything of significance for the Army's development':

> They actively promote the revolutionary and all-people's character of the Army; educate Army men in the spirit of the Yugoslav socialist revolution; develop socialist morale; consolidate the brotherhood and unity of the nations and nationalities of Yugoslavia; [and] foster Yugoslav socialist patriotism and internationalism.[77]

In a reform of the organisation of the SKJ in 1974, a Central Committee was formed in which the JNA was given fifteen seats (10 per cent of the total), the same proportion as Vojvodina and Kosovo each had, giving it a 'stronger voice ... than ever before' and making it the most politically represented military in Europe (except for Albania).[78]

The military was an institution which embodied the society that many in the Yugoslav leadership aspired to build. In theory at least, it transcended the national divisions within Yugoslavia, was vehemently socialist, and was free from external pressures and commitments. The JNA's position as the vanguard of socialist Yugoslav society placed it in a uniquely privileged position in which it was offered a high degree of formal autonomy and sovereignty within the state. It was not until 1966 that its finances were even scrutinised, and until the 1980s the budget was linked to national income.[79] In addition, the JNA controlled large parts of the economy (most significantly, the entire defence industry) and conducted its own foreign trade. Indeed, estimates suggest that the JNA produced 80 per cent of the combat material it required, and Yugoslav arms exports to non-aligned countries exceeded the value of arms imported by Yugoslavia.[80] The power and wealth acquired by the JNA was manifested in the everyday lives of the officers and personnel of the JNA, as Vašić illustrates: '[They] had their own apartment blocks, their privileged shops, their medical care, their courts of law; the army bank offered them privileged credits, their wives were employed without problems.'[81] Petrović describes the system as a 'society within a society' as they also holidayed in specific JNA resorts and attended exclusive concerts, dance evenings, and theatre in JNA *dom vojske* (Home of the Army) cultural centres.[82] Furthermore, the JNA had its own political representation, enjoyed generally high social esteem among the country's population, and its leadership was 'in a unique position in the communist world to comment publicly and critically on sensitive public issues'.[83] The elevation of the JNA to such a position in society represents a tangible effort to supplement the ideological focus of Yugoslav socialism with incentives to literally 'buy-in' to the idea. Through establishing legitimacy and utilising ideology, education, party membership, and the privileged position it enjoyed in society, the JNA went to great lengths to push integrative measures and forge bonds between its soldiers that transcended national divisions and would ensure unity.

The JNA was also employed in integration efforts that spanned broad aspects of society such as memorialisation, culture, and sport. The considerable number of

Yugoslavs who died in the Second World War provided a shared experience of loss, victimhood, and tragedy. The struggle of the Partisans against a militarily superior foe conveyed a message of shared sacrifice and heroism, and the Partisan victory offered a narrative of strength in unity and shared triumph. Together, this collective memory of the Second World War provided the fertile ground for the founding myth of the state and the JNA to be developed.

In his Victory Day speech Tito had envisioned 'eternal monuments' and 'monuments of our national pride' being created to honour the fallen and celebrate the heroism of the Partisans.[84] Following the war, such monuments were built at the sites of enemy atrocities and Partisan battles across Yugoslavia. The importance of these locations was emphasised, and such sites became the 'altar of the homeland, the holy grounds of the new socialist religion'.[85] Vladana Putnik describes the memorials thus: 'They depicted the martyrdom of the partisans and the civil victims as sacrifices in the struggle against fascism and for the establishment of communism'.[86] The Battle of Sutjeska, one of the significant engagements of the war, was memorialised with an initial monument at Tjentište in 1949, which was then replaced in 1958 and further enriched by an additional memorial complex completed in 1974. Putnik observes that memorials such as Tjentište, often built in inaccessible locations, were symbols of the state which became 'obligatory places for the student excursions to visit'.[87] In addition to the monuments, public holidays marked significant days of the Second World War. The beginning of the uprising against the Axis occupiers was marked on 4 July during Fighter's Day, while the formation of the NOP was commemorated on 21 (later 22) December. Monuments across Yugoslavia and the public holidays enjoyed across the country dispensed a message of the shared, Yugoslav, nature of the conflict.

The SFRJ also employed cinema in the memorialisation process, most significantly the production of *Partizanski filmovi* (Partisan films). Jurica Pavičić notes that 'throughout the forty-three years of Yugoslav cinema, partisan film was commercially the most successful, ideologically the most representative and culturally the most typical film of all genres'.[88] Partisan films often depicted the great tales of the struggle and ultimate victory of the Partisans, in productions such as Battle of Neretva (1969), Walter Defends Sarajevo (1972), and Battle of Sutjeska (1973). Pavičić argues that 'all of them organise their narrative around the legitimisation of the new regime through its war merits'.[89] Partisan films served to illustrate a clear narrative of the righteousness of the Partisan cause and the importance of unity, whilst also highlighting the martyrs and heroes' sacrifices to the causes of liberation and socialism, reinforcing and promulgating the founding myth of both the state and the JNA.

The JNA was even embedded in the sport of the SFRJ. Indeed, the country's largest stadium and 'flagship project of the physical culture movement' was built in Belgrade by soldiers and simply named the JNA upon its completion in 1951.[90] The stadium was the home of the army's own football team, Partizan, which was directed and administered by senior JNA officers and became one of the most successful teams of the socialist period. Partizan competed for the Marshall Tito Cup in the Yugoslav domestic league, a competition in which each season's victor was presented the trophy by senior JNA generals and party members. Richard Mills observes how 'publicly, the game's relationship with the regime was impossible to ignore' and notes that football itself became a vehicle 'to reinforce the popularity of the state and its institutions at a local level' as lower league teams and factory teams played matches in celebration of the Day of the Army.[91]

The JNA itself, whilst often the object of memorialisation, conducted commemorative events of its own. Ceremonies and military parades can be regarded as a common feature of most societies and serve to commemorate the fallen and reiterate a national narrative. The JNA was no exception to this, but it did develop a rather unique perspective on memorialising the Partisans. The plan for responding to a NATO invasion from the north-west, for example, was named 'Sutjeska 2', while large-scale training exercises were given names such as 'Freedom-71' and would often take place on the site of Partisan battles. 'Podgora-72' was a demonstration in celebration of the thirtieth anniversary of the navy and air force, and enacted a hypothetical attack on Tito's wartime headquarters on the island of Vis. As part of the 'Kornati-74' exercise, wreaths were laid in memory of the Partisans 'to remind the younger generation of the national liberation struggle'.[92] The evocation of the Partisan legacy in planning and training illustrates an attempt by JNA officers (who were mostly former Partisans) to imbibe recruits and conscripts with a sense of the wartime struggle, celebrate the founding myth of the JNA, and promote the ideology of brotherhood and unity.

The celebration and commemoration of the Partisans gave the JNA a clear identity and offered it a glorious and, importantly, shared founding myth. It was the multiethnic Yugoslav communists and Partisans who, through struggle and sacrifice, had defeated the occupiers. Memorialisation in this manner legitimised the regime, laid the foundation for the 'Yugoslav socialist patriotic' identity, and celebrated Partisan ideals such as brotherhood and unity. Whilst impossible to quantify, the impact of such culturally significant messages doubtlessly catalysed the ideological and structural integrative efforts of the JNA.

## A changing approach and Organic Yugoslavism

Between 1948 and 1952, a series of domestic and international political events instigated a dramatic reconsideration of the SFRJ's state structures and geopolitical position. For inspiration, the Yugoslav leadership returned to Marx and Lenin for inspiration and devised the doctrine of workers self-management. The new approach aimed to delegate control of the means of production to the workers themselves, rather than the creation of a state to control it in their name. This was manifested in practical terms by a reduction of central planning in favour of a decentralised structure which offered more power to the republics.[93] These changes were gradually introduced throughout the 1950s and the early 1960s, but it was not until 1964, at the Eighth Party Congress, that a firm commitment was made dispelling any assimilationist intent:

> The erroneous opinions that our nations have, in the course of our socialist social development, become obsolete and that it is necessary to create a unified Yugoslav nation [are] expression[s] of bureaucratic centralism and unitarism. Such opinions

usually reflect ignorance of the political, social, economic, and other functions of the republics and autonomous provinces.[94]

Ramet notes that 'this was unquestionably a turning point both for Yugoslav nationalities policy and for interrepublican relations' and resulted in the republics becoming 'fully legitimate agents of popular sovereignty' while the Yugoslav state became genuinely federal in its structure.[95] Although the 'Yugoslav' category (introduced in 1961) was retained as an option in the census, the period in which a Yugoslav identity was assumed to be gradually replacing those of the nations of Yugoslavia came to an end.

From 1964 onwards, the policy of Integral Yugoslavism was replaced with 'Yugoslav socialist patriotism'. The new approach lacked the supranational, assimilationist element of its predecessor, and was conceptually defined as 'the identification with, feeling for, and love of the socialist self-managing community' which represented a 'moral force for the unity of the socialist self-managing community of nations and nationalities of Yugoslavia'.[96] Ramet describes this new approach to the national question as 'Organic Yugoslavism', and argues that it included devotion to Yugoslavia as a whole, as well to one's republic.[97] The move away from Integral Yugoslavism was cemented following the removal of Ranković, one of its most influential sponsors, from his positions of power in 1966.[98] Robert Dean notes that 'as the decentralization of party and state authority proceeded in the late 1960s, the army remained something of an institutional anomaly – monolithic, hierarchical, centralized' and observes that 'the all-Yugoslav JNA seemed a threat to the rights of Yugoslavia's constituent republics', a situation which led nationalists to demand the reorganisation of the JNA into monoethnic units, each with their own language of command.[99] Although the nationalist demands were ignored, scrutiny of the JNA continued and the federal defence budget was subjected to serious criticism in the Yugoslav parliament in December 1966, for the first time.[100] The developments within the political apparatus of the SFRJ, coupled with concerns regarding its budget, demanded that the JNA reform its own structures. This pressure was compounded in 1968, when Soviet-led forces invaded Czechoslovakia, raising concerns of an offensive on Yugoslavia.[101]

Upon hearing of the invasion, Tito convened an extraordinary meeting of his top civilian and military leadership on the island of Brioni to assess the military capabilities of the SFRJ. The gathered leaders agreed that the JNA was unready for a Soviet invasion, and that Yugoslavia's defensive capacity needed to be significantly increased.[102] The JNA had been supplementing its standing army with a significant reserve of Partisan formations since the Warsaw Pact was established in 1955, and had formalised this practice in 1959 by focusing JNA doctrine on 'combined open-partisan warfare'.[103] The delegates at Brioni decided that this doctrine, which utilised Yugoslavia's knowledge, experience, and geography, was appropriate, but needed to be rapidly and considerably expanded. The promise of comprehensive military reform also provided an opportunity for the JNA to be brought in line with socio-political developments within Yugoslavia.

The most significant outcomes of the meeting on Brioni were gathered under the umbrella of the new Total National Defence (*Opštenarodna odbrana*, ONO) strategy. This approach offered an affordable and effective countermeasure to invasion, placated those calling for an increase in the power of the republics, and was largely drawn from the Yugoslav experience of the Second World War. Nikola Ljubičić, one of the architects of ONO, offers this explanation:

> The National Liberation War of the Yugoslav peoples, waged under unfavourable international military-political circumstances and with inferior military equipment, graphically illustrates what can be accomplished by a people who are well-organised, smartly led, and ready and resolved to fight for their vital interests. The Yugoslav liberation war confirmed that the morale of the people and their armed forces – though military weapons and equipment are hurled at them in massive quantities and the war is protracted and exhausting – is the most important, the decisive factor in victory.[104]

At its most basic level, ONO proposed to arm and train as much of the population as possible in Partisan warfare. Whichever armed force attempted to occupy Yugoslavia could, the theory went, win some significant victories against the JNA, but would then be faced by millions of trained, armed, and organised citizen-soldiers. Estimates suggested that a force of two million soldiers would be needed to effectively subjugate the country.[105] Although ONO was, in many ways, inspired by the Yugoslav experience in the Second World War, it was not the product of nostalgia. Ljubičić observed the successes of technologically inferior forces in China, Algeria, and interwar Indochina, but recognised the unique significance of Vietnam on their thinking:

> There, a relatively small, poor, impoverished, long suppressed but unified, resolute, morally strong and invincible people for eleven years successfully fought off the million-strong army of the USA and its quislings. Enormous quantities of technical equipment, numerical superiority, the most up-to-date combat equipment, including chemical and biological weapons, the appalling terror and devastation – none of these could defeat the morally firm and determined Vietnam people.[106]

The National Defence Law of 1969 formally introduced ONO, and established Territorial Defence (*Teritorijalna Odbrana*, TO) formations in each of the republics and provinces.[107] The new defence policy was believed to be consistent with the workers self-management tenet of Yugoslav socialism, and was therefore considered to be wholly appropriate. Mijalko Todorović, a member of the Executive Bureau of the SKJ, asserts:

> To expand the rights and responsibilities of federal republics, communes, working organisations and other self-managing units does not imply any weakening of our people's unity and defensive power but on the contrary, strengthens and raises them to a new, higher level of self-management.[108]

The TO forces were financed by their respective republics and provinces, utilised the relevant local language for administration and command, and stored their weapons locally. Although the commanders were usually from the JNA, in every other regard the

TO units were organised by regional defence ministries, which were given jurisdiction to direct national defence efforts within their respective territories.[109] This made each one an essentially separate and distinct army. Herrick describes the introduction of TO forces as 'a defence structure that allows for the national character of each of its republics and provinces', whilst Cynthia Enloe notes that, for the first time, 'racial-ethnic categories … were openly accepted'.[110] In addition, the ONO framework dictated that 25 per cent of each republic's troop contribution would be stationed in their home republic, limiting the exposure of conscripts to other nations and nationalities.[111] ONO represented a dramatic change in the JNA's place in Yugoslavia. It was no longer a distinctly Yugoslav institution that was, to some extent, responsible for trying to forge a new Yugoslav identity; instead, it became a 'co-equal' military force alongside multiple republican armies which offered each republic (particularly Slovenia, which had the most homogenous population of the Yugoslav republics and therefore a TO force that was organised, financed, composed, and commanded by Slovenes) 'one of the trappings of national sovereignty'.[112]

The placement of over one million trained reservists, complemented by further civil defence organisations comprising another million, to the jurisdiction of the republics and provinces had a profound impact on the JNA and its role in society. It would retain command in joint tactical operations, but the JNA 'lost its monopoly of responsibility for defence and became nominally (although not de facto) one of two co-equal components of the newly named Armed Forces of Yugoslavia'.[113] However, the legal status of the two sections of the Yugoslav military remained ambiguous. Traditionally, territorial forces offer little more than support to the conventional army. Ljubičić argued that under the new structures, 'there is not a hierarchy of elements in the system of nation-wide defence, but a combination of reactions in which any success by one expands the radius for action by others'.[114] His assertions were later confirmed in the 1974 Constitution, which stated thus:

> The Armed Forces of the Socialist Federal Republic of Yugoslavia form a single whole and consist of the Yugoslav People's Army, as the joint armed forces of all nations and nationalities and of all working people and citizens, and of the Territorial Defence as the broadest form of organized defence forces.[115]

The 1974 Constitution also enshrined other modifications to the structure and organisation of the Yugoslav Armed Forces. The JNA became the first army in history that was constitutionally bound to be proportionally representative of the population it defended:

> In terms of composition of the officer cadre, and appointment to higher command and leadership positions in the Yugoslav People's Army, the principle of proportional representation of republics and autonomous provinces will be applied.[116]

To achieve this aim, promotion quotas were used to lessen Serb dominance, and recruitment was focused on attracting cadets from under-represented republics.

Indeed, the reorganisation of 1974 immediately led to proportional national representation in all officer schools, the reserve officer corps, and TO units.[117] However, proportional representation by republic did not imply proportional representation by national origin, and the significant numbers of Serbs living outside of the Republic of Serbia, for example, were free to serve in the military as representatives of the republic where they resided. Proportional representation was never achieved in the officer corps, and the proportion of Serbs steadily rose until 1991. Among the most senior officers, however, a degree of proportionality was achieved and parity was almost achieved among senior officers more generally, with only Montenegrins remaining significantly over-represented.[118] The ONO approach to military organisation illustrates the entrenchment of Yugoslav socialist patriotism in the SFRJ defence sector and signalled the end of efforts to utilise the JNA as the school of a new, Yugoslav nation.

The 1974 constitution also established the equality of languages and alphabets. This allowed the Slovenian and Macedonian languages (and the Cyrillic alphabet) to be used in command and training and permitted the publication of educational literature and material in multiple languages. JNA recruits were also offered local language courses wherever they were stationed.[119] These measures were expanded further in 1988, when the main journals of the JNA, *Narodna armija* (People's Army) and *Front*, were published in Slovenian and Macedonian and multilanguage signs were introduced in all barracks and military installations.[120] These measures illustrate a clear departure from earlier attempts to create a unifying language shared by all Yugoslavs, and a recognition of the linguistic diversity within the JNA.

The JNA remained broadly unchanged in its 1974 format until the fabric of the SFRJ itself began to unravel. The death of Tito in 1980, economic stagnation, and the collapse of the USSR and European communism placed tremendous obstacles in the path of the Yugoslav leadership. The SKJ was formally disbanded in 1990, leaving the structures and institutions of the Yugoslav state in an ideological and political void. In this context, calls for independence and support for nationalist political platforms grew in strength in many of the republics. As the last Yugoslav institution, the JNA became the final obstacle to independence for nationalist movements within some republics. The Slovenian administration refused to continue providing funds to the federal defence budget in 1990–1, and the JNA came to be depicted as a foreign occupying force in some Slovenian media.[121] As tensions between the republics increased, the JNA, seeking 'reliable and usable' forces, formed ethnically homogeneous Serbian units for special use in Slovenia in 1991.[122] When the Yugoslav crisis escalated, the JNA found itself caught between increasingly vitriolic debates among the leaders of the republics. The collective presidency that had replaced Tito was all but paralysed by the crisis, and General Veljko Kadijević, the minister of defence of the SFRJ and de facto leader of the JNA, refused to intervene (either in the name of Yugoslavia or Serbia) without a mandate from the presidency.[123] As tensions between the republics erupted into declarations of independence, the predominantly Serb JNA was left with few options.[124] Hadžić, a former JNA officer, offers this concise analysis of events: 'The Army could not save the country it belonged to and so in order to survive it had to lean towards the one that Milošević offered. And he was the only one making the offer.'[125]

# Conclusion

The Partisans founded the socialist Yugoslav state in the midst of war, establishing a federal system which they hoped would provide unity and stability once victory was achieved. The struggle, sacrifice, and ultimate triumph of the Partisans provided the founding myth of Tito's Yugoslavia and established the legitimacy of the nascent state. In the years following the Second World War, following the example set by the Soviet Union, Yugoslavia entered a phase of development focused on centralising authority and strengthening the power of the state. During this period, the military was an invaluable tool for advocates of Integral Yugoslavism. Its access to (and control over) hundreds of thousands of men from across Yugoslavia placed it in an unrivalled position to inculcate the population with an ideological framework that legitimised the socialist Yugoslav state and its belief that 'national differences would wither away'.[126] The military leadership's attempts to build a unified army out of the nations and nationalities of Yugoslavia during this phase mirrored the state's efforts to unify the population, with a strong party presence and a focus on shared loyalty to Tito and socialism. In this time, military personnel enjoyed one of the most privileged positions in society, while the military as an institution was the subject of memorialisation and became 'accustomed to official public praise and a virtual aura of sanctity'.[127] These factors helped to make service in the military, and with it regular exposure to the leadership's efforts to forge a Yugoslav nation, more legitimate and appealing.

Following decades of ideological and political development, integrational agendas were cast aside by the political leadership of Yugoslavia. Following this change of policy, attempts were made to reimagine the JNA as the protector of the rights and identities of the nations and nationalities of Yugoslavia rather than a monolithic, assimilationist threat. Tito remained as a shared focus of loyalty, and a more clearly defined brand of Yugoslav socialism served to provide a unifying ideology. However, the introduction of TO forces undermined the JNA's role as the protector of all the nations and nationalities of Yugoslavia and brought its legitimacy into question. After a series of crises in Yugoslavia in the 1980s, coupled with the rise of nationalist leaders across many of the republics, the JNA (and the Yugoslav state) came to be viewed, like its interwar predecessor, as a device of Serb dominance. With Tito gone and support for socialism coming into question, the only factors left holding the JNA together were the SFRJ's complex constitutional order, the fading legacy of the Partisans, and the political and economic privilege enjoyed by its increasingly isolated leadership.

Throughout its various incarnations the JNA remained vital to the Yugoslav state. Tanja Petrović notes that 'the Yugoslav army and its officers were considered one of the most important pillars of Yugoslav unity', while Johnson states that the JNA was 'the custodian and ultimate guarantor of the Yugoslav State and the Communist System'.[128] Arguably, ensuring the unity of Yugoslavia was the single main task of the military. According to a 1971 poll conducted by *Nedeljne informativne novine*, a Belgrade weekly, only 12 per cent of professional JNA personnel (officers and non-commissioned officers) thought that foreign aggression was the most likely source of conflict and over half of high-ranking officers (from the rank of Major up) believed that 'nationalism and chauvinism' were the greatest dangers facing Yugoslavia.[129] Such polls indicate that many within the JNA, particularly in the upper echelons, were fully aware that their primary concern was keeping the SFRJ together. Minister of Defence Admiral Branko Mamula, writing in the JNA journal *Narodna armija* in 1983, described the role of the JNA in Yugoslav society thus:

> The links between the army and the people have been confirmed and strengthened. The reputation that the army enjoys in our society, as the backbone of the system of nationwide defense; a breeding ground of brotherhood, unity, and Yugoslav socialist patriotism; and an important factor of security, internal cohesion, and stability of Yugoslavia has been maintained.[130]

The sheer range of duties the JNA was expected to perform (the backbone of defence, a breeding ground of Yugoslav socialism, and an important factor of state cohesion) by the Yugoslav leadership long after the Yugoslav nation-building project was abandoned illustrates the extent to which the state was wholly reliant on the military for cohesion.

The challenge of maintaining this cohesion grew steadily more complex until the SFRJ began to disintegrate in 1991. Part 2 charts the demise of the JNA and socialist territorial formations during the last months of socialist Yugoslavia, illustrating how three armies emerged from this framework in BiH and evolved during the complex armed conflict that erupted in April 1992. These armies fought the war, and, in its aftermath, became the components from which the contemporary OSBiH was built.

Part 2

# Components

# 3

# The Army of Republika Srpska

The *Vojska Republike Srpske* (VRS) was established as the military of the Serb Republic that was proclaimed by Serb leaders in BiH in May 1992. It was created from the framework of the JNA and maintained a significant supremacy over its wartime adversaries in numerous areas, including equipment, training, and organisation, offering it complete dominance on the battlefield throughout most of the 1992–5 War in BiH. Despite such advantages, the VRS failed to force the government of BiH to capitulate, and as the conflict developed, its opponents grew increasingly powerful and coordinated. By the final year of the war, the VRS was struggling to attain any significant victories or retain the ground it had conquered, its troops were demoralised and overstretched, and its logistics and communications infrastructure, key to its momentous early triumphs, lay in ruins. Faced with defeat on the battlefield and mounting diplomatic pressure from the international community and their allies in Belgrade, the Bosnian Serb leadership acquiesced first to a ceasefire and then to the Dayton Peace Agreement. The terms of the agreement offered the VRS a chance to escape total defeat on the battlefield but fell short of victory: the state for which it had fought, Republika Srpska (RS), would survive, but in a reduced form and within BiH. In the aftermath of the conflict, the VRS remained as one of three armies on Bosnian territory. These three armies became the components of the military integration process and were ultimately unified to create the OSBiH.

The VRS played a central role in the project to create a Greater Serbia out of the disintegrating SFRJ. The Greater Serbia ideology of the 1990s represented a revival of early twentieth-century narratives that were developed to justify the expansionist ambitions of the Serbian administration.[1] In the context of the disintegration of the SFRJ, the idea of forging a larger Serbian state from the ashes of the Yugoslav state received enough widespread support to unite a wide range of nationalist Serb leaders in Croatia, BiH, Montenegro, and Serbia under the leadership of Serbian President Slobodan Milošević.[2] However, beyond this relatively vague desire to unite their respective Serb populations, these leaders had little else in common and frequently competed with each other for power, often at the expense of their overall strategic position. The most significant divisions among the Serb communities of BiH stemmed from the Serb experience of the Second World War. Marko Attila Hoare observes,

For the first year of its existence the rank-and-file of the Partisan movement was overwhelmingly Serb and though this numerical dominance lessened as the war progressed, the Serbs continued to participate disproportionately in the movement at an all-Yugoslavia level until the end of the war.[3]

As a result, a considerable portion of the Serb population across Yugoslavia was directly linked to the legacy of the Partisans and identified with its heritage. In BiH, the Bosnian Serbs had been the driving force of the Partisan resistance, contributing approximately 70 per cent of the strength of the two major Partisan units in the republic and, after the war, receiving 64.1 per cent of Bosnian Partisan pensions.[4] This population was mostly spread across the northern regions of Bosnian Krajina and Northern Bosnia, and was centred on Banja Luka, the largest predominantly Serb city in the republic. However, many Serbs, particularly in BiH and Serbia, rejected the socialist ideology of the Partisans and favoured the advancement of Serbian Orthodox Christianity and the restoration of the exiled Serb monarchy, which had ruled Yugoslavia prior to the Axis invasion. Their wartime movement was focused on the remnants of the JKV and adopted the name *Četnici* (Chetniks). Although the Chetniks had collaborated with Axis forces before being soundly beaten, both militarily and diplomatically, by the Partisans, many Serbs continued to celebrate the movement after the war.[5] In BiH, the most vocal support of this nature came from Bosnian Serbs in the mountainous regions of the Drina Valley, which bordered Serbia and Montenegro. Such ideological and historical separations within the Serb community were only amplified by the personal rivalries and political differences within and between the leaderships of each constituency.

As the forces that supported the creation of a Greater Serbia gathered, such divisions became increasingly apparent. This not only led to friction over how the war should be conducted within the Serb leadership but was also the cause of confusion among their adversaries, as Ejup Ganić, a member of the presidency of BiH recalls. In October 1991, he visited a village near Trebinje which had just been burnt down by JNA soldiers. He recalls:

> On the way back I noticed these soldiers of the [JNA] – they had the long hair of the Chetniks and they greeted me with three fingers raised. Then I asked 'Is this the Yugoslav Army or Chetniks? What am I seeing?' The commander's deputy told me 'it's up to you Ganić to decide what they are, who they are'.[6]

A few years previously, a JNA soldier evoking such imagery (the three fingers, *tri prsta*, was once a religious invocation of the Holy Trinity but had become a symbol of Serb nationalism) would have been severely punished for discrediting the legacy of the military's Partisan founders and undermining the military's vehemently anti-nationalist reputation. However, as the JNA was 'Serbianised', both in terms of its composition and outlook, parts of it became increasingly Chetnik. When the VRS emerged from the JNA, this division deepened.

Ganić's confusion over the identity of the soldiers not only reflects the rapidly changing political landscape in BiH but also hints at another key division that beset the Serb leadership throughout the war: the question of who was in overall command of the VRS. The matter was complicated by the *de jure* separation of the VRS from the renamed Army of Yugoslavia (*Vojska Jugoslavije*, VJ) while it in fact continued to operate as an integral part of it. As a result, Slobodan Milošević, president of Serbia and the sponsor of Serb efforts in BiH, Ratko Mladić, commander and figurehead of the VRS, and Radovan Karadžić, president of Republika Srpska and the military's constitutional civilian commander, could all claim to wield supreme authority over the VRS. Although they essentially operated in concert, their relationship was beset with rivalry as each had different, and somewhat irreconcilable, visions for how the VRS should develop as a military and fight the war.

Like all of the armies that emerged from the war in BiH and were later unified to create the OSBiH, the VRS emerged from the multiethnic institutions of the SFRJ. The once proudly diverse and professional military that had been the JNA was rapidly stripped of non-Serb personnel and divided among the Serb leaders across former Yugoslavia. Between the allocation of JNA troops to Bosnian Serb leaders in 1992 and the signing of the DPA, the VRS underwent a dramatic transformation. Arms and munitions cached to defend against Soviet or NATO invasion were turned on the civilians they had been intended to help defend as the leaders of the Greater Serbia project sought to 'cleanse' as much land as they could of non-Serbs. The VRS was a key instrument in this endeavour. Its troops employed merciless tactics to drive people from their homes, and ultimately committed acts of genocide in pursuit of their objectives. These acts, particularly the massacre of over 8,000 Bosnian Muslims at Srebrenica, define the VRS in the eyes of many Bosnians as well as foreign observers, making its integration into a unified multiethnic military after the war exceptionally complex and challenging.

## Partisans, Chetniks and the Military Line: The origins of the VRS

Unlike its opponents, the core of the VRS originated from a well-established and professional military. Once considered a champion of 'brotherhood and unity' and a cornerstone in efforts to promote cooperation between the peoples of Yugoslavia, by early 1992 the JNA had been stripped of conscripts and many professional soldiers from Slovenia and Croatia at the behest of those republics' respective leaderships. This increased the Serb contingent of the JNA from a pre-June 1991 total of 35 per cent of conscripts and 40 per cent of professional soldiers to over 90 per cent in both categories, undermining its legitimacy as a Yugoslav institution while also offering an opportunity for Serb leaders to inherit a powerful tool of coercion.[7] Such a turn of events had been anticipated by a powerful network of political and military leaders within the disintegrating Yugoslav state which served as a 'chain of command which ran parallel to the old Yugoslav Army, through the state security department and the interior ministry'.[8]

Known as the Military Line (*Vojna linija*, VL), this network was established by Milošević and coordinated by Serbia's State Security Service (*Služba državne bezbednosti*, SDB), which became a crucial tool for the Serbian president to project power both within Serbia and into the rest of Yugoslavia. In essence, the VL rejected the Titoist leanings of many in the Yugoslav leadership in favour of the 'Serbianisation' of the state and the military.[9] Part of the SDB's operations in the years leading up to the collapse of Yugoslavia had been to create this network of like-minded influential individuals across the institutions of the Yugoslav state, ensuring that each was prepared to support their agenda by having them sign an oath of loyalty to Milošević.[10] One of their recruits was Mladić, who was duly promoted to the rank of major-general and, on 25 April 1992, reassigned to the JNA's Second Military District, which included eastern Croatia and almost all of BiH, as deputy commander. Two weeks later, on 10 May, he assumed command of the district.[11] His redeployment ran alongside that of thousands of other Bosnian Serb JNA personnel who were brought from across Yugoslavia to replace outgoing soldiers from other Yugoslav republics, in a manoeuvre designed to pre-empt demands that the JNA be withdrawn from BiH following independence. While the JNA itself would leave, its significant Bosnian Serb contingent (85 per cent of JNA troops in BiH in 1991) could legitimately remain.[12] President of Yugoslavia and close ally of Milošević, Borisav Jović, explained the rationale behind this manoeuvring in December 1991:

> When BiH is recognised internationally, the JNA will be declared a foreign army and its withdrawal will be demanded, which is impossible to avoid. In this situation, the Serb population in BiH … will be left unprotected and endangered. Slobo feels that we must withdraw all citizens of Serbia and Montenegro from the JNA in BiH in a timely fashion and transfer citizens of BiH to the JNA there … That will also create the possibility for the Serb leadership in BiH to assume command over the Serb part of the JNA.[13]

Thus, the VL was able to organise, prepare, and deploy the core of an army in BiH which could be formally handed over to a cooperative (Serb) source of authority within the newly recognised country if it became independent.

The Serb Democratic Party (*Srpska demokratska stranka*, SDS) was established in July 1990 and functioned as the political leadership of Serbs in BiH, despite numerous localised Bosnian Serb and multiethnic parties being established across the republic.[14] However, in the December 1990 elections, the SDS won both Serb seats in the presidency, as well as gaining the second greatest share of seats (behind the dominant Bosnian Muslim party) in both houses of BiH's parliament, cementing its place as the unrivalled Bosnian Serb authority in BiH. The strength of the SDS and its broadly pro-Milošević outlook made it an ideal candidate to receive support from Belgrade, and the party was provided with arms and resources throughout 1991.[15] However, despite wielding genuine power and retaining significant influence within the newly elected institutions of the state, the SDS leadership chose to reject the legitimacy of BiH entirely. Karadžić explains,

> President Milošević did not see the international recognition of [BiH] as an event of crucial importance … We even joked about this and he said that although

Caligula declared his horse a senator, the horse never became one, and added that the same applied to [President of the Presidency of BiH, Alija] Izetbegović. He had international recognition but no state. And we really thought that.[16]

The SDS orchestrated a campaign to undermine and de-legitimise the nascent Bosnian state and prepare for its collapse. In April 1991, several predominantly Serb municipalities formed an economic and cultural association, which initially held no power, but soon developed their own assemblies and police forces. Many of them also stopped sending taxes to the government in Sarajevo.[17] In September, these assemblies proclaimed the formation of an array of Serb Autonomous Regions (*Srpska autonomna oblast*, SAO) in BiH, including Krajina, Romanija, and Stara Herzegovina, 'with the aim of separating from the Republican government agencies in Sarajevo'.[18] In November, the SDS organised a plebiscite primarily for the Bosnian Serb population, asking voters whether they wished to remain in Yugoslavia. The outcome was purportedly 100 per cent in favour, and over the following months the JNA and SDS increasingly coordinated the establishment of municipal governments, paramilitary forces, and checkpoints.[19] On 19 December 1991, the SDS promulgated a document to the Serb administrations labelled as 'Top Secret' and titled *For the Organisation and Activity of Organs of the Serb People in BiH in Extraordinary Circumstances*. James Gow, who served as an expert witness for the ICTY on this topic, argues that this document 'indicates preparations for the creation of these para-governmental structures through the establishment of what are called crisis headquarters'. He notes that such preparations were made 'almost certainly under the tutelage of the Serbian [SDB]'.[20]

The SDS leadership took up residence at the Holiday Inn in Sarajevo in October 1991, following the formation of the SAOs. By January 1992, it had become 'something of an SDS stronghold' and housed the well-armed entourage of Karadžić along with a host of party officials.[21] From this base, the SDS orchestrated its complete withdrawal from the institutions of the Bosnian state and laid the foundations of a Serb state on the territory of BiH. This final phase began on 9 January, when the Serb People's Assembly (which evolved from the framework of the crisis headquarters) proclaimed the establishment of the Serb Republic of Bosnia and Herzegovina (*Srpska Republika Bosna i Hercegovina*, SRBiH) at the hotel. This political entity was renamed *Republika Srpska* (RS) in August 1992.[22] The referendum on Bosnian independence of 29 February and 1 March 1992 was boycotted by most of the Bosnian Serb population, at the behest of the SDS, but went ahead peacefully. However, a shooting at an Orthodox wedding in Sarajevo on the final day of voting led to a significant increase in tensions, and by the next morning, armed SDS supporters were manning barricades across the city that they had erected overnight. These paramilitaries were coordinated by the SDS from the Holiday Inn, where a team of snipers joined the protection detail of the leadership.[23] This declaration was followed in March by the promulgation of an SRBiH Constitution, the parliamentary session of which was broadcast live on television. One Bosnian Serb MP commented in the last session that 'at long last I have lived to see Bosnian Krajina become Western Serbia' while another said 'now the Turks will shake with fear from us'.[24] The constitution made the objectives of the SRBiH (and the military duties of its citizens) clear in its stipulations regarding national defence, with Article 109 stating, 'It is the right and duty of all citizens to protect and defend the sovereignty and territorial integrity of the [Serb] Republic and Yugoslavia by organizing themselves within the framework of the armed forces of the JNA and the territorial defence units.'[25] In short, the constitution made it the duty of all Bosnian Serbs to ensure that the Serb Republic remained a part of Yugoslavia.

The SDS campaign to sabotage the Bosnian state neared its conclusion in early April 1992 when Serbian paramilitaries, led by Željko 'Arkan' Ražnatović, brutally massacred dozens of Bosnian Muslims in the city of Bijeljina in north-eastern BiH in a move designed to create terror among the non-Serb population and drive them from their homes.[26] After the attack, Arkan welcomed Biljana Plavšić, one of the SDS members of the presidency of BiH, to the city and was publicly kissed and offered thanks by her for his efforts.[27] Similar events took place over the following weeks in Foča, Višegrad, and elsewhere. Two days after the massacre in Bijeljina, Karadžić decided to withdraw Plavšić and her colleague, Nikola Koljević, from the presidency of BiH. Their removal, he argues, meant that the presidency 'would then become illegitimate, because we were a part of that government, the Serb representation accounted for one-third of its membership'.[28]

As news of the attack in Bijeljina reached Sarajevo and the Bosnian presidency issued a call to mobilise in preparation for war, the SDS leadership in their Holiday Inn stronghold became increasingly isolated and paranoid. On 5 April, SDS paramilitaries attacked strategically important locations such as the police academy (where the government could access arms). As the attacks were taking place, increasingly large crowds of civilians from across BiH gathered in Sarajevo to demand peace. As one such peace protest made its way through Sarajevo, SDS gunmen shot two demonstrators as they crossed the Vrbanja Bridge. The shooting provoked a much greater demonstration the following day outside the Bosnian parliament building, which stood across the road from Holiday Inn. The protesters chanted Partisan slogans and called for a peaceful resolution to the crisis, before turning their attention to the SDS leadership ensconced in the hotel. Unfortunately, as the crowd approached the building, the snipers stationed on the roof opened fire, killing six and wounding many more. During the ensuing chaos, the SDS leadership escaped (first to Ilidža, on the outskirts of the city, and later to the town of Pale) but the sniper team was apprehended by armed police.[29] Karadžić had lost the Holiday Inn, but during his residency there the SDS had established an administration for Serb self-rule in BiH, successfully boycotted a host of multiethnic Bosnian institutions, and created terror among the Bosnian Muslim population with the attacks on towns such Bijeljina. In the ensuing weeks, Sarajevo was surrounded, marking the start of one of the longest sieges in modern history. By the time the city was relieved, approximately 11,000 Sarajevan citizens (including up to 2,000 children) had been killed and countless more wounded. The cumulative impact of these actions almost destroyed the nascent Bosnian state in its infancy and laid the institutional foundations of RS.

On 3 April, the day after the attacks in Bijeljina, Federal Defence Secretary of Yugoslavia General Blagoje Adžić had ordered the JNA to 'hasten the withdrawal' from BiH.[30] As the troops left while the events in Sarajevo unfolded, they took with them confiscated Bosnian TO weaponry, as well as ammunition, supplies, fuel, and even some industrial military facilities. However, only 20 per cent of the JNA soldiers (approximately 14,000 soldiers) that were stationed in BiH actually left, with most instead staying at their posts.[31] The following month, on 4 May, it was announced that the JNA was going to be formally divided into the VJ and VRS two weeks later. In the interim, both Mladić and Karadžić prepared the military and civilian frameworks which would govern the new army. Mladić's second-in-command, Manojlo Milovanović, recalls that on 11 May the 'narrow circle of the Headquarters of the future army was formed, comprised of four generals, seven colonels, and one captain – all of them professional military personnel, of the now-former JNA'.[32] He notes that this group of senior officers determined ten principles which would define how the VRS should function. Many of them concerned the transition from the JNA, stating that the VRS should 'use all manpower and material assets left from the JNA and territorial defence in the area of RS and make them the base for the future VRS', and advising that they did not need to 'create a new art of war – tactics or strategy, but should adapt JNA guidelines and rules of engagement to the needs of the VRS'.[33] Other principles concerned structure and administration of the VRS, such as the role of municipalities in supplying the military, or affirmed the VRS's commitment to upholding international law and UN regulations. Of most significance were the many items that focussed on establishing and strengthening the grip of the Headquarters over the military. The second item, for example, stipulated that 'all paramilitary formations that are formed on the territory of RS are to be included in the VRS, and those that refuse will be broken up and exiled', while the third explicitly stated that the SDS-controlled Crisis Centres were to be 'excluded from the system of command over VRS units'.[34] This brought any Serb militias that had been raised and armed by the SDS into the VRS and formally removed the influence of the political leadership from within the ranks of the military. Furthermore, the fourth principle determined that the military would 'exclude the already-resurrected Chetnik strategy of warfare' and proclaimed that there would be 'no Chetniks, no Partisans, just warriors for the defence of RS'.[35] These principles removed certain aspects of the emerging military that the SDS had influence over, even threatening their paramilitaries if they did not recognise the VRS monopoly on the use of force.

This message was made even clearer by item seven, which announced that the military would create 'strict subordination, senior officers in command will appoint by a top-down system and not by elections from the bottom', and item eight, which decreed that the 'military of RS has to be depoliticised as an organisation, and command staff including NCOs, officers, generals, and civil personnel in the service of the VRS can't be members of political parties'.[36] Indeed, the Headquarters even promulgated their own vision of the role and purpose of the VRS, a privilege usually reserved for the civilian commander of a military:

The moral fibre of the VRS is to be built and developed on Serb heritage, tradition, patriotism, awareness of war goals, religion, professionalism of its command cadre, and the sense of justice and humanity in relation towards the wounded, dead and captured soldiers and their family members.[37]

Of most note in this statement is the omission of any reference to RS and its institutions of state, including the presidency, suggesting they were viewed as superfluous. Through asserting military dominance wherever any ambiguity regarding command and authority over the VRS arose, Mladić and his deputies enforced a break with a long tradition of political involvement in the Yugoslav military, a tradition that was continued in the armies of its adversaries. The formal separation of the civil and military facets of the state in this way came at the expense of the SDS. The Party of Democratic Action (*Stranka demoktratkse akcije*, SDA), the main representative of Bosnian Muslims in the BiH state, and the Croatian Democratic Union (*Hrvatska demokratska zajednica*, HDZ), a BiH extension of the ruling party in Croatia, were both pivotal in raising troops and organising the armies they led through the war. This allowed them to embed their influence and control into their forces. For the SDS, the military of the state they governed was prefabricated, with an established chain of command, structure, and heritage. With an assertive figurehead such as Mladić in command, they had little hope of influencing the military by any means other than conventional constitutional channels.

The following day, the SDS established the legal framework for the formation of the military. The law also stated that 'the former units and headquarters of the territorial defence are renamed into commands and units of the Army, whose organisation and formation will be established by the President of the Republic'.[38] The SDS had reminded Mladić that it was the duty of the president to organise and form the army; however, they did not claim any privileges within the military sphere beyond constitutional authority and civilian oversight. While these preparations were underway in BiH, in Belgrade, Air Force General Božidar Stevanović, part of the VL network, escalated an 'intelligence operation' he had been running in order to strengthen Milošević's control of the armed forces. Having already had a number of generals fired earlier in the year, Stevanović presented Milošević with an additional 38 names, all of whom were removed from their positions. In total, over a third of the JNA's 150 generals were purged as a result of being deemed 'unreliable' or 'traitors' by the operation.[39] With all aspects of the military firmly under the control of the VL and extensive preparations for the transition already made in BiH, the *de jure* division of the JNA went smoothly on 19 May.

The VRS inherited an extensive array of personnel and equipment from the JNA. A military history of the conflict produced by the CIA suggests that in total, Mladić had between 100,000 and 110,000 former JNA troops at his command when he assumed the position of chief of VRS Headquarters.[40] Gow contests this figure, postulating that it was more likely to have been between 60,000 and 80,000, only 50,000 of whom were operational.[41] Such estimates are difficult to make, particularly in the case of Yugoslavia. As a result of conscription, almost every Yugoslav male served in the JNA for a period of time, and many of them were retained as reservists after completing their service. Furthermore, in a series of large mobilisations of the population by the JNA in the years prior to the establishment of the VRS, Serbs and Montenegrins were increasingly the only people to respond. As a result, most of the men who joined the VRS had at least some JNA experience. If considering the number of serving JNA troops that were transferred to Mladić's command, however, Gow's figure is far more plausible.

It was the established framework provided by the transfer of these standing units to the VRS which allowed it to rapidly expand to include Bosnian Serb personnel of varying experience, creating a figure that correlates more with the estimates of the CIA. The transfer of organised military units offered the VRS additional advantages, the most potent of which was the arsenal it received: approximately 300 to 500 tanks (including 50 advanced M-84s, a Yugoslav-updated T-72), between 200 and 300 Armoured Personnel Carriers (APCs), 400 field artillery pieces over 100 mm, 48 multiple rocket launchers, and 350 120-mm mortars, as well as a modest air force of 35 aircraft.[42] By contrast, its opponents were unable to acquire enough uniforms and rifles to send their soldiers into battle and were outnumbered in terms of heavy weapons by more than ten to one.[43]

The VRS enjoyed a significant number of other advantages as a result of its heritage. Key to the success of the VRS throughout the war was its ability to communicate across the entire Bosnian theatre (and beyond) almost instantly with subterranean telephone lines that converged on Han Pijesak. Here, a complex of tunnels, bunkers, and underground facilities had been purpose-built to be the headquarters of the entire JNA in case of an invasion of Yugoslavia. In addition to unparalleled communications, Han Pijesak also offered the VRS a vital secure location to base their command and intelligence units.[44] Prior to its withdrawal, the JNA was ordered to prepare 'a map analysis of [BiH] which will clearly show: what is situated in secure areas; what can be successfully defended, with adequate reinforcements, until the conditions for evacuation are created; what can be evacuated through threats and force'.[45] Maps and plans such as this, created by a professional military preparing for war, provided the VRS with the capability to move units and supplies across the country with maximum efficiency, whilst also denying resources to their opponents.

Such a wealth of materiel, infrastructure, and planning undoubtedly provided the VRS with an overwhelming advantage on the battlefield. However, while the VRS inherited a range of key strengths and capabilities from the JNA, the most significant was the continuing institutional link with the VJ. The support which the VRS received through this link was prominently manifested in three key areas. First, throughout the war the VRS was able to rely on the VJ and the Serbian SDB for a steady supply of ammunition, fuel, spare parts, and other materiel vital for resisting the ARBiH and its attritional doctrine. In addition, when the situation required it, contingents of the VJ were also deployed to BiH, with as many as 20,000 troops and 100 tanks being sent over the border to assist the VRS throughout the conflict.[46] Second, following the division of the JNA, the armed forces that emerged from it retained a shared officer corps.[47] This not only allowed for the relocation of proficient officers when necessary, but also maintained a broad pool of experience, ensured a ready supply of professional staff, and, most importantly, allowed newly promoted officers to receive adequate training for their roles away from the front. Finally, the link with VJ proved invaluable as it allowed Belgrade to subsidise the VRS during a long and costly war that was impossible for RS to finance independently: as a large and technically advanced army, the VRS simply represented an overwhelming and unsustainable economic burden on the relatively small Bosnian Serb population. More significantly, the VRS's failure to capture any cities other than Banja Luka and Bijeljina, coupled with the ethnic cleansing campaigns that were orchestrated in captured territory, left it with 'an economically and demographically bankrupt territorial base from which to wage a war'.[48] Bojan Dimitrijević, a prominent Serbian historian of the period, describes how an 'imaginary unit' of the VJ, the 30th Personnel Centre (*Kadrovski centar*) was established as 'some kind of shadow name for the VRS' in order to oversee 'all of its administrative tasks'.[49] Through the centre, the VRS was able to considerably offset the cost of its own upkeep as officers' wages, pensions, and social care for the injured as well as compensation for the families of fallen soldiers were all managed and paid for in Belgrade.

Two former JNA corps formed the core of the VRS. Not only were there a substantial number of troops, but the corps also had established chains of command, trained staff officers, as well as logistics and support units, allowing for rapid expansion through the incorporation of numerous other Serb military formations in BiH. The most significant of these formations were the elements of the Territorial Defence of the Republic of Bosnia and Herzegovina (*Teritorijalna odbrana Republike Bosne i Herzegovine*, TORBiH) which had rejected Izetbegović's call to arms and sided instead with the Serb Republic. Initially, these units were placed under local SDS jurisdiction but deferred to JNA command when its troops were present. Their numbers were significantly swelled by volunteers, many of whom were Bosnian Serb reservists and conscripts who had been mobilised by the JNA in April 1992 (in a move deemed 'invalid' by Alija Izetbegović, leading most other Bosnians to ignore it) and had been allowed to keep their weapons upon completion of their service.[50] General Milutin Kukanjac, commander of JNA forces in BiH at the time, later explained: 'I mobilised the troops and those who joined got arms. The Serbs responded to the mobilisation call and the Croats and Muslims did not.'[51] Some of these conscripts and reservists gathered into their old units, such as the Banjalučki Corps, a JNA formation which became the VRS I Krajina Corps, while others joined up with local TO units.[52] Together, these volunteers boosted the number of Serb TO troops from the original 11,000 who had defected from the TORBiH to a considerable force of almost 60,000.[53]

Not all volunteers joined the structure of the TO, however, with many men from both BiH and Serbia forming independent units of their own, contributing a paramilitary aspect to the growing military might gathering in the name of the SRBiH. The paramilitary troops rarely contributed to battlefield operations, and instead fulfilled other roles ranging from special forces operations, such as when the 'Wolves' seized the television transmitter on Kozara Mountain in the spring of 1992 (offering the Serb leadership a broadcasting monopoly across many parts of BiH), to ethnic cleansing campaigns such as the one carried out by Arkan and his volunteers from Serbia in Bijeljina.[54] The military forces of the SRBiH were supplemented by a 15,000-strong Ministry of the Interior (*Ministarstvo unutrašnjih poslova*, MUP) armed police force that had been formed on 1 April, mainly from Serbs who had formerly served in the MUP of BiH.[55]

Central to the rapid mobilisation of such significant numbers of men was an operation conducted by the VL network in the months prior. In 1990, the Serbian SDB began distributing Second World War–era rifles from Serbian MUP and TO stocks to 'groups likely centred on the local SDS municipality board'.[56] Weapons were also smuggled into BiH from Montenegro, with one such convoy being captured by police loyal to the Bosnian government in late 1991, leading Izetbegović to lament to Colm Doyle, head of the European Community Monitor Mission (ECMM), that he 'saw the JNA not only as an army of occupation but as a force providing logistical support to the Bosnian Serbs'.[57] His observation proved to be astute, as the testimony of Mustafa Candić, a Bosnian Muslim JNA intelligence officer at the time, illustrates. Candić remembers how the JNA distributed confiscated TORBiH weaponry to Bosnian Serbs from places such as ski lodges, and recalls a moment when a JNA officer, Major Čedo Knežević, responded to an enquiry about the weapons by saying, 'I have lots of them and I can give you some. Here is a friend of ours. He can confirm that I can arm half of the United States, if you want.'[58] Candić also notes that the distribution was not based on 'old friendships' as Milošević suggested to him, but was instead a coordinated series of military operations codenamed *Proboj* (Breakthrough) 1 and 2.[59] Additional weapons were transferred from the JNA itself. Doyle, whose role in the ECMM included escorting JNA 'troop and equipment convoys [from Croatia] through Bosnia in order to determine if their final destination was to be Serbia or elsewhere', reports that unregistered convoys travelling westwards led the ECMM 'to suspect not all JNA units withdrawing from Croatia were heading for Serbia'.[60] In one such instance, on his way to a meeting with Plavšić in Pale at the end of April 1992, he records being forced off the road 'in order to give way to a convoy of M-84 tanks heading in the same direction. Here was the first evidence of large elements of the JNA moving to Pale, and in the process reappearing as the VRS.'[61]

Through the various operations and manoeuvres discussed, the VL network was able to prepare a vast military force in BiH before conflict broke out. Serving JNA troops, Bosnian Serb reservists and conscripts, paramilitary formations, and MUP units were all armed, organised, and in position, ready to fight when the time came.

## Early victories and rival visions: 1992 and 1993

By the time the VRS was formally established on 19 May 1992, scattered incidents of violence across BiH had escalated into open conflict. One of the first major battles occurred in northern Bosnia during April and May 1992 and resulted in Croat and Muslim forces, operating under the banner of the HVO, severing the strategically vital 'Posavina Corridor'. The corridor linked Serb territory in Croatia, the Serb Republic of Krajina (*Republika Srpska Krajina*, RSK), and Serb-held areas in Bosnian Krajina with the Drina Valley and, most significantly, Serbia itself. Upon its formation, the first major task which the VRS faced was reversing the HVO offensive and re-establishing the contiguity of Serb territory. In early June, the VRS I Krajina Corps began preliminary operations in the area and reopened the Corridor within three weeks.[62] Over the following months, the VRS steadily pushed opposition forces back, capturing the towns of Modrica, Odžak, and Bosanski Brod in some of the largest engagements (sometimes involving 'more than 50,000 troops on both sides', according to CIA estimates, although this figure was likely lower) of the entire war.[63] The CIA explains that this operation, which was successful against 'experienced and numerically superior Croatian, Bosnian Croat, and Bosnian Army forces', was the result of the VRS's 'typical mixture of professional leadership, organisation, and fire-power, enhanced in these operations by the commitment of most of the VRS's battle-tested former JNA units'.[64]

The capture of the so-called 'Corridor of Life' and the establishment of the northern border of RS on the River Sava (upon the banks of which Bosanski Brod lies) had been the second of a number of war aims that had been approved by the Bosnian Serb Assembly in May 1992. The third reiterated the constitutional provision that RS would join the Federal Republic of Yugoslavia (*Savezna Republika Jugoslavija*, SRJ), which had been formed on 27 April from the remaining republics of Yugoslavia, Serbia and Montenegro. All that remained to completely fulfil this aim was to finalise the republic's borders, the parameters of which were outlined in the fourth war aim: the 'Muslim and Croat section of Bosnia should run along the Neretva and Una Rivers, in addition to the Sava', claiming the majority of BiH for RS.[65] RS also claimed part of Sarajevo, as well as access to the sea. Within months, most of these aims had been achieved by the VRS: the Posavina Corridor remained open throughout the war, VRS troops were stationed along much of the Sava and Una, and parts of Sarajevo were occupied while the rest was besieged. Although BiH government forces held some ground, much of which (including areas around the Drina, Neretva, and Una rivers) was coveted by the RS leadership, the VRS successfully facilitated the 'creation of a territorially contiguous Bosnian Serb state' which covered more than 60 per cent of BiH during 1992 (see Map 3.1).[66] The conquest of this territory included significant victories: at Jajce, where a beleaguered Croat-Muslim resistance collapsed; at Bosanska Krupa and Bosanski Novi, both on the Una River near Bihać; as well as at numerous towns in the Drina Valley. In all cases, the non-Serb population was expelled, often 'under a rain of mortar rounds', or hounded by paramilitaries.[67] On 19 November, Mladić issued Operational Directive 04, which escalated this process by ordering the VRS Drina Corps to 'inflict the heaviest possible losses on the enemy, and force them to leave the Eastern Bosnia areas of Birač, Žepa and Goražde together with the Bosnian Muslim population'.[68]

Despite its rapid advance and battlefield successes, the VRS faced serious challenges as soon as it was formed. It was a particularly large army (in 1992, it was second only to the VJ in all of former Yugoslavia), however the Bosnian Serb population only totalled 1.35 million. This left it with very little strength in depth, and almost no military reserves. As a result, the CIA concluded that the VRS

> would never have the ability to deliver a knock-out blow to its enemies or adequately hold a frontline of more than 1000 kilometres. Even during 1992, the VRS was repeatedly forced to shuttle units across the country from battle to battle.[69]

Although in most cases the former JNA units in the VRS such as the I Krajina Corps easily defeated their opponents, the large concentrations of volunteer and TO formations in eastern Bosnia struggled, revealing a considerable disparity in capability within the military. Milovanović explains that the quality of the TO formations depended on where they were recruited, as the 'economic condition of the municipality' would dictate what equipment and combat ability they had. He observes that this led 'the Headquarters and corps commanders to form strong support units, and the corps even trained individual brigades from their constituency for manoeuvre

**Map 3.1** *The disintegration of Yugoslavia, 1991–5*

in other areas'.[70] Such a solution could only be successful if the VRS retained advantages in communication and transportation over its opponents and was therefore able to reinforce vulnerable areas before they were overrun. As a result, converting 'the mob of TO personnel into properly organised, well-led light infantry brigades, while simultaneously reigning in many of the virtually autonomous volunteer units', was a challenge that dominated VRS operations away from the battlefield during 1992.[71]

As command and control, ideological outlook, and training standards were centralised in the first months of the war, the rivalry between Karadžić, Milošević, and Mladić over authority of the VRS began to manifest. Karadžić hoped to break with the heritage of the JNA, saying that he 'wanted to make an army which would not be communist, a true army of the people'.[72] However, the VRS Headquarters had distanced him from having much sway over the development of the military. Just days after the formation of the VRS, Mladić ordered the artillery and tanks of the Sarajevo-Romanija Corps, which was encircling Sarajevo, to begin shelling the city.[73] General Života Panić, the last minister of defence of socialist Yugoslavia (he replaced Adžić on 8 May) and first commander of the VJ, attests that in shelling Sarajevo, Mladić acted against the wishes of Milošević, who feared 'an anti-Serb media campaign' and was 'very opposed to it'.[74] UN Secretary General Boutros Boutros-Ghali reported to the Security Council that Mladić was to blame; however, in response sanctions were placed on the SRJ, vindicating Milošević's concerns.[75] Thus, within a fortnight of its formation, Mladić used his operational authority to consolidate control over all Bosnian Serb armed forces in BiH, outline his vision for the future of the army, and overrule his main rivals.

Another organisational task which the VRS had to overcome was managing the transition of its institutional identity away from that of its socialist predecessor. The first steps in this direction were made on 28 June, when VRS troops gave an oath of allegiance at a ceremony attended by members of the presidency, government, and much of the military leadership. The oath read: 'I (name and surname), swear by my honour and my life to defend the sovereignty, territory, independence and constitutional order of my fatherland and faithfully serve the interests of its people. So help me God.'[76] (See Figure 3.1.) On 28 June is *Vidovdan*, a Serbian Orthodox religious holiday and the designated memorial day of the 1389 Battle of Kosovo, making it the most significant celebration of the year for many Serbs. Following the oath-giving ceremony, it also became the day upon which the deeds and sacrifices of the VRS were commemorated. The association with noteworthy celebrations of both the Serbian nation and the Serbian Orthodox Church, coupled with the invocation of 'fatherland' and 'god' in the oath, illustrate that although the structures and personnel of the JNA remained, a complete severance with its ideological and symbolic heritage now took place. However, although it is clear that the Orthodox faith was used to fill the void, no mention of the RS or its institutions was made in the oath.

By the end of the year, the VRS had reorganised and given some level of training to the TO troops and volunteers that had joined it in May, and now had at its command at least 80,000 well-equipped soldiers organised in 7 Corps and 51 manoeuvre brigades.[77] Much of the administrative infrastructure of the JNA had been adapted for use by the VRS. A former military training centre was repurposed as 'The Military Training Centre of the VRS' and the socialist-era positions of organisation, mobilisation, and

**Figure 3.1** *Troops of the newly established VRS evacuate Sarajevo airport on 29 June 1992 under the supervision of the UN. The JNA livery on their vehicle has been replaced with the Serbian Cross.* Courtesy of Christophe Simon/AFP via Getty Images.

personnel officer and ideological-political officer were retained on the Headquarters staff, the latter being redesignated 'Head of Morale, Religious, and Legal Issues'.[78] The officers who held these posts (and commanded the training centre) all answered directly to Mladić. Furthermore, in all properly organised VRS formations, morale, religious, and legal officers took the place of JNA ideological-political officers.[79] Through these officers, Mladić could dictate what would replace the socialist political education and training which the soldiers received, further increasing his level of influence over the development and ideological outlook of the military. Maintaining structural continuity with the JNA also offered the VRS another considerable advantage over its opponents, who were forced to conceptualise and build the institutions, structure, and offices of their respective militaries whilst fighting a war. Despite this advantage, the VRS failed to prevent the Bosnian government from raising considerable armed forces of its own and holding many strategically significant cities, facilities, and transport routes. As a result, in 1993 disputes over the manner in which the VRS was prosecuting the war and how the conflict should be ended deepened the animosity between Milošević, Mladić, and Karadžić.

In January 1993, UN Special Envoy Cyrus Vance and European Community (EC) representative Lord Owen promulgated the first comprehensive proposal for ending the war. Vladimir Petrović notes that 'the leadership of the Bosnian Serbs was unanimously and adamantly resisting the peace offer' as they felt it was 'provocatively anti-Serbian'.[80] Milošević, however, feared a rejection of the plan could lead to increased sanctions or a military intervention, but was unable to force Karadžić to agree to the terms. Nina Caspersen argues that SDS resistance to the plan stemmed from Mladić, whose 'vehement opposition and thirty-five-minute-long impassioned speech against acceptance was one of the decisive factors in parliament's rejection of the plan'.[81] Indeed, while the negotiations were taking place, VRS operations continued, including significant offensives in Eastern Bosnia. It was in this period, Caspersen observes, that a faction within the SDS hailing from Krajina, along with some members of the opposition, began aligning themselves with Mladić, illustrating his growing political influence and also the emergence of a 'regional division of the RS'.[82] Owen recalls, 'I think Mladić became very powerful from then on. And that's not to say he was powerful as a military leader, but I think he began to have a political constituency'.[83] Although Mladić usually deferred to Milošević, it is evident by his actions that peace, at least under the terms set by Vance and Owen, was not a priority. Petrović argues that the Bosnian Serb leadership showed 'a lack of interest in economic difficulties posed by sanctions, as well as an absolute determination to terminate the statehood of BiH'.[84]

In September 1993, the position of the VRS was strengthened by an unlikely source. The majority-Bosnian Muslim town of Velika Kladuša lies near Bihać, just across the border from what was, during the collapse of Yugoslavia, RSK. During the socialist period, it was home to Agrokomerc, an agricultural business (industrial chicken farming) which developed into one of the biggest conglomerates in Yugoslavia under the stewardship of Fikret Abdić. In the 1990 elections, Abdić had run for a seat in the presidency on an SDA ticket, and had won more votes than any other candidate. However, for unknown reasons he did not claim his victory, and instead left the role of chairman of the presidency to Izetbegović. Abdić took a lower-ranking seat in the presidency of BiH, but returned to Velika Kladuša, leaving the coordination of the war to Izetbegović and his allies. Then, in the autumn of 1993, after representing the BiH government at the Owen–Stoltenberg negotiations in Geneva over the summer, Abdić proclaimed the establishment of the Autonomous Province of Western Bosnia (*Autonomna Pokrajina Zapadna Bosna*, APZB), centred on Velika Kladuša, and began raising his own private army.[85]

Such a move shocked Sarajevo but was welcomed by many government forces in the Krajina region. Two entire brigades and significant contingents from other units of the ARBiH V Corps mutinied and joined Abdić, who immediately came to terms with both the Bosnian Serb and Croat leaderships.[86] By the end of the year, the APZB could muster up to 10,000 men organised in six brigades.[87] The VRS had even armed their erstwhile foes, equipping them with all the small arms, mortars, and ammunition they needed, as well as offering them artillery support. In exchange, the VRS moved troops through APZB territory, allowing them to mount an assault on Bihać from RSK territory in Croatia, and APZB troops fought alongside VRS in Krajina.[88] This significantly boosted the strength of the 80,000 troops Mladić had left, and almost won him Bihać.[89] Furthermore, although the APZB troops were not integrated into the VRS, they did operate alongside them and ultimately deferred to VRS command, making them something of a semi-autonomous auxiliary force in a similar manner to the HVO units operating within ARBiH Corps.[90]

The APZB troops were not the only non-Serb troops fighting with the VRS. A significant number of mercenaries and volunteers, largely hailing from Russia and Greece, are known to have fought in the VRS. Most estimates place their number at a maximum of 1,500 throughout the war, however Aziz Tafro argues that 'the exact number will never be known as a large number of Russians fought under false names'.[91] He suggests that 'more than 10,000 Russian mercenaries' could have served in the VRS during the war in BiH.[92] While this number is unlikely, monuments have been raised in honour of fallen Russian fighters, including a 5.5-metre-high Orthodox Cross in Višegrad, highlighting the value placed on their contribution.[93] Later in the war, 100 Greeks formed the 'Greek Volunteer Guard' which was 'fully integrated into the [VRS] and led by Serb officers' within the VRS Drina Corps.[94] A surprising outcome of the unlikely alliance with APZB and the recruitment of foreign volunteers was that it resulted in approximately 10 per cent of the soldiers under the overall command of Mladić being non-Serb. This means that, for a time (roughly April 1994–August 1995) at least, the war-weary forces under Mladić's command were the most multiethnic in BiH as both the ARBiH and HVO had become highly monoethnic organisations at that stage of the conflict.[95]

## Stalled Progress and Deepening Divisions: 1994 and 1995

In the early stages of the conflict, the VRS enjoyed complete supremacy on the battlefield. By 1994 'they had achieved virtually all of their territorial objectives at acceptable costs' and VRS troops persistently held their ground against the increasingly powerful and effective ARBiH.[96] Despite the strong position their forces were in, Serb leaders became increasingly fractured over control of the military and what to do next. In January, General Dušan Kovačević, RS minister of defence and an officer of the VRS Headquarters, argued that command should be left to Mladić and the Headquarters, writing in the VRS journal, *Srpska vojska* (Serb Army): 'We are one nation, one state, and we should have a single army under a single commander with the same badge who will complete the mission.'[97]

At this point, Karadžić and Milošević favoured negotiating the most favourable deal they could garner and declaring the war a triumph, while Mladić still sought 'a decisive close with a signal military victory over the Muslims'.[98] Such a prospect was becoming increasingly unlikely. A number of VRS offensives at the end of 1993 and beginning of 1994 had initially been successful, but the ARBiH retook the ground in every case. Indeed, the ARBiH had grown into the largest armed force in BiH and had developed an effective, although costly, doctrine which was beginning to grind the VRS down. Furthermore, the March 1994 Washington Agreement ended the conflict between parts of the ARBiH and HVO, allowing both to focus their efforts on defeating the VRS. Developments such as this soon translated into a change in the pattern of the war. The hitherto solid VRS lines began to falter, and as winter settled in Krajina, ARBiH V Corps managed to punch a hole through VRS defences and launch a penetrating offensive, recapturing Kupres and taking more ground for government forces in a few weeks than had been achieved throughout the entire war.[99] During this crisis, Karadžić 'insisted on his role as Supreme Commander and he donned a uniform', presenting himself as an alternative military leader to Mladić at the first moment when the general appeared strategically fallible.[100] In response, Mladić ordered a remarkably successful counter-attack, retaking all of the lost territory and almost defeating ARBiH V Corps entirely. Sensing his chance for decisive victory, Mladić prepared to conquer Bihać.

Both Milošević and Karadžić had other priorities. Milošević had accepted a peace plan drawn up by the Contact Group (composed of the United States, UK, Russia, Germany, and France) in August 1994 which had replaced the previous Owen–Stoltenberg process.[101] The plan was generous to the Bosnian Serbs, delineating the separation of BiH's population along ethnic lines and offering the fulfilment of almost all of their strategic objectives. Indeed, aside from the continued existence of a few Bosnian Muslim exclaves in the Drina Valley, having to share Sarajevo, and not attaining access to the sea (a particularly optimistic goal), the plan offered the Serb leadership precisely what it wanted. Despite this, Karadžić predicted 'carnage' if the Bosnian Serb Assembly voted yes, and after considerable debate he and the SDS rejected the plan.[102] In response, Milošević placed political and economic sanctions on RS and its leadership, heralding the most significant rift to date.[103] The introduction of 'inter-Serb' sanctions also reveals the extent to which the VRS was separate from the state it was supposedly fighting for, as fuel, ammunition, officers, and logistical and maintenance support from Belgrade continued unabated.[104] Furthermore, those VRS personnel who were working in the institutions of the state, such as Minister of Defence Kovačević, were simply withdrawn.[105] That the military was totally unaffected by the imposition of severe sanctions against the state suggests that, after more than two years of war, the VRS remained very much a Yugoslav institution, rather than one of the Serb Republic.

The economic sanctions placed on RS, coupled with the concomitant political isolation, severely undermined Karadžić's authority. He could no longer claim to be a conduit of Belgrade's designs, and thanks to the ambiguity of RS's constitutional status, any attempt to utilise legitimate institutional channels to assert his influence could easily flounder. Indeed, his new civilian minister of defence, Milan Ninković, recalls:

> Although I was defence minister, my main task was to organise the mobilisation of civilians, I had no power to order anything operational … Mladić issued the orders to the troops, he was not obliged to inform me. I only received orders to supply rations. It wasn't like in your country, where ministers have power.[106]

Karadžić's position was further weakened by the increasingly divided Bosnian Serb Assembly. Since his rejection of the Contact Group Plan, Milošević had gradually been enlisting agreeable 'rank and file' Bosnian Serb politicians with the goal of eventually ousting the RS president.[107] Sensing his authority was waning, Karadžić made a bid to assert his dominance. The VRS assault on Bihać was well underway, with Serb troops holding about a third of the UN-declared Safe Area around the city and fighting taking place near the Headquarters of V Corps. One UN report stipulated that there may have been only 300 V Corps soldiers left in the city, illustrating just how close Mladić was to eliminating an entire enemy corps and striking his decisive blow.[108] However, in attacking Bihać, the VRS not only violated a UN-declared Safe Area but also breached the no-fly zone over BiH by conducting numerous bombing runs against the city utilising Serb aircraft operating out of Udbina in RSK.[109] This led the UN Security Council to authorise NATO airstrikes against Serb forces. Karadžić's first response was to warn the United States of the dangers of 'another Vietnam', but he soon called for the offensive to stop and, a few weeks later, announced on television that he had personally invited Jimmy Carter, former US president, to act as an 'honest broker'.[110]

Carter, already widely regarded as an effective diplomat and peacemaker for his previous successes around the world, held talks which, true to form, soon culminated with an agreement on a four-month ceasefire across BiH. As Brendan O'Shea notes, 'the peanut farmer from Plains, Georgia, had once again succeeded where all the rest had failed'.[111] The ceasefire raised Karadžić's profile as a leader and probably saved him from being removed, perhaps forcefully, from his position. With few other options, Milošević was forced to accept that he had been outmanoeuvred and publicly backed the agreement. Mladić, who had already accused the RS president of promoting another Chetnik–Partisan split following the failure of the Contact Group Plan (Mladić had tacitly backed Milošević) and had been angered when the Bihać offensive was stopped, was furious with Karadžić.[112] Karadžić failed to defuse the situation, instead saying that the military leadership of the VRS were communists.[113] In January 1995, *Srpska vojska* published a thinly veiled attack on Karadžić:

> The development of the RS political system is quite difficult because of the war. Some political parties, primarily their leaders, feel that the war is over and are trying to secure the most favourable positions possible in the struggle for power. This has resulted in a change of behaviour that deserves the attention of the general

public to ensure the normalisation of the situation, and that the struggle for the freedom of the Serbian people is brought to an end soon.[114]

The article also proclaimed that 'the allegations against the officers of being communists are unacceptable'.[115] In such a climate, divisions within RS political and military leadership were at their most severe. Indeed, Milovanović recalls that following the NATO air strikes, VRS I Krajina Corps Commander Momir Talić suggested dividing the VRS into two, ostensibly to improve efficiency. He proposed the following:

> The first Army would have a zone of responsibility from the Una River, to Zvornik somewhere, and the other from there, to the south, including Herzegovina. The command of both armies would be directly linked to the [RS government], which would make the Headquarters unnecessary.[116]

Although the suggestion was dismissed, the fact that a senior VRS commander was contemplating the division of the military along the traditional axis of the Chetnik–Partisan split reveals the extent of disharmony within the Bosnian Serb leadership. This is further reflected by the decision of the SDS to begin strengthening the police, 'which they believed was completely loyal to them'.[117] Filip Švarm attests that it was 'thoroughly cleansed of anyone who was considered even remotely dangerous' and then recognised (and armed) as a military organisation, leading to the formation of special units of between six and seven hundred hand-picked men which quickly earned a reputation on the battlefield.[118] Such a move indicates that the SDS not only recognised its impotence over the VRS but also suggests that by the end of 1994 they were threatened by it.

On the battlefield, the long-overstretched VRS began losing ground to the combined forces of the ARBiH, HVO, and Croatian Army (*Hrvatska vojska*, HV) in 1995. Despite the ceasefire, fighting continued around Bihać, with ARBiH troops going up against APZB and VRS forces. A key factor in these engagements was the decline in fortunes of the SVK in Croatia: if RSK fell, the VRS would be left facing the entire HV, as well as its Bosnian adversaries. This no doubt informed the decision to abandon the operation around Bihać, the capture of which would be costly and was essentially untenable without the SVK. The failure to agree to a more comprehensive peace agreement following the ceasefire led to a resumption of fighting across BiH at the end of March 1995. This was triggered when 21,000 troops of the ARBiH VII Corps launched an offensive against VRS positions on Mt Vlašić, inflicting a significant defeat.[119] Just two weeks later, the VRS instigated its own offensive, which was lauded once again as 'war-winning', with the aim of widening the Posavina Corridor near Brčko. The attack managed to take some ground from the HVO, but an ARBiH counter-attack reversed all VRS gains. In *Balkan Battlegrounds*, the CIA analysts note:

> The VRS defeat was the Serbs' last effort at a war-winning offensive to break the Bosnian Government's will ... VRS forces – despite their advantages in armor, artillery, and other heavy weapons – were almost completely unable at this point in the war to break through ARBiH positional defenses ... The VRS was unable to

defeat the ARBiH's fortifications, and ARBiH troop reserves allowed the ARBiH to block any penetration the VRS made. The shift in the military balance between the ARBiH and the VRS that began in early 1994 was now complete.[120]

In June 1995, the ARBiH launched its largest offensive of the war. In a desperate bid to break the siege of Sarajevo, 80,000 troops from four corps attacked VRS positions across the Sarajevo operational area. The assault proved costly and ultimately fruitless. Furthermore, by drawing troops away from other fronts, it left some government-held territory exposed. The VRS triumph was lauded by *Srpska vojska*, which published an article at the end of June titled 'Grown with the Nation', which argued:

> the VRS today commands responsive forces, modern fighting equipment, and highly qualified fighters and officers for leading the armed struggle. With the activation of all human and material potential for defence, the equal distribution of the war effort on all structures of society, and the preservation of the unity of the army, government, and citizens, the tasks demanded by the Serb people can be fulfilled.[121]

Milošević was quick to recognise the opportunity and directed Mladić to move his forces against the remaining BiH enclaves in the Drina Valley. The defenders of Goražde, with some assistance from the Royal Welch Fusiliers, managed to hold the town, but the VRS's two other targets, Srebrenica and Žepa, fell in July. In both cases, the actions of Mladić's troops against the civilian population they captured, including the murder of over 8,000 Bosnian Mulsims at Srebrenica, were later declared to be acts of genocide.[122] In strategic terms, the capture of the towns did little more than fill in some spots of non-Serb territory on a map that already covered more than two-thirds of BiH. For the VRS, however, the atrocities committed by its soldiers that summer would come to define it in the eyes of the world.

After taking Srebrenica, Bosnian Serb and Greek soldiers under the personal command of Mladić made their way to the ruins of the town's Orthodox church and raised their respective national flags, along with those of Vergina (the unofficial flag of Greek Macedonia) and Byzantium, in victory.[123] This display of Orthodox pageantry encapsulates the underlying ideological currents that were prevailing within the VRS at the time. Although the military contribution of the Greek volunteers was minor, their presence, symbolically manifested by the assemblage displayed and the location selected for the ceremony, elucidated what united the VRS troops fighting in the Drina Valley above all else: the Orthodox faith. Furthermore, the people they massacred were portrayed (through a wide range of derogatory terms for Muslims) in religious terms, suggesting VRS forces, or at least parts of them, viewed the entire conflict as a holy war for the 'liberation' of Christian territory. The extremity and objectives of these beliefs obviously hearken back to the days of the Crusades; however, a similarity can be identified with the National Liberation War fought against the Axis and their local allies by the Partisans. That conflict had been portrayed by the socialist leadership of Yugoslavia as a titanic struggle between the forces of socialism and fascism in which the Partisans fought to liberate territory from an existential threat. Ideological-political officers in JNA units had lauded the sacrifices and victories of the Partisans for decades and had been responsible for ensuring troops were well acquainted with socialist ideology and theory. With such structures repurposed for morale, religious, and legal affairs by the VRS, the leadership, perhaps informed by their experience in such a system, aimed to motivate their troops in the same way that they had experienced when in the JNA. The promotion, utilisation, and celebration of the Orthodox faith within the VRS indicates that, despite the political divisions that had emerged between Karadžić and Mladić throughout the war, they continued to share fundamental ideological goals.

By the end of July, Croatian Serb forces were severely overstretched. The RSK had committed a lot of forces to the last-ditch effort to take Bihać, leaving much of the rest of that republic exposed to the HV forces that were gathering across the frontlines. When the Croatian attack came on 4 August 1995, it was rapid and effective, sweeping aside SVK defences and quickly capturing many strategically significant targets.[124] In a response that appears more political than strategic, Karadžić utilised the 'war conditions' powers which the SDS had invested him with a week previously to claim responsibility for the defence of RSK and declare himself commander of the VRS via a newly established Supreme Council.[125] Mladić was relieved of his command and reassigned to the civilian role of special adviser for the defence of RS and RSK.[126] The Serbian daily *Politika* speculated that the move was to prevent a coup d'état by the VRS Headquarters; however, such an initiative would most likely not have been stopped by these measures.[127]

Karadžić's announcement came the same day that RSK President Milan Martić ordered the evacuation of all Serbs from RSK territory, making it all but meaningless.[128] Through claiming personal authority over RSK and RS, Karadžić attempted to present himself as the key to peace in both polities. As one diplomatic source told *the Independent*: 'There is a power struggle going on, Karadžić's only chance in the struggle with Mladić is to consolidate the RSK and the RS as a single entity and present the case to Milošević and the international community.'[129] The next day, the RSK capital, Knin, fell and Karadžić's gambit began to unravel. Mladić had been in Belgrade negotiating with EU representative Carl Bildt at the time of his dismissal, but upon hearing the news he scheduled a meeting of the entire VRS Headquarters in Banja Luka for the next day. The outcome of the meeting was a letter to the RS Assembly, signed by the seventeen most senior officers of the VRS, which declared that Mladić was the commander of the VRS.[130] Karadžić publicly blamed Mladić for the loss of Knin:

> There are some commanders who have been interfering with civilian responsibilities or even wanted to negotiate with Bildt or Stoltenberg, that has to stop. Something like that is equal to treason. The army cannot negotiate with our enemies or with the international community.[131]

Nevertheless, the VRS leadership had made its choice, recognising its talismanic and influential commander over the constitutional order of RS (see Figure 3.2). The rivalry and divisions that had gradually worn away the unity and shared purpose of the three key Serb leaders had escalated into a public political battle over authority

**Figure 3.2** *VRS General Ratko Mladić (second right) is flanked by Generals Živomir Ninković (right), Milan Gvero (second left) and Jovan Marić (left) as he salutes his troops at a parade ceremony held at the Zaluzani air base near Banja Luka on 12 August 1995.*

of the military, and Mladić had won. Although he and Milošević remained relatively close, and the VRS continued to receive support from Belgrade, they did not agree on the war. For Milošević, there was little left to gain from the conflict in BiH, and international sanctions and war weariness threatened to foment widespread unrest in Serbia. As a result, he lent his support to the ongoing peace process, only to be frustrated by his erstwhile allies in BiH. Milošević's failure to end the fighting and Karadžić's inability to relieve Mladić of his command illustrates how, by August 1995, the VRS was unaccountable to any civilian authority. Indeed, the refusal to recognise Mladić's dismissal constituted mutiny. However, a coup d'état remained unlikely; as one Belgrade observer noted: 'Don't expect to see the [VRS] chiefs try to destabilise the political leaders. That would be deadly to both and would not be pleasing to Belgrade either.'[132]

For its part, the VRS was already losing a war of attrition against its increasingly large and capable opponents in BiH. It stood no chance whatsoever if the relatively small contingents of HV troops already operating alongside HVO forces were reinforced by the experienced and well equipped 65,000-strong army that had just defeated the SVK, particularly if it had to defend RS's 300-mile frontier with Croatia.[133] However, before the HV assault came, the VRS was dealt a crippling blow by a much more powerful assailant. In early August, the 'dual-key arrangement' which governed NATO's involvement in the Bosnian War was reworked. Previously, one key was held by NATO commander of allied forces in South Europe and the other was held by the UN secretary-general's special representative in Yugoslavia, Yasushi Akashi.

In the new arrangement, Akashi's key was handed to the UN's military commander in BiH.[134] Following the shelling of a marketplace in Sarajevo on 28 August, and no doubt emboldened by the events at Srebrenica a month earlier, acting UN Commander Lieutenant-General Rupert Smith 'turned the UN key' along with his NATO counterpart in Naples, and Operation Deliberate Force was launched.[135] The operation entailed a 'two-week campaign against the Bosnian Serbs, in which 3,500 aircraft sorties were flown, nearly 100 cruise missiles fired and almost 400 different Serb targets engaged.[136] (See Figure 3.3.) These targets included most VRS positions near government-held cities, ammunition dumps and transport routes, anti-air batteries, and, most significantly, the nerve centre of the RS war effort, Han Pijesak, along with a plethora of other communications and radar sites across the country. The destruction of many of the facilities at Han Pijesak increased the time it took for communications to reach the field from the Headquarters 'from minutes to 48 hours, or more'.[137] This entirely negated one of the VRS's greatest advantages and prevented its corps from coordinating their operations and effectively supporting each other. Furthermore, left isolated and with limited information on the course of the fighting, Mladić travelled to Belgrade, where he was admitted to a military hospital, supposedly with gallstones.[138] The VRS was impotent against NATO airstrikes and, with its commander away and communications down, it quickly lost ground to the combined ARBiH–HV–HVO offensive, which began on 8 September.

The offensive, codenamed Mistral-2, made considerable progress in Bosnian Krajina. The troops of the APZB had suffered significantly since the split from the government in Sarajevo, particularly when ARBiH V Corps troops temporarily captured the town of Velika Kladuša in December 1994.[139] In July 1995, Abdić had ambitiously proclaimed the Republic of Western Bosnia, but just two months later his forces, along with their VRS allies, were driven out from the territory.[140] News of the HV's 'stunning victory' over the SVK and its rapid impact on the conflict in BiH caused significant tension in the Bosnian Serb leadership. The 'improvements made in its force structure and doctrine before the operation' had a 'profound impact on the VRS leadership's thinking and crystallised their belief that a political-military settlement had to be negotiated as soon as possible'.[141] This added pressure on Karadžić to allow the formation of a negotiating team. Trevor Minter, who was commander of British forces in BiH at the time, observes that although the VRS was 'exhausted and outmanoeuvred' it 'did not collapse', its 'chain of command was maintained in defeat', and it would have 'fought on desperately had their home areas been attacked'.[142]

Just weeks later, Milošević announced the formation of a joint Bosnian Serb–Serbian peace delegation, which he would lead, preventing Karadžić from sabotaging any negotiations by superseding his position. Holed up in his stronghold of Pale in Eastern Bosnia, however, the RS president remained bellicose, declaring that the VRS was 'holding firm' and would 'win in the end', and saying of Deliberate Force, 'I think those bombs can destroy the peace process' and the strikes are 'a moral disaster for the Western World and for the UN'.[143] Mladić, meanwhile, returned to BiH once the NATO airstrikes stopped and oversaw the stabilisation of the frontlines, even orchestrating a number of counter-offensives which, under the circumstances, were remarkably successful, particularly when the VRS faced the

**Figure 3.3** *F-16 Falcons from the 510th Fighter Squadron, Aviano Air Base, Italy, take fuel from a KC-135 over northern Bosnia as part of a combat air patrol mission in support of Operation Allied Force.* Courtesy of USAF via Getty Images.

ARBiH by itself.[144] The unexpected reversal was enough to convince the Bosnian government to prioritise peace talks, although how much resilience the VRS had left at this point is debatable.

The string of triumphs against the ARBiH signalled that Mladić could still defeat his adversaries on the battlefield, but the damage inflicted by NATO was terminal. Without its ability to relay information and coordinate the rapid movement of reserves, the VRS was unable to enact the effective defensive doctrine that had served it so well, rendering its units isolated and outnumbered. Indeed, Gow argues that 'NATO's use of air power was, without a doubt and contrary to the predominant opinion of Western commentators, the decisive element in ending the war in BiH'.[145] Furthermore, although Mladić initially chose simply to ignore Karadžić and the SDS rather than remove them from power, the rift that had developed between them could easily have worsened had the war continued, with a military coup, the division of RS between Banja Luka and Pale or even a Bosnian Serb civil war representing perfectly plausible outcomes. However, on 9 October 1995, under the supervision of Milošević, both Mladić and Karadžić signed a ceasefire agreement with Izetbegović, who represented Bosnian Muslims and Croats.[146] The following month, a permanent peace agreement was negotiated in Dayton, Ohio, between Milošević, representing the Bosnian Serbs, Izetbegović, representing Bosnian Muslims, and President Franjo Tuđman of Croatia, who represented Bosnian Croats (see Figure 3.4). On 5 December 1995, the three presidents formally signed the General Framework for Peace in BiH in Paris, finally ending the brutal conflict.

**Figure 3.4** *Gathered statesmen applaud the signing of the Dayton Peace Accords at the Elysée Palace on 14 December 1995.* Courtesy of Peter Turnley/Corbis/VCG via Getty Images.

# Conclusion

Throughout the 1992–5 War the VRS shared the goals and ideology of the state it ostensibly served. However, while the SDS government dominated every other aspect of the nascent Serb republic, it was unable to assert its authority over the military. Its influence within the army was removed by the VRS leadership in the early months of the conflict, and as the war progressed, Karadžić consistently failed to establish his control, as president, over Mladić and his troops. This left the state and the military as two essentially monolithic, separate entities, exemplified by the necessity of having both Karadžić and Mladić sign the October 1995 ceasefire with Izetbegović. Furthermore, the VRS's reliance on locally raised armed forces left it unable to effectively address the Chetnik–Partisan divide by acting as a social agent. Instead, most troops raised in eastern Bosnia, for example, remained in that theatre and were led by local officers, most of whom would have identified more with the heritage of the Chetniks than the Partisans. Although the rigid structure of the chain of command maintained cohesion within the military, the suggestion of a senior officer that the VRS should be divided in two, with half serving the 'Partisan' leadership in Banja Luka and the other serving the 'Chetnik' stronghold of Pale in eastern Bosnia illustrates the pervasiveness of this divide.

Milošević did not have constitutional or military authority over the VRS, however, it was his VL network that went to great lengths to establish the army. The ongoing provision of vital support to the VRS was also given at his command. In addition, he was the unrivalled leader of the project to forge a Greater Serbia from the SFRJ, making him the main ideological driving force behind the VRS, and indeed all of the Serb armies that emerged from the JNA. Although he was ultimately able to assert his control over both Karadžić and Mladić, proving that he was the power behind the VRS, his ambiguous role completely undermined the emergence of civil–military relations in RS. Indeed, it would not be until the following year that the VRS was subject to oversight by the Bosnian Serb parliament. Despite the chaotic nature of the relationship between those who claimed authority over it, the VRS was able to emerge from the JNA rapidly and effectively. It had clear military objectives, and the tools with which it was equipped to achieve them were the most potent in the conflict. As a result, it quickly conquered considerable swathes of territory and established RS. Although Karadžić, Mladić, and Milošević disagreed with each other as to how the war should be fought and when it should end, their ideological motivations remained the same. By repurposing the ideological dissemination framework of the JNA, Mladić was able to inculcate his troops with a shared motivation for fighting: the 'liberation' of Serb lands from non-Serb oppressors in the name of the Orthodox faith. The contribution of non-Serb forces to these objectives did little to dilute this message. There appears to have been very little friction between APZB troops and their VRS allies, although their input is also largely ignored by their erstwhile Bosnian Serb allies in commemorations of the war; the presence of Greek and Russian soldiers only served to amplify the religious aspect of the conflict. This message was enough to gloss over divisions within the Serb community and maintain the cohesion and unity of the military.

The VRS was able to achieve almost all of its strategic objectives very quickly. Utilising its superior firepower, organisation, communications, logistics, and defensive doctrine, it was able to hold the territory it had claimed against its numerically superior adversaries. Having failed to subjugate the BiH government when its advantage was greatest, the VRS became increasingly overstretched. When NATO initiated Operation Deliberate Force, the damage inflicted left the VRS incapacitated. This left it, and RS, in a vulnerable position, particularly considering the entrance of significant numbers of HV forces into Bosnian Krajina. Facing an inevitable, although possibly drawn-out defeat on the battlefield and ever-deepening divisions within its leadership, the VRS and the RS were saved by the Dayton Peace Agreement, which ensured a place for both in the future of BiH.

# 4

# The Army of the Republic of Bosnia and Herzegovina and the Croat Defence Council

The ARBiH was the military of the nascent Bosnian state that emerged following the Republic of Bosnia and Herzegovina's declaration of independence from Yugoslavia in 1992. In the initial months of the war, the chances of the Bosnian government organising an effective defence seemed unlikely: it was essentially powerless against the superior training, heavy weapons, and air support of the VRS and held just 30 per cent of the country by the end of 1992 (see Map 3.1 in Chapter 3, in this book).[1] The territorial claims of some Bosnian Croat leaders further undermined the position of the embattled government in Sarajevo. From this unfavourable beginning, the ARBiH grew into a large military force which 'developed a war-fighting method commensurate with the material and human resources available to it' and was regarded as an effective light infantry fighting force.[2] 'The Bosnian defiance of the odds and formation of an army while already largely overrun', Gow argues, 'was heroic and, on many levels, partly successful.'[3] Indeed, although the ARBiH failed to obtain an absolute military victory, after almost four years of war the once-dominant VRS had been manoeuvred into a position where it was forced to negotiate peace terms or face increasingly frequent defeats on the battlefield.

The struggle to make the ARBiH capable of forcing the Bosnian Serb leadership (or their sponsors in Belgrade) to the negotiating table was complex. From the outset of the war, much of the army was under-equipped, untrained, and lacked the strategic, operational, and tactical capabilities to conduct anything other than static defence. Furthermore, the ARBiH was composed of a group of armed forces formed under the auspices of a range of state institutions and paramilitary organisations. Fusing these groups into an effective military while maintaining their legitimacy in the eyes of this diverse range of groups only magnified the challenge faced by BiH's wartime political and military leadership. In addition to the conflict on the battlefield, rival visions for the future of BiH competed for control and influence within the halls of power in government-held territory during the war. In November 1995, during the final days of the war, ARBiH III Corps Commander General Sakib Mahmuljin stated, 'we are still not a professional army. We are a people's army. To be precise, we are a nation in uniform.'[4] In this statement, Mahmuljin identifies the relationship that had developed between the military and society, and highlights how, due to the extent of the conflict, the two became fused. However, exactly what this nation constituted or should constitute was open to contention, and due to its omnipotent societal presence in government-held territory during the war, the ARBiH was an arena in which proponents of rival visions for the future of the nation-elect competed. Was the ARBiH a secular, multiethnic military which regarded all loyal Bosnian citizens as equals, or was it a Muslim army fighting to further the interests of Bosnian Muslims and their elected representatives?

The evolution of the ARBiH was impacted by another Bosnian military force, the HVO. Formed in 1991 by the leading Croat nationalist political party in BiH, the HDZ, the HVO entered the war as a highly decentralised organisation of Bosnian Croat local defence forces and was nominally tasked with defending the self-proclaimed Croat state on the territory of BiH, Herceg-Bosna (HB). This led to a complicated relationship with the ARBiH. In parts of BiH, historic ties between Croat and Muslim communities and straightforward military necessity ensured a considerable degree of cooperation and the two armies fought side-by-side against the VRS throughout the conflict. In other areas, a costly civil war between them erupted for over a year.[5] This dynamic was complicated further by divisions within the Bosnian Croat community, some of whom envisioned union with Croatia while others advocated a future in BiH.[6] Such divisions, coupled with the challenges that resulted from being the smallest force to fight in the Bosnian War, placed a great strain on the HVO throughout the conflict. Ultimately, both armies faced momentous challenges during the war. After emerging from the multiethnic institutions of the SFRJ as they became increasingly divided and separated throughout 1991 and 1992, the ARBiH and the HVO represented the armed forces of rival state-building projects on the territory of BiH. As a result, they had tremendous value for their respective civilian leaderships as vehicles for legitimising their efforts to build states and consolidating their political control over them, not to mention the immeasurable symbolic and ceremonial importance of the military in the efforts of some leaders to forge distinct and cohesive nations from the diverse Bosnian population. Evolving in this framework while in the furnace of a terrible war meant that by the time the DPA ended the war, almost every vestige of their multiethnic heritage had been stripped away and two very separate military organisations existed. Thus, while the overarching struggle to defend against the VRS remained a key feature of this period, institutional developments within the ARBiH and HVO and changes in the relationship between them are just as key for understanding the individual components of the post-war military integration process and the political context within which it took place.

## Origins of the ARBiH

The origins of the ARBiH can be traced to before its official formation on 15 April 1992. This date signifies the time at which a plethora of armed groups were symbolically unified into a single army, but numerous military units had been raised, armed, organised, and trained throughout the previous year. Many of the units and much of the structure of the ARBiH was inherited from the TO of BiH, which had been established as an independent reserve armed force of the SFRJ in 1974.[7] Although the TO of each Yugoslav republic was financed and organised entirely by the administration of that republic, the TO formations had been a central pillar of Yugoslav defence policy: if Yugoslavia was attacked, the professional troops of the JNA would meet the invader head-on and aim to inflict heavy losses and slow the advance, giving the TOs time to mobilise and present an armed populace that was impossible to defeat. Most TO forces in Yugoslavia were highly decentralised organisations, specifically designed to remain operational even following a devastating attack which could, potentially, destroy Yugoslavia's entire chain of command.[8] As a result, the structure of the TOs encouraged local commanders to act independently against an aggressor. The pursuit of Workers' Self-Management, a unique Yugoslav interpretation of socialism, added an ideological and constitutional aspect to the decentralisation and placed the responsibility and duty of defence upon workers themselves, rather than the federal or republican governments. This led to a situation in which, while the JNA had a relatively regular relationship with the Yugoslav state (demarcated by its adherence to the chain of command and respect for the constitutional order of Yugoslavia), the TOs were so localised and autonomous that their relationship with formal state structures was distant. Instead, they were offered leadership by the League of Communists and unified by Yugoslav Socialist Patriotism.[9]

By 1990, the ability of these twin pillars to provide leadership and galvanise public support had crumbled and in the elections of November and December that year, the SDA rose to power in BiH, attaining the greatest share of seats in the presidency, the Chamber of Citizens, and the Chamber of Municipalities.[10] With BiH still a constituent republic of Yugoslavia, the fledgling SDA government found itself 'at the apex of a state apparatus it hardly controlled' and a TO that was becoming increasingly fragmented.[11] In 1991, the Bosnian TO comprised 37,223 Muslims, 29,276 Serbs, 14,326 Croats, and 5,339 'Others'.[12] In the absence of the League of Communists, little was left to hold this diverse institution together, and with no constitutional measures in place for such a development, the legitimacy of what remained soon came to be questioned. The state inherited from Yugoslavia had been designed, developed, and staffed by communists, many of whom remained loyal to the idea of Yugoslavia or reinvented themselves as nationalist leaders of their respective ethnicities. As a result, institutions such as the MUP and SDB were 'riddled with Serb and Croat nationalists' who were willing to help 'subvert and conquer the Bosnian state from within'.[13] The SDA's position was further weakened by its continued acquiescence to the Yugoslav military leadership's May 1990 demand that all TOs in Yugoslavia be disarmed, despite BiH's being the only one to adhere to the decision. In total, over 300,000 assorted firearms, light mortars, artillery pieces, and armour were surrendered by the TO of BiH prior to April 1992, leaving the state increasingly defenceless.[14]

The September 1991 attempts of the other members of the Bosnian presidency to demand the withdrawal of Yugoslav forces and begin the mobilisation of the TO were thwarted by the veto of Biljana Plavšić of the SDS, one of two Bosnian Serb members of the collective leadership. When the Bosnian parliament began preparing for secession from Yugoslavia the following month, Bosnian Serb nationalists, including Plavšić and the SDS, instigated a campaign to undermine the republican government. First, they formed a parallel administration for the Serb people of BiH and declared numerous Serb Autonomous Districts, and then, in the first months of 1992, proclaimed the formation of the Serb Republic of BiH (which was later renamed Republika Srpska) and adopted a constitution which stated that it remained part of Yugoslavia.[15] On 12 May 1992, the Bosnian Serb Assembly approved the formation of its own army, the Army of the Serb Republic of BiH, which was renamed a few months later, becoming the VRS.[16] According to Stjepan Šiber, a Bosnian Croat who later served as deputy commander of the ARBiH, prior to the formation of the VRS, the ethnic composition of the senior commanders of the TO was 'around 60 percent Serb, around 30 percent Muslim, and around 10 percent Croat. Here [in BiH] there was no mention of the national key or equal representation of the peoples.'[17] Until many of them left the TO for the VRS, these mostly Serb upper echelons of the TO sought to continue working alongside the JNA (and assist its efforts in Croatia) by disarming non-Serb TO units, distributing arms among the Serb population, and mobilising some Serb units for deployment in Croatia.[18] However, TO units commanded by, or composed of, non-Serbs (which constituted a majority of the TO as a whole) became increasingly reluctant to cooperate.[19]

After the independence referendum of 29 February and 1 March 1992, Izetbegović, acting as chairman of the presidency of BiH, declared independence from Yugoslavia. Over the ensuing month, the SDS wrought chaos on the streets of Sarajevo from their headquarters in the Holiday Inn and on 27 March, paramilitary units from Serbia began a series of attacks on towns in north-eastern BiH, first terrorising Bosanski Brod, a small but strategically significant town bordering Croatia and then killing many Bosnian Muslim residents of Bijeljina and forcing the rest from their homes a few days later.[20] In his memoir, Izetbegović unequivocally states that, for him, it was the 1 April attack on Bijeljina that signalled the beginning of the war.[21] On 4 April, Plavšić and her colleague, Nikola Koljević, tendered their formal resignation from the presidency.[22] Over the next few days, BiH was recognised by numerous states and organisations around the world, including the European Community, the United States, and Croatia.[23] The start of hostilities, coupled with the complete withdrawal of Bosnian Serb nationalists from the apparatuses of the Bosnian state meant that the TO of BiH had, for all intents and purposes, ceased to exist. The presidency, now facing a war without an army, elected to form a new TO on 8 April, the same day the word 'socialist' was dropped from the name of the republic and an official state of 'war-danger' was declared.[24] Over the course of the following week, 40 of 48 former TO staff members, 7 of 9 regional TO staffs, and 73 out of 109 municipal staffs pledged their loyalty to the newly established Territorial Defence of the Republic of Bosnia and Herzegovina (*Teritorijalna obrana Republike Bosne i Hercegovine*, TORBiH), and 75,000 individuals (of 86,000 registered in the old TO) volunteered to join the new force.[25] The TORBiH was administered by the Bosnian Ministry of Defence and was commanded at an operational level by its own Supreme Command, a dynamic that remained from the socialist period. Indeed, the only significant institutional development at this stage was the reallocation of overall strategic command from the JNA to the TO Supreme Command.[26]

Both the military and the state of BiH emerged from the apparatus of socialist Yugoslavia. As the TO and the Republic approached the transition from devolved administrations within the framework of a federal state to the sovereign institutions of the government in an independent country, the nature of the relationship between them remained uncertain. The TO was far from a professional military, and significant portions of its personnel had rejected the presidency's call to mobilise, leaving it an untested and potentially fragile force.[27] Other state institutions were equally weakened, with many bureaucrats either leaking intelligence or leaving their posts and offering their services to Belgrade, Pale (the wartime Bosnian Serb capital) or Zagreb.[28] These factors combined to make the military and the wider state apparatus of BiH weak, undermanned, and subject to external influence.

With the threat of armed conflict becoming increasingly plausible, the SDA immediately began considering the establishment of a national paramilitary force outside the control of compromised state institutions. Marko Attila Hoare observes:

> The SDA as the leading party of government was forced to organise its own clandestine resistance movement independently of the Bosnian state institutions, while these same institutions in large part collaborated with the external enemy in attempting to suppress this resistance.[29]

In March 1991, Izetbegović approved the formation of such a force, and in June 1991, a 'Council for the National Defence of the Muslim Nation' was established within the SDA, signifying the moment when, according to Rasim Delić, future ARBiH commander, the party 'accepted historical responsibility for preserving BiH and Bosniaks'.[30] The military organisation formed by the party received the name 'Patriotic League' (*Patriotska liga*, PL), and although its ranks were open to all nationalities, Delić concedes that its units 'were primarily based on the participation of Bosniak people'.[31] A PL Main Headquarters, which included the PL's military leadership as well as a range of political, public, and cultural figures, was established, with Izetbegović himself overseeing its activities.[32] Sefer Halilović, the PL's military commander, offered a summary of the goal of the organisation in an interview with the BBC, stating, 'our objective was the defence of BiH as a state and the Bosnian Muslim people from genocide and eradication. So we existed as an armed force that protected BiH and Bosnian Muslims.'[33] Hasan Čengić (Izetbegović's closest confidant and later the Minister of Defence for BiH) concisely notes why the SDA, as the party of government, chose to raise an armed force outside the framework of the state: 'We decided to form the [PL] organisation through the structure of the [SDA] party because that was the only structure we could rely on.'[34] Speaking to the Second SDA Congress in 1997, Izetbegović reflected on the evolution of the PL, offering some important insights into its development:

> In July 1991 the first military experts joined the PL and provided the first directives for the defence of BiH. The first truckload of weaponry arrived in August 1991. The first military training began in September. The first units were formed in October. In November a long-range radio transmitter was acquired to cover all of BiH, and the training of communications operators began. In December, the organising of personnel and the arming of police reserve units of the BiH Interior Ministry began at the initiative and under the leadership of the PL. In January

1992 the first unit of the PL with military training was created, and the distribution of TO arms began at the initiative of the PL, an action that was carried out through the highest organs of BiH.[35]

Izetbegović's account of the formation of the PL understandably ignores many of the issues the organisation failed to overcome in this period. In *Balkan Battlegrounds*, the authors note that 'the PL failed miserably to acquire and distribute weapons' and the number of weapons it was able to stockpile 'fell far short of its requirements'.[36] Halilović claims that in March 1992 the PL had 126,000 organised members, 80,000 of whom were armed; however, external estimates suggest that at this time this figure was more likely to have been closer to 40,000.[37] Despite these shortcomings, the PL boasted a 'fairly evolved organisational structure' with eight BiH regional commands located in Sarajevo, Doboj, Cazin, Prijedor, Livno, Mostar, Višegrad, and Tuzla, as well as one in the Sandžak, a multiethnic region straddling Serbia and Montenegro that is home to a large Muslim population.[38] ARBiH General Rifata Bilajac later commented that 'the foundation of the ARBiH is in the Patriotic League, which grew through the TO to become the ARBiH'.[39] Comments such as this suggest that, for its commanders at least, although the multiethnic TORBiH provided the personnel and military structure of the ARBiH, it was the PL that provided its ideological foundations.

While the TORBiH and PL represent two military formations which would play pivotal roles within the ARBiH, in the earliest months of the conflict they were poorly equipped and inexperienced. During this period, particularly in April and May 1992, armed police, SDB, and other MUP forces played 'a decisive role in the defence of areas with a majority Bosniak population, especially in Sarajevo'.[40] On 4 April, the same day that the Bosnian Serb members left the presidency, Izetbegović ordered the mobilisation of all police units and reservists in Sarajevo in an attempt to bolster the city's fragile defences. Steven Burg and Paul Shoup argue that this decision, which was immediately followed by a call from Bosnian Serb nationalists to evacuate Sarajevo, signifies the 'definitive rupture between the Bosnian government and the Serbs'.[41] The next day, police stations and MUP buildings were attacked by Bosnian Serb units, many of which were also formed from policemen.[42] On 5 April, VRS troops began firing into Sarajevo, beginning an almost four-year siege of the capital. It was at this crucial moment that police units provided the Bosnian government with the ability to assert its control in the city, capturing, for example, six snipers who fired on a peace demonstration outside the BiH parliament and defending the TV tower on Hum, a hill overlooking the city.[43] A 200-strong unit of special police led by Dragan Vikić, a Bosnian Croat, played a pivotal role in these operations, highlighting how, much like the TO, the MUP was a multiethnic force.[44] According to Jovan Divjak, the most senior Bosnian Serb commander in the ARBiH throughout the war, the defensive actions of the police in cities were 'of vital strategic importance for the defence of BiH as a whole against the more powerful aggressor forces, [and] bought time for organising and planning the defence'.[45] Bosnian police units also contributed significantly to the overall strength and capabilities of the Bosnian government, and later to the ARBiH. In total, the MUP mobilised approximately 70,000 men, as many as the TORBiH.

Furthermore, as Charles Shrader notes, the troops of the MUP were 'mainly armed with small arms and had few vehicles but [were] generally well equipped and well trained'.[46] Hoare argues that at this time, the forces of the MUP were 'the most powerful armed force under Bosnian government command'.[47]

The Bosnian government managed to mobilise significant numbers of troops in this initial period and successfully established a framework for the organisation and operational control of its forces. However, as the head of the European Community's Monitor Mission in Sarajevo, Colonel Colm Doyle, observes, 'at this early stage, the fledgling Bosnian army was little more than a name'.[48]

## Origins of the HVO

In 1991, the Bosnian Croat population was broadly divided into two political constituencies. Laura Silber and Allan Little note that 'one-third of the Bosnian Croats lived in western Herzegovina, a notorious hot-bed of extreme right-wing nationalism, where Croats formed close to a hundred percent of the population'.[49] That year, many people from this region volunteered to fight with Croatian forces against the JNA and SVK in that theatre, reflecting a broader commitment among much of the community for union with Croatia. This constituency was represented by Franjo Boras of the HDZ in the Bosnian presidency.[50] The rest of the Bosnian Croat population lived across BiH, with the majority living in central and northern Bosnia in mixed towns and cities. Silber and Little observe that this constituency was 'much more inclined to live in a multiethnic Bosnian state than to seek its partition into ethnically pure units'.[51] Stjepan Kljuić, the other Bosnian Croat member of the presidency and leader of the HDZ in BiH, preferred to work within the framework of a united BiH and supported Izetbegović, representing this more inclusive outlook despite hailing from the same party.[52] His views were shared by many influential Bosnian Croat figures, including some in Herzegovina such as another influential HDZ leader, Miro Lasić. He stressed that the 'optimum solution is to "retain Bosnia and Herzegovina as a whole, not altering its borders", for such a future would be favourable to Croatia'.[53] Archbishop of Sarajevo Vinko Puljić echoed such statements, publicly declaring: 'The unified message, and I stand by this, is that an integral, sovereign Bosnia and Herzegovina is the best solution for the Croat people in Bosnia and Herzegovina.'[54] The HVO's main political rival, the Croat Peasants' Party (*Hrvatska seljačka stranka*, HSS), also favoured the preservation of BiH. Ivo Komšić, the party's leader from 1993 to 1995, reflects that the HSS feared that the majority of Bosnian Croats (those living outside of Herzegovina) were left 'unprotected' by the policies discussed by some within the HDZ and sought to build an alternative platform:

> We wanted to become an independent political subject in BiH, one that would make its own decisions, and not be instructed what to do... Of course, we knew we would be faced with fierce reactions. The very establishment of the Party was fiercely attacked by Grude and Zagreb. Even by the HSS in Zagreb.[55]

The influence of such figures was significant and represented key communities, but it was eclipsed by the power of Croatian President Franjo Tuđman. His command over the Croatian state and military, combined with his influence as leader of the HDZ in Croatia, placed him almost entirely in control of the future of the Bosnian Croat community.

Although he did offer some support to Boras in the presidency, Tuđman largely chose to circumvent the Bosnian state in order to influence events in BiH. An emerging leader from Herzegovina, Mate Boban, was selected to lead efforts to form an independent Croat 'political, cultural, economic and territorial whole' and, upon its declaration on 18 November 1991, he became its first president.[56] According to Article 2 of the *Decision on the Establishment of the Croat Community of Herceg-Bosna*, Herceg-Bosna (HB) consisted of the following municipalities: Jajce, Kreševo, Busovača, Vitez, Novi Travnik, Travnik, Kiseljak, Fojnica, Kakanj, Vareš, Kotor Varoš, Tomislavgrad, Livno, Kupres, Bugojno, Gornji Vakuf, Prozor, Konjic, Jablanica, Posušje, Mostar, Široki Brijeg, Grude, Ljubuški, Čitluk, Čapljina, Neum, Stolac and parts of Skender Vakuf (Dobretići), Trebinje (Ravno), and, added a year later, Žepče.[57] This encompassed approximately 30 per cent of the territory of BiH, and included many areas which were not majority Croat. Kljuić, the most prominent Croat critic of the attempt at self-rule, was formally stripped of his authority to represent Bosnian Croats in any negotiations by the HB leadership a month later.[58] On 8 April 1992, as conflict was erupting in Sarajevo, the HB leadership declared the formation of the HVO, which it described as 'Herceg-Bosna's supreme executive, administrative and defence body'.[59] Boban contended that this was necessary because 'thirteen Croatian villages in the municipality of Trebinje – including Ravno – were destroyed and the Bosnian government did nothing thereafter'.[60]

A series of crisis staffs established in predominantly Bosnian Croat areas served as nuclei for HVO military units to muster. With the ARBiH using the structures of the TO, and Serbs dominating the JNA, the HB leadership was forced to build the organisational structures of the HVO from scratch. The framework of the TO was copied, linking Bosnian Croat reservists and volunteers across BiH through the municipal administrations controlled by the HDZ. As many units had been covertly organised for the war in Croatia, fully formed HVO units surfaced 'within days of the Bosnian war's beginning, complete with officers, staffs, organisations, and weapons'.[61] On 16 April, Tuđman ordered the HV to set up a forward position in Grude, a municipality in Herzegovina. Milivoj Petković, a former JNA lieutenant-colonel from Croatia, was placed in command of the position in his capacity as an HV officer and was subsequently appointed chief of the HVO Main Staff. He was assisted in his duties by Slobodan Praljak, a Bosnian Croat who served as an HV Major-General, Assistant Minister of Defence of Croatia, and senior representative of the Croatian Ministry of Defence to HB.[62] The ICTY, in its initial indictment of Praljak, noted:

> He served as a conduit for orders, communications and instructions from President Franjo Tuđman, [Croatian Minister of Defence] Gojko Šušak and other senior officials of the Republic of Croatia to the HB/HVO government and armed forces, and reported to and kept Croatia's senior officials informed of developments in [BiH].[63]

With Petković and Praljak in control, the level of direct influence exercised by Zagreb over the HVO was absolute at the highest levels. The CIA observed: 'Organized and directed from Zagreb, the HVO in 1992 was for all practical purposes a subordinate command of the Croatian Army.'[64] Up to 20,000 Bosnian Croats mobilised under the HVO's banner before April 1992, and by the end of that year, this figure had grown to approximately 45,000, including contingents of HV troops.[65] These troops were equipped with small arms seized from TO stockpiles in HDZ-controlled municipalities, but were entirely dependent on their counterparts in Croatia for leadership, logistical support, heavy weapons, and additional arms. Tuđman was forthcoming in these regards. The HV commanders deployed to BiH raised a brigade-sized formation, the Ante Bruno Bušić Regiment, over the spring of 1992. It was composed entirely of volunteers organised in four battalions, and was well-equipped and manoeuvrable, making it the HVO's most effective unit. Additional support from Zagreb came in the form of considerable financial backing, the supply of approximately 50 tanks, up to 500 artillery pieces, and a 'very important' small fleet of helicopters, as well as small arms and ammunition.[66] As a result, despite being the smallest army in BiH (by a significant margin), the HVO was in 'organizational second place at the war's outbreak in April 1992 – lacking the fully formed military infrastructure of the VRS but far ahead of the virtually non-existent Bosnian Army'.[67] This led many Bosnian Muslims to join up, particularly in local defence units that were raised in majority-Croat areas. Klejda Mulaj argues that, in 1992, up to 30 per cent of the HVO was composed of Bosnian Muslims 'whose preference for joining this formation rather than local Muslim militias was informed by the HVO's ability to provide weapons'.[68] There was also plenty of precedent for such formations in BiH, particularly during both world wars. Indeed, given the high quantities of captured German equipment that was cached in TO stockpiles across BiH during the socialist period, it is entirely plausible that, initially at least, these troops carried the same weapons that their grandparents had been issued fifty years earlier.

Another Bosnian Croat army emerged in the months prior to the outbreak of war in addition to the HV/HVO. The Croat Defence Forces (*Hrvatske obrambene snage*, HOS) were formed by the Croat Party of Rights (*Hrvatske stranke prava*, HSP), an extreme right-wing Croatian political party. Indeed, the abbreviation HOS itself invoked the identity of the Axis-aligned Croat Armed Forces (*Hrvatske oružane snage*) of the Second World War. On 3 January 1992, Blaz Krajlević and Mile Dedaković were appointed to establish headquarters in Ljubuški, a municipality in Herzegovina, and lead the HOS against the JNA and VRS.[69] Burg and Shoup note that the HSP and HOS favoured 'an alliance of Croats and Muslims against the Serbs, and the creation of a republic made up of Croats and Muslims that would eventually be absorbed into a greater Croatia'.[70] The HOS raised approximately 5,000 troops, many of whom hailed from the diaspora or were hired as mercenaries.[71] They wore a black uniform, openly sported fascist insignia, and found significant support from both Bosnian Croats and Muslims.[72]

Despite the apparent display of separatism that the establishment of HB represented, the relationship of its leaders with the Bosnian state was ambiguous. Jure Krišto contends that for Tuđman, 'it was in the interest of the Croatian people at that time for there to be a "demarcation" *inside* Bosnia and Herzegovina'.[73] Thus, initially at least, both the HVO and HOS shared the goals of the Bosnian government and fought alongside the forces it had gathered against the VRS.

## Formation of the ARBiH

The emergence of the PL, coupled with the institutional separation of the TORBiH and MUP and the establishment of the HVO and the HOS, led to a situation in which five separate armies (in addition to numerous paramilitary groups) fought in the name of the Bosnian government during the first weeks of the war. Each was administered and received orders from different institutions, only two of which, the Ministry of Defence and the Ministry of Interior, represented the Bosnian state. In a bid to assert its authority and bring both organisation and legitimacy to the array of armies fighting for BiH, the presidency declared the unification of all armed forces on the territory of BiH under the banner of the Armed Forces of the Republic of Bosnia and Herzegovina (*Oružane snage Republike Bosne i Herzegovine*, OSRBiH) on 9 April 1992, and gave a deadline of 15 April for all units to accept the decision.[74] This largely symbolic gesture was accepted by each armed force, including the HVO and HOS, and was followed by the absorption of the PL into the structures of the TORBiH on 12 April. An appeal on 13 April by Hasan Efendić, a former JNA officer and the newly appointed chief of staff of the TORBiH, called for Bosnians in the JNA to desert, join the OSRBiH, and help defend the Republic of BiH and its peoples.[75] Upon being offered the position of chief of staff on 8 April, Efendić reportedly asked the Minister of Defence: 'Will our army be multi-national or mono-national? If it is mono-national I would not want to be commander'.[76] The promise of a Bosnian Croat and a Bosnian Serb deputy, Stjepan Šiber and Jovan Divjak respectively, convinced Efendić to take the role.

Just under 40 per cent of Bosnian TO commands refused the presidency's request to join the newly formed TORBiH, a figure roughly equivalent to the proportion of Serbs in the population, suggesting that the force that was emerging to defend BiH would be heavily dominated by Bosnian Muslims.[77] However, the TORBiH successfully retained much of the character of its Yugoslav predecessor in the initial months of the conflict and remained a distinctly multiethnic organisation. Efendić suggests that 'Bosniaks, Croats, and a small number of Serbs responded to the mobilisation', while Divjak reports that in 1992 the proportion of Croats in the army was 'higher than their proportion of the overall population', which was 17.3 per cent in 1991, and the proportion of Serbs 'stood at about half their percentage proportion of the population', which was 31.21 per cent.[78] He also notes that the ARBiH Supreme Command was composed of 18 per cent Croats and 12 per cent Serbs, which reflected the proportions of overall troop numbers.[79] Thus, in 1992 the ARBiH was approximately 65 per cent Bosnian Muslim (and 'Other'), 20 per cent Croat, and 15 per cent Serb, a composition which was reflected in the leadership to the highest levels. Such a balance in composition and distribution of power suggests that, as Delić argues, the ARBiH at this time was indeed an organised armed force of BiH and its peoples and citizens defending not only their own country and citizens, but also the values of democracy and civilisation and a thousand-year long history, as well as the multiethnic, multiconfessional, and multicultural character of BiH.[80]

The presidency's decision to create the OSRBiH went some way in establishing a framework for the coordinated management of the separate armed groups on paper, but few practical changes were made. The integration of the TORBiH and PL under the auspices of the Ministry of Defence (rather than the SDA) and the establishment of the TORBiH on 12 April had represented a more significant development toward a democratic model of civil–military relations, but it was not until the following month that the legal status of the OSRBiH was clarified. The Law of the Armed Forces of RBiH, introduced on 20 May 1992, enshrined the OSRBiH as the 'common armed forces of all citizens and nations of the Republic', while the Law on the ARBiH of 1 August 1992 stated:

> Service in the Army is carried out by the citizens of RBiH. Citizens of the Republic have the right, under the conditions determined by this Law, to serve in the Army, to perform military and other duties, to acquire the rank of military officers and other professional titles and to advance in the service.'[81]

The promulgation of such laws, at a time when prospects on the battlefield were bleak, illustrate the extent to which the leadership of BiH were committed to establishing at least the appearance of an inclusive and legitimate armed force, in which all citizens of BiH could serve and fight to preserve the constitutional order of BiH. It was this image that Izetbegović iterated to the world at the International Conference on Former Yugoslavia in August 1992, when he declared some 'fundamental principles' upon which he hoped the future constitution of BiH would be based. The first was that 'BiH will be a democratic, secular state, based on the sovereignty of its citizens and equality before the law of its nations'.[82] However, even while drafting inclusive laws and presenting democratic visions for the future, Izetbegović and the SDA began a series of political manoeuvres which bypassed the nascent institutions of state and ignored the legal framework that was being established, immediately undermining the emergence of democratic civil–military relations in BiH.

Divjak contends that after the PL was officially incorporated into the TORBiH, 'there was still a dual command structure in place' in which Colonel Hasan Efendić, a former JNA officer, led the TORBiH while Halilović retained command of the PL.[83] Halilović, a former JNA officer originating from the Sandžak, had deserted in September 1991 because he felt that 'my place was with my people' and had travelled to Sarajevo in order to put himself 'at the disposal of the SDA and Bosnian Muslims'.[84] On 25 May, the impractical dual command structure was abolished; however, rather than the PL becoming fully incorporated into the TORBiH, Efendić was replaced by Halilović, signifying something of a coup within the military, and the ascension of the armed wing of the SDA to the height of military power within the OSRBiH.[85] Just over a week later, Rasim Delić, another former JNA officer (and SDA supporter) who had defected a few months earlier, was placed in command of the newly established Operational Command in Visoko, near Sarajevo. His tasks included forming new military units and serving as a conduit through which weapons smuggled into BiH could be distributed, arguably making him the most significant figure in the formation and development of the armed forces loyal to the BiH government. In direct contravention of the established chain of command, Delić answered directly to Izetbegović, rather than through the TO Supreme Command and Chief of Staff Halilović, who (despite his own irregular selection process) protested that such an arrangement was a violation of military protocol.[86] Following the formal declaration of war on 20 June 1992, the presidency assumed direct control over the OSRBiH from the Ministry of Defence, in part due to alleged obstructionism on the part of the 'Croat-oriented' Jerko Doko, who led the ministry.[87] Although such a transfer of authority was constitutional in a time of war, by July 1992 many of the original members of the presidency had left the institution, leaving it firmly in the hands of the SDA, although a Bosnian Croat, Mile Akmadžić, remained prime minister.

The efforts of the Bosnian government in the spring and summer of 1992 to establish the necessary legal, administrative, and organisational frameworks to send the ARBiH into battle ran alongside the struggle to arm and equip the thousands of soldiers it now had under its command. During this period, the JNA was still deployed across BiH, and held its own stockpiles and confiscated TO arms in warehouses and barracks across the country. With an international arms embargo placed on Yugoslavia and its seceding republics, these weapons became a jealously guarded resource.[88] In mid-April, PL troops stormed the Pretis factory in Vogošća, on the outskirts of Sarajevo, and seized 800 anti-tank rockets. However, no compatible rocket launchers could be found in the city, so Colonel Sulejman Vranj flew a helicopter at great risk from Sarajevo to the town of Visoko, picked up a single rocket launcher, and flew back, providing the defenders with a vital capability that was driven around the city to face subsequent attacks.[89] One such attack by the JNA on 2–3 May was successfully defeated; however, hundreds of JNA troops remained trapped inside their barracks in the city. Some within the OSRBiH, such as PL Commander Halilović, advocated seizing all confiscated TO weaponry at the JNA's warehouse in Faletići, in Sarajevo. Izetbegović preferred to allow the JNA to leave the city, with the weapons, unhindered.[90] As a result, the defence of Sarajevo was, initially at least, bereft of even the most basic weaponry.

According to Divjak, in 1992 the defenders of Sarajevo possessed only six sniper rifles (in contrast with the besiegers' 285), one tank (opposed to 91), and no heavy artillery.[91] OSRBiH forces in some areas of BiH were more successful in acquiring arms and, sometimes, heavy weaponry. On 15 May, a JNA convoy was captured in Brčkanska Malta, near the old mining city of Tuzla. This had a 'crucial impact in raising morale among our troops and strengthening their resolve to defend the area'.[92] An additional 9,000 infantry weapons were seized from the JNA barracks at Kozlovac, which was just outside Tuzla, providing the defenders of the city with a veritable arsenal in comparison to the rest of the OSRBiH.[93] In Zenica, TO units managed to acquire heavy weaponry, including 20 tanks and 19 anti-aircraft guns.[94] Although Bosnian government forces remained significantly outmatched, particularly in terms of heavy weaponry, artillery, and air power, enough arms and ammunition were acquired in this crucial period to prevent a complete rout.

On 22 May, the TORBiH was given the order to fully mobilise, and five days later, the creation of twelve brigades of the OSRBiH was formally announced.[95] Although most of the army remained in scattered TO units, the OSRBiH now had soldiers organised in sizeable units, a much clearer chain of command, and was beginning to look less like a collection of militias and more like a military. However, despite these developments, the OSRBiH remained limited in both its capabilities and effectiveness. Defensive lines established in the first months of the war would, in many cases, remain unchanged for the duration of the conflict. In Sarajevo, for example, two thirds of the defence lines were left unaltered from June 1992 until the DPA brought an end to the fighting in December 1995.[96] The story was similar across most of the country, with OSRBiH troops able to halt enemy advances, but unable to mount any offensive actions, plan coordinated manoeuvres or increase their operational capability. For many of these soldiers, their experience of the conflict was limited to participating in 'shifts' on static frontlines. Shrader describes this process thus:

> The available military weapons were kept on the frontline position and transferred to the relieving shift. The men participating in the shifts were only skimpily supplied with uniforms and other equipment and were considered soldiers only during the time they were actually on shift.[97]

Divjak offers a further insight into the problems the OSRBiH faced in the first phase of the war, many of which, he argues, remained unresolved until the end of the conflict. He notes that in addition to the lack of weapons and munitions, the OSRBiH also severely lacked signalling and engineering equipment, lamenting that 'we did not even have shovels to dig simple trenches, to say nothing of mechanical diggers, especially in the cities which had been surrounded since day one'.[98] He estimates that approximately 75 per cent of the OSRBiH spent the first year of the war fighting 'in jeans and trainers' and did not even possess a single, unifying insignia (see Figure 4.1). Instead, OSRBiH troops wore the badges of the TO, PL, Yugoslav-era civil defence and youth workers' brigades or simply the emblem of their respective city.[99] The most significant shortcoming Divjak identifies is the lack of professional personnel and the limited training that could be offered to recruits. He illustrates the extent to which the OSRBiH was an amateur force by discussing the case of one particularly large brigade (with more than 5,000 men) which boasted that they did not have a single officer or non-commissioned officer (NCO) from the former JNA. He also notes that in some places, such as Sarajevo, there was essentially no opportunity to conduct training exercises due to uninterrupted military activity and the lack of space.[100]

During the summer of 1992, following the declaration of a state of war by the presidency on 20 June, the OSRBiH underwent a comprehensive reorganisation. On 4 July, the TORBiH (which already included the PL) was renamed the ARBiH, and the MUP and most Bosnian Muslim paramilitary units were incorporated into the new

**Figure 4.1** *Bosnian soldiers wearing a variety of uniforms walk among civilians in Sarajevo on 19 June 1992.* Courtesy of Christophe Simon/AFP via Getty Images.

force. New formations within the ARBiH were also established at this stage, including the 700-strong *Prva sandžaka brigada* (First Sandžak Brigade). Composed of volunteers who had come to defend Sarajevo, this brigade was the military manifestation of an interest in the outcome of the conflict in BiH which attracted many *Sandžaklije* to the city. Morrison and Elizabeth Roberts observe, despite the reservations of the local population (some of whom referred to the volunteers as the *Sandžačka linija* (Sandžak Lobby), 'the influence and political clout of the Sandžak new-comers increased throughout the Bosnian war and the years that followed'.[101]

ARBiH leaders planned to structure their forces in much the same way as a conventional army. However, a Supreme Command (rather than a General Staff) would preside over regional- and municipal-level commands. The predominantly Croat elements of the OSRBiH, the HVO and HOS, remained operationally independent of the new army, although a largely symbolic link was retained by the framework of the OSRBiH. This link was strengthened, for a time, following an agreement signed between Izetbegović and Croatian President Franjo Tuđman on 21 July that recognised the HVO and the ARBiH as distinct elements of the OSRBiH and called for the creation of a joint staff.[102] Despite the challenges faced in the period between April and July 1992, forces loyal to the BiH government managed to mobilise enough manpower, acquire enough weaponry, and mount a strong enough defence to prevent themselves from being completely overrun. Amidst this often-chaotic struggle, the myriad armed groups which had mobilised and fought for the government of BiH were slowly merged into a single, relatively cohesive army: the ARBiH.

## A giant rises: 1992

Following its formation, the ARBiH was divided into seven military districts (Sarajevo, Doboj, Tuzla, Banja Luka, Zenica, Mostar, and Bihać), a system which reflected the structure of TORBiH.[103] The commanders for these districts were selected by Chief of Staff Halilović, although the ability to communicate and exert command and control over all units remained limited.[104] These districts, originally designed to coordinate the defensive operations of TO militias in their respective areas, were transformed to a more conventional military structure on 18 August 1992, when they officially became ARBiH Corps Areas: The Sarajevo Military District became ARBiH I Corps, Doboj and Tuzla became II Corps, Banja Luka and Zenica became III Corps, Mostar became IV Corps, and Bihać became V Corps. Two additional corps were added in 1993, VI Corps located in Konjic, and VII Corps, headquartered in Travnik.[105] The reorganisation took months to complete, but by the beginning of December 1992, the ARBiH possessed five corps, each with its own headquarters and staff, which commanded a number of operational groups (a collection of brigades gathered 'to facilitate the conduct of operations and command and control in combat'), in addition to artillery, signals, engineering, logistical troops, and varying numbers of independent and tactical brigades.[106] Due to the nature of the fighting in BiH, each corps was essentially isolated from the others and operations involving multiple corps were rarely coordinated until the final year of the war.

By the end of 1992, the ARBiH commanded approximately 170,000 troops organised in 28 brigades, 16 independent battalions, 1 armoured battalion, and 2 artillery divisions, in addition to 138 smaller units of various types.[107] These figures had rapidly increased following the influx of refugees (mostly to central BiH) from places such as Jajce, which was captured at the end of October 1992. Many of these people that had been driven from their homes formed mobile units that could operate across BiH and conduct offensive operations, offering the ARBiH a capability it had hitherto lacked.[108] A considerable number of women also volunteered to fill the ranks of the ARBiH through organisations such as the PL, with official records showing that 5,360 female soldiers served during the war as frontline troops, logistical support, and medical staff.[109] (See Figure 4.2.)

By the end of 1992, the ARBiH had grown both in terms of its size and its capabilities. This was reflected by several successes on the battlefield. At the end of October 1992, troops from II Corps repulsed VRS forces near Gradačac and managed to capture an entire JNA armoured train, acquiring significant quantities of arms and equipment in the process.[110] The journal of II Corps, *Armija Ljiljana* (Army of the Bosnian Lily), later reported that the artillery captured that day had been formed into a unit nicknamed 'The Division of Earthly Thunders' which 'had led the enemy to despair' during the fighting around Brčko and could be used in operations in Banovići and Gradačac.[111] In an interview with *Armija Ljiljana*, the commander of the unit, Feriz Šehanović, noted:

We have excellent gun crews, and the composition of the unit is multinational. But I still urge our fellow citizens, Orthodox Bosnians, to report to our unit, according

**Figure 4.2** *Emina Bakić of the ARBiH on Mount Trebević, outside Sarajevo.* Courtesy of Chris Sattlberger/Sygma via Getty Images.

to their knowledge and abilities, so that tomorrow our city can walk with its head raised up.[112]

Šehanović is evidently implying that Tuzla, the city in which II Corps was based, found pride in its diversity, even during the conflict. Interviews conducted by Anna Calori corroborate this suggestion, with interviewees (former ARBiH soldiers) commenting that there were more Serbs in II Corps 'than in any other part of Bosnia', 'most of my Serb colleagues remained here during the war, and we went together to the front-line to fight against nationalists', and 'I wasn't protecting Serbs or Croats or Muslims, I was protecting people'.[113] Calori suggests that this can be attributed to the city's unique heritage, but also highlights the role of the local leadership:

> The Tuzla government's measures were aimed for the collective defence of the city rather than the protection of a singular ethnic group. This was perhaps due to the leadership's anti-nationalist stance, derived from their ideological, cultural and political background.[114]

The election of a reformist candidate, Selim Bešlagić, as mayor in the 1990 municipal elections and the formation of a multiethnic cabinet not only contributed to the II Corps' diversity, but also led to a situation in which, according to a former II Corps soldier, 'you left your weapons outside the city' as the police maintained internal security.[115] This denotes a clear separation between the civil and military aspects of security, as well as the development of an armed force which, in this part of BiH, was not only proving to be effective on the battlefield but was also representative of the population and subservient to civilian authority.

Over the course of the first six months of the conflict, relations between the HVO and the HOS worsened. The HOS had proved valuable due to the supposed enthusiasm of its troops for combat; however, their autonomy soon came to be viewed as a liability by the HVO leadership. On 9 August 1992, HOS Commander Kraljević and seven staff officers were killed at an HVO checkpoint, and two weeks later the majority of the HOS was incorporated into the HVO, with a small component joining the ARBiH.[116] Combined with a gradual expansion, the incorporation of the HOS brought the strength of the HVO to over 30,000 troops, which were supported by an additional 15,000 HV soldiers when necessary.[117] A December 1992 instruction by the commander of HVO forces in Mostar, Ivan Primorac, reveals the concerns of the leadership regarding the incorporation of former HOS units. It ordered all commanders 'to ensure that unit members wear only HVO insignia and remove other emblems' which could 'compromise the reputation of HVO and HV members by implying ideas which the world media may interpret as fascistic'.[118] HV troops deployed to BiH were required to 'wear HVO insignia during their deployment'.[119] Such actions indicate a gradual process in which a degree of uniformity was brought to the various units under HVO command. However, while the ARBiH grew considerably, both in terms of size and organisation, throughout 1992, the HVO 'had in large measure failed to evolve since the war's beginning'.[120]

## Advances and setbacks: 1993

The ARBiH which survived 1992 served the constitutional order and territorial integrity of BiH, and was inclusive of all components of the population, making it a uniquely Bosnian institution. However, Divjak argues that even by the end of 1992, the percentage of Bosnian Croats and Serbs serving in the ARBiH declined as the SDA 'radicalised its position' and 'started saying that the Bosniaks were the "central nation" in Bosnia and appropriated the name Bosniak, which historically refers to all inhabitants of Bosnia, thus relegating local Serbs and Croats to their "reserve homelands"'.[121] In September 1993, the leading Bosnian Muslim parties in BiH and Sandžak formally adopted the designation *Bošnjaci* (Bosniak), a moniker used during the Ottoman period for all inhabitants of Bosnia, to replace the term Muslim as a national label. While Bosniak now serves as the official lexicon for the Bosnian Muslim population, many within BiH (including Bosnian Muslims) dispute the use of the term due to the role of Islam as the basic attribute of the identity and continue to extend its meaning to Bosnian Croats and Serbs.[122] Divjak also notes that, beginning in 1993, the clergy became involved in the ARBiH and religion was introduced within the military. He argues that, when coupled with the appropriation of Bosniak identity, this 'led to the genesis of a mono-national structure and politics that contradicted the presidential platform for the defence of multi-national, multi-religious, multicultural BiH'.[123] Developments such as this were reflected in the upper echelons of the ARBiH, where Šiber, the highest ranking Croat in the ARBiH, was 'promoted' to a diplomatic posting in Switzerland at the start of the year, effectively removing him from the inner circle of the army.[124] Thus, while the ARBiH of 1992 was an army for all BiH, as 1993 developed it increasingly became the domain of the SDA and the Bosnian Muslim population. However, although the numbers of Bosnian Croats and Serbs in the ARBiH were dwindling, the overall strength of the ARBiH was rising steeply.

By January 1993, Halilović suggests that the ARBiH had grown to 'an impressive figure' of 261,500 troops, which he states is 'the time when the *Armija* reached its peak' and controlled the most free territory.[125] Divjak claims that in 1993 the ARBiH 'had as many as 200,000 people on our list', while the International Institute for Strategic Studies' (IISS) *Military Balance*, widely lauded for its precision, puts the total at 180,000, although it does concede that there was a 'lack of accurate information' and it should be noted that only 'regular' troops are included in IISS estimates.[126] Nonetheless, even at the lowest estimate, 180,000 troops made the ARBiH considerably larger than any other force operating in BiH, and gave it an edge over its opponents in one aspect of the conflict.

The impact of the ARBiH's numerical dominance was severely constrained by two key factors. On 14 January 1993, open conflict broke out between the ARBiH and its erstwhile allies, the HVO. Although Bosnian Muslims and Bosnian Croats in many parts of BiH continued fighting alongside each other, in Central Bosnia and Mostar vicious fighting over the control of territory and supply routes drew considerable resources and manpower away from both armies' frontlines facing the VRS. In Central Bosnia, for example, the 26,000 troops of ARBiH III Corps fought over 8,000

HVO Operative Zone Central Bosnia soldiers, gaining some ground at great cost but having little impact on the overall course of the war.[127] In addition to having to supply and conduct operations on a second front, the ARBiH's manpower advantage was also blunted by the pervasive difficulty it faced in sourcing even the most basic arms and equipment. Izetbegović estimates that by mid-1993 the BiH government had successfully acquired 30,000 rifles and machine guns, 20,000,000 bullets, 37,000 grenades, 46,000 anti-tank missiles, 20,000 uniforms, and 120,000 pairs of boots.[128] Although considerable, particularly considering the arms embargo and the difficulties transporting supplies into and across the country, such figures remained far lower than was necessary to properly arm the ARBiH. By the end of the year, the ARBiH 'still showed serious deficiencies in equipment and skills, lacking both armour and artillery and, in some units, even basic infantry weapons and ammunition'.[129]

The conflict between the ARBiH and the HVO began just two days after the Vance–Owen Plan was announced, and was welcomed by VRS Commander Ratko Mladić, who declared: 'I will watch them destroy each other and then I will push them both into the sea.'[130] The conflict had a considerable impact on the HVO and exposed many of its organisational and operational limitations. While many units in Herzegovina were well-equipped and had gained considerable combat experience, most forces raised in Central Bosnia and Herzegovina 'had little to do in their hometowns other than keep a watchful eye on their Muslim neighbours'.[131] The Croats of Northern Bosnia had witnessed the most fighting, but were largely contained to a small pocket around Orašje and were considered loyal to the Bosnian government. As a result, when the conflict with the ARBiH intensified, the considerable variations in the capability of HVO units soon became apparent. Furthermore, many were found to be understrength and the army as a whole suffered from a severe lack of reserves. Additional problems stemmed from the HVO's formation as both a governmental and military body. Shrader notes instances of local HVO commanders ignoring the orders of their military superiors and argues that 'without the assent of the local civilian authorities, even the major regional commander might find it difficult to relieve a subordinate commander' who might be a 'local favourite'.[132]

The HVO leadership began addressing these issues on 10 February 1993, when all municipalities in HB were ordered to raise a Home Guard unit for the protection of military facilities and the manning of checkpoints. This would free HVO troops for frontline operations. However, before such measures could be implemented, the ARBiH's overwhelming numbers soon translated into victories on the battlefield, leading to the capture of both Travnik and Kakanj from the HVO in June 1993.[133] This led Jadranko Prlić, the HVO's political leader, to order all Bosnian Croats between eighteen and sixty to report for military service, indicating how vulnerable HB had become.[134] By the end of July, about a quarter of HB territory had been lost to the ARBiH, and the entire project stood at the verge of disaster.[135] Praljak, reflecting on the fall of Bugojno, contends that the town's defenders were defeated 'in spite of being the best armed brigade of the [HVO]' because 'there were no clear political ideas about what to defend'.[136] He also blamed the civilian leadership for losses in Travnik and Vareš, labelling them 'a group of thieves … getting rich'.[137] In some areas, such as Konjic and Žepče, HVO forces were so desperate that an unprecedented and highly utilitarian alliance with local VRS forces was formed against the ARBiH.[138] Further south, the HV took responsibility for the defence of much of Herzegovina, freeing up additional HVO units to stem the tide in Central Bosnia.[139] The most significant change, however, came at the end of 1993 when Ante Roso, a former French legionnaire from Croatia, was appointed as commander of the HVO. He was responsible for establishing the Zrinski Battalion of the HV (centred around his fellow ex-legionnaires), which saw extensive combat in Croatia and was regarded as one of the best units of the HV.[140] His task in BiH was to bring the organisational methods used by the HVO in line with the HV and create a Bosnian Croat force which could operate alongside its Croatian counterpart in sophisticated and demanding manoeuvres.

While the HVO overcame its own struggles with extensive assistance from Croatia, the SDA began subordinating the ARBiH to its political goals. Hoare observes that this was initially manifested by 'the sidelining or dismissal of commanders who did not follow the SDA line'.[141] On 8 June 1993, this process was escalated by the appointment of Delić, a close ally of Izetbegović, to the newly created post of commander of the ARBiH. Delić assumed complete operational control of the army, with Divjak and Šiber remaining as deputies, although, as both were not Bosnian Muslims, their strategic input was reportedly ignored.[142] Halilović, the erstwhile leader of the ARBiH, claimed his demotion was unconstitutional as it had not been approved by a majority of the presidency, and allegedly attempted to incite a *coup d'état* which was only just averted. However, he was technically not demoted, as he retained the position of chief of staff, despite it being made largely defunct by the new position of commander. In October 1993, the SDA also began increasing its grip on the Bosnian state, replacing Prime Minister Mile Akmadžić, a Bosnian Croat, with Haris Silajdžić of the SDA. Although this served to bring an end to crippling divisions between Muslim and Croat ministers within the government, it left Izetbegović and the SDA with a near-monopoly on the institutions of governance.

Many ARBiH units were, in 1993, still largely autonomous formations that had answered the call to defend their towns and cities in 1992 but were yet to be brought under the effective command and control of the Supreme Command and the presidency. The IX and X Brigades, which had both made vital contributions to the defence of Sarajevo, came under scrutiny following a direct appeal from Divjak to Izetbegović regarding their mistreatment of Serbs. The commanders of the brigades, Mušan 'Cace' Topalović and Ramiz 'Ćelo' Delalić, were widely known to have been criminals prior to the war, but had become charismatic leaders with significant followings after their early military successes, and Izetbegović speculated that it had been Halilović's 'insufficient personal courage' and 'insufficient authority among the troops' that had allowed them to ignore orders and persecute civilians.[143] Following the rise of Delić, plans were made to bring the rogue units to heel. However, Izetbegović chose to circumvent both military and state institutions and instead use the SDA and its affiliates to achieve this. On 23 October 1993, the SDA issued a statement condemning certain units in the I Corps for their 'unlawful behaviour' and 'arbitrary conduct', precipitating military intervention.[144] The planning of the intervention, which was given the name Operation Trebević, was confined to an inner cabal of Izetbegović, Delić, and MUP Commander Bakir Alispahić. It involved moving the elite (and personally loyal to Izetbegović) *Crni labudovi* (Black Swans) paramilitary unit from Kakanj into Sarajevo in order to, in the words of Izetbegović, 'take action against our own units'.[145] The presidency was consulted just a few hours before the operation began, but endorsed the use of violence anyway, and on 26 October Delalić was apprehended and Topalović was killed.

Alongside efforts to consolidate their control over the ARBiH, Izetbegović and Delić also targeted numerous units composed mostly of Bosnian Croats which had been formed under the auspices of the HVO but, in practice, fought as integral parts of the ARBiH, even as the Muslim–Croat civil war evolved in other parts of the country. The Kralj Tvrtko Brigade in Sarajevo, for example, was formally part of the HVO and operated under its banner, but in practice coordinated its efforts with the ARBiH and held a 2-km front along the north bank of the Miljacka with its 1,500 troops.[146] In the Bihać area, the relatively small Croat community formed the 101st HVO Brigade, which in practice operated as a battalion-sized, semi-autonomous formation within the ARBiH V Corps, while in Tuzla, the 107th, 108th, and 115th HVO Brigades had minimal links to the rest of the HVO, and served as key units within the ARBiH II Corps.[147] This history of relatively successful cooperation did little to temper the effort to consolidate all troops under the banner of the ARBiH following the success of Operation Trebević. In November 1993, the HVO military leadership in Sarajevo were captured and detained during Operation Trebević 2. What remained of the Kralj Tvrtko Brigade was then forcibly incorporated into the I Corps, resulting in the loss of more than half of its troops, who refused to join the ARBiH. Similar operations were attempted, to varying degrees of success, against HVO units which had participated in the defence of majority-Muslim areas such as Bihać, Tuzla, and the Posavina region.[148]

## Consolidation and offensive operations: 1994

The Washington Agreement, signed on 18 March 1994, brought an end to the fighting between the ARBiH and the HVO. Described by Izetbegović as 'the result of force, not conviction and political will', the Agreement contained provisions to not only end the conflict but also established a lasting alliance between the two.[149] The newly established alliance was strengthened by Tuđman, who dismissed Boban as president of HB and replaced him with a more moderate candidate.[150] These developments led to an abrupt end to the efforts to forcefully incorporate units into armed forces (either HVO into ARBiH, or vice versa) in the manner displayed by Operation Trebević 2. The conflict in Central Bosnia had already stimulated the ethnic homogenisation of both the ARBiH and the HVO, but the Washington Agreement formalised this process by establishing ethnic identity as the basis for the division of power in the new alliance and encouraging separation, leaving little reason or incentive for Bosnian Croats to remain in the ARBiH and Bosnian Muslims to remain in the HVO.[151] The proportion of Serbs in the ARBiH (15 per cent in April 1992) had steadily fallen as the war progressed due to attrition and the mobilisation of the much larger Bosnian Muslim population in government-held territory. As a result, from 1994 onwards both the ARBiH and the HVO were virtually monoethnic armies, with examples such as Divjak, who remained in a senior position in the ARBiH throughout the war, representing a symbolic vestige of diversity.

During 1992 and 1993, the efforts of both the ARBiH and the HVO were invested in holding as much ground as possible, arming their soldiers, and providing them with whatever training and organisation they could. With the renewed alliance, significant quantities of troops and materiel from both armies could be redeployed, offering a significant boost to the operational capacity of the forces facing the VRS. Furthermore, support and logistics were able to reach pockets of resistance that had been isolated for over a year, while the respite offered by the Washington Agreement presented an opportunity for another reorganisation of the ARBiH. Operational Groups gathered with the purpose of conducting the ARBiH's first major offensives of the war and fully equipped mobile battalions were established within brigades, greatly improving their individual manoeuvring capacity and effectiveness.[152] Additional 'manoeuvre' and 'liberation' brigades, capable of operating across BiH, were also formed, providing a capability which had, for the most part, been limited to small units such as the *Crni labudovi*, *Živiničke ose* (Zinc Axes), and *Kalesijski vukovi* (Calvary Wolves), all of which were essentially paramilitary formations serving as special forces.[153]

The cessation of hostilities also offered the HVO the time it needed to fully implement the ambitious reforms being implemented by Roso. The new HVO was a two-tier force. The top cadre was composed of four newly formed Guards Brigades, in which only professional soldiers served and most of the HVO's heavy weaponry was concentrated. These brigades were designed to operate independently throughout BiH and were in every way copies of the Guards Brigades of the HV. Their creation, however, led the rest of the HVO to be devoid of its best soldiers, officers, and equipment. These units were remodelled as well, becoming the second-tier Home Defence Regiments (*domobranska pukovnija*) that had originally been envisioned to supplement the HVO. These reforms left the Bosnian Croats with a very small but capable offensive component, and an excess of operationally useless militias, most of which were soon dismissed. As a result, the CIA observes, 'though it could manage some local attacks on its own, during the offensive operations of the year, it would function as a mere supporting auxiliary of the HV'.[154]

Until 1994, most of the ARBiH was so under-resourced and inexperienced that coordinating its efforts on a national level was all but impossible. It had, however, increased its overall troop capacity to 228,000 and was becoming increasingly capable as it adapted to the conflict.[155] As a result, it began providing the Bosnian government with

> an overall offensive strategy, a doctrine and tactics that fit this strategy but could be carried out with the Army's limited resources, and a training programme which would produce a force disciplined and proficient enough to execute the manoeuvres required by the strategy.[156]

Formulated by newly appointed Commander Delić, the strategy aimed to grind the VRS down in a war of attrition that, given its numerical superiority, the ARBiH would inevitably win. This was translated into a doctrine in which the ARBiH would 'seek to achieve a continual series of limited gains sustainable without artillery support or motorised transport and roll the frontline back a kilometre at a time'.[157] A more sophisticated doctrine was reflected in the evolution of battlefield tactics employed by the ARBiH. During 1994, elite units, designed specifically to facilitate such a style of combat, began to emerge. One such example is the 'recon-sabotage' unit which scouted the battlefield prior to an offensive. The would identifying weak points in the opposing lines, which were then targeted with sabotage operations aimed at disrupting command and control links and artillery observation posts, isolating enemy frontline units prior to an infantry attack spearheaded by elite assault units.[158] Strategies, doctrine, and tactics such as these allowed the ARBiH to maximise its strengths, while doing as much as possible to negate the extent to which it was hindered by shortcomings such as the lack of artillery, armour, and mechanised transport. The result was a limited but significant change in the nature of the conflict. The ARBiH conducted a range of offensives across the country, and although many failed in their objectives, some ground was taken (almost 100 sq km around Konjic, for example). Furthermore, in some battles, such as at Vozuća in the Ozren Mountains during the summer of 1994, the ARBiH came close to defeating the Bosnian Serb I Krajina Corps, proving to the VRS that 'winning battles against the Muslims was becoming a near-run thing.'[159] An article published in the ARBiH journal, *Prva linija* (First line), the following year reflected on the progress made:

> The new mode of warfare required the introduction of several manoeuvring brigades and the coordinated activities of two or more corps. This implies the extraordinary operational coordination of units involved in the operations, a high level of discipline and responsibility for the execution of plans, providing connections, communications, logistical provisions, and all of the other components of organisation and planning.[160]

Such an analysis suggests that the ARBiH leadership was fully aware of the scale of the challenge they were facing but was also becoming increasingly confident in the capabilities of the army they were building.

Away from the frontlines, Izetbegović continued publicly to proclaim the inclusivity of the ARBiH throughout 1994. On 4 August, he stated:

> Our army in which both Serbs and Croats are serving, is not an avenging army. It is not an anti-Serb army. It is the golden *fleur-de-lis* that flutters on its flag, not Death's head. Our common homeland of Bosnia and Herzegovina meets all the conditions to become, finally, a state in which the rights of all will be respected and protected.[161]

A few weeks later, in a speech to the UN General Assembly, he reiterated that 'for many of us, Bosnia is an idea. It is the belief that people of different religions, nations and cultural traditions can live together.'[162] On the anniversary of Bosnian Independence on 1 March 1995, he proclaimed:

> Our aim is a Bosnia of free people, a Bosnia in which the human being and human rights will be respected. We oppose the concept of mono-national, mono-religious,

one-party parastates – in the plural – with our concept of a free and democratic Bosnia.[163]

This image presented by Izetbegović and the SDA was becoming increasingly distant from reality and continued to be undermined by the decisions they made. As Sabrina Ramet observes: 'Izetbegović tried to be all things to all men, presenting himself as a devout Muslim to some audiences and as a champion of tolerance and secular liberal democracy to other audiences.'[164] On 19 November 1994, ARBiH II Corps Commander Hazim Sadić was replaced by an SDA-approved candidate, Sead Delić, and was sent to Turkey to serve as a military attaché to BiH's diplomatic delegation there.[165] Sadić had been a successful leader who, with the cooperation of Tuzla's reformist mayor, had advocated for the ARBiH to be as multinational and inclusive as possible, and had even formed Bosnian Serb 'Liberation' units, inspired by the Partisans, within his forces. Hoare contends that Sadić may have been suspected of harbouring autonomist designs for the Tuzla region, offering a pretext for his removal. By this stage of the war, Sadić's lack of SDA membership was unusual in the upper echelons of the ARBiH, and may have been considered reason enough to warrant his removal.[166] The substitution of ARBiH officers with SDA-selected replacements, coupled with the elevation of Rasim Delić above the established chain of command in 1993, illustrates the extent to which the ARBiH was increasingly becoming the armed wing of the SDA, rather than the military of the Bosnian state.

## Exclusivity and endgame: 1995

The SDA's attempts to consolidate its control over the ARBiH in 1993 and 1994 led to a clash between Izetbegović and the other members of the presidency in January 1995. At a ceremony in Zenica on 20 October 1994, Izetbegović had been made the honorary commander of the VII Muslim Brigade, one of the ARBiH's elite units, infamous for its Islamic character, Mujahidin volunteers, and combat effectiveness. During the ceremony he received a certificate written in Bosnian and Arabic, which stated:

> We fighters of the VII Muslim Illustrious Brigade, by the Lord Allah the Almighty in whose name we fight, proclaim our immense honour in awarding this certificate to the hadji Alija Izetbegović, the worthiest son of Bosnia, most beloved brother of the Bosniak-Muslim nation, proclaiming you first honorary commander of the VII Muslim Illustrious Brigade. It is our principle: May the mercy of Allah, and His protection from the crime committed against the Bosniak-Muslim nation, always be with you.[167]

In response, at the beginning of 1995 the non-SDA members of the Bosnian presidency, one of the 'last feeble bastions of multi-ethnicity in the state', condemned the politicisation of the ARBiH as manifested at Zenica, and its transformation into an Islamic, Bosniak, and SDA army.[168] Izetbegović responded by demanding full authority over the military be invested in him as president of the presidency, rather than shared collectively between all of its members, as the case had been since June 1992. This coincided with the establishment of *Dan šehida* (Day of Martyrs) on 23 January by the *Islamska Vjerska Zajednica* (Islamic Religious Community, the organisation of BiH's Muslim clergy), which was to be celebrated annually on the second day of Ramadan, and would entail the faithful visiting the local *šehidsko mezarje* (martyr's cemetery) for prayers.[169]

The term *šehid*, derived from the Arabic for witness or martyr, increasingly became applied to fallen Bosnian Muslim soldiers of the ARBiH as the war progressed. Although it was often used alongside a more inclusive term (*šehidi i poginuli borci*, martyrs and fallen warriors), the widespread use of such a term, its institutionalisation as a public holiday, and the creation of cemeteries specifically to inter fallen Muslim ARBiH soldiers illustrates the extent to which the ARBiH had become increasingly Islamic in its identity, at the expense of its former inclusivity. Indeed, the commander of British UN (and later NATO) forces in Bosnia from August 1995, Trevor Minter, observes that 'in my time the ARBiH was entirely Muslim'.[170] The concerns of the non-SDA members of the presidency were validated by Izetbegović's response, yet their intervention came at the expense of the little power they had left. Following such events, the carefully maintained image of the equality of BiH's constituent nations within government-held territory began to slip. In an interview with the *Times* in February 1995, for example, Izetbegović commented that his aim was 'to preserve Bosnia and to ensure that the Muslim people have their own place there', while in a speech to the Bosnian parliament at the end of the year, he proclaimed that 'the Bosniak people were the backbone of the state'.[171]

Despite the political turmoil, on the battlefield the ARBiH continued to develop into an organised, experienced, and increasingly confident force. The ceasefire orchestrated by former US president Jimmy Carter put the fighting on hold for the first four months of 1995, offering Delić an opportunity to make 'organisational and formation changes' and bolster the logistical support and training ARBiH troops received.[172] In addition, the staff of the Supreme Command, the highest body in the ARBiH, was reorganised along more conventional lines and renamed, becoming the General Staff of the Army. *Prva linija* reports that the reorganisation 'aimed at strengthening the defence capabilities of the Army and increasing its efficiency', as well as improving leadership and command.[173] Although strengthened, the ARBiH still remained very limited in its operational capabilities due to shortages in arms and equipment. Indeed, it still had 'fewer weapons than people' and, for an army with approximately 250,000 troops, the ARBiH could only put 31 tanks, 35 APCs, and a total of around 100 artillery pieces of all sizes into the field.[174] This compared with the 370 tanks, 295 APCs, and 700 heavy artillery pieces of the VRS.[175] Furthermore, 'this haphazard collection of captured vehicles and weapons was a hodgepodge of varying calibres and types, and each gun crew knew its ammunition reserves had to last for the remainder of the war'.[176]

The extent to which the ARBiH had evolved, in terms of its organisation and ambition, yet remained hindered in terms of its capabilities, is best illustrated by the June 1995 attempt to break the siege of Sarajevo. Misha Glenny suggests that in the months leading up to the operation, 'a carefully planned campaign of disinformation' was promulgated by the Bosnian government, in which many potential scenarios were disseminated into the public discourse to ensure the real campaign was a surprise.[177] Furthermore, he notes that Sarajevo TV punctuated 'lengthy explanations of passages from the Koran' with 'sequences romanticizing the preparations of the [ARBiH] for the spring offensive', further illustrating the growing fusion between the Islamic elements of the SDA's ideology and the ARBiH itself.[178] When the operation was finally launched, it was unprecedented in size, involving the coordination of 80,000 troops from four separate ARBiH Corps. Although it did achieve some successes, the well-prepared troops of the VRS stalled the attack with artillery and the rapid redeployment of mechanised units, followed by 'the judicious commitment of elite infantry units at key moments to eliminate ARBiH territorial gains'.[179] Even with its well-developed organisation and strategic planning, the ARBiH was unable to deal a significant blow to the VRS.

It was not until September 1995, following the defeat of the SVK by the HV in Croatia and the subsequent distribution of a wealth of captured military equipment and supplies that ARBiH forces were able to pose a significant threat to the VRS. The deployment of significant firepower on the battlefield, for example, allowed the ARBiH V Corps to conduct manoeuvres that had been unimaginable just months previously, resulting in considerable gains on the ground, as well as the capture of further substantial quantities of equipment and supplies. The II Corps was also able to widen the scope of its operations, organising its own captured artillery into division-level reserves, allowing for more coordination and offensive manoeuvres, and introducing 'pursuit detachments' (composed of tanks, APCs, light vehicles, and elite mobile infantry units) in order to allow operations 'against the enemy's rear in a manner never before possible and [afford] the II Corps a new degree of offensive depth'.[180] Delić argues that by the end of 1994 and throughout 1995, the military supremacy of the VRS had been reduced to the extent that the Bosnian Serb leadership and their sponsors in Belgrade had to consider negotiating peace (see Figure 4.3). This was compounded, he notes, by the establishment of a military alliance between the ARBiH, the HVO, and the HV, the decline in morale of the VRS and the Bosnian Serb people, and the damage inflicted upon VRS logistical and communications infrastructure by NATO in August and September 1995.[181] On 12 October 1995, another ceasefire was signed, heralding negotiations held in Dayton, Ohio, in November, and the formal signing of the General Framework Agreement for Peace in BiH in Paris in December.[182]

## Conclusion

The ARBiH became an effective army only in the last months of the war. From April 1992 until the end of 1993, the priority on the battlefield was simply to hold ground, as the political and military leadership of the Republic of BiH attempted to build an army. With considerable numbers of troops organised, an appropriate doctrine introduced, and parts of the army developing the capability to conduct offensive operations, the ARBiH was no longer a rag-tag militia of volunteers fighting in 'jeans and trainers' in 1994, but still significantly lagged behind both the VRS and the HVO in terms of operational capability. By 1995, it was able to coordinate manoeuvres

**Figure 4.3** *Bosnian government soldiers atop a truck wave a captured Serb flag in Zenica on 11 October 1995, the day before the final ceasefire of the war. The troops were coming back to their base in Zenica after capturing a strategic point near Ozren, on the main road between Zenica and Tuzla.* Courtesy of David Brauchli via Getty Images.

involving units from across the country, utilise more complex offensive tactics, and ultimately move beyond the static-defence operations that it had largely been limited to for most of the war. By the time the peace agreement was signed, the ARBiH was an organised army, with relatively high levels of discipline, experience, and morale. Furthermore, it had developed a strategy, a doctrine, and the tactics that offered it a way to attain victory on the battlefield. Over the course of the war, it had evolved from a loose organisation of disparate armed groups into an army that was recognisable as a reasonably effective and cohesive fighting force. Despite these successes, it remained unable to properly equip, train, and provide professional officers to its soldiers throughout the conflict, and many of its victories on the battlefield owed much to the efforts of the HV, NATO airstrikes, and the subsequent decline of VRS morale. The extent to which the ARBiH remained limited in the final months of the war is illustrated by Minter, who notes that even in the final months of 1995, ARBiH units were 'very local forces and [were] dependent on local personalities and leadership'.[183] Its troops were 'not soldiers at all but people given a uniform and a gun. I was not aware of any training, certainly not above individual level'.[184] Delić concludes his account of the conflict with a frank assessment of the ARBiH's capabilities at the end of the war:

The ARBiH was in a condition to continue waging the war of liberation of BiH, if it had been supported by the international community and if it continued with joint operations with the Croatian Army and the HVO. Without such support, the ARBiH could not continue the war.[185]

As Delić concedes, although the ARBiH had grown and matured as a military, the support of the HVO, and more importantly the HV was vital. At the beginning of the conflict, the HVO was relatively well-organised and armed, and as a result was successful in its defence of the territory claimed for HB. Despite ostensibly being a Bosnian Croat organisation, it was financed by Zagreb and 'during the entire Bosnian war – but especially during the first several months – the HVO's chain of command, both political and military, [ran] all the way back to Tudjman's desk in Zagreb'.[186] For many of their most significant engagements, HVO units were deployed alongside HV troops, and were subject to command by HV officers. By 1995, the HVO had developed into a force designed specifically to augment the HV, to the extent that it was entirely reliant on Croatia to safeguard the territorial claims of the HB. Under the framework of the Washington Agreement, the HVO was formally allied with the ARBiH. However, the reality on the ground was that, for all intents and purposes, it represented an expeditionary force of the HV. This ambiguity would be the cause of much consternation in the future. For the months either side of Dayton, it allowed the HVO to serve as the crux of the ARBiH–HVO–HV alliance which threatened the VRS with defeat.

This alliance survived and recovered from countless VRS offensives and, by doing so, successfully removed the possibility of Mladić attaining a military victory and ending the conflict on his terms. Combined with mounting international pressure on the architects of the Greater Serbia project, manifested most significantly by NATO's bombing campaigns, this forced Milošević to the negotiating table. Given the position of the ARBiH and HVO in 1992, this was a considerable achievement. However, while this did constitute a victory of sorts, the democratic aspirations that the Bosnian government had established as its aims at the beginning of the war had not triumphed. Although efforts were initially made to create the constitutional and institutional framework for an inclusive and democratically accountable military to develop, particularly in Tuzla, all progress in this direction was subverted by the SDA's gradual consolidation of control over both the civil and military facets of the Bosnian state. The SDA succeeded in removing any meaningful opposition, either through allocating the portfolios of obstructionist ministers to the presidency, or by replacing them outright with SDA members. Furthermore, Izetbegović slowly gathered more and more authority over military affairs, first through bypassing the conventional chain of command, then by replacing non-SDA approved officers, and finally by investing full authority over the ARBiH in himself.

Thus, by the time the Dayton Agreement was signed in December 1995, power in all areas held by the ARBiH was in the hands of the SDA. As a result, the relationship between the state and the military (although both were diminished in size and diversity) had essentially reverted to what it had been during the socialist period: both were dominated by the same political party, making any formal separation between them purely symbolic. Indeed, as Hoare argues, 'the Bosniak national interest was identified solely with the president, the ruling party and the army, in consequence of which these three institutions became increasingly fused'.[187] In a speech to a large crowd in the Bilino Polje Stadium in Zenica in April 1996, Izetbegović stated: 'Without the SDA Bosnia would either be a province of Greater Serbia today, or it would have been destroyed.'[188] This statement underlines the extent to which the ARBiH and the remaining structures of the Bosnian state had become subordinated to the SDA, which for all intents and purposes had simply replaced the Communist Party as *the* source of authority within both the government and the military, and across government-held territory as a whole.

Part 3

# Construction

# 5

# The entity armies, 1995–2002

The DPA brought peace to BiH after more than three and a half years of brutal conflict. Approximately 100,000 people died as a result of the war, more than half of the population were forced from their homes, much of the housing and infrastructure lay in ruins, and almost 10 per cent of the country was left contaminated with landmines and unexploded ordnance. Well over 200,000 troops (up to 400,000–430,000, including reservists) remained armed and divided into three armies that were ready to continue fighting each other, while the institutions and structures of the young state tasked with maintaining the peace were largely untested, their only experience of state-wide multiethnic governance being the disastrous months leading up to the outbreak of war in 1992.[1] In this climate, the likelihood of BiH following the path of most post-conflict states and relapsing into war remained a distinct possibility.

Faced with the herculean task of establishing a lasting peace from such an unpromising situation, the architects of the DPA laid the institutional foundations of the Bosnian state in addition to ending the conflict. Annexes included stipulations on a wide range of issues, including elections, refugees and displaced persons, the preservation of national monuments, policing, and the constitution.[2] Furthermore, the integral role that the international community would play in BiH was enshrined, and 60,000 NATO troops were mandated to enter the country to 'assist in the implementation of the territorial and other militarily related provisions of the agreement'.[3] (See Figure 5.1.) However, despite the considerable attention given to certain aspects of the future of BiH in the DPA, the fate of the armies that had fought in the war was almost entirely unaddressed. Indeed, Richard Holbrooke, a US diplomat who was the driving force behind the negotiations at Dayton, later lamented that 'the most serious flaw in the DPA was that it left two opposing armies in one country, one for the Serbs and one for the Croat-Muslim Federation'.[4]

On the ground, the military commanders of all three armed forces faced myriad challenges. Initially, they had to ensure that the armies they commanded abided by the terms of the peace agreement while they began demobilising the considerable numbers of troops that they led. In the medium term, they had to develop structures and systems to maintain forces that could hold their ground should the conflict resume without draining the severely diminished resources of their respective patrons. Although many of these tasks were completed within a few years, the challenge of maintaining a credible military force without any resources or investment dominated

**Figure 5.1** *A Bosnian family on a horse-cart makes its way through the M1 Abrams tanks of a US IFOR checkpoint outside the town of Kalesija, on 28 April 1996.* Courtesy of Odd Anderson/AFP via Getty Images.

this period for military personnel across BiH. The VRS also continued to serve as a vital tool for the RS political elite to consolidate their authority in peacetime, while the Bosnian Muslim and Croat components of the VF proved equally valuable to the elites of their respective constituent peoples. Indeed, throughout the first post-war decade, military personnel and veterans served key symbolic functions in ceremonies and parades that the wartime leaderships from across BiH employed in their efforts to consolidate their authority and influence over their respective constituent peoples. In addition to this considerable range of duties, the VF was also tasked with carrying out a major transformation of its structure and doctrine, which remained based on what had been inherited from the socialist era, to a system focused on producing a small but professional military akin to the armed forces of NATO states. Further layers of complexity were added to the security sector in post-Dayton BiH by the sustained presence of a series of multilateral peace operations, external interest and investment in building the Bosnian state, and the ongoing hunt to capture indicted war crimes suspects, many of whom were prominent military commanders.

In this complex environment, the principles upon which each military was built and maintained diverged considerably. By 2002, the entity armies of BiH were administratively separate organisations that were not only divided by the bitter legacy of the war but also by the completely different approaches to training, structure, and organisation that each employed. Thus, while the armies that emerged from the war in 1995 remained largely based on ideas and structures that had been inherited from the SFRJ and were therefore, in that respect, quite similar forces, the entity armies grew further and further apart, making the construction of a unified army from them an unlikely prospect. The process of military integration in post-conflict BiH was not a linear process that began with Dayton; it became a more challenging proposition in the period 1995–2002.

## Three armies in one state: The Dayton Peace Agreement

The DPA divided BiH into two entities, the term given to the semi-autonomous devolved administrations which each governed approximately half of the country. Republika Srpska (RS) covers 49 per cent of the territory of BiH (see Map 5.1). Its population is almost wholly Serb, and the entity is governed by a centralised administration. Constituting 51 per cent of the territory of BiH, the Federation of Bosnia and Herzegovina (*Federacija Bosne i Hercegovine*, FBiH) is composed of ten cantons, to which many powers are devolved: six are majority Bosnian Muslim, two are majority Bosnian Croat, and two are mixed. Although many people eventually returned to homes outside their respective ethnic enclaves, governance of the entities remains the preserve of the dominant ethnic group. In addition, there is one small 'shared' district, Brčko.[5] Brčko owes its unique status to its strategically vital location on what was known by the VRS as the Posavina Corridor: It is the sole link between the two halves of RS, and also provides access to the rest of the FBiH for the Posavina Canton, which is otherwise encircled by RS and Croatia.

At the national level, BiH is governed by a bicameral parliament composed of a House of Representatives (composed of 28 members from the federation and 14 from Republika Srpska) and a House of Peoples (composed of five Muslims, five Croats, and five Serbs). Executive power is held by a three-member presidency, composed of a Bosnian Muslim, a Croat, and a Serb.[6] Overseeing all elements of political activity is the Office of the High Representative (OHR), an organisation which represents the international community, in the form of the Peace Implementation Council (PIC).[7] The High Representative leads the OHR and has the responsibility to monitor the implementation of the peace settlement, coordinate with the signatories of the DPA and report back to the PIC. In 1997, at a PIC conference in Bonn, the powers of the High Representative were extended, giving them the authority 'to remove from office public officials who violate legal commitments and the Dayton Peace Agreement, and to impose laws as he sees fit if [BiH]'s legislative bodies fail to do so'.[8][9] These responsibilities have since been referred to as the 'Bonn Powers'.

Governance in BiH has, for the most part, remained restricted to the collection of nationalist parties which came to prominence in the 1990 elections and retained their positions throughout the war. The SDA, which positioned itself as the protector of Bosnian Muslims, generally favoured strengthening the central state at the expense of the entities, not least because they would likely form the largest party in parliament. The HDZ remained close to its sister party in Croatia, and sought to maximise Bosnian Croat autonomy, with little regard for the FBiH or BiH itself. The SDS, which had led RS through the war, managed to retain its position initially, but lost ground to

**Map 5.1** *Bosnia and Herzegovina after the Dayton Peace Agreement*

other parties from 1997.[10] All parties which governed RS in the period, however, remained firmly committed to their entity's autonomy and continue to frequently threaten secession from BiH. Together, these parties filled seats at various levels of the consociational power-sharing arrangements embedded throughout the Bosnian state councils and formed uneasy coalitions which, thanks to pervasive political deadlock, generally achieved little to improve the material well-being of the Bosnian population for most of the 1995–2002 period.

The establishment of such structures of governance and the arrival of the largest peacetime deployment of military force since post–Second World War Germany led to the rapid de-escalation of the military situation in BiH. According to the World Bank, within four months of the DPA, 100,000 soldiers of the ARBiH, 45,000 HVO troops, and an additional 150,000 from the VRS had left their units.[11] Tobias Pietz notes that 'it is not accurate to talk of demobilisation or controlled reduction but rather of the disintegration of the armed forces of all groups'.[12] Greatly reduced in size, the armies that remained in BiH after Dayton were composed of the core staff of each military and a fraction of the operational forces that they commanded during the war. The practice of conscription, a legacy of the socialist period as much as the war, continued in all three armies, providing a ready supply of cheap troops to fill the ranks and maintain high numbers of reserves. Military service also offered civilian and military leaders the opportunity to use their militaries as a 'school of the nation' with which they could attempt to embed approved values and beliefs in the youth of their respective constituencies.[13] Rohan Maxwell (senior political-military analyst at NATO Headquarters Sarajevo from 2005 to 2019), notes that conscription was regarded as a 'rite of passage', which 'remained important – to the leadership and politicians, if not the increasingly disenchanted, unpaid, and maltreated conscripts – and each ethnic group of soldiers saw itself, and was generally seen, as protectors of its constituent people'.[14]

The continued presence of multiple opposing armies in post-Dayton BiH was not a product of design. Holbrooke notes that 'since NATO would not disarm the parties as an obligated task, creating a single army or disarming [BiH] was not possible'.[15] Carl Bildt, the EU's wartime negotiator, contends that rather than NATO's timidity, it was the desire of Washington to be able to exert influence on and offer assistance to the armies in BiH that resulted in the DPA's vagueness concerning the military.[16] While there was clearly plenty of political manoeuvring at Dayton, the constitution that was eventually negotiated recognised, but did not enshrine, the presence of entity armies:

> Neither Entity shall threaten or use force against the other Entity, and under no circumstances shall any armed forces of either Entity enter into or stay within the territory of the other Entity without the consent of the government of the latter and of the Presidency of [BiH]. All armed forces in [BiH] shall operate consistently with the sovereignty and territorial integrity of [BiH].[17]

The armed forces were obliged to defend and preserve the territorial integrity of BiH but were also restricted to their respective entities. The omission of any further detail regarding the status of the militaries in the constitution put them, by default, under the control of the entities, as 'all governmental functions and powers not expressly assigned in this Constitution to the institutions of [BiH] shall be those of the Entities'.[18] Additional negotiations regarding the finalisation of two military articles of the DPA were held in 1996 in Florence and Vienna, but concerned arms control, de-escalation, and the promotion of cooperation between the entity armies.[19] Such initiatives were largely successful, but did little to address many underlying problems, as the commander of the US contingent of the Peace Implementation Force (IFOR), Major General William Nash, observes:

> All four armies [including IFOR] have done their job pretty well in achieving the objectives set out in Annex 1-A of the Dayton Accord. But I don't know if the military aspects bring peace as much as bring the absence of war.[20]

As a result, the FBiH formed its own Ministry of Defence and General Staff, and the RS retained the military institutions it had built during the war. Furthermore, the RS constitution was amended in order to reserve the right of the RS National Assembly (the entity-level parliament) to declare war.[21] Coordination at the state level with regard to defence was limited to the Standing Committee on Military Matters

(SCMM), which held no power and merely served to provide a 'tenuous link between the three militaries'.[22] Indeed, the SCMM failed to meet until 1998, and even then was periodically boycotted by all parties involved.[23] NATO, burdened as it was with enforcing the ceasefire, controlling BiH's airspace, and supervising the boundaries between the entities, was reluctant to disarm the armies in the years immediately after conflict. The recent US experience in Somalia no doubt informed the decision to prioritise caution and avoid mission creep. As a result, even paramilitary units were left armed until August 1997.[24] Rather than building Bosnian institutions or rushing to integrate former combatants, the absolute priority of the peacekeepers in the initial years after Dayton was to stop the war from restarting. This entailed practical measures rather than reforming policy, as a US IFOR engineer explains: 'We've blown up two thousand bunkers, that's a lot of bunkers … We're going to make it so it's hard for these guys to go back to war.'[25] The ambiguity of the DPA with regard to the armies in Bosnia and the prioritisation of other tasks provided each entity with plenty of scope to possess and develop its own armed force.

## The Army of the Federation

The VF was one of the two entity armies that existed in Bosnia after Dayton. It was the product of the March 1994 Washington Agreement, which brought an end to the conflict between Bosnian Muslims and Croats in parts of BiH, forged a military alliance between them and laid the foundations for what, upon the signing of the DPA, became the FBiH.[26] While this served to strengthen both the ARBiH and the HVO in their struggle against the VRS, it also led to the ethnic homogenisation of each force. Due to the localised nature of much of the fighting, in many cases whichever ethnicity was dominant in an area led the defence against the VRS and the minority ethnicity would serve under the other's banner. As a result, many HVO units had been up to 50 per cent Bosnian Muslim, and a significant proportion of the ARBiH was Bosnian Croat and Serb.[27] When conflict broke out between the ARBiH and HVO in Herzegovina and Central Bosnia in October 1992, this practice quickly stopped in those areas, although in some places, such as Sarajevo, the instability led to the forced incorporation of semi-autonomous Bosnian Croat units into the ARBiH.[28] After the Washington Agreement, both armed forces became increasingly monoethnic as troops were ushered into formations representing their ethnic identity. By the end of the war, although they were officially unified by Article 6 of the Washington Agreement, which stated that 'both sides agree to the establishment of a unified military command of the military of the Federation', the ARBiH and HVO existed as separate, monoethnic institutions.[29]

The rhetoric of political and military leaders in the years after Dayton illustrates the extent to which they disregarded the VF, and instead focused on consolidating their ethnically demarcated political constituencies. Indeed, Herceg-Bosna, the wartime Bosnian Croat state, was not formally dissolved until August 1996, more than two years after the FBiH was established. The following year, it was replaced with a political association, demonstrating the ongoing interest in the territorial division of BiH.[30] At an SDA convention in 1997, Alija Izetbegović, the Bosnian Muslim member of the presidency, stated that there was

> no turning back to a colourless, non-national Bosnia. After becoming aware of itself and its name and after the unmeasurable sufferings it has gone through, the Bosniaks will never again give up their nationality and Islam as its component.[31]

Speaking at another convention in March 2000, he proclaimed that the SDA had been the organiser and leading power of the resistance to Serb aggression, and had fought 'for the political and spiritual survival of Bosnia and the Bosniak people'.[32] Such statements contrast with many speeches he gave during the conflict itself, when he often emphasised the secular, multiethnic, and inclusive character of BiH, but were echoed by ARBiH military commanders. At a ceremony held in Zenica on [ARBiH] Army Day (April 15) in 1996, Brigadier-General Vahid Karavelić reminded the gathered troops and civilians that, 'We defended the Bosniak people … The ARBiH grew from our people, and remember, from now, as long as this world exists, we are the Army of our people. Our foundations are our faith, our fallen heroes, and our injured.'[33] At another Army Day event the following year, Rasim Delić, the wartime commander of the ARBiH, asked the audience to 'be firm in the commitment to the survival of the whole of Bosnia and … the Bosniak people, our culture, traditions and faith in this region … we all have to be the army'.[34] From such statements it is clear that for most Bosnian Muslim political and military leaders, the ARBiH and the SDA were institutions that had become permanently intertwined with Bosnian Muslim (or Bosniak) people during the war, even though the ARBiH did not formally exist in post-Dayton BiH.[35]

The legacy of conflict between the two component parts of the VF was reflected in its structure and development. Most prominent was the continued segregation of the lower ranks on the basis of ethnic identity. As a result, the approximately 18,000 Bosnian Muslims and 6,000 Bosnian Croats who made up the army only served together for ceremonial purposes, at VF Headquarters, or in the Rapid Reaction Force, which was composed of a battalion from each ethnicity.[36] A 2005 NATO report reflected on the presence of parallelism in the VF, and illuminates the extent to which it was, in practice, two separate armies. The report notes that property and equipment seized by the ARBiH and HVO during the war was held separately, each component maintained their own separate logistics and support processes, and despite a Federation Intelligence Service being established in 1997, work within it was divided. Furthermore, veterans' affairs and wartime archives were not consolidated, and both the ARBiH and HVO kept separate bank accounts, leaving the joint federation account being all but empty.[37] Indeed, each component of the VF was funded from entirely different sources. A 1998 report from the International Crisis Group concluded that the Bosnian Muslim element was largely financed domestically, although 40 per cent of funds came from Arab states in the Gulf. The Bosnian Croat element, by contrast, was financed entirely from abroad, with 83 per cent of its funds coming from Croatia and much of the rest coming from the diaspora.[38] This situation led some observers to claim that the Croat forces constituted a 'foreign force', and thus were in contravention of the DPA.[39]

The extent to which the VF remained a deeply divided institution is illustrated by events that took place in 2001. The November 2000 elections, in which the HDZ lost ground to a ten-party coalition, initiated a tumultuous year in Bosnian Croat politics which culminated with the withdrawal of the HDZ from the institutions of the FBiH and an attempt to (re)establish self-rule in Herzegovina.[40] HDZ leaders requested that Croats in the VF refuse orders from non-Croats, meetings were held between Croat VF officers and the wartime HVO leadership to discuss forming a new army, and numerous Croat soldiers removed the Federation insignia from their uniforms (see Figure 5.2). This campaign was mostly financed by funds held by the Hercegovačka Bank (subject to one of the largest corruption scandals in post-Dayton BiH), some of which were used to pay Croat VF officers if they left their posts.[41] Crisis was only averted following an international investigation into the dealings of Hercegovačka Bank, the intervention of the Croatian Foreign Ministry (which pledged its support for the state and entity institutions of BiH), and the appointment of a new federation minister of defence. Despite this, General Dragan Ćurčić, deputy commander of the VF (and the highest-ranking Croat), resigned, citing his desire to remain loyal to the Croat people.[42] Thus, while the VF remained intact until the creation of a unified Bosnian military, it was an army only in name.

The VF was structurally fragile but had significant resources at its disposal. A combined 1998 budget of over 400 million Deutschmarks (the currency of choice in post-war BiH) dwarfed the 70 million that was allocated to VRS. Much of this

**Figure 5.2** *Bosnian Croat soldiers of the VF stand in support of Croat self-rule at a stadium in Kiseljak on 11 May 2001.* Courtesy of Reuters via Alamy.

was spent on maintaining an army more than twice the size of its former adversary, as well as a considerable pool of reservists. However, a significant focus was placed on modernisation.[43] An American military consulting firm, Military Professional Resources Incorporated (MPRI), had earned itself a reputation in the region after it had helped professionalise the Croatian Army (*Hrvatska vojska*, HV) prior to Operation Storm. While MPRI was nominally in Croatia to train Croatian officers in democratic civil–military relations and managing the transition from socialism, the HV rapidly became a highly capable force and was soon able to successfully launch complex military offensives, suggesting some level of strategic input. When Operation Storm was launched in August 1995, the offensive defeated the Serb state in Croatia, Republika Srpska Krajina, in a week and brought HV, HVO, and ARBiH troops to within 16 miles of the largest Bosnian Serb-held city, Banja Luka. Paul Williams, who served as a legal counsel to the Bosnian delegation at Dayton, reported that his clients sought similar assistance for the nascent VF at the accords, and even hoped to make it a precondition for signing the treaty.[44] British and French concerns that arming the Bosnian Muslims could lead to a return to war prevented such provisions being included formally, but the Bosnian Muslim delegation received verbal assurances from their US counterparts that assistance would be provided in future.[45] These assurances were quick to manifest themselves, and just six months later, in May 1996, MPRI officially began working with the VF under the Train and Equip Program (see Figure 5.3).[46] The US State Department established the Joint Interagency Taskforce for Military Stabilisation of the Balkans to administer the programme, and US Ambassador James Pardew led the initiative.[47] He described its aims frankly:

> We do not seek an offensive force, but in the future if somebody wants a fight it will be more than fair. This war had an aggressor, and it had a victim. The program [seeks] to ensure that there will be no future victims and no easy prey for partisans of war.[48]

The journal of the VF, *Prva linija* (Frontline), heralded Train and Equip with the headline 'The Professionals Come!'[49] It explained that the programme 'creates conditions to enhance the combat power and efficiency of our units, and in this way modern weapons, professionalism and expertise compensate for the significantly reduced and limited numerical strength of our units'.[50]

Through Train and Equip, the VF acquired an array of small arms, hundreds of artillery pieces, armoured vehicles, tanks, and even a squadron of helicopters, with almost all of the new equipment being of American or French origin.[51] MPRI oversaw the establishment of the federation Ministry of Defence and Joint Command, which were completed in 1997 and 2001, respectively. They also introduced the US Army concept of a Training and Doctrine Command, and began using modern training methods used in the US military, including a computer simulation centre and a field combat training centre.[52] Such was the transformation of the VF that conscripts even translated and learnt US Army chants for use on exercises.[53] Chris Lamb, of the US Department of Defense, regarded the Train and Equip Programme as successful, and noted that it 'rectified the military imbalance between Bosnian Serb and Federation

**Figure 5.3** *MPRI consultants train Bosnian and Croatian army soldiers at a joint training and operations centre in Hadžići, BiH, on 12 December 1997.*

forces, reassuring the Federation and sobering the Serbs'.[54] Recognising the advantages Train and Equip offered, RS President Biljana Plavšić requested the programme be extended to the VRS. However, her unwillingness to hand over all remaining persons indicted for war crimes to international authorities led the United States to dismiss her request.[55] As a result, Bosnian Serb commentators such as former VRS General Vinko Pandurević argued that as 'RS is unable to allocate more extensive financial resources for the development and modernisation of its military' the Train and Equip Program could 'significantly disturb the balance of military forces and encourage the FBiH to launch a new offensive against RS'.[56]

In 2002, 10,000 VF soldiers were demobilised, completing a series of troop reductions that began with Dayton, leaving the VF with a standing force of 14,000 men. This quantitative shortfall was more than offset by modern equipment and a greater quality of training and education, most of which was offered by friendly states and brought the troops up to the standards of many NATO armed forces.[57] By January 1998, 1,500 VF personnel had received education and training abroad, most significantly in Turkey, and another 500 were being trained as far afield as the United States, Malaysia, Qatar, and Pakistan.[58] Schools were established for personnel to learn foreign languages, predominantly English, German, and Turkish, and new accommodation was also built, with the aim of creating 'quality living and work conditions'.[59] The rapid transformation of the VF, with the assistance of MPRI and friendly states, established a modern professional army in the FBiH, and represented a significant shift from the armed forces that had fought in the war. The developments were welcomed by *Prva linija* as they promised 'training to world standards' and the creation of 'armed forces for the 21st Century'.[60] However, despite professionalisation and modernisation, the VF failed to integrate its Bosnian Croat and Bosnian Muslim composite elements at any level below that of the most senior leadership throughout the period. It remained an army only in name.

## The Army of Republika Srpska

Just weeks after the DPA was signed and VRS forces withdrew from the front (see Figure 5.4), the talismanic leader of the Bosnian Serb military, General Ratko Mladić, published a Christmas and New Year's message in *Srpska vojska*, the journal of the VRS. In it he lauded the exploits of his army, stating: 'The VRS, in the defensive and liberation war that was imposed on us, in exceptionally difficult conditions, unrivalled in the history of warfare, against a many times stronger and more powerful enemy and the most powerful part of the international community, defended the Serb people and most [RS] territory'.[61] He remained bellicose, reminding his readers that 'the signing of the [DPA] created the conditions ... for the ongoing struggle of the Serb people for their own sovereignty, statehood, and cultural, spiritual, and general development to continue in the diplomatic, political, economic, and other spheres of life in peace'.[62] Foreseeing 'numerous and complex tasks in the coming years', he also outlined his vision for the VRS after the war, declaring that 'the entire Serb people will be the builders of a happier future, but also a strong and invincible army to guarantee their

**Figure 5.4** *A column of VRS M-84 tanks in Lepnica, northern Bosnia, inside the Posavina Corridor on 30 December 1995. A total of seven tanks were moved 2 km from the Orasje frontline in the Posavina Corridor as agreed upon in the Dayton Peace Agreement.* Courtesy of Odd Anderson/AFP via Getty Images.

survival in this region'.[63] His message ended with a stern reflection on the sacrifices that had been made: 'We must never forget that our freedom was paid for with the lives of the best sons of the Serb people. Their sacrifice permanently obliges us to preserve the freedom and peace of the Serb people and all citizens in [RS]'.[64] Through such statements, Mladić clearly conveys a simple message that although the war had stopped, the fight continued, and the VRS remained central to success.

Despite Mladić's sabre-rattling rhetoric, the VRS faced an array of momentous challenges in the years following the war, the most pressing of which was addressing the dismal relationship it had with the political leadership of the entity it served. In August 1995, the entire high command had rebuked the orders of their constitutional leader, RS President Radovan Karadžić, in favour of Mladić. This amounted to mutiny and provided President of Serbia Slobodan Milošević the pretext he needed to act on behalf of the divided Bosnian Serb leaders in the final months of the war. By bringing peace to BiH, the DPA reduced Milošević's authority over the Bosnian Serb leadership, but did little to narrow the gulf between the civilian and military commanders of RS. The extent to which the VRS remained independent of civilian control is best illustrated by the words of the RS Minister of Defence (1994–8) Milan Ninković: 'At the time of Dayton I piloted a law through the assembly to increase civilian control of the military, and Mladić didn't like that. He arrested me. I thought I was going to be executed. I was released because Patriarch Pavle, the head of the Serbian Orthodox Church, intervened.'[65] While it is possible to speculate that Patriarch Pavle's intervention may have taken place at the behest of Milošević, indicating his ongoing influence in BiH, the arrest of the minister of defence by the military was the second clear act of mutiny which the VRS committed in the interest of strengthening Mladić's authority at the expense of their civilian commanders and the constitutional integrity of RS.

Before tensions could escalate much further, however, the hunt for Mladić on behalf of the ICTY, which had indicted both him and Karadžić after the massacre of Bosnian Muslims in Srebrenica in July 1995, began to have an impact on the Bosnian Serb leadership. Although he technically remained in command of the VRS until the end of 1996, Mladić largely retired from public life to the shelter of a bunker disguised as a hunting lodge near Han Pijesak, his wartime headquarters.[66] He is believed to have remained in the bunker until the summer of 1997, when he moved to Serbia.[67] In July 1996, Karadžić was ordered to step down as RS president and head of the SDS by Milošević, who feared renewed sanctions against the Federal Republic of Yugoslavia (*Savezna Republika Jugoslavia*, SRJ).[68] Mladić and Karadžić remained influential, the former from his bunker near Han Pijesak and latter from his stronghold in Pale; however, their control over the civil and military pillars of RS was over. Holbrooke, who negotiated Karadžić's removal, made this clear: 'He [Karadžić] will not appear in public, or on radio or television or other media or participate in any way in the elections', which were scheduled for September.[69]

Karadžić's chosen successor was one of his wartime deputies, Biljana Plavšić. She served as interim leader until elections were held, and successfully secured a two-year term as RS president. Plavšić was known for her extreme views, having been an active supporter of the ethnic cleansing campaigns of Serb paramilitaries and having stated during the war that 5 million dead Serbs was a price worth paying if it secured 'the survival and freedom of the other 5 million'.[70] Indeed, even Vojslav Šešelj, a notorious war criminal, described how she 'held very extremist positions during the war, insufferably extremist, even for me, and they bothered me as a declared Serb nationalist'.[71] He noted that she refused to shake hands with Milošević after he agreed to the Vance–Owen Plan in 1993.[72] In November, she moved to do what Karadžić had failed to do fourteen months previously, and asserted constitutional authority over the military. Manojlo Milovanović, Mladić's deputy throughout the war, recalls Biljana Plavšić's actions on 7 November 1996:

> The complete Headquarters [of the VRS] was removed by the order of the President of RS, Ms. Biljana Plavšić, after 1,697 days of existence. Some senior officers were reassigned to other duties, part of them retired, and several generals were made available to the VRS or the [SRJ] military. The Headquarters, as an institution, was renamed the General Staff, and was led by retired colonel Pero Čolić.[73]

Mladić had been unanimously supported by the military leadership during the previous effort to assert civilian control in August 1995. This time around he was not even present to protest, and the transition proceeded smoothly. Plavšić and Čolić remained in office until the 1998 elections. Although they achieved little else, their actions lessened the divide between the VRS and the other state institutions of RS.

Throughout the war, the VRS was dependent on the significant support of the SRJ. This link with Belgrade remained central to the VRS as an entity army, with observers describing it as 'an integral part of the Yugoslav Army'.[74] In 1998, 40 per cent of VRS funding came directly from the SRJ, and until 2002 its officers' wages were still being paid from Belgrade.[75] The continued reliance on Yugoslav support following Dayton can be explained as much by necessity as by fraternal bonds. By the end of the war the VRS was on the verge of defeat, with some estimates suggesting that once reservists and formations of extremely limited value were discounted, its operational force had been whittled down to just 30,000 troops.[76] Much of the equipment that the VRS had inherited from the JNA had served its purpose in a war against armies without heavy weapons but had since become obsolete. The T-55 tank, for example, was employed widely during the war to great effect, but it was originally designed in 1945 and stood little chance against the M60 Pattons received by the VF through Train and Equip: the Pattons were a modernised model of a tank that had been designed specifically to destroy T-55s. Problems with outmoded equipment were compounded by a chronic shortage of spare parts, which meant that almost all of the VRS's equipment was difficult to maintain. Moreover, it had depleted almost all of its considerable ammunition reserves in the war.[77] RS was, however, able to retain a small air force, including 30 fixed-wing light attack jets and 12 helicopters, which were kept stored in hangars near Banja Luka and Zalužani.[78] Although the equipment was dated, the VF had no fixed-wing capability whatsoever, offering the VRS a noteworthy advantage in that field.

The total budget of the VRS in 1998 was 70 million Deutschmarks, half of what the Bosnian Croats received, and a fraction of the total VF budget.[79] As a result, the VRS was limited to a comparatively small force of 10,000 men, although the Total Defence system inherited from Yugoslavia was maintained, allowing for the rapid mobilisation of reserve troops.[80] Little was done to improve the quality of training offered to VRS personnel, although senior officers began to attend training seminars in Oberammergau, Germany, alongside their VF counterparts, in 1998.[81] The food and accommodation offered to VRS conscripts deteriorated in quality over time, and no official arms imports were made by RS between Dayton and military unification in 2006.[82] Although equipment may have been sourced covertly from the SRJ, such materiel would have been compromised by the same problems as the VRS's existing reserves. Maxwell explains that 'the RS Army had not moved, they were still on the old system, and quite proud of it … although maybe the VRS would have recognised that they were probably outgunned by the stuff that had been given to the Federation'.[83] An interview conducted by *Srpska vojska* with Plavšić offers insight into the condition of the VRS. Discussing the reduction of personnel, she observed:

> Of course, the reorganisation should have been followed with a much stronger material base than was the case … As far as I know, people in the General Staff and in the Army in general are performing to the level of their capabilities. However, much of it depends on material assets.[84]

In 2003, the VRS demobilised an additional 3,500 soldiers, leaving them with a standing force of only 6,500 men, less than half the strength of the VF.[85] By the time the reform process began, a significant discrepancy in the relative military capability of each entity had developed, with the VF being twice the size of the VRS, possessing superior equipment, and receiving better training.

The VRS did, however, retain significant symbolic value, offering RS considerable power and 'one of the trappings of national sovereignty'.[86] A 1996 article in *Srpska vojska* underlined its importance, stating: 'All those on whom further building of the Army depends must know that it still remains the only guarantee to the Serb people for a peaceful life and development of RS.'[87] Plavšić emphasised the link between the VRS and RS's aspirations for statehood: 'A Yugoslav soldier did not know what he was fighting for, whereas a Serb soldier knows that he is fighting for his Serb state. By keeping such an attitude, we will have both our state and our future.'[88]

VRS Day is celebrated on 12 May, and commemorations have focused on the role of the army in the founding of RS.[89] In May 1997, the editors of *Srpska vojska* remarked: 'In a little over four years of war thousands of fighters fell, giving their lives for what we have today – and that is Republika Srpska.'[90] The following year, the publication ran the headline: 'The Army is the pillar of unity of RS.'[91] This invoked the words of Plavšić at a ceremony held in Banja Luka in which she proclaimed, 'may remembering the victims be a measure of our love for RS' and contended:

> In peacetime, it is the VRS' task, as well as its obligation as the creator of this Serb country, to use its authority, professionalism and proven patriotism, to be a pillar of our society inside, and a barrier to the outside, if needed.[92]

In comparison with the VF, the VRS developed very little as an entity army. This can be explained in part because of its formation, originating as it did from the well-equipped and professional Yugoslav army, but much of this stagnation stemmed from a severe lack of funds and resources. However, where the VF symbolised little more than an alliance of necessity between its composite elements, the VRS was hailed as the founder, unifying focus, and guarantor of the Serb entity in BiH. RS gave the VRS a state to serve as Yugoslavia collapsed. In return, the VRS fought to establish RS. For many Bosnian Serbs, the survival of one was intertwined with the other.

## Military integration: An unlikely prospect?

The divergent paths of development that were followed by the post-war entity armies not only symbolised the ongoing division within BiH and increased the likelihood of a conflict relapse, but also raised extensive practical challenges to reform and integration. Concerns regarding the development of the entity armies were raised by the PIC in 1998:

> The Council is concerned at the increasing divergence in doctrine and training between the Entity Armed Forces, and urges the development during 1999 of plans for a training and development programme common to all the armed forces of Bosnia and Herzegovina.[93]

The inability of the VF to address the legacy of conflict between its composite elements and integrate them at a meaningful level offered an indication of the difficulties that would emerge in the face of any efforts to unify the armed forces in BiH. The PIC described the integration efforts in the VF as 'superficial and inadequate' and noted that efforts to implement confidence and security building measures had been delayed, resulting in 'a lack of real progress towards improving the level of co-operation and confidence between the Entity Armed Forces (and within the Federation army)'.[94] David Lightburn, a NATO analyst, observes that 'de facto, however, there were, and remain (in 2000), three armies, since the Croat and Bosniac forces have not been integrated either in structure or in practice, and cooperation between the two is minimal and superficial'.[95]

The extent of external sponsorship of all armed forces in BiH following Dayton exacerbated the practical difficulties facing integration efforts, raised concerns regarding legitimacy and jurisdiction, and presented a direct threat to the viability of the Bosnian state. The PIC also voiced its concern regarding this matter: 'The Council requires immediate and full transparency in all aspects of external support to military forces ... all such external support should promote integration and cooperation among and between all elements of the armed forces'.[96] The problems in the defence sector were apparent to international observers, and the PIC itself identified 'the instability that is inherent in having two – and in practice three – armies present in one country'.[97] However, few actions were taken to address this beyond maintaining a large multilateral peace operation in BiH. The lack of progress in this area can in part be explained by the omission of many specifics regarding defence in the DPA, and the initial focus on de-escalation and reconstruction following the war. However, implementing reforms across almost every sector of post-Dayton BiH society proved to be a slow and difficult process.

A report to the US House of Representatives illustrates the frustration faced by those wishing to establish a functioning state: 'Bosnian leaders from all three ethnic groups have not made a concerted effort to curb corruption and have often acted to obstruct the reform process in general'.[98] It was in the face of such corruption and obstructionism that the Bonn Powers were introduced. Initially, the Powers were used to establish basic aspects of the state, such as promulgating a Law on Citizenship, and introducing a passport, flag, currency, national anthem, coat of arms, and a common licence plate for vehicles, none of which could be agreed upon by Bosnian politicians.[99] The continued failure to build a political consensus within the country led the Office of the High Representative to increasingly rely on the Bonn Powers to force through reforms, including the creation of a state-wide public broadcasting system, judicial reform, constitutional amendments, and the formation of a state-wide tax system.[100] Throughout the period, however, the entity armies remained relatively untouched due to the protection provided by their ambiguous legal and constitutional status and the significant symbolic value of the VRS to the RS administration. Put simply, the international community (through the PIC and High Representative) considered that, as long as the armies were not fighting each other, it was too destabilising to interfere with them.

In December 1999, Croatian President Franjo Tudman died. He had been key in facilitating financial and political support for the HDZ in BiH and the Bosnian Croat component of the VF, and although he 'repeatedly proclaimed his public support for the [DPA], he never abandoned hopes of creating a Greater Croatia'.[101] In elections held following his death, the HDZ was ousted from power in Croatia, severely weakening their allies in BiH and shifting priorities domestically. The Social Democrat–Liberal coalition government prioritised integration in Euro-Atlantic institutions, reforming the constitution and, in May 2000, joining NATO's Partnership for Peace (PfP), a bilateral programme that promotes multilateral military cooperation and the modernisation and democratisation of armed forces. In 2002, the Croatian Ministry of Defence published a revised National Security Strategy, which 'sees Croatia's military as a smaller, more professional force, able to participate in peace support operations in cooperation with NATO countries and to fulfil Croatia's obligations as part of the PfP'.[102] In doing so, the Croatian state made clear its ambition to reform its military to conform with the conventions and practices of NATO member-states, making the potential for a return to the illicit support of Bosnian Croats particularly difficult.

Croatia's PfP membership coincided with renewed calls from the PIC for the creation of a 'state defence establishment' in BiH, a reduction in the size of armed forces, and a military configuration that could be 'balanced against projected budgets'.[103] An audit of the defence budgets of 2000, sponsored by the governments of the United States, UK, Switzerland, and Germany, concluded that the entity armies were spending far more than they were allocated, and warned that by 2002 the VF would be able to pay only one in three of its soldiers, and the VRS two in three.[104] In addition, it was found that both armies often failed to pay salaries and bills, and almost nothing was spent on purchasing equipment, providing quality training within BiH, maintaining infrastructure, investing in research and development, or adequately funding the SCMM, the only state-level military institution.[105] Sergeant Peter Fitzgerald, a peacekeeper deployed to BiH with the Stabilisation Force (SFOR, the successor to IFOR), noted the fiscal impact of BiH's bloated defence sector:

> The primary purpose of any armed force is to defend a country's territorial integrity and sovereignty. The situation in BiH is unique, however, with two distinct armed forces in defence of one country. Such a defence structure has led to armed forces that have become an economic burden on the country.[106]

He points out that steady personnel reductions had greatly reduced the number of troops, from an end-of-war estimate of 430,000 to 34,000 in 2001. However, at this number the BiH defence budget was still consuming approximately 6 per cent of the country's Gross Domestic Product (GDP), quadruple that of the European average.[107] Even following a programme of troop reduction in both entities, in 2003 there remained 20,000 soldiers in Bosnian armies, in addition to a combined total of 250,000 reserves. Compared with total population figures, this amounted to 1 soldier for every 21 citizens: In the US the ratio is 1:200.[108] Having three armies in one state, regardless of the political or symbolic value, was an expensive luxury that BiH could not sustain.

The December 2000 general election in Serbia resulted in Zoran Đinđić becoming prime minister after he led the Democratic Opposition of Serbia to victory and formed a coalition government. Widely favoured by many Western leaders for his role in the September presidential elections which toppled Milošević, the victory of Đinđić represented a sharp change in outlook for the Serbian state. Furthermore, it dealt a significant blow to the aspirations of the RS leadership to join the SRJ, as two of the new government's first moves were to establish diplomatic ties with BiH (symbolising its formal recognition of the sovereignty of BiH) and express interest in PfP membership.[109] This led to a reconsideration of priorities in BiH, particularly after January 2001, when a coalition of ten parties convinced to cooperate by the American and British ambassadors formed a government. Known as the Democratic Alliance for Change (*Demokratska alijansa za promjene*), the new government ousted the incumbent nationalists, whose 'stewardship since Dayton had left Bosnia poor, dysfunctional, divided, corrupted, unreconstructed and hopeless' in the eyes of many, for the first time since 1990.[110] The arrest of Milošević in April 2001, followed by his extradition to The Hague in June, offered a definitive end to an era which had started to recede with the election of Đinđić. In March of the following year, Mladić was officially retired from the military (by the SRJ) and in April a warrant was issued for his arrest.[111] This was immediately followed by the announcement that Serbia formally aspired to join the PfP.[112] The recognition of BiH, the arrest of Milošević, the forsaking of Mladić by Serbia, and the declared intention to join a NATO programme represented a seismic shift in the political environment in Serbia. This, combined with the formation of a relatively progressive coalition government in BiH, left the SDS isolated. With the possibility of secession receding, the party was left with few options but to try and obstruct the state-building process in BiH on its own.[113]

The accession of Croatia to PfP and the interest signalled by the Government of Serbia inevitably led to the consideration of the programme in BiH. In July 2001, the collective presidency of BiH formally expressed its desire to become a partner. Such declarations were welcomed by the NATO Council, but many conditions had to be met before BiH could join the programme. NATO Secretary-General Lord Robertson outlined the requirements at a press conference in Sarajevo:

> A common security policy, democratic parliamentary oversight and control of the armed forces, the provision at a state level of command and control of the armed forces, including a state level ministry responsible for defence matters, full transparency for plans and budgets, and a development of a common doctrine and common standards to train and equip the armed forces of this country.[114]

The conditionality offered by NATO demanded significant reforms for progress towards PfP membership to be made. However, although the creation of state-level oversight was required, the integration of the armed forces in BiH was not.

On 27 May 2002, Paddy Ashdown, the former leader of the British Liberal Democrats, became High Representative. He brought with him new ideas, a new approach, and a willingness to intervene in BiH domestic politics at an unprecedented level, to the extent that his critics gave him the moniker 'the Viceroy of Bosnia'.[115] In his inaugural speech to the Bosnian parliament, Ashdown highlighted the burden that the entity armies were placing on BiH's finances, noting that 'BiH spends twice as much on defence as the United States, and four times more than the European average …

there is no alternative to reform'.[116] Later, reflecting on his time as High Representative, Ashdown offered an interesting insight into his aims for BiH:

> I felt that the process of creating the peace was over, the job was now to put BiH irreversibly onto the path to a sustainable peace as a member of the European institutions. Note the word European institutions, it doesn't just mean the EU, it means Brussels-based institutions which includes NATO. In making that the aim of my mandate, I was clear that in order to become a member of NATO they would have to create a united army, a single army. It was contained within the framework of what I thought the aim of my mandate was.[117]

Ashdown's interpretation of his mandate did not correlate exactly with the official NATO position, which allowed for multiple armies if they had state-level oversight. He explained this discrepancy, stating: 'Mostly I decided I was a better judge of what was possible in Bosnia than they were sitting in Brussels'.[118] When asked where the idea for military integration originated from, Ashdown explained: 'It started with me. I saw my job as to build in BiH the framework for a light level state. One of the parts of that framework was a single army under the control of the Presidency'.[119]

The events of 2000–2 constituted a seismic shift in the political discourse and strategic environment of the region. The divergence of the entity armies and associated instability had been highlighted by the international community, along with the economic unsustainability of the post-Dayton defence sector in BiH. Regional interest in NATO, coupled with the formation of the 'least obstructive' BiH government since the war ended, initiated serious discussion within Bosnian society about the long-term future of the armed forces in the country.[120] With the goal of joining the PfP agreed, NATO's conditions outlined, and the arrival of an ambitious High Representative, the climate for reform was as conducive as it had ever been.

Before any significant progress could be made, however, several prominent Bosnian Serb leaders moved to sabotage the process. The Bosnian Serb member of the presidency, Živko Radišić of the Socialist Party, vetoed legislation that aimed to reorganise military organisation at the state level just weeks prior to Ashdown's arrival, and, on Ashdown's first day as High Representative, RS Prime Minister Mladen Ivanić of the SDS 'flatly refused, with threats' to enact the last act of Ashdown's predecessor, Wolfgang Petritsch.[121] In September 2002, *Glas srpski*, a newspaper from RS, reported that the NATO director for the Balkans, Robert Serry, did not deem unification a necessary step to NATO integration, reporting that 'officials of [RS] and NATO confirmed that the abolition of the [VRS] and the [VF] is not a condition for BiH to join the Partnership for Peace'.[122] Serry is quoted as saying, 'according to the Dayton Agreement BiH is entitled to two armies, but it is required to provide guarantees to the [SCMM]'.[123] The statement was leapt on by Bosnian Serb leaders, who could argue that any attempt to disband or merge the VRS was a violation of the DPA.

This understanding differed from Ashdown's interpretation. He recalls that in October 2002 he hoped to introduce another reform: 'the disbandment of Bosnia's two entity-based armies and the creation of a single army, under the control of the state. This was an essential requirement for membership of NATO'.[124] These contrasting statements illustrate the pervasive ambiguity of the constitutional position of the armed forces in BiH. According to some international observers, the armies were entitled to exist separately as a result of the DPA. However, to others, the entity armies represented a barrier to integration into international institutions and were not protected by the agreement. The delays caused by such tactics lasted until the October elections, when the main nationalist parties returned to power at the state level and were able to protect their military interests more effectively. In 2003, five Bosnian Serb parties agreed to harmonise parliamentary activities in order to block any talks regarding defence reform.[125] Ashdown notes that he was aware that any attempt to reform the VRS 'would be furiously resisted by the RS, who regarded their army as a mark of "statehood"'.[126] Military integration, it seemed, remained an unlikely prospect.

## Conclusion

The DPA established a lasting peace; however, it did little to address a broad range of issues which together created an extremely complex and unstable security environment in post-war BiH. In practical terms, the three armies that had fought each other in an extremely divisive and polarising conflict were left to navigate this environment by themselves, with the stipulations of the DPA and the efforts of the international community for the most part being restricted to demobilisation and de-escalation. This led the administrations of both entities, fearful of a return to conflict, to retain considerable armed forces, to establish prerogatives and structures of military administration and organisation usually the preserve of sovereign states, and to maintain doctrine and training focused on the potential resumption of the war.

The consociational nature of BiH's governing structures allowed politicians who identified as leaders of the Serb, Croat, or Muslim communities of BiH (rather than of the citizenry as a whole) to dominate the administration of the country. By extolling the glories and sacrifices that their respective armies had made, such leaders utilised a powerful tool which helped them maintain the focus of BiH politics on the divisions brought about by the conflict and consolidate their positions. As Berg explains: 'Across all areas, ties between ethnic-nationalist networks and security forces remained strong. Many political leaders in all three ethnic groups had been military leaders, and used military officers and veterans' groups to mobilize public support.'[127] This made it politically prescient to keep the militaries as separate as possible and resulted in the VF being essentially bereft of any identity or cohesion. Furthermore, although the international community recognised the 'inherent danger' of having three armies in one state, particularly one as unstable as BiH, the various intergovernmental agencies and state-led initiatives that called for significant defence reform were unable to incentivise (or demand) such action. Lightburn asserts:

> The main obstacle remains the lack of political will in the area of defence, at both state and entity levels. A radical change in the attitude of members of the joint presidency and of other state and entity leaders is required.[128]

An array of measures and reforms was gradually implemented throughout the period with the explicit goal of strengthening the state-level governance of BiH. Meanwhile, Croatia progressed towards Euro-Atlantic integration, the era Milošević was brought to an end in Serbia, and international observers increasingly came to recognise that the instability caused by presence of multiple armies in BiH was the greatest threat to peace in the region. Rather than developing in line with these trends and moving towards coexistence or integration, the entity armies maintained and promoted distinct ethnic identities, remained ideologically and doctrinally prepared to resume fighting each other, and ultimately evolved into two very different institutions.

The perspective offered by peace and conflict scholars Johan Galtung, Anders Themnér, and Thomas Ohlson illustrates how these developments 'limited' the peace in post-Dayton BiH. Galtung identifies two types of peace: negative, which he defined as 'the absence of violence'; positive, which he characterises as the 'integration' of human society.[129] Themnér and Ohlson contribute an additional category, 'legitimate peace', which they place midway between positive and negative peace. Legitimate peace, they contend, is when 'loyalty to the idea(s) of the state' are strengthened and 'the attitudes and practices of individuals and groups within the state toward each other' are improved.[130] Viewed in this way, it is apparent that throughout the 1995–2002 period, the peace in BiH did not advance beyond negative. Central to this lack of progress was the institutionalisation of the separation of the formerly warring armies, manifested by the entity armed forces: As long as they stood ready to fight each other, peace in BiH was limited to the absence of violence. This was reflected in the observations of military leaders on the ground, such as VF Commander Atif Dudaković, whose 2003 assessment summarises the limited nature of the changes in the security sector of post-Dayton BiH:

> So far, some cosmetic changes have occurred, but it has, so to speak, kept the dynamic from the war, which is the HVO, the [ARBiH], and the VRS. So, this is what has been done so far on the issue of the military: the reduction of personnel, weapons, and bases, which are mainly cosmetic transformations. There aren't divisions anymore but brigades, not corps but development groups, not 100s but 30s, but the structure, and even the thinking remains the same.[131]

# 6

# The Orao Affair and military unification

By 2002, the 'inherent instability' of having three armies in one state was widely recognised by the range of international organisations that were working to strengthen the Bosnian state and consolidate peace in the region. With deadlock in the Bosnian parliament preventing the emergence of any local solutions and the risk of intervention deemed too great by the OHR, the only progress that had been made was the geographic separation of the armies from each other, the destruction of military infrastructure by IFOR personnel, and the somewhat chaotic demobilisation (or disintegration) of some military units.[1] For all intents and purposes, the ARBiH, HVO, and VRS remained entirely separated from one another, poised to continue the war: all three continued conscription and maintained large standing forces after Dayton, they all acquired large arsenals of weaponry, and interaction between them was minimal. Raffi Gregorian, a US State Department official who later led defence reform efforts in BiH (and also served as Brčko supervisor and deputy High Representative), summarises the efforts to reconcile the militaries in the years immediately following the war:

> The military leaders of the international community (various commanders of SFOR, and the deputy commanders) were all trying to get the entity armed forces to work together, to get into the habit of doing that. They would have exercises: civilian emergency response, build a bridge with engineers, and they would put them on retreats and workshops. Across the board they would really do whatever. And they got nowhere. That is because, and I think this is something Paddy [Ashdown] appreciated, these were not military technical problems, they were political problems.[2]

This situation changed dramatically in 2002–3, in the aftermath of the most severe and potentially destabilising political crisis to take place since the war. The revelation that a business in the Bosnian Serb entity had been selling weapons to Iraq while it was under a UN-mandated arms embargo caused widespread international condemnation and raised the genuine possibility of damaging sanctions being placed on BiH. This crisis, which became known as the 'Orao Affair' after the business involved, encompassed the entire RS administration as well as the VRS leadership. The political fallout caused a seismic shift in the public conversation about the armed forces in BiH, led to the arrest of seventeen senior officials of the RS defence establishment and the dismissal of many more, and drove powerful and cohesive calls for reform from both international and Bosnian political figures.

In response to the Orao Affair, High Representative Paddy Ashdown established a Defence Reform Commission (DRC). Over the course of two years, various delegates from the US government, NATO, OSCE, and the EU worked alongside Bosnian officials from state-level institutions and both entity administrations within the framework of the DRC. They were tasked with developing a method of military organisation that was suitable for PfP membership, could be maintained with BiH's modest resources, and, most importantly, was acceptable to constituent peoples of the country. After years of research and negotiations, the DRC produced the final blueprint for the contemporary OSBiH in 2005. Under the proposals, each army would be preserved in a reduced form as a ceremonial infantry regiment, while three battalions of infantry from each army would be brought together in the new Bosnian force to create three multiethnic brigades. All units other than the infantry battalions (constituting about half of OSBiH personnel) would also be multiethnic. Despite some serious reservations and emotional moments, representatives of all three constituent peoples approved the plans and the three armies which had fought the war and remained powerful symbols in its aftermath were unified. This not only significantly reduced the likelihood of a return to armed conflict, but also represents a defining moment of political consensus in which Bosnian leaders worked together to build the largest multiethnic institution in the country and strengthen the fragile state which they shared. These factors make the defence reform and military integration processes that were implemented in response to the Orao Affair the most significant acts in consolidating peace in BiH and the wider region since the DPA ended the war.

## The Orao Affair

Links between the SFRJ and Iraq were first established following Saddam Hussein's rise to power in 1976–9 and manifested themselves in the ensuing years through the construction of numerous infrastructure projects and bunkers in Iraq by *Jugoimport* and *Aeroinženjering*, two Yugoslav companies. Prior to the break-up of Yugoslavia, the Iraqi Air Force used repair and maintenance services at a facility in Zagreb. However, following the secession of Croatia from Yugoslavia, nineteen Iraqi MiGs that were being serviced were transported to Serbia, where they remained.[3] The relationship continued into the 1990s despite UN sanctions on both states remaining in place (not to mention the anti-Islamic rhetoric of the Milošević regime), with contractors from the Federal Republic of Yugoslavia constructing the new Ba'ath Party headquarters and several bunkers in Baghdad throughout the period.[4]

On 9 September 2002, the US Embassy in Sarajevo voiced concerns that a business in BiH was engaged in trade with Iraq and demanded an investigation as it was believed that arms were involved, in contravention of the UN embargo. The business in question was the *Vazduhoplovnog zavoda 'Orao'* (Eagle Aviation Institute), a former JNA manufacturer based in Bijeljina which produced jet engines for the entire fixed-wing fleet of the SFRJ. As with so many parts of the JNA that were based in BiH, the

Orao company was inherited by the VRS and continued to work closely with partners in Serbia following Dayton. Embassy staff told the press that they had 'information which raises the question of whether violations of the UN resolution regarding Iraq had taken place, which is why the issue is raised with Bosnian governments, both at state and entity level'.[5] The following day the Investigative Commission of the RS Ministry of Defence reported that 'there is no evidence that the Orao Aviation Institute from Bijeljina delivered weapons, military equipment or spare parts, nor provided any services to any country under UN embargo, especially not Iraq'.[6] For its part, Orao announced that it would file charges 'against those who gave statements and the alleged information about this (the delivery of weapons to Iraq), as well as against the media that reported this without checking the information'.[7] The same press release emphasised that 'the "Orao" Aviation Institute, in its long tradition, never produced weapons or any type of ordnance, and jet engines are not weapons'.[8]

The RS Commission presented its findings to the BiH presidency a few days later, which accepted the conclusion that Orao did not arm Iraq and that BiH had not violated the UN embargo.[9] However, a number of ambiguities in the report left the issue unresolved. It stated that 'the commission could not confirm whether one of Orao's partners hadn't misused business arrangements and commitments to divert weapons to Iraq', and that it had been unable to complete 'the verification of the residence of people employed at Orao, to determine whether any of them were living in Iraq'.[10] On 8 October 2002, the Sarajevo daily *Oslobođenje* published allegations from 'well informed Western officials, who requested anonymity', that 'in the last two years engineers and other employees of the "Orao" Aviation Institute regularly travelled to Iraq and worked on maintaining Iraqi aircraft, and received nine times more pay'.[11] *Oslobođenje* elaborated that 'Orao has allegedly worked on the overhaul of jet engines for MiG-21 "Fishbed" and MiG-29 "Fulcrum" fighters in Iraq'.[12] The Western source revealed that the US Embassy had privately discussed the matter with RS officials prior to going public, but had been dissatisfied with the response:

> Representatives of the United States deliberately did not make a fuss in the media, because they want to give the RS authorities the opportunity to clear this up. Also, they did not want the affair to influence the current election. BiH needs to choose the path to Europe, rather than to Iraq. Cooperation with Iraq prevents BiH's integration with international institutions. This is an opportunity for the military and civilian officials of RS to show that they are not part of the problem, but that they are able to investigate the matter and solve the problem. The response of the US government will depend on how serious and genuine their investigation and its results are.[13]

On 11 October, after Orao had closed for the weekend, SFOR troops began an inspection of its factories and warehouses in Bijeljina. Major Sean Mel of SFOR informed reporters in Bijeljina that it was a 'regular check and that these inspections cannot be connected with the affair concerning the involvement of Orao in the sale of weapons to Iraq'.[14] The search continued throughout the weekend as, supposedly, the keys for a number of safes could not be found by Orao staff. However, SFOR soldiers remained at the complex until they were located.[15] Before SFOR publicly announced the results of its search, representatives of the US Embassy met with the RS Investigative Committee in Banja Luka. Deputy Minister Lieutenant-General Nikola Delić, who chaired the committee, gave assurances that 'trade with Iraq halted from mid-September, and that no official of Ministry of Defense or an official at a higher level in the RS has approved such a trade'.[16] Despite his assurances, the results of the inspection revealed that Orao had indeed been supplying aircraft spare parts and technical assistance to the Iraqi Air Force, and was continuing to do so: A letter was found pertaining to multiple shipments of materials for the maintenance and repair of MiG jet engines, at least five experts were thought to still be in Iraq, and evidence was found indicating that Orao officials had asked the Iraqi Air Force to remove the Orao emblem from all documents and equipment and hide the Serbian-language technical manuals. The most damning piece of evidence discovered by the search, however, was the discovery that communications between Orao and its partners in Iraq were ongoing and shipments were continuing two weeks after the US Embassy had issued its first warnings.[17]

In a statement published by *Oslobođenje*, US officials made clear how they viewed the situation and what response they expected from those authorities accountable for the trade:

> In fact, work with Iraq is not suspended, trade with the material and the movement of people into and out of Iraq is not interrupted. Investigations so far have not been adequately extensive, and the United States expects it to continue, and to show fully and in detail how the trade was actually conducted, who was included, in particular who was in charge, how many people travelled to Iraq, when and how many times. They expect to be provided with the details of the material which was sold to Iraq, as well as details on the payment of such activities. The US also expects to be told what measures will be taken against those responsible for these actions.[18]

The statement also made clear that the repercussions of the escalating scandal had the potential to be severe for BiH. Antonio Prlenda, an *Oslobođenje* columnist, reflected: 'BiH could be facing international sanctions because of the slow and insufficiently serious investigation by the Ministry of Defence of the Republika Srpska.'[19] Just days later, the newspaper ran the headline 'BiH has 24 hours to avoid sanctions'.[20] At the time, the Bosnian economy remained in a fragile state, with high unemployment, low wages, and Gross Domestic Product standing at approximately half of its pre-war total. Furthermore, both the state and entity governments were reliant on foreign aid to meet their respective expenditures.[21] Depending on what shape the sanctions took, financial assistance could cease, goods could be embargoed, or individuals and institutions targeted. Such a response was guaranteed to destabilise the fragile Bosnian state and ran the risk of inviting a return to conflict.

Ashdown understood that 'in the worst case, this breach of international law by the RS could have opened up Bosnia to the possibility of UN action'.[22] He was, however, also the first to see the opportunity which the crisis presented, recording in his memoir: 'We knew at once that this would give us the opportunity I had been looking for to try to push through defence reform in order to abolish the two opposing entity armies and create a single Bosnian army under state control'.[23] Moving quickly to take the lead in the international response to what was being dubbed the 'Orao Affair', he outlined the 'required action' that was needed to avert a crisis on 28 October:

> In the short term there must be a full and public enquiry. This will need to involve the State authorities as the State ultimately has responsibility for ensuring BiH respects UN resolutions. Those politically responsible for bringing BiH to the brink of international condemnation and pariah status must face the consequences.[24]

He called for new standards and regulations regarding trade to be implemented, including the provision that state (rather than entity) institutions had to approve weapons exports.[25] Ashdown also ordered reviews of BiH's border control and the entity defence structures, arguing that democratic civilian control of the security sector needed to be consolidated and stating that 'it is clear that the current system appears to allow parts of the defence industry to operate outside of transparent political control'.[26] Furthermore, he added that oversight of the defence sector needed to be properly established at the state level, demanding that 'clear lines of responsibility must be established through a strengthened Standing Committee on Military Matters'.[27] All of these measures were directed towards the strengthening of the BiH state at the expense of the entities, a process that the leadership of RS had vehemently fought since Dayton.

In RS, opinion was divided over who should be held accountable. Most parties agreed that the RS President Mirko Šarović and Prime Minister Mladen Ivanić were ultimately accountable. However, whether or not they, or indeed anyone else, should be removed from their positions was the cause of much debate.[28] Eventually, at the request of the BiH presidency 'to dismiss all officials responsible for the cooperation between Bijeljina and Baghdad within 24 hours', RS took action.[29] The director of the Orao Aviation Institute, Milan Prica, the commander of the RS Air Force, Colonel Miljan Vlačić, and the director of the Department for Military Logistics, Spasoje Orašanin, were all quickly dismissed.[30] Although Prica continued to protest, reiterating that 'Orao has never sold weapons', the Bosnian Serb leadership considered the matter dealt with.[31] Following the dismissals, the Serb member of the BiH presidency, Mirko Šarović, announced: 'The government and the relevant authorities of RS took concrete measures to sanction any institution which violated the embargo on exports of arms and equipment to Iraq.'[32]

The US administration was unsatisfied. A press release issued by the Embassy the next day stated:

> The United States government welcomes the first steps which have punished a violation of UN Security Council resolutions, the Dayton Agreement and BiH export control regulations, but we expect new steps from those responsible in the state and entity to stop cooperation with Iraq and carry out a full investigation. We expect that the officials who bear political, military and business responsibility are not only dismissed, but are also criminally sanctioned.[33]

The Bosnian Muslim member of the BiH presidency, Beriz Belkić, also called for more punishment. He told *Oslobođenje*:

> The dismissals that have occurred in the RS itself are a signal that we have started to understand the situation. But, those dismissed were in the military structure, and now we need to establish the responsibility of the civilian structures, which command the army.[34]

Ashdown was also critical of the response of the RS leadership and, after returning from a meeting with the UN Security Council regarding the affair, commented that 'it is worrying that the measures taken by the RS in September to clarify this issue were very tepid and unconvincing', although he did concede that 'the latest measures by the RS are encouraging'.[35] A more ominous warning came from US Secretary of State Colin Powell (see Figure 6.1), who wrote to Ivanić and told him that his government faced serious consequences because of the scandal and informed him that 'this topic has now gained attention at the highest level in the Government of the United States'.[36] He described the RS investigation as a 'mockery', and said that 'you were warned about these activities and did not do anything to prevent them'.[37] Further pressure was applied as Powell reminded Ivanić that 'the United States also has access to numerous sanctions and penalties that can be applied to your government and to all individuals who are involved'.[38] Powell made it clear that RS was facing diplomatic isolation if it did not go further, and that the United States could act unilaterally and punish the Serb entity if it was deemed appropriate.

As the leadership of RS assessed its options, others began to see the opportunity that the unfolding events presented. Belkić declared that 'we must learn from this and reform defence'.[39] In the media, Aldijana Omeragić argued that 'the US threat of sanctions has become a great opportunity for BiH, more than seven years after the war, to reorganize and eventually curb all legal and secret weapons and armaments'.[40] She also recognised that the Orao Affair had stimulated a discussion 'about creating a single BiH Army. Or maybe even a new, state-level Ministry of Defence'.[41] Zira Dizdarević contended that 'to punish the whole of Bosnia and Herzegovina because of Orao would be meaningless because the central government does not have a mechanism for control over the military industry'.[42] She reasoned that 'the most important question is what lesson can be brought from this case on a system level. The Orao Affair and the behaviour of the authorities on this occasion favours the strengthening of the powers of the central authorities and giving more responsibilities to them'.[43]

Meanwhile, more details of Orao's dealings were emerging. On 27 October 2002, *Oslobođenje* reported that SFOR had found a link between Orao, a Belgrade firm called Jugoimport, and Al-Bashair Trade Companies of Iraq. The findings confirmed the role of Orao in the provision of parts, maintenance, and mechanical training for two series of engines for MiG fighters in a contract worth US$8.5 million. The *Oslobođenje* article concluded that Orao 'has enabled Iraq, with highly specialised Yugoslav help, to get the damaged fleet of MiGs back to the heavens'.[44] This came just two weeks after US President George W. Bush told the UN that Saddam Hussein's regime in Iraq posed a 'grave and gathering danger' and issued an ultimatum that unless weapons inspectors

**Figure 6.1** *US Secretary of State Colin Powell (R) shakes hands with Lord Paddy Ashdown, High Representative of the International Community for Bosnia-Herzegovina, at the State Department in Washington on 5 March 2004.* Courtesy of Reuters/Jason Reed JIR via Alamy.

were allowed into Iraq, action would be taken.[45] Bush's declaration coincided with an escalation in the bombing of Iraq (a regular occurrence between the First Gulf War and the Second) by US and British aircraft, which used the UN-mandated no-fly zone to 'destroy the country's air defence systems in anticipation of an all-out attack'.[46] By helping the Iraqi Air Force in such a political climate, Orao (and by association, BiH as a whole) was not only contravening a UN arms embargo, but was also posing a threat to US and British military assets in the Middle East. Indeed, in the final weeks of 2002, an Iraqi MiG destroyed a US Predator Drone, although it is not possible to verify if it was one included in the Orao deal.[47]

In response to the mounting severity of the case, the commander of SFOR (see Figure 6.2), US General William Ward, called on the RS authorities to conduct

> a thorough inspection of the Orao complex at the Ministry of Defence level, as well as to make an overall inspection of RS Ministry of Defence and all other institutions and companies engaged in the production of military equipment or weapons.[48]

Ward's approach presented the RS leadership with multiple opportunities to conduct its own investigations and present its findings to the Bosnian public and the international community. However, a growing body of evidence indicated that the RS administration

**Figure 6.2** *SFOR and its successor, EUFOR (pictured here), continued supporting peace and stability in BiH throughout the period. Here German soldiers destroy weapons at their base in Rajlovac, near Sarajevo, on 21 March 2005.* Courtesy of Stringer/AFP via Getty Images.

was not only involved in the original deal but had also approved further trade since the US Embassy first raised the issue. As a result, Ward warned that 'only strict control of the Ministry of Defence of the RS, the RS Government and the Government of Bosnia and Herzegovina can ensure that in future there is no serious violation of the trade embargo'.[49] In response to this increased pressure, two further high-ranking officials resigned their positions: RS Minister of Defence Slobodan Bilić and the VRS chief of staff, General Novica Simić. The RS government stated that 'this act helps to improve the international position of the Republika Srpska'.[50] Whether this would be enough to satisfy domestic observers and the international community remained unclear.

With the RS leadership firmly implicated in the Orao Affair, Ashdown presented his case for using the unfolding crisis to fundamentally reform the security sector to the international community. On 29 October, he flew to Brussels to brief the North Atlantic Council, informing the gathered ambassadors and secretary-general of NATO that BiH was facing its 'most severe crisis since the war'.[51] Ashdown warned that when his enquiry was complete, it would likely show some high-level political culpability for the Orao Affair. He also used this meeting to gauge the response to his planned reforms, noting that he 'intended to use this scandal to initiate a complete reform of the defence structures in BiH'.[52] Secretary-General Lord Robertson agreed that NATO would supervise the defence reform process, giving some strong credibility to any proposals that would follow.[53] Ashdown also received the endorsement of the UN Security Council for the 'priority reform measures'.[54] In the following days, General Ward told *Oslobođenje* that the only solution to the problems arising from the Orao Affair was the creation of a BiH State Ministry of Defence, and US Ambassador Clifford Bond spoke of the need for a unified Bosnian army.[55] Ashdown was able to quickly establish a consensus among the international community and, crucially, a range of Bosnian political figures on the appropriate response to the actions of Orao and the RS administration by highlighting the danger that sanctions posed to BiH as a whole and advocating assessment and reform rather than punishment. His position was strengthened by the direct involvement of the RS political and military leadership in the trade and ensuing cover-up, which left those individuals discredited and isolated.

Before the planning phase of the reform process could begin, the RS Investigative Committee was given a final opportunity to meaningfully participate. In accordance with parliamentary procedure, the Bosnian parliament and the international community waited until the committee had completed its (second) investigation and reported its findings. This took over two months, and when, on 7 January 2003, Ashdown was offered a 'first, private sight of the latest RS government report' he found the 1,600-page document to be an 'attempt to provide a snowstorm of paper which would obscure the issue of political culpability'.[56] Indeed, the report placed the burden of responsibility on former RS president Biljana Plavsić, a 'sworn enemy of the current administration, who was, very conveniently, already in jail, having been convicted by the Hague Tribunal'.[57]

The incumbent Bosnian Serb member of the presidency, Mirko Šarović, was also implicated in the report. He had been elected to his position as news of the Orao Affair was first breaking just months earlier, with 70 per cent of the Bosnian Serb vote, but prior to that he had served as RS president and the chairman of the RS Supreme Defence

Council, its highest military body and the one responsible for overseeing the deal with Al-Bashair Trading Companies in Iraq.[58] However, the report was absent of any concrete evidence linking Šarović to Orao. Frustrated again by what was deemed to be an attempt to obscure the truth, Ashdown ordered a fresh investigation by intelligence officers from NATO countries. This investigation identified Šarović as the key culprit in the Orao Affair.[59] Just days after his links to Orao were confirmed, Ashdown publicly accused Šarović of being engaged in yet another politically damaging scandal. The High Representative had been shown evidence of 'aggressive intelligence operations against [BiH] institutions and citizens, and international organisations working in BiH' that 'compounded the damage done by the Orao Affair'.[60] Documents and equipment to back these allegations had been gathered in a raid by British troops on 7 March which proved that VRS intelligence, with the cooperation of its Serbian counterpart, had been intercepting the phone calls of international organisations and bugging briefing rooms in the Bosnian parliament.[61]

The evidence linking Šarović with criminal and unconstitutional activities made his position increasingly untenable, and by the beginning of April it became apparent that he would have to resign or be removed by the High Representative. Ashdown records that on 1 April, 'to my huge surprise, Bosnian Muslim President Sulejman Tihić, backed by his Croat colleague, warned that I should not remove the Serb president as this would destabilise the whole country'.[62] He notes that 'my big fear is not riots or instability as predicted by the French and the Germans yesterday, but a Serb withdrawal from the whole process'.[63] In response, Ashdown privately asked Šarović to step down, which the member of the presidency eventually acquiesced to do the following day, although his aides indicated that it was a 'tactical resignation, forced on him by Lord Ashdown, and that he would make a political comeback'.[64] Ashdown later reflected that this was 'a very dangerous moment', but contends that he was left with few options: 'He had broken a UN Security Council sanction, he continued to provide weapons and weapons assistance to Iraq, and you just can't ignore that. It was not something which I enjoyed doing or something I particularly wanted to do.'[65]

Šarović joined a multitude of other Bosnian Serb government officials and military officers who were removed from their positions, including the VRS's military and civilian leadership. Seventeen of those dismissed were later charged with illegal trading, either for being involved in the trade or helping to cover it up.[66] The following day *Glas srpski* reported: 'Yesterday BiH Presidency Chairman Mirko Šarović tendered his resignation from his duties, which was accepted by the High Representative Paddy Ashdown, who consequently explained that it put an end to the "Orao affair."'[67] Dragan Mitrović, the new RS prime minister (Ivanić was shuffled to foreign affairs), reflected: 'I regard his resignation as a personal and moral act with the aim to establish new standards of behaviour by those holding public positions.'[68]

Ashdown's public response was clear. He declared that 'the Orao Arms-to-Iraq affair has done more damage to BiH's international reputation than any other event since the end of the war', and noted that 'it is no exaggeration to say that these activities could have placed this country's stability in jeopardy'.[69] He targeted RS specifically, stating that 'too many in the RS think the RS is a state not an Entity. Signing arms deals with foreign governments are the actions of a state' and observing that 'if the RS had truly accepted its role as part of BiH, [the arms deals] would not have happened'.[70] Commenting on Šarović's resignation, Ashdown emphasised:

> Mr Šarović was President of the RS when [Orao] signed arms contracts with Iraq in direct contravention of UN Security Council Resolutions. With war now underway in Iraq, possibly involving weaponry exported from this country, I cannot overstate the seriousness of this affair.[71]

With those responsible for the Orao Affair being held to account, Ashdown announced a package of preliminary reform measures, which were duly approved by both entity administrations. The package abolished the RS Supreme Council, amended entity legislation and their constitutions to remove all inference of statehood, independence, and sovereignty, and requested plans and legislation from the state and entity governments for bringing the arms industry and international trade more broadly under accountable and transparent civilian control. Furthermore, all Bosnian senior military officers were required to submit details of travel abroad to the state-level Ministry of Foreign Affairs, and measures were planned to reduce dual structures in the VF. In addition, Ashdown established a commission to 'identify constitutional and legal barriers to effective state-level command and control' of the military.[72] Introducing the reforms, Ashdown stated:

> With the resignation of Mirko Šarović from the BiH Presidency, to take responsibility for the Orao Affair, and the reform package which I announced today, I am satisfied that the Arms-to-Iraq affair and the VRS espionage scandal have been effectively addressed.[73]

The Orao Affair triggered a momentous shift in political discourse and activity in BiH. It exposed numerous flaws in the structures and laws which governed post-Dayton BiH, particularly regarding the management of borders and oversight of the military. The revelation that the military autonomy of the VRS had been utilised to spy on international and domestic institutions during the entire investigation served to further illustrate the disregard with which RS leaders held both the Bosnian state and the international community. The Serbian government was proven to have been the 'mastermind' of the trade and a co-conspirator in the spying scandal, and as a result the Orao Affair had a 'huge impact' in Serbia.[74] The coordination between the defence institutions of Serbia and RS highlighted many unresolved security issues inherent in post-Dayton BiH. As a result of the affair, all financial and logistical support that the VRS received from Belgrade and all military collaboration between the RS and Serbia became heavily scrutinised at the state-level, while the Serbian government was forced to hand over all records and information concerning Belgrade's cooperation with Iraq over previous decades, including details of a host of military infrastructure projects. This intelligence was procured just as US and British forces were making their final preparations to invade the country.[75] Discredited and isolated, and with most of its political and military leadership removed, the RS administration was unable to prevent comprehensive reform from becoming a political priority, nor could it offer an alternative. For the first time since the DPA was signed, the future of the armies that had fought the war and the place they had in society became the subject of scrutiny and debate.

## Root and branch reform: The response to the Orao Affair

The DRC established by Ashdown had a profound impact on the shape that the response to the Orao Affair in BiH would take. It had a broad remit to examine and analyse the complex security environment in post-Dayton BiH and was ultimately tasked with suggesting reforms which could be implemented by the Bosnian parliament if a consensus could be found. If it could not, the Bonn Powers offered a route for Ashdown to force the reforms through, although such action was considered extremely risky. Ashdown announced the main aims of the DRC in May 2003:

> Bosnia and Herzegovina needs to establish transparency and proper civilian control of its armed forces, in the interests of BiH and its people, but this process will also help BiH achieve its stated desire of joining Euro-Atlantic structures, and in particular, NATO's PfP Programme.[76]

For the DRC to have a chance of achieving its somewhat ambitious objectives, it was imperative to establish its legitimacy within BiH while also ensuring that its proposals remained viable and fit for purpose. As a result, the commission was composed of representatives from a broad range of organisations and was overseen by observers from across the international community. At the helm was James Locher III, a veteran US policymaker with experience of reforming the American military, and serving alongside him were the following: the secretary general of the SCMM (the Bosnian state-level military administration) and his two deputies, representatives of the entity presidents, the entity ministers of defence, the head of the OSCE Mission to BiH, the commander of SFOR, a representative of NATO, and a representative of the EU. Observers included representatives of the Organisation of Islamic Conference and the EU presidency, as well as both the Russian and US ambassadors to BiH.[77] Thus, the work of the DRC was done by Bosnian and foreign delegates working together, with representatives from all relevant institutions forming working groups, each of which focused on a particular area marked for reform. In some cases, former belligerents were now designing reforms alongside each other, such as in the Policy Working Group, where former ARBiH commander Rasim Delić, worked alongside former HVO chief of staff Slavko Marin and Dragan Kapetina, a leading member of RS's wartime civilian leadership.[78]

Despite the potential for discord to hinder the work of the DRC, its progress was rapid. An Executive Order issued by President Bush on 29 May undoubtedly offered some impetus as it imposed unilateral sanctions on 150 individuals in the former Yugoslavia, most of whom were either war crimes suspects or people believed to be helping them.[79] The response from the leading political parties in BiH (all of whom had members on the list) was unanimously one of outrage: a former SDA minister described the list as 'the greatest post-war evil to be committed against the Bosniaks' while the HDZ published a statement labelling it 'humiliating'.[80] However, it served as a prominent reminder of the fragile position the Bosnian political leadership was in and encouraged cooperation with priority measures such as the DRC. This allowed the commission to submit a comprehensive report on 25 September 2003, just five months after it had been formed.[81] The commissioners identified a number of key problems which undermined the emergence of democratic civil–military relations and BiH's integration into the security apparatus of the PfP programme. These were as follows:

> [The] lack of adequate State-level command and control of the armed forces of [BiH]; ambiguity and inconsistency in the law regarding the competencies of the State and entities for defence matters; insufficient democratic oversight and control of the armed forces, especially by parliaments; lack of transparency at all levels for defence matters; non-compliance with international obligations, primarily OSCE politicomilitary accords; an unjustifiable number of reserves and the small arms and light weapons to arm them; excessive, deteriorating arms at too many locations; waste of human and financial resources in the defence sector; forces sized and equipped for missions no longer appropriate for the security situation.[82]

To address these problems, the DRC recommended fundamentally restructuring the Bosnian security sector. It proposed transferring all authority over military matters to the Bosnian parliament and establishing accountable civilian oversight at the state level by establishing a Bosnian Ministry of Defence. This was viewed as being within the parameters of the DPA and articulated 'a fundamental principle of Statehood: a State must have the capacity to defend its territorial integrity and sovereignty. To have this capacity, a State must control its armed forces'.[83] The report also suggested considerable reductions in arsenals, military property, and troop numbers. The 19,090 professional soldiers serving in the entity armies, the DRC concluded, should be reduced to 12,000, and the majority of the 240,000 troops kept as reserves should be dismissed, leaving just 60,000. In addition, 'the intake of conscripts would be reduced by 50 percent, and the conscript training period shortened from six to four months. The headquarters and field staffs of the entity Ministries of Defence would also be reduced by 25 percent'.[84] Although much reduced in size and capability, these initial proposals of the DRC envisioned a system in which state-level institutions such as the Ministry of Defence oversaw the entity armies, which would be maintained, trained, and paid for by the entities.

Following the publication of the report, significant diplomatic pressure was placed on Bosnian politicians to accept and implement the findings. The OHR issued a statement informing the Bosnian public that 'the eyes of Europe and the world are on BiH as its leaders decide whether to seize the opportunity to take the first historic steps into NATO and European security structures'.[85] The following day, the ambassadors of EU member-states lobbied the BiH presidency to support the reforms.[86] Within months, most had passed through the relevant legislatures, and at the end of 2003 the Bosnian government was informed that enough progress had been made for NATO ministers to consider its membership of PfP at a summit scheduled for the following June.[87] The state-level Ministry of Defence was established in March 2004, and the entity armies conducted their first joint exercise in May. Six months later, an 'honorary unit' was formed from soldiers of all three ethnicities.[88] Although the reforms were extensive and brought the entity armies under a single command and administration, making them eligible for international integration, they did little to address the underlying issues which continued to threaten to destabilise BiH. Below senior ranks and outside of ceremonial units, the bulk of the soldiers remained segregated from other ethnicities and were still, to an extent, autonomous of the state. Indeed, although the three armies which had fought the war in BiH were now governed by a single administration, they still remained, for all practical purposes, separate forces that were maintained primarily to fight each other. The lack of significant change is best illustrated by the revelation that in 2004, after many reforms had been implemented, the VRS was still using its autonomy to help Ratko Mladić evade international authorities.[89] These concerns led the ambassadors discussing the issue at the NATO Summit in Istanbul to conclude that BiH was not ready for PfP membership and should instead make 'continuous progress towards the establishment of a single military force'.[90]

At the end of 2004, Ashdown extended the mandate of the DRC for another year and appointed Bosnian Minister of Defence Nikola Radovanović and Dr Raffi Gregorian of NATO Headquarters Sarajevo to replace Locher as co-chairmen. They were instructed to focus on the key areas in which BiH fell short of qualifying for PfP membership and use their time to 'examine and propose the legal and institutional measures necessary to transfer the competencies of the Entity [Ministries of Defence] to the State level, to enhance State level command and control, and to promote co-ordination with the ICTY'.[91] The rest of the commission was, like its predecessor, composed of delegates from across state and entity security institutions and the various organisations of the international community.[92] Gregorian recalls that Ashdown was determined to implement whatever reforms were needed to ensure PfP membership, even if it meant using the Bonn Powers to 'come down like Zeus' and overrule the Bosnian Serbs, who were 'furious' about the mandate of the DRC and said that 'they could never cooperate with NATO, or me. They weren't going to engage in any talks'.[93] At the time, the PIC legal team judged that using the Bonn Powers in this instance would be unlawful, making any such action by Ashdown to have been unlikely unless the circumstances changed significantly. Gregorian reflects that due to these factors, the situation demanded thorough negotiations with the concerned parties and an understanding of what Bosnian political leaders *needed*, rather than wanted. He provides this summary of their priorities:

> The Bosniaks really wanted a central army, a state army. The Serbs were definitely afraid of this large conscript-based reserve force that the Bosniaks had, hundreds of thousands of supposedly trained people. The Croats felt overwhelmed by everybody and didn't feel they were getting a good deal in the Federation Army. If you moved it up to the state level then the Croats would have a third of the assistant ministers and one of the three power positions, both in the Ministry and the Joint Staff.[94]

Even with these needs under consideration, negotiations concerning the implementation of the recommendations of the DRC's final report were fraught. Progress was marred by the upcoming tenth anniversary of Dayton, which inspired much reflection and antagonism over the war. Heightened tensions were exacerbated by the emergence of video footage, just two weeks prior to when the DRC was supposed to sign off the final agreement, of the *Škorpioni* (Scorpions) Serbian paramilitary unit executing a group of bound Bosnian Muslim boys during the war. Gregorian notes that this almost led the Bosnian Muslim leadership to back out of the process as it gave weight to concerns regarding the termination of conscription, but recalls an emotional meeting with Tihić in which he reminded the Bosnian Muslim member of the presidency that 'here I have a single army for BiH. This is what your people fought for and died for. And over here, you have conscription and more of the same'.[95] Gregorian's point was reinforced by military analysis conducted by the DRC which concluded that the conscript-based reserve force 'had shown to be a paper tiger, not ready for anything. Thus, it was a dangerous deceit to think the reserves offered real protection to anyone'.[96]

Consensus was eventually found among the commissioners and their final report was presented to Ashdown in September 2005. The report noted that the commission 'bases its recommendations on the continuing endeavour to secure credible [PfP] candidacy for [BiH]' but was 'sensitive to the unique circumstances of [BiH] as a state with three constituent peoples and others and the needs for its armed forces to belong to and protect all its peoples'.[97] As a result, the reforms suggested in the report were very much the product of compromise between the various interests represented on the commission. However, while lengthy negotiations were held over some of the finer points of the reform, a surprising unanimity was found among the participants of the DRC, including the Bosnian Serb representatives, that any reform package they produced should in fact go beyond their original mandate. Gregorian explains:

> The terms of reference of the second DRC didn't require the ending of the entity armed forces, they just said that they have to have a single personnel system, a single pay system, and so on. So administratively they'd be completely linked, but still be separate armies in terms of combat power. The process we led and the way we did it, and the leadership in place at the time, created that political moment to go beyond [the terms of reference].[98]

He elaborates that it was the RS leadership who requested that the reforms being implemented should be comprehensive enough to meet the requirements to join NATO, not as a partner but as a member, as each reform process cost them a significant amount of political capital and was regarded as being 'incredibly painful'.[99] As a result, the final report of the DRC not only strengthened the state-level Ministry of Defence, but also proposed a complete restructuring of the security institutions in BiH in order to create 'a single defence establishment and single military force in Bosnia and Herzegovina under fully functioning state-level command and control'.[100]

The major obstacle to creating a unified military was the challenge of how best to integrate soldiers (or units) from 'three essentially mono-ethnic brigades' which carried the heritage of opposing wartime armies.[101] This task was complicated further as all of the Bosnian representatives were ardent that some degree of ethnic identification be retained in the new structure.[102] Such demands were consistent with the DPA, which structured BiH as a consociational state composed of three constituent peoples, and had some precedent in several militaries already in NATO, validating it as a method of organising armed forces.[103] Indeed, a strong contingent of former and serving British Army officers were delegates on the commission and had extensive experience with such methods: Retd major-general John Drewienkiewicz represented the OSCE as vice-chairman of the DRC; John Colston, a senior British Ministry of Defence civil servant, represented NATO; and Major-General David Leakey represented the EU Peacekeeping Force (the successor to SFOR, EUFOR).[104] Furthermore, Gregorian, one of the commission's co-chairmen, had earned his PhD researching Gurkhas in the British Army.[105] A logical conclusion of the demands of the entities and the expertise on the panel, therefore, was the decision to adapt the regimental system developed by the British Army to the needs of BiH.[106] Gregorian elucidates that the inspiration for applying the model to BiH came from his knowledge of how the British Indian Army arranged brigades of three battalions, each of which came from a different regiment, and one of which had to be British. This concept was developed into a practical model by Rohan Maxwell and Gregorian's Canadian military attaché, Colonel MacGillivray, who 'were the real experts who advised on the finer points of the regimental system as they knew it from Canada'.[107]

It can be argued that endorsing ethnic separation within the military served to further entrench divisions within a very polarised and fragile state. The alternative, 'integral organisation' in a manner reminiscent of the early JNA, had considerable precedent in the region and there is evidence to suggest that it could help stabilise states recovering from conflict. In Lebanon, soldiers of all eighteen official religions were enlisted into a unified, fully integrated Lebanese Army following a long civil war. While the post-war state was structured in a manner similar to BiH, with ethnic representation guaranteed in government, the military emerged from the conflict as a truly Lebanese institution and is widely viewed as being pivotal in preventing a return to war.[108] The unique heritage of the Lebanese Army, however, prevented it from serving as a template for BiH. Owing to the influential legacy of its first commander, Fuad Chehab, the military remained aloof of the conflict fought between various ideological and sectarian militias. In doing so, it failed to maintain stability in Lebanon but preserved its reputation as a non-partisan institution. This allowed it to serve as a vehicle to reconcile divisions and, utilising its heritage and reputation, assert an inclusive Lebanese identity once a political settlement to the conflict was reached. In BiH, the pre-existing military structures had been repurposed to fight the war and were, for the most part, resented by the parts of the population that they did not represent. Furthermore, while the Lebanese Army's pre–civil war heritage was very much identified with the sanctity of the republic, which was compatible with the post-war political climate, the long history of multiethnic military organisation in BiH is largely shrouded by the memory of more recent conflicts. Thus, any military claiming to represent an overarching identity, including a Bosnian one, was likely to be viewed as a foolish and illegitimate revival of the JNA, which had quite demonstrably collapsed. Additionally, any notion of providing the government in Sarajevo with a mandate to begin moulding new Bosnian citizens out of OSBiH recruits would be viewed as a direct threat by many Bosnian leaders, particularly those political parties that dominated parliament at the time, and would likely force their withdrawal from the entire process.

The regimental system agreed by the DRC, on the other hand, found 'a solution for maintaining military heritage and identity within a single military force' which was 'in keeping' with the multi-ethnic constitution and laws of Bosnia and Herzegovina.[109] Indeed, the merits of such a system in the Yugoslav context was highlighted in 1992 by James Gow, who argued that 'it seems self-evident that an empirically homogenous, regimental system could have improved [JNA] effectiveness'.[110] In the proposed system, the Bosnian Croat component of the VF would contribute three battalions to the new military, the Bosnian Muslims another three, and three would come from the VRS. Together, they would form the OSBiH. Operationally and administratively, they would be organised in three brigades, which was the standard (and thus interoperable) model for NATO militaries. Each brigade was to be composed of an infantry battalion from each ethnicity, while command, support, and specialist units were to be formed anew and would be multiethnic. The leadership was to be provided by a Joint Staff, which would oversee both the Operational Command and Support Command.[111] The report also stipulated that the three constituent peoples should be 'equally represented in each senior decision-making level' and, as a result, the minister of defence, chief of the joint staff, the commander of operational command, and the commander of support command would 'each have two deputies whose responsibilities are defined in the law. The principal and his deputies cannot be from the same Constituent Peoples'.[112]

The DRC recognised that 'the brigade structure addresses basic structural operational requirements but it does not address the need to maintain a military heritage and identity'.[113] As a result, an iteration of the tried and tested regimental system was embedded within the OSBiH for 'ceremonial and military heritage purposes'.[114] Each Bosnian regiment was to embody 'the historical military lineage of the component from which it is descended', although it was reiterated that 'regiments are purely ceremonial organisations and unlike brigades have no operational, training or administrative roles'.[115] The regiments were legally defined as multiethnic organisations, although no meaningful measures were taken at this stage to encourage the mixing of personnel.[116] While the identity of the infantry regiments was inspired by ethnicity, non-infantry units were to be affiliated to regiments based on speciality, such as artillery. In practical terms, the regiments were composed of a handful of staff led by a regimental major. Their tasks were designated as the management of the regimental museum, the regimental fund, and the regimental mess; preparation, research and maintenance of regimental history and the preservation of regimental artefacts; and providing guidance on conduct at ceremonial events and direction on regimental custom, dress, and deportment.[117] This correlates exactly with how regiments in the British Army operate, but there is clearly a lot of scope for interpretation by those entrusted with regimental duties. The rest of the proposals contained within the 2005 DRC report largely focussed on reducing overall troop numbers, abolishing conscription entirely, and restructuring the reserve system so that only well-trained soldiers were retained.[118]

Both entities were largely receptive to the plans, although Rohan Maxwell and John Andreas Olsen explain that the proposals were met with calls for even greater ethnic representation. They recall proposals to 'group non-infantry functions into three non-infantry regiments ... so that each of the three constituent peoples would get one non-infantry regimental command position', and others that called for the infantry brigades (rather than battalions) to be monoethnic, or for all OSBiH personnel to belong to one of the infantry regiments, regardless of their position in the military, in order to maintain ethnic identification.[119] Maxwell and Olsen argue that extending ethnic identification beyond the infantry would result in 'an [OSBiH] divided into three distinct ethnic groups', whilst having no ethnic identification at all 'would destroy the regimental compromise that allowed for agreement on a single military force'.[120] 'The application of the regimental system to the infantry', they concede, 'is the concession to ethnic identity within the [OSBiH]'.[121]

By the end of December 2005, most of the relevant legislation had been passed at the state and entity levels, establishing the state as the sole authority over the military. On 1 January, the OSBiH officially entered service and the implementation of the reforms on a practical level began.[122] In July 2006, the Bosnian parliament approved a decision by the BiH presidency to reduce military personnel to 10,000 professional soldiers, 5,000 reservists, and 1,000 civilian staff, and introduce a system of ethnic quotas based on data from the 1991 census, with the intention of ensuring ethnic representation in proportion to the pre-war population. As a result, its target composition is 45.9 per cent (4,826 people) Bosnian Muslim/Bosniak, 33.6 per cent (3,533 people) Serb, 19.8 per cent (2,084 people) Croat, and 0.7 per cent (74 people) Other.[123] This policy, which is highly reminiscent of the socialist period, created yet another layer of ethnic identification in the OSBiH and arguably undermined the regiments that had so recently been introduced, as their function of preserving heritage and identity became a responsibility of the military as whole.

In December 2006, the freshly unified OSBiH was admitted to the PfP programme, marking the culmination of four years of dramatic change in the post-Dayton security sector in BiH. Attaining access to the programme was a significant feat and illustrated the extent to which the military situation in BiH was becoming normalised. Indeed, transforming three large formerly warring armies into a unified, professional, and democratically accountable military was the most significant step in stabilising BiH since the signing of the DPA. Not only had the presence of multiple armies within a single country been removed, but the Bosnian state had secured its monopoly on the legitimate use of force, greatly strengthening its position as the sovereign authority in the territory of BiH. Indeed, reflecting on the key reforms (creating a state-level judiciary, strengthening tax collection, and military unification) that were made in BiH under his oversight, Ashdown offers this insight into what he was trying to build: 'What is it that defines a state? It is a region bounded by borders in which a single law operates, and the instruments of lethal force lay in the hands of state and no one else'.[124] Integration into the PfP offered the OSBiH access to training, exercises, and assistance from the most modern militaries in the world, improving its effectiveness and reinforcing its professionalism. Ashdown argues that 'we could not have created a single army responsible to the state in BiH had there not been NATO as the magnetic pull', noting that the military leaderships in BiH 'were professional, and they immediately saw the advantage of having a unified army up to NATO standards, and saw a single army in Bosnia as the best context to be professional soldiers ... That was crucial.'[125] Thus, in the eyes of many Bosnians and the international organisations that operated in the country, military unification and international integration represented a significant step in BiH fulfilling the criteria of a 'successful state' with a military recognised as a modern and professional force that was on the 'path to a sustainable peace as a member of the European institutions'.[126]

Although the OSBiH made rapid and considerable progress in certain areas such as operability and administration, the 'ethnic identification' concession included in the reforms began veering off track almost immediately. Gregorian concedes that one of the aspects of the DRC's recommendations that he was unsatisfied with were the names that were selected for the regiments. He noted that he would have preferred 'something innovative like the Una, the Bosna, and the Neretva regiments', which alluded to the former armies by reference to the geographic location of their headquarters, but did not explicitly state ethnic allegiance.[127] Unsurprisingly, the names and symbols eventually selected were, for the most part, inspired by ethnicity. The Bosnian Croats chose *Pješadijski gardijski puk* (The Guards Infantry Regiment) and issued the Croatian *šahovnica* (checkerboard) as their regimental emblem, the Bosnian Muslim regiment was called the *Pješadijski rendžerski puk* (The Rangers Infantry Regiment) and received the *Zlatni ljiljan* (Golden Lily) as its emblem, and the Bosnian Serb regiment was called the *Pješadijski Republika Srpska puk* (Republika Srpska Infantry Regiment) and would wear the coat of arms of RS as its emblem (see Figure 6.3). Whilst such variations in appearance are common to the regimental system and are usually encouraged by its proponents to foster a unique regimental identity, all of the emblems that were chosen in BiH were prominent wartime symbols. Furthermore, the Guards Regiment now appeared, in both name and iconography, almost identical to its counterparts in the Croatian Army, and the RS coat of arms which the Republika Srpska Regiment had as its emblem was only two small *fleurs-de-lis* and some crossed sabres away from being that of the Serbian Army. While it should be noted that the troops in each regiment are required to wear the BiH flag in a superior position to any regimental symbol, and those symbols that are worn are set on a blue background (indicating infantry) and fringed with yellow, a pattern which happens to reflect the colours of the Bosnian flag, the imagery employed by the AFBiH regiments remains unconventional.

The use of imagery associated with other states raises obvious questions regarding the loyalty of such units and highlights the potential for them to serve as a potential fifth column or Trojan Horse in the case of a conflict. By subscribing to an existing identity, the individuality and uniqueness of the regimental identities themselves are undermined. The Royal Irish Regiment of the British Army has perhaps the most in common with the Guards and RS Regiments of the OSBiH, as it historically draws its soldiers from a population who may primarily identify with a neighbouring state, Ireland. However, rather than drawing on imagery from the Irish State, the Royal Irish wear a clover leaf as their insignia, use a motto in the Irish language (*Faugh a Ballagh*; Modern Irish: *Fág an Bealach*; English: Clear the Way), and their regimental colours depict a crown, symbolising loyalty to the British monarchy, and a harp, an

**Figure 6.3** *The regimental patches of the 1 (Guards) Infantry Regiment, the 2 (Rangers) Infantry Regiment, and the 3 (Republika Srpska) Infantry Regiment.*

established cultural symbol of the Irish. As a result, the regiment's Irish identity is clearly displayed, yet it remains clear to what the regiment owes its loyalty, and furthermore, the regimental identity is free to develop separately from Irish national identity. In a similar manner, the Royal 22E Régiment of the Canadian Army displays its Francophone legacy through the use of the French language rather than imagery from France itself, successfully preserving its cultural heritage without styling itself as being in service to the French state.

## Conclusion

Between the conception of the first DRC in April 2003 and the OSBiH's accession to the PfP programme in December 2006, the security environment in BiH was transformed. In 2002, over a quarter of a million soldiers and reserves stood ready to go to war with each other, the state had no real military authority, and security had to be provided by external forces. By the Autumn of 2005, the number of soldiers and reserves had been reduced to a total of 15,000, democratically accountable civilian oversight of the military was established at the state-level, and the number of peacekeepers was dramatically reduced, with responsibility for them also being transferred from NATO to the EU. Such changes went far beyond what was needed to satisfy the demands and conditionality of the international community, and undoubtedly contributed to increasing stability in BiH and the wider region. Viewed through the prism of peace and conflict studies, it is possible to illustrate the scale of change this represented. The 'loyalty to the ideas of the state' displayed by the leaderships of BiH's constituent peoples by disbanding their wartime armed forces and supplying troops to the state-level military, compounded by the 'improvement in attitudes and practices toward each other' this represented, signifies the most significant step in the transition from a 'negative' peace to a 'legitimate' one.[128] Indeed, when viewed through this lens, the unification of the armies following the Orao Affair is the single most important act in consolidating peace in BiH, and with it the wider region, since the DPA was signed.

Although a military that was inclusive and representative of the multiethnic population of BiH was successfully created in the wake of the Orao Affair, the OSBiH continues to face myriad obstacles that impede its development and hinder its pursuit of the tasks assigned to it by the Bosnian parliament. Such pervasive challenges must not be understated. However, the significance of the defence reform and military integration processes that took place in this period is remarkable, representing the most important step in consolidating peace in BiH and the wider region since the DPA ended the war. Within a year, US forces withdrew from Eagle Base near Tuzla, handing over authority for the strategically important airfield to the OSBiH (see Figure 6.4), signalling the extent to which the US administration was satisfied with the progress that had been made.

Ashdown contends: 'I think most people who know anything about Bosnia regard the fact that you have a unified army, responsible to the Presidency, as a miracle.'[129] Considering the potential for the OSBiH to serve as a model for other Bosnian institutions, he argues that the military is 'the place where the nation's interests and

**Figure 6.4** *Bosnian soldiers raise the flag of Bosnia and Herzegovina during a handover ceremony at the former US Eagle Base, near Tuzla, on 30 June 2007.* Courtesy of Elvis Barukcic/AFP via Getty Images.

the interests of those in the organisation have superseded, or mostly superseded, nationalistic tendencies'.[130] Central to achieving this 'miracle' was the Orao Affair. Gregorian argues that it was 'crucial' and 'vital' for the success of defence reform in post-Dayton BiH, while Ashdown summarises the significance of the opportunity that the affair presented thus: 'In politics you use what levers you can use which are presented to you. If one is presented to you, you use it. And the Orao Affair was certainly a lever to achieve what I wanted to achieve'.[131] The Orao Affair was pivotal in highlighting the need for urgent reform and building the political and diplomatic capital that was needed to achieve it. Without the affair, military integration in post-conflict BiH (along with all of the associated benefits for stability and international integration) may not have happened at all.

# 7

# The Armed Forces of Bosnia and Herzegovina

During the war, the large reinforced runway of Mostar Airport and the old military bunkers that had been dug into the adjoining mountainside by the JNA represented an important strategic location. Between 9 April and 21 June 1992, local HVO and ARBiH forces drove both the JNA and the VRS from the area in a series of relatively rare coordinated offensives. A year later, the erstwhile allies fell into conflict and the runway became, quite literally, part of the frontline between them until the Washington Agreement established the federation in May 1994. During this period of the conflict, in an even rarer example of coordination, VRS troops stationed in the hills to the east of the city provided artillery support to ARBiH troops as they assaulted HVO positions, firing their shells over the runway towards the emerald waters of the Neretva River. These prolonged periods of intensive conflict make the airport one of the few parts of the country where the ARBiH, HVO, and VRS all fought each other during the war.

This complex history made the resurfaced runway a fitting venue for a scene which anyone who witnessed the conflict would have thought to be unlikely just a decade later. In May 2005, twelve soldiers of the VRS stood to the side of tarmac, armed and ready for combat. Nearby were twelve Bosnian Croat and twelve Bosnian Muslim troops of the VF, all of whom were also prepared to fight and carrying weapons. It was perfectly plausible that less than ten years previously, these very soldiers had been fighting each other. Had they been wearing their normal uniforms that day, the different styles of clothing and the various wartime insignias on display would have made the heritage of each soldier abundantly clear. Instead, the whole group wore Desert Camouflage Uniforms issued by the US military, adorned with a simple Bosnian flag on their arm. In contrast to what happens in most post-conflict states, the soldiers were not preparing to fight each other and restart the war, but were instead going on an operational deployment as an integrated (and specialist) unit of Bosnian soldiers to support an ongoing multilateral peace operation. After leaving the country as personnel of separate entity armies, all thirty-six troops swore a fresh oath of allegiance to the newly established OSBiH within a month of returning from their tour of duty. Their departure from Mostar Airport aboard a C-17 Globemaster of the US Air Force (captured on the cover of this book) marked the first operational deployment of a unified Bosnian military unit and represents the beginning of a new chapter in the development of the post-war Bosnian security sector.

Since its creation, the duties of the OSBiH have been governed by Article 4 of the 2005 Law on Defence of Bosnia and Herzegovina. The Article places 'participation in collective security operations, peace support and self-defence operations' as the top 'mission' of the OSBiH, before going on to list defending BiH and its citizens, responding to natural disasters, removing landmines, and 'fulfilling the international obligations' of BiH as the only other responsibilities of the military.[1] Article 5 of the law clarifies the limited domestic role of the OSBiH even further, simply specifying that 'the Armed Forces cannot be used for political purposes or political partisan activities'.[2] Within this framework, OSBiH personnel and Ministry of Defence officials have been entrusted with a challenging range of responsibilities, from conducting demining programmes and responding to natural disasters at home to supporting a growing portfolio of multilateral peace operations around the world. The OSBiH is also required to continue evolving as an institution, while also maintaining high standards of professionalism among its personnel and ensuring that they safely navigate the complex and often fractious political environment of contemporary BiH. The effort to meet these challenges continues to be framed by the fundamental need to maintain the legitimacy of the military as a Bosnian institution, rather than an agent of one of its constituent peoples. In this context, Bosnian soldiers have availed themselves commendably and the OSBiH represents an increasingly capable military. However, serious challenges remain, most notably the concerted campaign of certain political constituencies to starve state-level institutions such as the Ministry of Defence and the OSBiH of funding. If the political consensus cannot be found to provide the OSBiH with the resources it requires, its future remains uncertain.

## Multilateral operations

As stated in the Law on Defence, the primary task of the OSBiH is participating in multilateral operations of all kinds alongside the armed forces of other states. Such deployments present opportunities for individual soldiers to gain experience and provide the impetus for the OSBiH to develop, but also reflect a concerted campaign on the part of the Bosnian Ministry of Defence to challenge BiH's reputation as a 'a country in need of military assistance' and become a state which can 'provide the conditions of security for others'.[3]

Bosnian contributions to multilateral operations began in 2000, when a small contingent of police officers were seconded to the United Nations Transitional Administration in East Timor.[4] This deployment was supported by the United Nations Mission in Bosnia and Herzegovina (UNMIBH), which identified Bosnian participation in UN peacekeeping operations as one of six 'core programmes' that had to be implemented before responsibility for security in BiH was handed over to local institutions. Service on such operations was regarded 'as beneficial for harmonizing police and military cooperation'.[5] The following year, Bosnian military observers from both entity armies joined the United Nations Mission in Ethiopia and Eritrea (UNMEE), and in 2002 additional observers were sent to the United Nations Mission in the Democratic Republic of Congo (*Mission de l'Organisation des Nations Unies en République démocratique du Congo*, MONUC).[6] These deployments marked the fulfilment of UNMIBH's mandate and the mission was terminated in 2002. Amidst the institutional upheaval in the Bosnian security sector over the ensuing years, BiH maintained its contributions to the UN operations and thus, upon the formation of the OSBiH in 2005–6, a relatively small cadre of Bosnian troops had been serving on multilateral operations for almost five years.

In May 2005, the Bosnian presidency approved the deployment of a single thirty-six-person UXO disposal team to support international efforts to bring stability to Iraq. Given the ongoing defence reform and military integration processes that were taking place that year, a unique Bosnian unit composed of troops from the VF and VRS was created for the mission. By the time they returned to BiH in December 2005, the two entity armies that these troops had left earlier in the year had been dismantled and a month later the troops officially became OSBiH soldiers. A total of eight UXO teams (each composed of twelve Bosnian Croats, twelve Bosnian Muslims, and twelve Bosnian Serbs) were rotated to Iraq (see Figure 7.1), where they joined the 8th Engineer Support Battalion of the US Marine Corps in the west of the country alongside a contingent of Polish troops.[7] Reflecting on his two deployments to Iraq, Sergeant Major Ivo Lukačević points out that with the 'quality specialist training initially conducted by the American instructors' every mission that the Bosnian UXO teams were sent on was successful.[8] In August 2008, the UXO specialists were joined by a forty-nine-person infantry platoon which was tasked with guarding Victory Base in Baghdad and carrying out missions with the rest of Multi-National Division Baghdad.

**Figure 7.1** *A Slovakian lieutenant (left) and an OSBiH sergeant look for information on a case of ammunition discovered at a cache site near Ad Diwaniyah, Iraq, on 19 December 2006.* Courtesy of Stocktrek Images, Inc. via Alamy.

The contingent was composed of sixteen Bosnian Croats, sixteen Bosnian Muslims, and sixteen Bosnian Serbs, with a single ethnic Ukrainian representing the other nationalities of BiH.[9] Bosnian troops remained in Iraq until December 2008, when the UN mandate for the multinational force was terminated. A total of 288 OSBiH personnel served in Iraq over a period of three and a half years.[10]

The decision to contribute only multiethnic units to multilateral operations was informed by two key factors. Maxwell points out that OSBiH deployments were reliant on bilateral support and, in the case of Iraq, the US administration 'made it clear that they expected the units to be multiethnic'.[11] However, given the preponderance of consociational arrangements in Bosnian state institutions and the promulgation of a law requiring 'national representation' to be taken into account when selecting personnel for operations abroad in 2005, such an outcome was likely even without such pressure, as Maxwell suggests:

> I suspect that the units would have been multiethnic even without external conditionality, as this is the approach taken in BiH to most external activities: where it is not possible to send three participants to a given activity, then – as far as I have seen – the position is filled in strict rotation between the constituent peoples.[12]

In March 2009, the Bosnian ministers of defence and foreign affairs signed a pair of agreements with NATO Secretary-General Jap de Hop Scheffer in Brussels, formally bringing BiH into the framework of the International Security Assistance Force (ISAF).[13] Before Bosnian soldiers set foot in Afghanistan, they were put through a rigorous NATO-observed training programme in BiH and a separate assessment process by troops of the Danish Armed Forces, who judged the OSBiH personnel to be highly motivated, disciplined, and ready for deployment.[14] BiH's first contribution (BIHCON-1, in NATO parlance) to the operation in Afghanistan came with the deployment of two staff officers to Regional Command South-West, where they served as part of the Danish contingent of ISAF.[15] In September 2009, eight additional OSBiH staff officers flew to Afghanistan, serving in Regional Command North as part of the German ISAF contingent. The following year, a forty-five-person OSBiH infantry platoon joined the Danes, providing security within ISAF bases in Helmand. As with the deployments in Iraq, every unit which rotated to Afghanistan was multiethnic. Successful participation in ISAF inspired further Bosnian contributions, with a contingent of OSBiH military police and instructors joining troops of the 115th Military Police Battalion of the Maryland National Guard for their deployment in 2012.[16]

The OSBiH continued deploying troops to Afghanistan when ISAF was replaced with Operation Resolute Support in 2014, providing an infantry platoon (see Figure 7.2) and a contingent of staff officers.[17] In 2018, these troops were joined by a small contingent of OSBiH military police, bringing the total Bosnian contribution to Operation Resolute Support to sixty-six personnel.[18] Three OSBiH officers were commended by the US military for their actions in Afghanistan, with one receiving the Bronze Star Medal and two being awarded Army Commendation Medals.[19] Since Bosnian contributions began, approximately one thousand OSBiH troops have

**Figure 7.2** *Specialist Rebekah Wall, Headquarters and Headquarters Company, Special Troops Battalion, 1st Cavalry Division Resolute Support Sustainment Brigade, pulls security with an OSBiH Soldier at Bagram Airfield, Afghanistan, on 23 January 2017.* Courtesy of Chuck Little via Alamy.

served in Iraq and Afghanistan and sixty-eight are currently deployed with Resolute Support.[20]

Alongside its commitments in Iraq and Afghanistan, the OSBiH has continued to participate in UN peacekeeping operations. The small team of OSBiH officers in MONUC and its successor, the United Nations Organization Stabilization Mission in the Democratic Republic of the Congo (*Mission de l'Organisation des Nations Unies pour la stabilisation en République démocratique du Congo*, MONUSCO), have been maintained for most personnel rotations that have taken place since 2002.[21] In their efforts to protect civilians and support the government of the Democratic Republic of Congo, OSBiH troops have operated in a complex environment as part of the largest peace support operation in the world.[22] In some cases, Bosnian officers have risen to command positions within the mission, leading multinational contingents of military observers as they monitor events.[23]

Between 2006 and 2008, the Bosnian contingent of UNMEE was increased from a few officers to fourteen personnel. In this period, OSBiH military observers served alongside troops from fifty-five countries as they monitored and patrolled the demilitarised zone between Eritrea and Ethiopia.[24] As with MONUSCO, Bosnian observers rose to command positions within the mission.[25] UNMEE was terminated in 2008, when the Government of Eritrea imposed crippling restrictions on its activities. In 2014, two OSBiH staff officers joined the United Nations Multidimensional Integrated

Stabilization Mission in Mali, again serving in extremely demanding conditions as part of a major international peacekeeping operation.[26] Another contingent of OSBiH staff officers was deployed to the Central African Republic in 2017, where they are assisting Spanish troops of the European Union Training Mission in the Central African Republic (EUTM RCA) as they help to build 'modernised, effective, inclusive and democratically accountable' armed forces in a society divided by years of armed conflict.[27] The Bosnian troops of EUTM RCA were cited for commendation by their EU commanders and received the National Order of the Central African Republic for their services to the country.[28]

Throughout these deployments, OSBiH personnel have served with distinction alongside some of the most capable troops in the world. In the demanding environments of Afghanistan and Iraq, Bosnian troops stood as equals alongside US forces and were frequently cited for commendations and praised in internal assessments for promoting the reputation of BiH 'in the best possible way'.[29] In UN peacekeeping operations, OSBiH officers have risen to command positions and earned the plaudits of their commanders, while the Bosnian contributions to EUTC RCA have been similarly praised. To date, no Bosnian troops have been killed during deployments abroad. By successfully participating in multilateral operations led by the UN, EU, NATO, and the US military, the OSBiH has fulfilled its primary mission and met BiH's international obligations with distinction. The deployments have also helped to bring BiH closer to achieving its goal of transforming from a security consumer to a security exporter. This process resonates with OSBiH personnel who have served abroad, as former UNMEE team leader Major Nermin Hasić explains: 'One of the most pronounced motives [for volunteering] was the knowledge that for several years now officers from various countries of the world came to our country in order to help create and preserve peace. That proved to me that we could help someone too.'[30]

Participation in multilateral operations provided OSBiH personnel with operational experience and a host of professional development and training opportunities that would have otherwise been unavailable. The UXO teams in Iraq, for example, were mentored by their US counterparts, while every Bosnian soldier that was sent to Afghanistan was vigorously assessed prior to their deployment. By embracing such opportunities and excelling in every assessment, OSBiH troops developed and improved their operational capabilities while also establishing themselves as reliable partners. Reflecting on his time as an ISAF staff officer and leader of BIHCON-1, OSBiH Colonel Taib Karaica highlights how his experience demonstrates that Bosnian troops 'have not the slightest reason to feel inferior to the officers of foreign armies in terms of training' and emphasizes that, for a professional soldier, such a mission is 'definitely the best opportunity to apply what they have learned in real war conditions, thereby complementing their skills and gaining professional and life experience'.[31]

OSBiH contributions to multilateral operations also represent a demonstration of BiH's suitability for NATO membership, a long-standing foreign policy goal of the Bosnian state. In a 2010 interview with *Bilten* (the official journal of the OSBiH), Bosnian Minister of Defence Selmo Cikotić explained:

In order for BiH to become a member of NATO, it must show that it is capable of sharing the risks and difficulties of peace support operations, as well as other collective security mechanisms, which is the essence of NATO. Our soldiers who have been on missions so far have presented the [OSBiH] in the best possible way, and with their readiness and training proved that they can cope with the greatest challenges in extremely difficult conditions.[32]

This sentiment is reciprocated by the leadership of NATO. Brigadier General David Enyeart, who was the commander of NATO Headquarters Sarajevo when the OSBiH joined ISAF, outlined the connection between service in Afghanistan and accession:

The participation of a single state force in an operation to counter an internationally recognized security threat is among the best ways to demonstrate the will and ability to contribute to international security. The ability to do that is one of the things that NATO expects from future members.[33]

The decision to send only multiethnic OSBiH units on multilateral operations has proven wise, not simply because there have been no recorded incidents among the personnel. The maintenance of these strict quotas has ensured that the opportunities for professional development and financial gain that serving abroad represents are shared equally among the constituent peoples. This prevents the military from becoming perceived as an institution in which only one group can advance, as has happened in many other multiethnic armed forces built in the aftermath of armed conflict, thus preserving its legitimacy within Bosnian society.[34] Furthermore, Maxwell offers this concise summary of the potential operational benefits that such multiethnic units can offer the OSBiH:

Although fully half of the [OSBiH] works daily in multiethnic units, they do not associate much outside of working hours. It has therefore been beneficial for members of the [OSBiH] to live and work together, for months, in operational theatres. Shared experience of working and living conditions, facing a degree of risk together, and engaging with other countries' contingents as a single BiH contingent under a single flag, have combined to build relationships and to create some level of trust and mutual understanding. It's not clear whether and to what extent those bonds survive the return to normal life, but at minimum they have created at least the possibility of improved cohesion in future scenarios, whether related to external political pressure on the [OSBiH], or to something like a Bosniak infantry company reinforcing a Serb unit in a disaster response task.[35]

Service in multiethnic units has made an impression on OSBiH personnel, as Lieutenant Edin Osmić observes in an interview concerning his deployment to Iraq:

The friendship that developed between the members of the Unit, which continues today, proves that coexistence in BiH between peoples exists and lives. You need to turn around and see that this is what this country needs. Here [in Iraq] we are all equal and rely only on each other, because when you are in a convoy, first of all you pray to dear God that nothing hits you, and then you look at each other and think about how you will protect yourself and the person next to you.[36]

The OSBiH does not serve as a school of a Bosnian nation. However, sentiments such as those expressed by Lieutenant Osmić demonstrate, as far as is possible, that service on multilateral operations has helped to harmonise personnel and build institutional cohesion.

## Defending (and demining) BiH and responding to natural disasters

The OSBiH's capacity to defend BiH and its citizens from military attack has never been tested. Given the peaceful relations that have prevailed between BiH and its neighbours since the DPA and the ongoing presence of an international military force in Bosnian territory, assessing the OSBiH in terms of its capabilities in this regard would ignore the geopolitical situation in which it exists. In the years since the war, the greatest threat faced by the Bosnian population is not invasion by an external force but the appalling legacy left by the previous conflict: landmines, cluster munition remnants, and other explosive remnants of war have killed an estimated 600 people and seriously injured 1,100 more since the DPA was signed.[37] With approximately 2 per cent of Bosnian territory still contaminated by various forms of UXO, the effort to remove this threat represents the OSBiH's greatest contribution to defending the Bosnian population.

The OSBiH is one of twenty-six accredited organisations that remove UXO in Bosnian territory.[38] In total, these organisations field approximately 1,200 personnel in demining and support activities in BiH.[39] The overall effort is coordinated by the Demining Commission, a multiethnic body composed of three representatives from the state-level ministries of civil affairs, security, and defence. The commission works alongside the Bosnia and Herzegovina Mine Action Centre, which administers the ordnance disposal activities of the OSBiH, the Federal Administration of Civil Protection, the Civil Protection Administration of Republika Srpska, Brčko District Civil Protection, and the Red Cross Society of Bosnia and Herzegovina. Norwegian People's Aid (NPA) has assisted with mine clearance in BiH since 1996 and, as a result, is 'well respected in BiH and treated almost like a national asset' because it alone has cleared more than 20 per cent of the total land that has been demined since the DPA.[40] Within this framework, the OSBiH provides approximately half of the UXO teams and much of the heavy equipment required for some demining activities (see Figure 7.3). The OSBiH's entire arsenal of UXO disposal assets are fully engaged from March to November each year and, thanks to considerable institutional experience gained in both BiH and Iraq, are limited only by the difficulties in finding adequate insurance for deminers and ongoing shortfalls in equipment such as personal protective equipment, batteries for detectors, and fuel for demining machinery.[41] EUFOR and its predecessors

**Figure 7.3** *An OSBiH soldier working to clear landmines in BiH on 17 July 2014.* Courtesy of Martyn Aim/Corbis via Getty Images.

have provided extensive assistance to the OSBiH in these areas, and have also made their own individual contributions to the demining effort. In recent years, further support from NPA and Swiss donors has allowed the OSBiH Demining Battalion to establish additional teams to increase the pace of land clearance.

The efforts of successive peacekeeping missions, a host of NGOs, and several Bosnian state institutions have reduced the amount of land contaminated by UXO from over 4,000 sq km (roughly 9 per cent of the country) to an estimated 1,000 sq km (2 per cent of the country) at the time of writing. Although considerable progress has been made, BiH has consistently fallen far short of its annual land release targets and the pace of clearance has decreased significantly in recent years. The original target for the removal of all landmines and UXO on Bosnian territory was 2009. This date was set in 1999 in accordance with the Convention on the Prohibition of the Use, Stockpiling, Production and Transfer of Anti-Personnel Mines and on Their Destruction, but has since been revised several times. The current target is 2027; however, a report by Mine Action Review (an independent annual survey of global demining efforts financed by the NPA) states that even this date is unlikely to be met.[42] The report highlights the challenges posed by the difficult terrain in which the remaining mines are located as a cause for the delay, but also cites the failures of the Bosnian parliament to approve reforms to the governance and management of the demining effort, and the declining capacity of local institutions such as the OSBiH as contributing factors: 'BiH reported a decrease in operational capacity over recent years, with an average of 52 teams deployed in 2014–17 and 36 teams deployed in 2018 and 2019.'[43] This sentiment was echoed in

2020 by the head of the EU Delegation in BiH and the commander of EUFOR, who warned that the decline in demining capacity was 'a safety threat to BiH citizens' in a joint statement.[44]

The Law on Defence also requires the OSBiH to assist civil authorities in responding to natural disasters and other accidents. Efforts in this regard were largely limited to responding to wildfires, such as the 2013 fires on Mt Ozren which required the deployment of 510 OSBiH personnel to combat the blaze and support the hospital in Bihać.[45] In May 2014, Bosnian disaster response capabilities faced a much greater test when most of BiH was struck with unprecedented flooding. A total of 750 OSBiH troops were mobilised to help rescue and evacuate civilians in 46 of BiH's 74 municipalities. Their efforts were supported by 450 soldiers from an Austrian–British–Slovenian EUFOR battalion and 22 US cadets who volunteered for service via the US Embassy in BiH. Together, this response force rescued 8,669 civilians, provided humanitarian assistance to thousands more, repaired 8 bridges and 83 km of road, and destroyed 396 UXO items exposed by the floods.[46] The response was praised by Bosnian Minister of Defence Zekerijah Osmić, who declared at an award ceremony for OSBiH personnel:

> The Armed Forces responded to this challenge with great ability, which is the result of good training, but also with the courage, motivation and patriotism acquired in their units and commands. They showed that they are an indispensable factor in the affirmation of Bosnia and Herzegovina.[47]

## Institutional development and international partnerships

Upon its formation, the OSBiH represented a merger between two distinct armed forces and a political compromise between three constituent peoples. In such circumstances, forging a cohesive and effective military capable of fulfilling the entire spectrum of duties it was assigned constituted a major challenge, particularly given the extremely limited resources with which the Bosnian Ministry of Defence had to work. As a result, a host of partner armed forces have helped to drive forward the institutional development of the OSBiH, fashioning it with new competencies and providing specialist training to its troops. In most areas, this process has been successful. However, the OSBiH remains reliant on bilateral support and donations to fulfil many of its key functions.

The OSBiH's oldest partnership is with the Maryland National Guard (MDNG), which established links with the entity armies in 2003 and continues to maintain ties with BiH (see Figure 7.4). This bilateral arrangement is facilitated by the US Department of Defense's State Partnership Program (SPP), an initiative developed in the aftermath of the Cold War to build ties with the armed forces of states emerging from the Soviet Union. As Yugoslavia disintegrated, the programme was extended to many states emerging in the Western Balkans. Slovenia and Macedonia joined the SPP in 1993, Croatia followed suit in 1996, and Serbia, Montenegro, and Kosovo have all signed up since BiH. Since the SPP began, a total of 82 partnerships have been forged 'with one third of the world's countries and the National Guard of every US state

**Figure 7.4** *US and Bosnian troops conduct a colour guard parade during the Bosnian–US Friendship Day ceremony in Mostar on 5 June 2008.* Courtesy of Elvis Barukcic/AFP via Getty Images.

and territory.'[48] The most recent audit of the SPP conducted by the US Government Accountability Office stresses that one of the main benefits of the programme is that it encourages partner countries to join multilateral operations such as those in Afghanistan and Iraq.[49] However, the broad range of countries that are participating in the SPP (including formally neutral states such as Serbia) illustrate the extent to which the programme is designed to be politically unobtrusive and maintain as broad an appeal as possible.

In 2006, the MDNG began its partnership with the freshly established OSBiH by providing disaster response training, deploying medical and engineering contingents to BiH to provide humanitarian assistance to the civilian population, and conducting joint exercises with the OSBiH military police.[50] Since these initial activities, more than 5,000 MDNG and OSBiH personnel have trained together, forging a relationship strong enough to allow Bosnian troops to serve within MDNG units in Afghanistan. In 2015, seven OSBiH soldiers were invited to participate in the US military's annual trials for the Expert Infantry Badge alongside nineteen MDNG personnel.[51] The badge is a prestigious accolade awarded to a fraction of those who attempt the trials. Although no Bosnians met the requirements needed to attain the badge, participation in such events highlights the benefits of the partnership with the MDNG and demonstrates the growing capabilities of the OSBiH. In recent years, OSBiH soldiers have also competed in the US National Guard's annual 'Best Warrior' competition, where they put their skills to the test alongside MDNG personnel. In 2020, the OSBiH team won a silver medal in the competition.[52] Celebrating fifteen years of the MDNG's partnership with BiH at a 2018 event in Sarajevo, Bosnian Minister of Defence Marina Pendeš highlighted the deployments to Afghanistan to demonstrate the effectiveness of the SPP:

> By adopting the knowledge and skills passed on to them by their colleagues from the United States, our Armed Forces are strengthening their competencies, interoperability, and compatibility with NATO forces every day. Proof of this was the deployment of our military police officers in 2013 to joint duties with members of the Maryland National Guard in Afghanistan, where they were fully integrated into the 115th Battalion of the Maryland National Guard Military Police.[53]

Brigadier General Janeen Birckhead of the MDNG offered a similarly positive appraisal at the event, declaring:

> The [MDNG] has proudly served alongside the [OSBiH] for well over a decade now. It is with great pride and distinction that today we celebrate our partnerships together as brothers and sisters striving to accomplish common goals in advising and assisting one another to collectively be better.[54]

Evelyn Farkas of the US Department of Defense echoes Birckhead's statement, noting that 'the partnership with Bosnia yields benefits that are hard to quantify on paper, but definitely result in forces that are now better equipped, more credible and making progress toward meeting NATO standards – which ultimately creates efficiencies'.[55] She adds that 'the Bosnians display a great sense of pride, confidence and teamwork that has, in part, been built during these military and security exchanges' and highlights how 'the work they're doing with the [MDNG] has not only primed them to support [ISAF] Afghanistan missions, but prepared them for international security involvement around the world'.[56]

On 14 December 2006, BiH joined the PfP programme. Much like the SPP, the PfP emerged in the aftermath of the Cold War to support the armed forces of democratising states in Eastern Europe and has since expanded to encompass countries across the world. Partners are free to select their level of participation and are not required to aspire to NATO membership. These criteria have facilitated the inclusion of countries that are traditionally wary of NATO, such as Belarus, Russia, and Serbia. Among other benefits, PfP membership provides access to the Partnership and Cooperation Menu, a list of over 1,600 training and development activities that NATO can provide to its partners, ranging from military cooperation exercises to lessons on civil–military relations and environmental issues.[57] In addition, partner countries qualify for participation in NATO military exercises and manoeuvres.

Since May 2007, OSBiH participation in the PfP has been guided by the biennial Planning and Review Process, which 'provides a structured approach for enhancing interoperability and capabilities of partner forces that could be made available to the Alliance for multinational training, exercises and operations', and serves as a significant step towards full membership.[58] The following year, BiH also joined the Individual Partnership Action Plan, which provided a framework for strengthening democratic civilian control and oversight of the military.[59] In 2009, the OSBiH was given the chance to demonstrate its abilities when it was selected to host Exercise Joint Endeavour, a training event involving 150 OSBiH troops and 435 personnel from 27 NATO member states and partners. The exercise, which focused on testing telecommunication equipment, was conducted successfully, leading the chairman of the BiH presidency, Željko Komšić, to declare:

> For me personally, this is proof of the maturity of the structures that lead the [OSBiH], the BiH Presidency and the Ministry of Defense, as well as the [OSBiH] themselves. It proves that, when we truly want, we can equally participate in the most complex military activities.[60]

In 2014, BiH joined NATO's Partnership Interoperability Initiative (PII) alongside Serbia and 21 other partners. The initiative focuses on harmonising standards, doctrines, procedures, and equipment to ensure that NATO partners 'can contribute to future crisis management, including NATO-led operations and, where applicable, to the NATO Response Force'.[61] Participation in the PII has opened up a broader range of development opportunities for OSBiH personnel, from interoperability training with the Croatian and Hungarian armed forces to building OSBiH capacity to operate alongside the US Air Force through 'Air-Ground integration' bilateral exercises.[62] OSBiH participation in such exercises has not only furnished Bosnian soldiers with the knowledge and skills of NATO armed forces, but has also laid the foundation for a marked increase in Bosnian contributions to multilateral operations.

In 2019, the OSBiH conducted a Self-Evaluation Level 1 (SEL-1) of its Light Infantry Battalion Group, a formation composed of 840 personnel replete with combat support functions such as artillery, engineering, and air defence.[63] The SEL-1 is the first of four steps that must be completed before the group can be declared fit for operational deployments with NATO, the EU, and the UN. In September 2020, the OSBiH successfully conducted the NATO Evaluation Level 1 (NEL-1) exercise, and is expected to complete the evaluation process in 2023.[64] The exercises are demanding, testing command and control and logistics alongside combat capabilities. Maxwell notes that 'despite sincere efforts by BiH, the Light Infantry Battalion Group had many, many shortfalls – primarily in equipment and supplies – that must be remedied if it is to complete the evaluation and certification process'.[65] He warns that the current condition of the OSBiH 'makes it unlikely that the unit will survive as a long-term, steady-state unit' but highlights how 'the attempt to form and certify the unit has its own value in terms of catalysing reforms and providing a concrete focus for modernisation efforts'.[66] Should the OSBiH prove capable of meeting the requirements of the evaluations scheduled for the coming years, BiH will have at its command an entire battalion of highly competent troops which can be deployed as an integrated and cohesive Bosnian contribution to a broad spectrum of multilateral operations. Regardless of whether BiH eventually joins NATO, the PfP mechanism would allow the OSBiH Light Infantry Battalion Group to serve as a fully integrated component of multinational NATO brigades.

The US military and NATO have provided the most significant levels of assistance to the OSBiH since its formation; however, several other partners have helped to shape its development. The Peace Support Operations Training Centre (PSOTC) was established in 2003 by twelve partner nations (this later grew to eighteen) under the leadership of the UK. The centre trains both civilian and military personnel from BiH and beyond in a wide array of skills required for peace support operations. Between 2008 and 2010, there was considerable debate, both in BiH and among the international sponsors of the centre, over its future. The key axis for division was whether the PSOTC should become a Bosnian national military academy or remain as a specialist institution. The centre ultimately remained a specialist institution and the Training and Doctrine Command established for the VF with US assistance in 1997 has since become the main provider of higher military education in BiH.[67]

The PSOTC was recognised as a PfP Training and Education Centre in 2007 and became fully accredited by NATO in 2011. The following year, additional courses were formally certified by the UN. In 2009, an OSBiH officer was appointed as commandant of the PSOTC and, on 12 December 2012, the British government formally transferred authority over the centre to the Bosnian Ministry of Defence. In the ensuing years, the PSOTC has retained its international character through the retention of some foreign staff and continues to broaden the organisations with which it is accredited, receiving recognition from the US State Department in 2014 and the European Security and Defence Centre in 2018.[68] The presence of such an institution within the framework of the Bosnian security sector provides OSBiH personnel with an exceptionally high level of training in peace support operations, to the extent that troops from around the world now come to BiH to learn from Bosnian experts. In fact, in a rather unusual development, EUFOR personnel ostensibly deployed to BiH to keep the peace regularly receive internationally accredited training from Bosnian instructors at the PSOTC. Few other post-conflict states have the capacity to provide genuine professional development opportunities to the peacekeepers deployed within their borders.

The British government has also helped to develop the OSBiH by sponsoring initiatives via diplomatic channels and providing training opportunities in the UK. Following the successful handover of the PSOTC to local authorities, the British government provided much-needed assistance to the Bosnian Ministry of Defence as it attempted to rejuvenate the ranks of OSBiH. The most pressing challenge was the ageing officer corps and the inadequate recruitment structures that had developed since the end of the war. Although a handful of OSBiH officers were trained at military academies in friendly states, the vast majority were produced simply by commissioning soldiers from the ranks, many of whom were already nearing the end of their careers. Alongside NATO Headquarters Sarajevo, the British Embassy in BiH spent sixteen months supporting Bosnian efforts to develop a new selection and training system, with the goal of attracting 'bright young graduates into the Armed Forces directly from the civilian sector'.[69] In February 2014, the first of the new generation of OSBiH officers began their training.[70] In addition to building domestic capacity, the UK government also provides many OSBiH personnel with training at institutions such as the Royal Military Academy Sandhurst. Bosnian cadets have attended with distinction: Cadet Martin Mlakić, for example, graduated at the top of his class at Sandhurst in 2017–18.[71] Similarly, serving OSBiH troops receive specialist education in the UK and participate in rigorous training exercises hosted by the British Army such as Cambrian Patrol, in which the deep reconnaissance abilities of soldiers are rigorously tested.[72] Limited numbers of OSBiH personnel also receive training in over thirty other states, most notably Serbia, Croatia, and Turkey.[73] While such training opportunities abroad provide the OSBiH with the expertise it requires, reliance upon them means that there are significant disparities in the education that OSBiH officers receive. Until BiH can provide its officers with a consistent baseline of training, integrating cadets trained around the world poses an ongoing challenge to the cohesion of the military.

Many important developments to the structures and organisation of the OSBiH have been implemented with minimal external support by the Bosnian Ministry of Defence. The most significant of these has been the ongoing effort to increase the size of the small contingent of female soldiers inherited from the entity armies. This has partly been driven by the dual requirements of bringing the OSBiH in line with Bosnian equal opportunity laws and maintaining its legitimacy as an institution, as Bosnian Deputy Minister of Defence Marina Pendeš observes: 'Women's access to the armed forces is a significant segment of the democratisation of the military environment and is a matter of non-discrimination, equal career opportunities for men and women, equal access to different functions, and equal pay.'[74] From a strictly operational perspective, the recruitment of female soldiers into the OSBiH was given much greater impetus by the promulgation of UN Security Council Resolution 1325. Among its many provisions, the resolution called for an expanded role for 'women in United Nations field-based operations, and especially among military observers, civilian police, human rights and humanitarian personnel'.[75] The UN Department of Peace Operations is currently aiming for 25 per cent of its military observers and staff officers and 15 per cent of total troop deployment to be female by 2028, unequivocally stating: 'Women peacekeepers improve overall peacekeeping performance, have greater access to communities, help in promoting human rights and the protection of civilians, and encourage women to become a meaningful part of peace and political processes.'[76]

In 2010, BiH became the first country in the Western Balkans to adopt the Action Plan for the implementation of Resolution 1325 and has since made noteworthy progress in its efforts to recruit female soldiers, with the proportion of female personnel in the OSBiH rising from 6.07 per cent in 2014 to 8.1 per cent in 2020.[77] This process has been driven by increased interest from female applicants and a successful effort on the part of the Bosnian Ministry of Defence (in concert with the BiH Agency for Gender Equality, the Ministry for Human Rights and Refugees, and the British Embassy in BiH) to ensure at least 10 per cent of the total number of OSBiH recruits and 20 per cent of officer cadets are female.[78] Women remain relatively underrepresented (at just 2.5 per cent) in senior positions; however, inspiring figures such as the now-retired brigadier Mersida Mešetović, a veteran of the wartime ARBiH and the first female sector leader of UNMEE, demonstrate that it is possible.[79] Although BiH's current implementation plan for Resolution 1325 concedes that 'increasing the participation of women in the defence and security sectors, including participation in decision-making, is a long-term process', the document contains many measures to increase female representation in the OSBiH.[80]

A CSS report on Bosnian participation in peace support operations notes that an average of just 4 per cent of the total number of Bosnian personnel who were deployed abroad between 2001 and 2017 were women.[81] By 2018, this figure had risen to 7.58 per cent, highlighting a significant increase.[82] If the OSBiH can sustain this growth and reach the target laid out by the UN of having 15 per cent female personnel (at least on operations abroad) by 2028, it will be in a unique position to contribute to peace support missions. Indeed, combined with the expertise provided by the PSOTC, the institutional knowledge gained from decades of deployments abroad, and the operational capabilities demonstrated in the current assessments of the Light Infantry Battalion Group, the OSBiH could be among the most fit for purpose peacekeeping forces in the world if it can continue to recruit more women.

# Challenges

Despite all the progress that has been made in forging a unified military in BiH, a major challenge remains which could ultimately cause the disintegration of the OSBiH without a shot being fired. The OSBiH is reliant on donations and support from partner forces to fulfil its duties and sustain itself. Although a cohesive institution and a capable and professional fighting force, the resources required to properly maintain the OSBiH are relatively limited, representing less than half of what was being spent on the entity armies before they were disbanded. In other words, even for a state with a modest budget like BiH, the issue is not financial. In the contemporary political climate, furnishing the Ministry of Defence with the resources it requires to properly maintain the OSBiH represents a commitment to the Bosnian state that is not shared by the political parties in power. As this section demonstrates, the entire project to build a multiethnic military in post-Yugoslav BiH will be terminally undermined if the budget continues to shrink or if support from partners becomes less forthcoming. This challenge encompasses far more than the OSBiH, ultimately requiring a moment of political consensus and a sustained nationwide commitment to adequately fund Bosnian state institutions before it can be considered resolved.

BiH's military expenditure has fallen dramatically since the defence reform process began, dropping from 3.9 per cent of GDP in 2002 to 1.4 per cent in 2006.[83] This latter figure is in line with most NATO member-states and, had it been maintained, would have provided the OSBiH with the resources it needs. However, the defence budget has continued to shrink since 2006, reaching a low of 0.86 per cent in 2017 and remaining below 1 per cent in 2021.[84] Under these constraints, the Bosnian Ministry of Defence is able to pay the relatively poor salaries (in comparison to the civilian sector) of the soldiers and staff under its command and maintain some of the equipment it has under its jurisdiction, but little else. This situation has had a major impact on the OSBiH. Declining wages (the salary of 80 per cent of OSBiH personnel is below the Bosnian average) and living standards (reportedly there was no food available at some barracks) have led to serious shortfalls in recruitment and problems retaining staff.[85] Furthermore, dozens of modernisation projects, most of which have already been planned and are ready for implementation, have been mothballed until the appropriate resources are in place and the sustainability of valuable institutions such as the PSOTC is in question.[86] The scarcity of OSBiH resources neared a crisis point in 2020, when

Bosnian political parties failed to agree on funding for UXO disposal operations in BiH, preventing the OSBiH from pursuing one of its core objectives and jeopardising the nationwide demining effort. A last-minute donation of demining equipment from the United States furnished the OSBiH with the tools it needed to put eighteen UXO teams in the field, providing a temporary solution to a pervasive problem.[87]

From its formation in 2003 until 2019, the Bosnian Ministry of Defence did not make a single purchase of arms or equipment. In a recent interview with local media, defence officials bluntly stated that procurement took place 'exclusively on the basis of donations, and never with their own funds'.[88] This changed in December 2019 with the purchase of four UH-2 helicopters, although the US government subsidised more than half the cost of this purchase.[89] Including this subsidy, the US has donated arms and equipment valuing over $100 million to the OSBiH, with items including 45,000 automatic rifles, dozens of light vehicles, communication devices, computers, and demining equipment.[90] Further donations have been received from around the world, including the governments of the following: China, which offered engineering equipment; Germany, which fitted Bosnian helicopters with side cranes; Saudi Arabia, which financed the refurbishment of Bosnian arms depots; Switzerland, which handed over fifty hydraulic forklifts; Turkey, which also provided communications equipment; and the UK, which recently donated three military ambulances.[91] When such donations are not forthcoming, the Bosnian Ministry of Defence resorts to hiring military equipment from partners, as was done to facilitate OSBiH participation in NATO Exercise Immediate Response 19.[92]

This scarcity of resources is the product of the domestic political environment. One of BiH's leading political parties, the Alliance of Independent Social Democrats (*Savez nezavisnih socijaldemokrata*, SNSD), has won every election in RS and three of four candidacies for the Bosnian Serb member of the presidency since the OSBiH was established. Dodik, who remains the leader of the SNSD, recently offered his views on the OSBiH, stating, 'these are not the armed forces of Bosnia and Herzegovina, but some other foreign forces' and lamenting that 'the cost is huge and increasing'.[93] He argues that 'demilitarisation should have been carried out' and 'we should begin reducing the OSBiH'.[94] Such statements mask some of the nuances of the SNSD's position: they played a noteworthy role in getting the legislation that established the OSBiH through parliament and were considered 'open to strengthening state powers to enable the country to efficiently participate in European integration' in international assessments at the time. The party continues to participate in OSBiH events, agreed to further progress toward NATO accession in 2019, and also recently approved joint exercises between the OSBiH and the Serbian Army.[95] However, Dodik's words perfectly encapsulate the extent of domestic political opposition to the very existence of a Bosnian military among some constituencies.

The SNSD rhetoric on the OSBiH must be viewed with scepticism, not just because the party's current platform represents a complete reversal from fifteen years ago. At 0.9 per cent of GDP, the 2019 Bosnian defence budget was less than 25 per cent of what it was before the Orao Affair. According to data collected by the Stockholm International Peace Research Institute, this figure is the second lowest in the Western Balkans (after Kosovo) and one of the lowest in Europe.[96] In its current form, the OSBiH requires an annual budget equivalent to 1.5 per cent of GDP to sustain itself.[97] This figure remains less than 40 per cent of the amount that was spent on maintaining the entity armies, even at their most streamlined. Simply put, the economic cost of maintaining a unified military is much less than preserving two parallel defence structures. Dodik first floated the idea of demilitarising BiH on the grounds of economic cost in 2012. The suggestion was immediately met with cynicism from across the rest of the Bosnian political spectrum and dismissed by High Representative Valentin Inzko, who stated:

> This issue would have to be examined at a time when Serbia, Croatia and Montenegro would disarm their forces and there would be no more soldiers in the Balkans. That would be the moment when BiH could think that there are no more Armed Forces.[98]

The SNSD's case for disbanding the OSBiH is severely undermined by their activities in other areas. While calling for the demilitarisation of BiH, the SNSD has been attempting to furnish RS with paramilitary capabilities by militarising the police force. This has been achieved by repurposing thousands of weapons handed in by civilians, purchasing thousands of automatic rifles from Russia, acquiring five helicopters for the RS Ministry of Interior, and establishing a heavily armed RS Gendarmerie (*Žandarmerija Republike Srpske*, ŽRS).[99] The ŽRS appears well funded (see Figure 7.5), as the head of RS Police Dalibor Ivanić highlighted to local media:

**Figure 7.5** *Armed police from Republika Srpska and the Republic of Serbia train together during Operation Drina 2016 in Loznica, Serbia, on 28 August 2016.* Courtesy of Serbia Ministry of Interior/Anadolu Agency via Getty Images.

They have state-of-the-art weapons for efficient use in urban areas, but also for the eventual need to engage in rural areas. They use special vehicles and also have armoured vehicles, popularly called BOVs [*Borbeno oklopno vozilo*, Armoured Personnel Carrier], sniper rifles, chemical weapons, and the like.[100]

Under such circumstances, disbanding the OSBiH would simply return BiH to the post-war situation in which multiple armed forces operated within a single state. Rather than a process of demilitarisation, such a development would likely lead to an arms race among Bosnian police forces and foster instability across the region.

Although Dodik's economic argument for disbanding the OSBiH rests on shaky foundations, his opposition to strengthening BiH and its institutions has received consistent support from the Bosnian Serb population at the polls; in 2018, he secured 54 per cent of Serb votes for the presidency and the SNSD won 16 per cent of votes across BiH.[101] Rhetoric and political manoeuvring aside, the representatives of one of two political entities and one of three constituent peoples continue to be elected on a platform of strengthening RS at the expense of BiH. In this political climate, a consensus on state-level defence spending is unlikely to emerge. Ashdown was cognizant of the difficulties that lay ahead, observing:

> In the end, it is the military who will, in the last analysis and at the last case, ensure the survival of the state – and I think they would. But, the state's survival can just as easily be undermined by a failure of the economic structures to provide taxes that the state can use.[102]

To provide a 'a single, assured source of state finance', he introduced the Value Added Tax (VAT) system to BiH. This new source of state revenue came into force on 1 January 2006 (the same day that the OSBiH officially entered service) and remains a key source of income for the Bosnian state.[103] By establishing reliable sources of revenue through measures such as this, Ashdown provided Bosnian state institutions with a degree of protection against internal efforts to undermine them. As long as Bosnian political parties of all persuasions continue to uphold the DPA and, with it, Bosnian territorial integrity, a change in electoral fortunes or an event such as the Orao Affair could provide the impetus for the OSBiH to be provided with the resources it needs. Such an outcome is plausible: In a change of heart mirroring the SNSD, the leadership of the SDS (a party which was, of course, once fiercely opposed to the very existence of BiH) now supports strengthening state institutions, including the OSBiH. In 2017, for example, Chairman of the Bosnian Presidency Mladen Ivanić (previously dismissed for his involvement in the Orao Affair) stated: 'let us take steps forward to modernise our armed forces because we need that to develop a good relationship with NATO'.[104] Similarly, Mirko Šarović (also dismissed for his role in the Orao Affair) was recently declared a 'loser' by Dodik for supporting the formation of an intelligence component in the OSBiH.[105]

Securing a reliable source of revenue to sustain itself is undoubtedly the greatest challenge faced by the OSBiH today. However, there is another connected, yet in many ways entirely separate, issue that has inspired much political debate about the future of the OSBiH: Bosnian accession to NATO. A 2018 poll of 1,513 Bosnian citizens conducted by Ipsos suggests that while only 11 per cent of Bosniaks and 18 per cent of Bosnian Croats are opposed in any way to BiH joining NATO, 74 per cent of Bosnian Serbs 'strongly oppose' NATO accession and an additional 8 per cent are 'somewhat opposed'.[106] These figures resonate with the results of similar polls conducted in Serbia, where 72 per cent of citizens are against NATO membership.[107] During the conflicts that took place as Yugoslavia disintegrated, NATO conducted extensive bombing campaigns targeting locations in contemporary BiH, Croatia, Montenegro, Kosovo, and Serbia. These campaigns proved decisive on the battlefield, hammering the VRS into submission in BiH and ending the conflict in Kosovo in seventy-eight days. However, many targets of limited military value were destroyed, and hundreds of Serb civilians were killed. In some cases, targets were a great distance away from the fighting: Novi Sad, a city in Vojvodina that was administered by the political opponents of Milošević, is over 500 km from Kosovo and had little bearing on the conflict, yet it was bombed extensively. According to Human Rights Watch, approximately 500 civilians were killed during Operation Allied Force in 1999, 40 per cent of them outside Kosovo.[108] In the 2018 Ipsos poll, 60 per cent of Bosnian citizens who were opposed to NATO accession cited these interventions as their primary reason; of those polled in Serbia, this figure was 63 per cent.[109]

The constitutional guarantees enshrined in the DPA mean that the elected representatives of the Bosnian Serb population will always have a veto on the decision to join the alliance. However, at the political level, attitudes among Bosnian Serbs appear more flexible than public polling might suggest. Dodik and the SNSD are currently opposed to NATO membership, arguing recently that it would 'justify the illegal aggression of the North Atlantic Alliance on the former Yugoslavia', and passing legislation in 2017 declaring the military neutrality of RS.[110] However, the SNSD voted in favour of the 2005 Law on Defence which listed NATO membership as a national objective, signed off on BiH's Membership Action Plan application in 2009, and it was Dodik who co-wrote the Reform Programme (*Program reformi*) in 2019, bringing BiH a step closer to NATO membership for the first time in almost ten years.[111] Reflecting on Dodik's political record, Bosnian Croat member of the presidency Željko Komšić said:

> We did not even have a decision on the Membership Action Plan ten years ago, but we made one. We didn't even have a decision on the Defense Review, so we made one. We did not even have a decision on registering military property, so we made one. We did not even have a decision on the Annual National Plan / Reform Program, so we made one. We will also make a decision on NATO membership. Dodik will take part in it again. Let him be intimately against NATO as much as he wants, just let him sign the decisions as before.[112]

The SDS readily denounces Dodik as a traitor for facilitating closer ties with NATO and, after he approved the Reform Program, accused him of 'fraudulently excluding RS institutions and its citizens from the decision to join NATO'.[113] However, in sharp contrast to such rhetoric, their formal position in recent years has broadly been in favour of completing the steps required for NATO membership. Standing alongside

NATO Secretary-General Jens Stoltenberg in 2017, Ivanić emphasised his support for BiH meeting the requirements to join the alliance but argued that 'it is too soon for this question of fully fledged membership, because this generation of politicians will not decide on it'.[114] In practical terms, the SDS position appears to be in favour of cooperation until BiH has met all the criteria for membership, at which point a decisive referendum on the subject of accession should be held.[115] BiH continues to inch towards NATO membership. However, whether or not the final step of accession will be taken depends on future developments in the RS political arena.

Ongoing political developments regarding NATO accession have had minimal impact on the development of the OSBiH in practical terms. As a military, it has made good progress under the circumstances and is almost at the point where it meets the requirements to join the alliance, proving itself to be a professional force and a valuable operational partner. Indeed, through the mechanisms of the PfP and other programmes, the OSBiH already has access to most of the benefits enjoyed by full members and has contributed personnel to NATO operations for over a decade. Similarly, the strategic benefit of collective defence provided by Article 5 of the Washington Treaty is largely superfluous to BiH as long as EUFOR and NATO Headquarters Sarajevo remain in Bosnian territory. The countless delays that have stymied the accession process do not stem from a lack of OSBiH capability but from political recalcitrance on the part of the elected representatives of the Bosnian Serb population. Whether BiH eventually joins NATO or remains a partner, the OSBiH is likely to remain at the centre of political debates on the subject until a moment of consensus emerges. Maxwell concisely summarises the current position of the OSBiH regarding NATO:

> A country does not have to be a military or economic powerhouse to join NATO, nor does it have to have completely fixed things like corruption and organised crime and rule of law. However, it has to have made a credible effort in those areas, with evidence of sustained intent, and it has to be a country whose elected leaders and state institutions can agree and implement a foreign policy that conforms broadly to NATO's approach. No matter how capable it might become – and it's not going to become very capable with current and projected funding – the OSBiH can't bring BiH into NATO. It can at best make BiH a credible long-term NATO partner.[116]

## Conclusion

Between 2006 and 2021, over 1,600 Bosnian soldiers participated in multilateral operations around the world, serving as military observers on UN peacekeeping missions across Africa, UXO disposal experts in Iraq, and riflemen in Afghanistan.[117] OSBiH personnel now provide training to peacekeepers from around the world and are even helping to build a cohesive, multiethnic military in the Central African Republic after years of armed conflict and instability. Bosnian troops have also been put to the test at home, clearing land contaminated by UXO and rescuing civilians from natural disasters. The experience gained at home and on deployments has been supplemented by the development and training opportunities provided by partners, from the relatively modest offerings of the MDNG and the British government to the institutional support and large-scale exercises provided by NATO. Furthermore, along with successfully maintaining a balance between BiH's constituent peoples, the OSBiH has also made noteworthy progress recruiting women into its ranks, demonstrating its ability to adapt to the changing requirements of the international security environment. Throughout all these endeavours, the OSBiH has availed itself commendably, earning the plaudits of a diverse range of governments and organisations. It has also made significant progress towards completing the missions formally assigned to it in the Law on Defence, with its capacity for further progress being limited only by the scant resources at its disposal.

The Bosnian Ministry of Defence was established in December 2003, just eight years after the DPA was signed. The OSBiH entered service in January 2006, just over two years later. Both were among the first institutions that were built to span the myriad divisions of post-war BiH and bring all three constituent peoples into a unified, professional, multiethnic organisation. In this context, there was no guarantee that the process of military integration would be successful, particularly given the fraught domestic political environment. In these challenging circumstances, the OSBiH has consistently acted in accordance with the values of a professional military, upholding the constitutional order and subordinating itself entirely to the Bosnian presidency and Ministry of Defence. Indeed, the only act of insubordination by OSBiH personnel to have been documented came in January 2017, when, at Dodik's request, troops from the Republika Srpska Regiment attended an unconstitutional RS day parade in Banja Luka against the orders of Minister of Defence Marina Pendeš (see Figure 7.6).[118]

The key to ensuring the survival of the OSBiH was establishing its legitimacy within the society it serves. This has been achieved through three measures that were embedded in its structure upon its formation: Strict adherence to proportional recruitment (in line with the 1991 census) between constituent peoples; equal representation on deployments abroad; and the use of the regimental system. The OSBiH is not presented as an institution dominated by a single constituent people in political debates concerning its future, and troops from across BiH have historically been recruited without issue. Although Dodik has previously declared the OSBiH to be a foreign force, he participates in military ceremonies, offers plaudits to the Republika Srpska Regiment, and approves of joint exercises with the Serbian Army, suggesting a degree of recognition. More importantly, Deputy Minister of Defence Mirko Okolić recently observed that the OSBiH receives more applications from Bosnian Serbs than Croats or Bosniaks, suggesting that the OSBiH enjoys a good level of legitimacy across Bosnian society.[119] With BiH's Croat population declining significantly in recent years and careers in the military becoming less competitive, the OSBiH will soon struggle to recruit its quota of Bosnian Croat personnel. This could undermine its legitimacy among this constituency in future.

Unlike other multiethnic armed forces built in post-conflict states (such as Lebanon), the OSBiH has not been tasked with instilling its personnel with an official form of Bosnian nationalism or any other ideology. Instead, the symbols of BiH's three

**Figure 7.6** *Soldiers of the Republika Srpska Regiment of the OSBiH attend an unconstitutional statehood day parade in Banja Luka.* Courtesy of Pierre Crom via Getty Images.

constituent peoples are enshrined in the three regiments of the OSBiH and, like all armed forces modelled on NATO guidelines, the only non-military tasks carried out by Bosnian troops are ceremonial. The OSBiH is celebrated nationally on 1 December with parades and other activities encompassing the entire military. In addition to these events, each regiment celebrates its own heritage independently of the rest of the OSBiH. The Regiment of Republika Srpska, for example, celebrates its founding on 12 May alongside commemorations of the VRS. While these events could be framed as divisive, particularly as many are often organised by the Committee for Nurturing the Tradition of the Liberation Wars of the Government of the Republika Srpska (*Odbora za njegovanje tradicije oslobodilačkih ratova Vlade Republike Srpske*), the speeches of OSBiH officers at such events suggest otherwise. At the 2019 event, for example, Brigadier Milan Radojčić declared:

> The 3rd Infantry (Republika Srpska) Regiment makes a huge contribution to strengthening trust between nations, but also to building peace and stability in this area. We must protect our own, but also respect others, and members of the 3rd Infantry (Republika Srpska) Regiment must be and remain worthy of the bright traditions of the Serbian people with their character and work. The main task of all of us today is to ensure lasting peace and stability for future generations in these areas. The past war must be a lesson and a warning to everyone. We must study the war and know it, so that it does not happen again in the future, but we must do everything so that future generations live in peace.[120]

The regiments were the product of compromise between representatives of the international community and all three constituent peoples. To date, the concessions made on their activities, structures, and associated symbols have paid dividends, helping to maintain the legitimacy of the military while having a negligible impact on peace and security in BiH.

The OSBiH has established itself as a professional, unified, and highly capable military. It stands as proof that the constituent peoples of BiH can serve alongside each other as equals and demonstrates that the divisions of war can be overcome. However, as an institution, the OSBiH represents a stronger and more unified BiH. This makes it a target for political constituencies who hope to strengthen the entities at the expense of the state. To date, efforts to undermine the OSBiH by reducing the defence budget have been foiled by the ongoing assistance of partner armed forces. As long as this assistance continues, the OSBiH can continue to serve as a stabilising influence within BiH and as a credible partner to other armed forces, at least until the political consensus can be found to either provide it with the resources it needs or develop a military which Bosnians can agree to fund.

# Conclusion

The construction of a multiethnic military in post-Yugoslav BiH was far from inevitable. As the socialist state disintegrated in the early 1990s, a range of competing and ultimately irreconcilable visions for the territory emerged. The establishment of RS, Herceg-Bosna, and the Autonomous Province of Western Bosnia all directly challenged the existence of BiH. The architects of these alternatives raised armies from the population and launched armed campaigns against the Bosnian government. While that government successfully mobilised a diverse coalition of armed forces to protect itself, forging the multiethnic ARBiH, the secular and inclusive identity of this military was lost on the battlefield. By the end of the conflict, three monoethnic armies had emerged, each inextricably linked to the hopes and history of one of BiH's constituent peoples.

The DPA ended the war and established the constitutional framework of the contemporary Bosnian state. Many of the structures of that framework (such as decentralisation and constituent peoples) were inherited from the SFRJ and built upon a long tradition of consociational arrangements in the region. The use of these structures created a state that was composed of three constituent peoples, each of whom enjoy a considerable degree of autonomy. RS was preserved as a political entity, while Bosnian Croats were provided with a framework to govern themselves in certain federation cantons. The war was over. Yet, for all intents and purposes, three armies designed exclusively to fight each other remained on Bosnian territory. Not a shot was fired in anger in post-Dayton BiH; however, these armies continued to serve as vehicles for certain political constituencies to pursue their war aims in the aftermath of the conflict, furnishing them with the trappings of sovereignty and the option to achieve political goals with the threat of violence. The VRS in particular was very much entwined with RS, symbolising not just the wartime heroism and sacrifices that established the entity but also representing one of the few remaining institutional links with Belgrade.

The DPA also provided for extensive international involvement in upholding the peace and building the institutions of the Bosnian state. By the time Paddy Ashdown was appointed as High Representative in May 2002, he felt that 'the process of creating the peace was over' and his main responsibility was to put BiH firmly on the path to integration in Euro-Atlantic institutions such as the EU and NATO.[1] BiH's geographic proximity to these organisations inspired considerable international interest in preventing another armed conflict in BiH, illustrated most clearly by the presence of peacekeepers in Bosnian territory for almost thirty years. These peacekeeping missions have served as the ultimate guarantee of security in post-Dayton BiH, creating the political space in which Ashdown could pursue his mandate. In addition to the expertise it has offered through SFOR and its Sarajevo Headquarters, NATO has also provided impetus for the construction of the OSBiH. Ashdown observes:

> We could not have created a single army responsible to the state in BiH had there not been NATO as the magnetic pull – people wanted to belong to NATO and NATO was the overarching structure in which we had to work. It also served as an instrument of leverage.[2]

A key requirement that had to be met before BiH could progress towards Euro-Atlantic integration was the creation of a security framework which was, at the least, governed by a unified state-level Ministry of Defence. As the cost of maintaining the entity armies became increasingly apparent to observers, the case for creating a single, unified military gained traction both in BiH and among international observers. However, taking the first steps towards military integration required a degree of political consensus that only emerged, albeit briefly, in the aftermath of the Orao Affair.

The construction of the OSBiH represents a compromise that was forged in the 2003–5 Defence Reform Commissions. By establishing these commissions, Ashdown created a framework in which personnel from each armed force and the elected representatives of BiH's constituent peoples could discuss the future of the armed forces together and negotiate a mutually acceptable method of organisation. The inclusion of experienced American defence officials and representatives of NATO and the OSCE ensured that the potential structures under discussion remained feasible, affordable, and capable of partnering with NATO. Years of analysis, negotiations, and compromise within the framework of the commissions produced the OSBiH.

Since its creation, the OSBiH has subordinated itself to the Bosnian presidency and Ministry of Defence with no major breaches of conduct, and has managed to maintain its legitimacy as an institution shared between the constituent peoples of BiH. Bosnian troops continue to serve commendably on multilateral operations around the world and have made noteworthy contributions to keeping citizens safe at home. Through partnerships and donations, the OSBiH has also increased its competencies to the extent that it is considered a credible partner to a wide range of highly trained armed forces. If solutions or compromises can be developed to properly fund the OSBiH, it can stand as a genuinely capable, multiethnic, and unified military that can continue contributing to peace and stability. Indeed, if such resources are made available and current programmes continue, the OSBiH will soon be in a position where it can provide a battalion of 840 highly capable peacekeepers to multilateral operations. This would not just represent the fulfilment of BiH's long-standing objective to transition from being a security consumer to a security exporter but would also provide lucrative opportunities for the OSBiH and its personnel.

The OSBiH connects with and continues a long tradition of multiethnic military organisation on the territory of contemporary BiH, from the territorial defence force of the Ottoman period and the Bosnian regiments of the k.u.k. Army, to the TO formations of the socialist period and the ARBiH in the early years of the most recent conflict. Like these armed forces, the OSBiH is a distinctly Bosnian institution, in the sense that it spans the diversity of the population who live in the mountains and valleys of Bosnia and Herzegovina. Its construction demonstrates that genuinely capable, professional, and multiethnic armed forces can be built out of formerly warring armies in states divided by armed conflict. Successful cooperation within the OSBiH proves that the people of BiH can construct cohesive and effective institutions and work alongside each other within them. Many challenges remain, particularly concerning current budget constraints and broader political divisions, but such concerns are beyond the remit of a professional military such as the OSBiH.

From its earliest beginnings, the OSBiH has represented a unique collaboration. Although commanded and staffed by Bosnians, it exists within a security environment dominated by external powers. The US government has played a pivotal role in the construction and development of a unified military in BiH, contributing vital expertise, equipment, and training. Reflecting on the history of the OSBiH at a 2019 ceremony in Sarajevo celebrating the acquisition of the UH-2 helicopters, US Ambassador to BiH Eric Nelson offered the following appraisal:

> The [OSBiH] is a success story worth investing in. Many of its members served on opposite sides during the war, and now they stand side-by-side in service of their country and their people. They have formed a united force for peace and stability across the globe, and have become a trusted NATO partner for peacekeeping and countering terrorism. Simply put, the Armed Forces are a shining example of what the people of BiH can achieve when they stand together and look towards the future. They have proven that every Pfennig invested in the Armed Forces pays enormous dividends for peace, security, and the future of the people of BiH.[3]

Such sentiments make it clear that the key external backer of the military integration process evaluates the time and resources it has committed to the construction of the OSBiH as a good investment. Maxwell (who originally advised the Defence Reform Commissions and remained at NATO Headquarters Sarajevo until 2019) offers some key qualifications concerning the success story of the OSBiH, noting that from an operational perspective, 'I would describe it as reasonable progress under crippling financial constraints and a very high degree of political interference'.[4] Considering the extent to which the OSBiH has achieved the objectives set out in the Law on Defence, he argues:

> The [OSBiH] has succeeded within its mandate to the extent that it can, given sustained resource starvation that prevents any real modernisation effort, and a dysfunctional political dynamic that constrains severely the ability of senior officers to take decisions on a purely professional basis, no matter that they would all like to be free of such considerations.[5]

With these shortcomings established, Maxwell highlights that 'from a political perspective, the OSBiH has certainly succeeded in creating a single, multiethnic force that does not in itself, pose a security risk to the citizens of BiH. That has been the real success.'[6]

As a key process within a much broader effort to build a functional Bosnian state, the creation and development of a multiethnic military remains a noteworthy achievement which proves that effective Bosnian institutions can be built. However, progress in the defence sector alone cannot sustain BiH. Ashdown argued that for the state to be preserved it required three pillars to be in place: The rule of law, security, and an assured source of state finance. He assessed the OSBiH positively and believed it served as 'one of the three pillars, yes, the ultimate one, *ultima ratia regis*, the last answer of the king' which could be called upon to defend BiH.[7] Yet, he was keenly aware that the Bosnian state 'can fail long before that, either through the rule of law or the failure of economics'.[8] Whether other institutions follow the example set by the military remains to be seen; ultimately, the entire state-building project requires consensus among the people of BiH to provide institutions such as the OSBiH with the resources that they require before it can be considered anything other than a work in progress.

The international effort to construct the Bosnian state was an unprecedented endeavour in terms of its scale and ambition. Since it began, similar strategies have been employed across the world by a growing number of intergovernmental organisations and national governments. Today, the African Union, EU, NATO, OSCE, and the UN are all committing personnel and resources to strengthening states that are recovering from armed conflict, with varying degrees of success. In almost every case, defence reform and military integration represent a key component of a much wider state-building effort. The case of BiH is, like every other, unique; however, some insights from the construction of the OSBiH can be applied to similar processes. The creation of the OSBiH shows that it is possible to work with established armed forces during a post-conflict transition to build a military which, at the least, is tolerable to all stakeholders. Its operational record and institutional development demonstrate that effective multiethnic institutions can be built, given sustained commitments of both expertise and resources. The case of BiH also illustrates that regardless of how capable an institution becomes, it risks being undermined if it is not backed by an assured source of finance. In the contentious political arena of post-Dayton BiH, symbols of state sovereignty and power (particularly cohesive, multiethnic ones) are anathema to politicians with an eye on independence. Without extensive international assistance to sustain it through its lifetime, such actors would have ensured that the OSBiH became a shadow of the military it is today.

Life in contemporary BiH is tough. Unemployment remains high, wages are low, people are leaving the country in considerable numbers, and ongoing political deadlock renders the state semi-functional at best. In this context, it is difficult to sustain an argument that BiH represents an entirely successful example of state building. If lessons can be taken from the process of creating the OSBiH, the first is that constructing a unified, professional military represents just one small step towards creating a functional and stable state. Unless concomitant progress is made in other areas, most notably securing an assured source of state finance, then the creation of such institutions remains a hollow accomplishment, no matter how competent they are. However, in the broader context of states recovering from armed conflict, the creation of the OSBiH is exceptional.

The proximity and cooperation of regional economic and security forums and their agencies played an integral role in the construction of the OSBiH, most demonstrably through the deployment of peacekeeping missions in Bosnian territory for over twenty-five years. In addition, the provision of financial assistance and technical expertise by such organisations has been considerable and sustained. The OSBiH was constructed in a state where the rule of law and electoral process enjoyed support across the country. Important decisions were made to incorporate all political and military stakeholders in the defence reform process, including the full spectrum of relevant international missions, while the Orao Affair (and resulting threat of international sanctions) provided the impetus for military integration to begin. By using the Bonn Powers to forge a favourable political climate in response to the scandal, High Representative Paddy Ashdown ensured that the window of opportunity presented by the Orao Affair was used to its full potential. Perhaps most importantly, the entire state-building project in BiH has taken place in a relatively benign and peaceful regional context. These factors combined to create an environment in which a multiethnic military could be built in post-Yugoslav BiH.

Although still a young military, the OSBiH has proven its value. The future of BiH remains uncertain, but the construction of a multiethnic military has helped to foster an environment in which the debate over that future can take place peacefully. The significance of that achievement should not be underestimated.

# Notes

## Introduction

1. Paddy Ashdown, interview with the author (22 March 2016).
2. BiH Ministry of Defence and Armed Forces of Bosnia and Herzegovina, *Brochure* (Sarajevo, 2011), p. 5.
3. Ibid., p. 12.
4. Maj. Kurt Rauschenberg, 'Bosnia and Herzegovina Armed Forces Celebrate Armed Forces Day, Marking 13 Years of Unified Military', *U.S. Army News* (1 March 2018).
5. British Embassy Sarajevo, 'Best and Brightest Required to Lead the Armed Forces of Bosnia and Herzegovina', *UK Government Announcements* (2 October 2013), available at: https://www.gov.uk/government/news/best-and-brightest-requi red-to-lead-the-armed-forces-of-bosnia-and-herzegovina (accessed 18 January 2021).
6. Raffi Gregorian, interview with the author (18 July 2017).
7. RFE/RL Balkan Service, 'Bosnian Parliament Breaks 14-Month Impasse, OKs Government', *Radio Free Europe/Radio Liberty* (23 December 2019), available at: https://www.rferl.org/a/bosnian-parliament-breaks-14-month-impasse-oks-gov ernment/30340670.html (accessed 25 January 2021).
8. Almir Bičakčić, 'Tegeltija je zakočio MAP', *Oslobođenje* (2021), available at: https:// www.oslobodjenje.ba/vijesti/bih/tegeltija-je-zakocio-map-619817 (accessed 18 January 2021).
9. Andrew Byrne, 'Bosnian Serb Forces Take Part in Illegal "Statehood Day" Parade', *Financial Times* (9 January 2017).
10. Alan Crosby, 'Bosnian Serb Leader's Call for Wartime Uniforms Tugs at Bosnia's Nationalist Threads', *Radio Free Europe* (13 May 2019).
11. Rauf Bajrović, Richard Kraemer, & Emir Suljagić, *Bosnia on the Chopping Block: The Potential for Violence and Steps to Prevent It* (Philadelphia, 2018), p. 6.
12. Thérése Pettersson & Magnus Öberg, 'Organized Violence, 1989–2019', *Journal of Peace Research*, Vol. 57, No. 4 (2020); Håvard Strand et al., 'Trends in Armed Conflict, 1946–2019', *PRIO Conflict Trends*, No. 8 (2020); Thomas S. Szayna et al., *Conflict Rends and Conflict Drivers: An Empirical Assessment of Historical Conflict Patterns and Future Conflict Projections* (Santa Monica, 2017); Elliot Short & Milt Lauenstein, *Peace and Conflict Since 1991: War, Intervention, and Peacebuilding Organizations* (New York, 2020).
13. One of the first peacekeepers to enter BiH, Colonel (retired) Colm Doyle of the Irish Defence Forces, later served as Chief of Staff of the UN Military Division, where he quite literally applied lessons learned in BiH to peacekeeping operations around the world. UN Secretary-General Kofi Annan cited the case of BiH when calling for more effective responses to gross and systematic violations of human rights in his 2000 Millennium Report, which inspired the formation of the

International Commission on Intervention and State Sovereignty. The Commission's final report, *The Responsibility to Protect*, also cited the case of BiH. See Kofi Annan, *'We the Peoples': The Role of the United Nations in the 21st Century* (New York, 2000), available at: https://www.un.org/en/events/pastevents/we_the_peoples.shtml (accessed 19 January 2021); International Commission on Intervention and State Sovereignty, *The Responsibility to Protect* (Ottawa, 2001), available at: https://www.un.org/en/genocideprevention/about-responsibility-to-protect.shtml (accessed 19 January 2021).

14. ICTY, *About the ICTY* (The Hague, 2020), available at: https://www.icty.org/en/about (accessed 27 October 2020).

15. See e.g.: Elliot Short, *Stopping War: 101 Successful Efforts to Reduce Armed Conflict* (Lesswar.org, 2020), available at: https://www.lesswar.org/publications-1 (accessed 28 January 2021).

16. Timothy D. Sisk, *Statebuilding* (Cambridge, 2013); Francis Fukuyama, *Statebuilding: Governance and World Order in the Twenty-First Century* (London, 2004); Michael Cox, 'Bosnia and Herzegovina: The Limits of Liberal Imperialism', in Charles T. Call & Vanessa Wyeth, eds, *Building States to Build Peace* (Boulder, 2008); Marina Ottaway, 'Rebuilding State Institutions in Collapsed States', *Development and Change*, Vol. 33, No. 5 (2002); Catherine Goetze & Dejan Guzina, 'Peacebuilding, Statebuilding, Nationbuilding – Turtles All the Way Down?' *Civil Wars*, Vol. 10, No. 4 (2008).

17. E.g.: Elliot Short, 'Assessing International Statebuilding Initiative Effectiveness at Preventing Armed Conflict Recurrence: The Cases of Burundi, Chad, Côte d'Ivoire, and Nepal', *The Better Evidence Project at George Mason University* (2020), available at: https://betterevidenceproject.squarespace.com/bepevents/bep-research-report-release-on-statebuilding-by-dr-elliot-short (accessed 19 January 2021).

18. Barbara Walter contends that civil wars that took place between 1945 and 2009 had a recidivism rate of 57 per cent, while more recent scholarship from the Peace Research Institute Oslo places this figure at 60 per cent. Barbara Walter, 'Conflict Relapse and the Sustainability of Post-Conflict Peace', *World Development Report 2011: Background Paper* (2011), p. 1, available at: https://openknowledge.worldbank.org/handle/10986/9069 (accessed 19 January 2021); Scott Gates, Håvard Mokleiv Nygård, & Esther Trappeniers, 'Conflict Recurrence', *PRIO Conflict Trends*, No. 2 (2016). See also: George Frederick Willcoxon, 'Why Do Countries Relapse into War? Here Are Three Good Predictors', *Washington Post* (29 March 2017), available at: https://www.washingtonpost.com/news/monkey-cage/wp/2017/03/29/why-do-countries-relapse-into-war-here-are-three-good-predictors/ (accessed 20 May 2020).

19. Central Intelligence Agency, Office of Russian and European Analysis, *Balkan Battlegrounds: A Military History of the Yugoslav Conflict, 1990-1995* (Washington, DC, 2002).

20. James Gow, *The Serbian Project and Its Adversaries: A Strategy of War Crimes* (London, 2003); Gow has also produced numerous other relevant works: *The Triumph of the Lack of Will: International Diplomacy and the Yugoslav War* (London, 1997); *Legitimacy and the Military: The Yugoslav Crisis* (London, 1992).

21. Marko Attila Hoare, *How Bosnia Armed* (London, 2004). Hoare has also written on the development of civil–military relations in the ARBiH: 'Civil–Military Relations in Bosnia-Herzegovina 1992–1995', in Branka Magaš & Ivo Zanić, eds, *The War in Croatia and Bosnia-Herzegovina 1991–1995* (London, 2013).

22. Kenneth Morrison, *Sarajevo's Holiday Inn on the Frontline of Politics and War* (London, 2018); Kenneth Morrison & Paul Lowe, *Reporting the Siege of Sarajevo* (London, 2021).
23. Anthony Loyd, *My War Gone By, I Miss It So* (London, 2000).
24. Colm Doyle, *Witness to War Crimes: The Memoirs of a Peacekeeper in Bosnia* (Barnsley, 2018).
25. Catherine Baker, *The Yugoslav Wars of the 1990s* (London, 2015).
26. The Peace Implementation Council and the Office of the High Representative were both established to monitor and assist with the implementation of the DPA, and the Organisation for Security and Cooperation in Europe and the North Atlantic Treaty Organisation were mandated to oversee certain provisions of the Agreement. The United Nations Development Program, the World Bank, and the International Crisis Group also established missions designed to monitor or assist BiH in its transition from conflict. All published reports and analysis on the situation in BiH. Florian Bieber and Sumantra Bose are the most prolific political analysts of the implementation of Dayton, and their relevant publications are listed in the bibliography.
27. Christopher Bennett, *Bosnia's Paralysed Peace* (London, 2016).
28. Rohan Maxwell & John Andreas Olsen, *Destination NATO: Defence Reform in Bosnia and Herzegovina, 2003–2013* (London, 2013); Maxwell has also published an insightful chapter on the subject in 'Bosnia-Herzegovina: From Three Armies to One', in Roy Licklider, ed., *New Armies from Old: Merging Competing Military Forces after Civil Wars* (Washington, DC, 2014).
29. Florence Gaub, *Military Integration after Civil Wars: Multiethnic Armies, Identity and Post-Conflict Reconstruction* (London, 2011).
30. Charles Tilly, *Coercion, Capital, and European States, AD 990–1990* (Blackwell, 1992), pp. 70–1.
31. Max Weber, *The Theory of Social and Economic Organisation*, trans. A. M. Henderson & Talcott Parsons (Oxford, 1947), p. 154.
32. Francis Fukuyama, 'The Imperative of State-Building', *Journal of Democracy*, Vol. 15, No. 2 (2004), p. 21.
33. In the original context, 'Who will guard the guardians?' was used to show the impossibility of imposing a moral code on women. Juvenal, *Thirteen Satires of Juvenal, Volume 1*, trans. John Mayor (Cambridge, 2010), Satire 6.
34. Samuel Finer, *The Man on Horseback: The Role of the Military in Politics* (London, 1962), p. 5.
35. Ibid., p. 83.
36. Ibid., pp. 8–10.
37. Samuel Huntington, *The Soldier and the State: The Theory and Politics of Civil–Military Relations* (London, 1970), pp. 7–11.
38. Anthony Forster, Timothy Edmunds, & Andrew Cottey, 'The Professionalisation of Armed Forces in Postcommunist Europe', in Anthony Forster, Timothy Edmunds, & Andrew Cottey, eds, *The Challenge of Military Reform in Postcommunist Europe: Building Professional Armed Forces* (Basingstoke, 2002), p. 6.
39. Ibid., p. 57.
40. Thomas-Durrell Young, 'Military Professionalism in a Democracy', in Thomas Bruneau & Scott Tollefson, eds, *Who Guards the Guardians and How: Democratic Civil–Military Relations* (College Station, 2006), p. 17.
41. Samuel Huntington, *Political Order in Changing Societies* (Yale, 1968), pp. 201–2.

42. Kees Koonings & Dirk Krujt, 'Introduction', in Kees Koonings & Dirk Krujt, eds, *Political Armies: The Military and Nation Building in the Age of Democracy* (London, 2002), p. 1.
43. William Odom, 'The Party–Military Connection: A Critique', in Dale Herspring & Ivan Volgyes, eds, *Civil–Military Relations in Communist Systems* (Boulder, 1978), pp. 32–3.
44. Ibid., p. 35.
45. Ibid., p. 36.
46. Gaub, *Military Integration after Civil Wars*, p. 9.
47. Zoltan Barany, *The Solider and the Changing State: Building Democratic Armies in Africa, Asia, Europe and the Americas* (Princeton, 2012), p. 1.
48. Ibid.
49. Alon Peled, *A Question of Loyalty: Military Manpower Policy in Multiethnic States* (New York, 1998), p. xiii.
50. Ibid., p. 1.
51. Cynthia Enloe, *Ethnic Soldiers: State Security in a Divided Society* (London, 1980), p. 8.
52. Benedict Anderson, *Imagined Communities: Reflections on the Origin and Spread of Nationalism* (London, 2016), p. 5.
53. Ibid., pp. 5–6.
54. Eric Hobsbawm & Terence Ranger, eds, *The Invention of Tradition* (Cambridge, 2010), p. 14.
55. Herodotus, *The Histories*, trans. Aubrey De Selincourt (London, 2003), pp. 439–45; Sun Tzu, *The Art of War*, trans. Lionel Giles (Minneapolis, 2006), p. 37.
56. Gaub, *Military Integration after Civil Wars*, pp. 17–18.
57. Oren Barak, *The Lebanese Army: A National Institution in a Divided Society* (New York, 2009); Edward Azar, ed., *The Emergence of a New Lebanon: Fantasy or Reality?* (Santa Barbara, 1984); Oren Barak. 'Commemorating Malikiyya: Political Myth, Multiethnic Identity and the Making of the Lebanese Army', *History and Memory*, Vol. 13, No. 1 (2001); Florence Gaub, 'Multi-Ethnic Armies in the Aftermath of Civil War: Lessons Learned from Lebanon', *Defence Studies*, Vol. 7, No. 1 (2007).
58. Sabrina Ramet, *Nationalism and Federalism in Yugoslavia, 1962–1991* (Bloomington, 1992), p. 51; these approaches, and their relation to the Yugoslav military, are discussed in detail in Chapter 2 in this book.
59. David French, *Military Identities: The Regimental System, the British Army, and the British People, c.1870–2000* (Oxford, 2007); Catriona Kennedy & Matthew McCormack, eds, *Soldiering in Britain and Ireland, 1750–1850* (Basingstoke, 2013); Laurence Brockliss & David Eastwood, eds, *A Union of Multiple Identities: The British Isles, c.1750–c.1850* (Manchester, 1997); Lieutenant General Sir Alistair Irwin, 'What Is Best in the Regimental System?' *RUSI Journal*, Vol. 149, No. 5 (June 2004).
60. Desmond Bowen & Jean Bowen, *Heroic Option: The Irish in the British Army* (Barnsley, 2005); Hew Strachan, 'Scotland's Military Identity', *Scottish Historical Review*, Vol. 85, No. 2 (2008); Stephen Conway, 'War and National Identity in the Mid-Eighteenth-Century British Isles', *English Historical Review*, Vol. 116, No. 468 (2001), p. 877; Peter Karsten, 'Irish Soldiers in the British Army, 1792–1922: Suborned or Subordinate', *Journal of Social History*, Vol. 17, No. 1 (1993).
61. John Cookson, *The British Armed Nation, 1793–1815* (Oxford, 1997), p. 129.
62. French, *Military Identities*, p. 98.
63. Ramet, *Nationalism and Federalism in Yugoslavia, 1962–1991*, p. 51.

64. Anthony Smith, 'When Is a Nation?' *Geopolitics*, Vol. 7, No. 2 (2002), p. 15; see also Anthony Smith, *National Identity* (London, 1991), p. 14.
65. Anthony Smith, *Ethno-symbolism and Nationalism* (London, 2009), p. 28.
66. John Hutchinson, 'Warfare, Remembrance and National Identity', in Athena Leoussi & Steven Grosby, eds, *Nationalism and Ethnosymbolism: History, Culture and Ethnicity in the Formation of Nations* (Edinburgh, 2006), p. 43.
67. Ibid.
68. Smith, *Ethno-symbolism and Nationalism*, p. 78.
69. Ibid.
70. Roy Licklider, 'Introduction', in Licklider, *New Armies from Old*, p. 1.
71. Ronald Krebs & Roy Licklider, 'United They Fall: Why the International Community Should Not Promote Military Integration after Civil War', *International Security*, Vol. 40, No. 3 (2015), p. 94.
72. Licklider, *New Armies from Old*.

## 1 The region before the Second World War

1. Cathie Carmichael, *A Concise History of Bosnia* (Cambridge, 2015), p. 12.
2. Marko Attila Hoare, *The History of Bosnia: From the Middle Ages to the Present Day* (London, 2006), pp. 35–7.
3. Ivan Lovrenović, *Bosnia: A Cultural History* (London, 2001), p. 46.
4. Noel Malcom, *Bosnia: A Short History* (London, 1996), pp. 22–3.
5. Ibid., pp. 43–4.
6. Rhoads Murphey, *Ottoman Warfare, 1500–1700* (New Brunswick, 1999), p. 144.
7. Hoare, *The History of Bosnia*, p. 38.
8. Ibid., p. 41.
9. Carmichael, *A Concise History of Bosnia*, p. 22.
10. Murphey, *Ottoman Warfare, 1500–1700*, p. 144.
11. Ibid., p. 144.
12. Carmichael, *A Concise History of Bosnia*, p. 31.
13. Hoare, *The History of Bosnia*, p. 43.
14. Malcom, *Bosnia*, p. 46.
15. Ibid., p. 46; Carmichael, *A Concise History of Bosnia*, pp. 22–3.
16. Malcolm, *Bosnia*, p. 47.
17. Ibid., p. 73.
18. Ibid., p. 83.
19. Hoare, *The History of Bosnia*, p. 46.
20. Ibid., p. 48.
21. Ibid.
22. Ibid.
23. Malcolm, *Bosnia*, p. 92.
24. Carmichael, *A Concise History of Bosnia*, p. 36.
25. Hoare, *The History of Bosnia*, p. 49.
26. Malcolm, *Bosnia*, p. 121.
27. Hoare, *The History of Bosnia*, p. 50.
28. Ibid., p. 65.
29. Ibid., p. 40.

30. Sabrina Ramet, 'Realpolitik or Foreign Policy Surrealism: A Reconsideration of the Peace Treaties of Berlin (1878), London (1913), Versailles (1919), and Trianon (1920)', in James Pettifer & Tom Buchanan, eds, *War in the Balkans: Conflict and Diplomacy since World War I* (London, 2020), p. 38.
31. Richard Bassett, *For God and Kaiser: The Imperial Austrian Army* (New Haven, 2016), p. 372.
32. Ibid., p. 374.
33. Clemens Ruthner, 'Introduction: Bosnia-Herzegovina: Post/Colonial?' in Pettifer & Buchanan, *War in the Balkans*, p. 5.
34. Lohr Miller, 'Politics, the Nationality Problem, and the Habsburg Army, 1848–1914 (Volumes I and II)', *LSU Historical Dissertations and Theses*, No. 5336 (1992), p. 137.
35. Gunther E. Rothenberg, *The Army of Francis Joseph* (West Lafayette, 1976), p. 102.
36. Carmichael, *A Concise History of Bosnia*.
37. Bassett, *For God and Kaiser*, p. 379.
38. Miller, 'Politics, the Nationality Problem, and the Habsburg Army, 1848–1914', p. 353.
39. Bassett, *For God and Kaiser*, p. 377.
40. James Lucas, *Fighting Troops of the Austro-Hungarian Army, 1868–1914* (Cheltenham, 1987), p. 41.
41. Ian Sethre, 'Occupation and Nation-Building in Bosnia and Herzegovina, 1878–1914', in Clemens Ruthner et al., eds, *WechselWirkungen: Austria-Hungary, Bosnia-Herzegovina, and the Western Balkans* (New York, 2015), p. 41; Aydun Babuna, 'The Story of *Bošnjastvo*', in Ruthner et al., *WechselWirkungen*, pp. 123–4.
42. Hoare, *The History of Bosnia*, p. 72.
43. Gunther E. Rothenberg, *The Military Border in Croatia, 1740–1881* (Chicago, 1966), p. 9.
44. John Paul Newman, *Yugoslavia in the Shadow of War: Veterans and the Limits of State Building, 1903–1945* (Cambridge, 2015), pp. 117–18.
45. Rothenberg, *The Military Border in Croatia, 1740–1881*, p. 196.
46. Bassett, *For God and Kaiser*, p. 380.
47. John Schindler, 'Defeating Balkan Insurgency: The Austro-Hungarian Army in Bosnia-Hercegovina, 1878–82', *Journal of Strategic Studies*, Vol. 27, No. 3 (2004).
48. Miller, 'Politics, the Nationality Problem, and the Habsburg Army, 1848–1914', p. 214.
49. Jiří Hutečka, *Men under Fire: Motivation, Morale, and Masculinity among Czech Soldiers in the Great War, 1914–1918* (Oxford, 2019), p. 167; Josef Váchal, *Malíř na frontě. Soca a Italie 1917–18* (Prague, 1929), p. 109.
50. Bassett, *For God and Kaiser*, p. 381.
51. Christoph Neumayer & Erwin Schmidl, eds, *The Emperor's Bosniaks: The Bosnian-Herzegovinian Troops in the k.u.k. Army, History and Uniforms from 1878 to 1918* (Vienna, 2008), p. 104.
52. Emir Numanović, 'Muslimani – pouzdani vojnici Austro-Ugarske Monarhije,' *Deutsche Welle* (25 June 2014), available at: https://www.dw.com/hr/muslimani-pouzdani-vojnici-austro-ugarske-monarhije/a-17734276 (accessed 13 January 2021).
53. Bassett, *For God and Kaiser*, p. 367.
54. Neumayer & Schmidl, *The Emperor's Bosniaks*, pp. 109–10.
55. Numanović, 'Muslimani pouzdani vojnici Austro-Ugarske Monarhije'.
56. István Deák, *Beyond Nationalism: A Social and Political History of the Habsburg Officer Corps, 1848–1918* (Oxford, 1989).
57. Rothenberg, *The Army of Francis Joseph*, p. 121.
58. John Cox, *The History of Serbia* (Greenwood, 2002), p. 55.

59. Siniša Malešević, 'The Mirage of Balkan Piedmont: State Formation and Serbian Nationalisms in the Nineteenth and Early Twentieth Centuries', *Nations and Nationalism*, Vol. 23, No. 1 (2017), p. 136.
60. Ibid., p. 138.
61. Ibid., p. 139.
62. Charles & Barbara Jelavich, *The Establishment of the Balkan National States, 1804–1920* (Seattle, 1993), p. 255.
63. Ibid., p. 257.
64. Cox, *The History of Serbia*, p. 64.
65. Malešević, 'The Mirage of Balkan Piedmont', pp. 148, 142.
66. Tim Buchanon, 'The Balkan Wars after 100 years', in Pettifer & Buchanan, *War in the Balkans*, p. 7.
67. Richard Hall, *The Balkan Wars, 1912–1913: Prelude to the First World War* (Abingdon, 2000).
68. Eric Beckett Weaver, 'Yugoslavism in Hungary during the Balkan Wars', in Pettifer & Buchanan, *War in the Balkans*, p. 54.
69. Malešević, 'The Mirage of Balkan Piedmont', p. 137.
70. Ibid., p. 144.
71. Carmichael, *A Concise History of Bosnia*, p. 56.
72. Eric Beckett Weaver, 'Yugoslavism in Hungary during the Balkan Wars', in Pettifer & Buchanan, *War in the Balkans*, p. 63.
73. Newman, *Yugoslavia in the Shadow of War*, p. 206; Malcolm, *Bosnia*, p. 158.
74. Alexander Watson, *Ring of Steel: Germany and Austria-Hungary at War, 1914–1918* (London, 2015), p. 248.
75. Neumayer & Schmidl, *The Emperor's Bosniaks*, p. 127.
76. Watson, *Ring of Steel*, p. 286.
77. Hoare, *The History of Bosnia*, p. 92.
78. Neumayer & Schmidl, *The Emperor's Bosniaks*, p. 127.
79. Mitja Velikonja, *Religious Separation and Political Intolerance in Bosnia-Herzegovina* (College Station, 2003), p. 141.
80. John Schindler, *Fall of the Double Eagle: The Battle for Galicia and the Demise of Austria-Hungary* (Nebraska, 2015), pp. 199, 233.
81. Hutečka, *Men under Fire*, p. 167.
82. Ibid.
83. Carmichael, *A Concise History of Bosnia*, pp. 57–8.
84. Ibid., p. 57; Schindler, *Fall of the Double Eagle*, p. 199.
85. Bassett, *For God and Kaiser*, pp. 3–4.
86. John Paul Newman, 'Forging a United Kingdom of Serbs, Croats, and Slovenes: The Legacy of the First World War and the "Invalid Question"', in Dejan Djokić & James Ker-Lindsay, eds, *New Perspectives on Yugoslavia: Key Issues and Controversies* (Abingdon, 2010), p. 47.
87. Bassett, *For God and Kaiser*, pp. 533–4.
88. Carmichael, *A Concise History of Bosnia*, pp. 58–9.
89. Mile Bjelajac, *Jugoslovensko iskustvo sa multietničkom armijom, 1918–1991* (Belgrade, 1999), p. 24; Newman, *Yugoslavia in the Shadow of War*, p. 42.
90. Dejan Djokić, *Elusive Compromise: A History of Interwar Yugoslavia* (New York, 2007), pp. 12–13.
91. Newman, *Yugoslavia in the Shadow of War*, pp. 39–40.
92. Hoare, *The History of Bosnia*, p. 107.

93. Newman, *Yugoslavia in the Shadow of War*, pp. 41–2.
94. Ibid., p. 42.
95. Ibid.
96. Ibid., p. 44.
97. Bjelajac, *Jugoslovensko iskustvo sa multietničkom armijom, 1918–1991*, p. 32.
98. Newman, *Yugoslavia in the Shadow of War*, p. 43.
99. Hrvoje Čapo, 'Former Austro-Hungarian Officers in the Army of the Kingdom of Serbs, Croats and Slovenes/Yugoslavia', *Review of Croatian History*, Vol. 5, No. 1 (2009), p. 120.
100. Bjelajac, *Jugoslovensko iskustvo sa multietničkom armijom, 1918–1991*, p. 37.
101. Čapo, 'Former Austro-Hungarian Officers in the Army of the Kingdom of Serbs, Croats and Slovenes/Yugoslavia', p. 136.
102. Newman, *Yugoslavia in the Shadow of War*, p. 44.
103. Hoare, *The History of Bosnia*, p. 102.
104. Ibid., pp. 151–2.
105. Djokić, *Elusive Compromise*, p. 235.
106. Ibid., p. 212.
107. Hoare, *The History of Bosnia*, pp. 102–3.
108. Newman, *Yugoslavia in the Shadow of War*, pp. 186–94.
109. Carmichael, *A Concise History of Bosnia*, p. 64.
110. Jakub Salkić, 'Dova za domovinu na bedme Bosne', *Stav arhiv* (14 August 2019), available at: https://arhiv.stav.ba/dova-za-domovinu-na-bedemu-bosne/ (accessed 15 January 2020).
111. Steven Pavlowitch, *Hitler's New Disorder: The Second World War in Yugoslavia* (London, 2008), p. 17.
112. Bjelajac, *Jugoslovensko iskustvo sa multietničkom armijom, 1918–1991*, pp. 43–4.
113. Pavlowitch, *Hitler's New Disorder*, pp. 19–20.
114. Ibid., p. 20.
115. Ibid., p. 18.
116. Hoare, *The History of Bosnia*, p. 152.

## 2 The Yugoslav People's Army

1. Nikola Ljubičić, *Total National Defence – Strategy of Peace* (Belgrade, 1977), p. 252; Richard Herrick, *The Yugoslav People's Army: Its Military and Political Mission* (Monterey, 1980), pp. 14, 45.
2. A. Ross Johnson, 'The Role of the Military in Yugoslavia: An Historical Sketch', in Roman Kolkowicz & Andrzej Korbonski, eds, *Soldiers, Peasants, and Bureacrats: Civil–Military Relations in Communist and Modernizing Societies* (London, 1982), p. 182.
3. Vladimir Dedijer, *Tito Speaks: His Self-Portrait and Struggle with Stalin* (Norwich, 1953), p. 145.
4. Ljubičić, *Total National Defence*, p. 57.
5. Dedijer, *Tito Speaks*, p. 153.
6. James Gow, *Legitimacy and the Military: The Yugoslav Crisis* (London, 1992), p. 43.
7. Ibid., p. 172.

8. Anton Bebler, 'Political Pluralism and the Yugoslav Professional Military', in Jim Seroka & Vukasin Pavlovic, eds, *The Tragedy of Yugoslavia: The Failure of Democratic Transformation* (New York, 1992), p. 106.

9. Ibid.

10. A. Ross Johnson, 'The Role of the Military in Yugoslavia: An Historical Sketch', p. 182.

11. Dedijer, *Tito Speaks*, pp. 186, 202.

12. Johnson, 'The Role of the Military in Yugoslavia', p. 182; Bebler, 'Political Pluralism and the Yugoslav Professional Military', p. 110.

13. Ibid., p. 182.

14. William Deakin, *The Embattled Mountain* (Oxford, 1971), p. 88; Sabrina Ramet, *Nationalism and Federalism in Yugoslavia, 1962–1991* (Indiana, 1992), p. 49.

15. AVNOJ, *The Declaration from the Second Session of the Anti-Fascist Council of National Liberation of Yugoslavia* (Jajce, 1943).

16. Tomislav Dulić & Roland Kostić, 'Yugoslavs in Arms: Guerrilla Tradition, Total Defence and the Ethnic Security Dilemma', *Europe-Asia Studies*, Vol. 62, No. 7 (2010), p. 1058; Johnson, 'The Role of the Military in Yugoslavia', p. 181.

17. Jelena Batinić, *Women and Yugoslav Partisans: A History of World War II Resistance* (Cambridge, 2015), p. 2.

18. Ivana Pantelić, 'Yugoslav Female Partisans in World War II', *Cahiers balkanique*, Vol. 43, No. 1 (2013), p. 3; Batinić, *Women and Yugoslav Partisans*, p. 2.

19. Gow, *Legitimacy and the Military*, p. 54; Sabrina Ramet, *The Three Yugoslavias: State-Building and Legitimation, 1918–2004* (Indiana, 2006), p. 153.

20. Deakin, *The Embattled Mountain*, p. 106.

21. Adam Roberts, *Nations in Arms: The Theory and Practice of Territorial Defence* (London, 1976), p. 124.

22. Marko Attila Hoare, *Genocide and Resistance in Hitler's Bosnia: The Partisans and the Chetniks, 1941–1943* (London, 2006), pp. 201–3.

23. Johnson, 'The Role of the Military in Yugoslavia', p. 182.

24. Dedijer, *Tito Speaks*, p. 244.

25. James Gow, *The Serbian Project and Its Adversaries: A Strategy of War Crimes* (London, 2003), p. 35.

26. Josip Broz Tito, *The Selected Works of Josip Broz Tito* (New York, 2013), pp. 25–9.

27. Branko Mamula, *Small Countries' Defence* (Belgrade, 1988), p. 201.

28. Roberts, *Nations in Arms*, p. 124.

29. Miloš Vasić, 'The Yugoslav Army and the Post-Yugoslav Armies', in David Dyker & Ivan Vejvoda, eds, *Yugoslavia and After: A Study in Fragmentation, Despair and Rebirth* (Harlow, 1996), p. 120.

30. Gow, *Legitimacy and the Military*, p. 42.

31. Jeronim Perović, 'The Tito–Stalin Split: A Reassessment in Light of New Evidence', *Journal of Cold War Studies*, Vol. 9, No. 2 (2007), p. 34.

32. Robert Niebuhr, 'Enlarging Yugoslavia: Tito's Quest for Expansion, 1945–1948', *European History Quarterly*, Vol. 47, No. 2 (2017), p. 287.

33. Perović, 'The Tito–Stalin Split', p. 60.

34. Dulić & Kostić, 'Yugoslavs in Arms', p. 1058; Johnson, 'The Role of the Military in Yugoslavia', p. 183.

35. Dulić & Kostić, 'Yugoslavs in Arms', p. 1058.

36. Gow, *Legitimacy and the Military*, p. 43.

37. Roberts, *Nations in Arms*, p. 147.

38. Gow, *Legitimacy and the Military*, p. 44; Johnson, 'The Role of the Military in Yugoslavia', p. 184.

39. Roberts, *Nations in Arms*, p. 149.

40. Constituent Assembly of the Federative People's Republic of Yugoslavia, *Constitution of the Federal People's Republic of Yugoslavia* (Belgrade, 1946).

41. Ramet, *Nationalism and Federalism in Yugoslavia*, p. 55.

42. Constituent Assembly of the Federative People's Republic of Yugoslavia, *Constitution of the Federal People's Republic of Yugoslavia*.

43. Almost all ethnic Germans left Yugoslavia by the end of the 1950s. Ramet, *Nationalism and Federalism in Yugoslavia*, p. 55; Steffen Prauser & Stanislav Sretenovic, 'The "Expulsion" of the German Speaking Minority from Yugoslavia', in Steffan Prauser & Arfon Rees, eds, *The Expulsion of the 'German' Communities from Eastern Europe at the End of the Second World War*, EUI Working Paper HEC (Florence, 2004), pp. 54–6.

44. Gow, *Legitimacy and the Military*, p. 31.

45. Johnson, 'The Role of the Military in Yugoslavia', p. 198; Mile Bjelajac, *Jugoslovensko iskustvo sa multietničkom armijom 1918–1991* (Belgrade, 1999), p. 80.

46. Florian Bieber, 'The Role of the Yugoslav People's Army in the Dissolution of Yugoslavia: The Army without a State?' in Lenard Cohen & Jasna Dragović-Soso, eds, *State Collapse in South-Eastern Europe: New Perspectives on Yugoslavia's Disintegration* (Indiana, 2008), p. 305.

47. Mile Bjelajac, 'The Military and Yugoslav Unity', in Dejan Djokić, ed., *Yugoslavism: Histories of a Failed Idea, 1918–1992* (London, 2003), p. 219; Bjelajac, *Jugoslovensko Iskustvo Sa Multietničkom Armijom 1918–1991*, p. 49.

48. Ramet, *Nationalism and Federalism in Yugoslavia*, p. 50.

49. Ibid., p. 51.

50. Ibid.

51. Ibid., p. 179.

52. Slobodan Stankovic, 'Aleksandar Rankovic – Political Profile of a Yugoslav 'Stalinist', *Radio Free Europe* (1983), p. 1.

53. Mensur Seferović, ed., *Armed Forces of the SFRY: On Guard of the Peace and Freedom* (Belgrade, 1977), p. 83.

54. Marko Milivojević, 'The Political Role of the Yugoslav People's Army in Contemporary Yugoslavia', in Marko Milivojević, John Allcock, & Pierre Maurer, eds, *Yugoslavia's Security Dilemmas: Armed Forces, National Defence and Foreign Policy* (Braford, 1988), p. 39.

55. Sabrina Ramet, *The Three Yugoslavias: State-Building and Legitimation, 1918–2005* (Bloomington, 2006), p. 603.

56. Mitja Ribičič, 'The Armed People in Defense of Socialism and Independence', in Olga Mladenović, ed., *The Yugoslav Concept of General People's Defense* (Belgrade, 1970), pp. 31–2.

57. Borba (Belgrade, 1971) quoted in Milivojević, 'The Political Role of the Yugoslav People's Army in Contemporary Yugoslavia', p. 21.

58. Bjelajac, *Jugoslovensko iskustvo sa multietničkom armijom 1918–1991*, p. 100.

59. Ibid., p. 52.

60. Robin Alison Remington, 'The Yugoslav Army in Transition', in Constantine Danopoulos & Daniel Zirker, eds, *Civil–Military Relations in the Soviet and Yugoslav Successor States* (Boulder, 1996), p. 157.

61. Ljubičić, *Total National Defence*, p. 19.

62. Edvard Kardelj, 'Tito and the League of Communists of Yugoslavia' (1967) quoted in Ljubičić, *Total National Defence*, p. 21.
63. Ann Lane, *Yugoslavia: When Ideas Collide* (London, 2004), p. 119.
64. Tamara Pavasović Trošt, 'A Personality Cult Transformed: The Evolution of Tito's Image in Serbian and Croatian Textbooks, 1974–2010', *Studies in Ethnicity and Nationalism*, Vol. 14, No. 1 (2014), pp. 46–7.
65. Miroslav Hadžić, *The Yugoslav People's Agony: The Role of the Yugoslav People's Agony* (Farnham, 2002), p. 56.
66. Slobodan Stankovic, 'Tito Praises Yugoslav Army', *Radio Free Europe* (1971), p. 2.
67. Johnson, 'The Role of the Military in Yugoslavia', p. 187.
68. Anton Bebler, 'Political Pluralism and the Yugoslav Professional Military', in Jim Seroka & Vukasin Pavlovic, eds, *The Tragedy of Yugoslavia: The Failure of Democratic Transformation* (New York, 1992), p. 108.
69. Hadžić, *The Yugoslav People's Agony*, p. 58.
70. Gow, *Legitimacy and the Military*, p. 52.
71. Remington, 'The Yugoslav Army in Transition', p. 156.
72. Dean, 'The Yugoslav Army', p. 85; Vašić, 'The Yugoslav Army and the Post-Yugoslav Armies', p. 116.
73. Anton Bebler, 'Political Pluralism and the Yugoslav Professional Military', pp. 108–19.
74. Seferović, *Armed Forces of the SFRY*, p. 81.
75. Milivojević, 'The Political Role of the Yugoslav People's Army in Contemporary Yugoslavia', p. 31.
76. Bebler, 'Political Pluralism and the Yugoslav Professional Military', p. 122.
77. Ljubičić, *Total National Defence*, p. 340.
78. Zdenko Antic, 'Yugoslav Army Influence to Be Strengthened', Radio Free Europe (1974); Bebler, 'Political Pluralism and the Yugoslav Professional Military', p. 109.
79. Roberts, *Nations in Arms*, p. 158; Bieber, 'The Role of the Yugoslav People's Army in the Dissolution of Yugoslavia', p. 303.
80. Roberts, *Nations in Arms*, pp. 195–6.
81. Vašić, 'The Yugoslav Army and the Post-Yugoslav Armies', p. 120.
82. Tanja Petrović, 'Officers without an Army: Memories of Socialism and Everyday Strategies in Post-Socialist Slovenia', in Breda Luthar & Maruša Pušnik, eds, *Remembering Utopia: The Culture of Everyday Life in Socialist Yugoslavia* (Washington, DC, 2010), p. 96.
83. Milivojević, 'The Political Role of the Yugoslav People's Army in Contemporary Yugoslavia', p. 33.
84. Tito, *The Selected Works of Josip Broz Tito*, p. 26.
85. Vladana Putnik, 'Second World War Monuments in Yugoslavia as Witnesses of the Past and the Future', *Journal of Tourism and Cultural Change*, Vol. 14, No. 3 (2016), p. 208.
86. Ibid., p. 208.
87. Ibid., p. 209.
88. Jurica Pavičić, 'Titoist Cathedrals: The Rise and Fall of Partisan Film', in Gorana Ognjenović & Jasna Jozelić, eds, *Titoism, Self-Determination, Nationalism, Cultural Memory: Volume Two, Tito's Yugoslavia, Stories Untold* (New York, 2016), p. 39.
89. Ibid., p. 43.
90. Richard Mills, *The Politics of Football in Yugoslavia: Sport, Nationalism, and the State* (London, 2018), p. 86.
91. Ibid., pp. 124–5.

92. Roberts, *Nations in Arms*, pp. 186–7.
93. Gow, *Legitimacy and the Military*, p. 23.
94. *Osmi kongres Saveza Komunista Jugoslavije* (Belgrade, 1964) quoted in Ramet, *Nationalism and Federalism in Yugoslavia*, p. 51.
95. Ramet, *Nationalism and Federalism in Yugoslavia*, pp. 51–2.
96. Milan Miladinović, *Jugoslovenski socijalistički patriotizm* (Belgrade, 1976) quoted in Ramet, *Nationalism and Federalism in Yugoslavia*, pp. 53–4.
97. Ramet, *Nationalism and Federalism in Yugoslavia*, pp. 51–4.
98. Dulić & Kostić, 'Yugoslavs in Arms', p. 1059.
99. Dean, 'The Yugoslav Army', p. 87; Johnson, 'The Role of the Military in Yugoslavia', pp. 191–2.
100. Roberts, *Nations in Arms*, p. 158.
101. Johnson, 'The Role of the Military in Yugoslavia', p. 184.
102. Bebler, 'Political Pluralism and the Yugoslav Professional Military', p. 122.
103. Gow, *Legitimacy and the Military*, p. 45.
104. Ljubičić, *Total National Defence*, pp. 276–7.
105. A. Ross Johnson, *Total National Defence in Yugoslavia* (Santa Monica, 1971), p. 4.
106. Ljubičić, *Total National Defence*, p. 277.
107. Excerpts from the 1969 National Defence Law can be found in Mladenović, *The Yugoslav Concept of General People's Defense*, pp. 318–21.
108. The Communist Party of Yugoslavia was renamed the League of Communists of Yugoslavia in 1952. Mijalko Todorović, 'The Essence of the Concept of General People's Defense', in Mladenović, *The Yugoslav Concept of General People's Defense*, p. 45.
109. Florence Gaub, *Military Integration after Civil Wars: Multi-Ethnic Armies, Identity and Post-conflict Reconstruction* (London, 2001), p. 83.
110. Enloe, *Ethnic Soldiers*, p. 173.
111. Constitution of the Socialist Federal Republic of Yugoslavia (Belgrade, 1974), Article 243.
112. Gow, *Legitimacy and the Military*, p. 31.
113. Johnson, 'The Role of the Military in Yugoslavia', p. 185.
114. Nikola Ljubičić, 'General People's Defense – The Guarantee of Independence for Socialist Yugoslavia', in Mladenović, *The Yugoslav Concept of General People's Defense*, p. 37.
115. Constitution of the Socialist Federal Republic of Yugoslavia (Belgrade, 1974), Article 240.
116. Ibid., Article 242.
117. Herrick, *The Yugoslav People's Army*, p. 76.
118. Zdenko Antic, 'National Structure of the Yugoslav Army Leadership', *Radio Free Europe* (1972), p. 3.
119. Bjelajac, *Jugoslovensko iskustvo sa multietničkom armijom 1918–1991*, p. 101.
120. Ibid.
121. Ibid., pp. 103–6.
122. James Gow, *The Serbian Project and Its Adversaries* (London, 2003), p. 55.
123. Ibid., pp. 56–7.
124. Miroslav Hadžić, *The Yugoslav People's Agony: The Role of the Yugoslav People's Army* (Farnham, 2002), p. 260.
125. Ibid., p. 259.
126. Ramet, *Nationalism and Federalism in Yugoslavia*, p. 50.

127. Bebler, 'Political Pluralism and the Yugoslav Professional Military', p. 125.
128. Petrović, 'Officers without an Army', p. 98; Johnson, 'The Role of the Military in Yugoslavia', p. 186.
129. Slobodan Stankovic, 'What Does the Yugoslav Army Think?' *Radio Free Europe* (1971), pp. 1–2.
130. Slobodan Stankovic, 'Yugoslav Defense Minister Calls the Army the "Backbone of the System"', *Radio Free Europe* (1983), pp. 4–5.

## 3 The Army of Republika Srpska

1. See Chapter 1, in this book.
2. Many Bosnian Serbs dismissed the nationalist leaders in favour of BiH's ostensibly inclusive government, including significant numbers from Tuzla and 80,000 Serbs from Sarajevo, many of whom helped defend their cities. Misha Glenny, *The Fall of Yugoslavia* (London, 1996), p. 218.
3. Marko Attila Hoare, 'Whose Is the Partisan Movement? Serbs, Croats and the Legacy of a Shared Resistance', *Journal of Slavic Military Studies*, Vol. 15, No. 4 (2002), p. 26.
4. Ibid., p. 27.
5. See Chapter 2 in this book.
6. Ejup Ganić, 'Interview for *The Death of Yugoslavia* by the BBC', Liddell Hart Centre for Military Archives (1995), p. 5.
7. Prosecutor vs. Duško Tadić, 'Opinion and Judgment', *IT-94-1-T* (ICTY, 1997), p. 38.
8. Julian Borger, 'Brutal Cog in Serb Machine', *The Guardian* (17 January 2000).
9. James Gow, *The Serbian Project and Its Adversaries: A Strategy of War Crimes* (London, 2003), p. 61.
10. Prosecutor vs. Slobodan Milošević, 'Mustafa Candić, Testimony before the Court', *IT-02-54* (ICTY, 2002), p. 12742.
11. Prosecutor vs. Ratko Mladić, 'Fourth Amended Indictment', *IT-09-92-PT* (ICTY, 2011), p. 2.
12. Central Intelligence Agency, Office of Russian and European Analysis, *Balkan Battlegrounds: A Military History of the Yugoslav Conflict, 1990–1995* (Washington, DC, 2002), p. 129.
13. Borisav Jović, *Poslednji dani SFRJ: Dnevne zabeleške iz perioda 15. V 1989–8. VII 1992* (Belgrade, 2000), p. 420.
14. Steven Burg & Paul Shoup, *The War in Bosnia-Herzegovina: Ethnic Conflict and International Intervention* (New York, 2000), p. 47.
15. *Balkan Battlegrounds*, p. 127.
16. Radovan Karadžić, 'Interview for *The Death of Yugoslavia* by the BBC', Liddell Hart Centre for Military Archives (1995), p. 3.
17. Burg & Shoup, *The War in Bosnia-Herzegovina*, p. 120.
18. Prosecutor vs. Tadić, 'Opinion and Judgment', p. 34.
19. Ibid., p. 35.
20. Prosecutor vs. Duško Tadić, 'James Gow, Testimony before the Court', *IT-94-1-T* (ICTY, 1996), p. 376; Gow, *The Serbian Project and Its Adversaries*, p. 122.
21. Kenneth Morrison, *Sarajevo's Holiday Inn on the Frontline of Politics and War* (London, 2018), pp. 83–4.

22. Vinko Pandurević, *Srbi u Bosni i Hercegovini: od deklaracije do konstitucije* (Belgrade, 2012), p. 34; Gow, *The Serbian Project and Its Adversaries*, p. 174.
23. Morrison, *Sarajevo's Holiday Inn on the Frontline of Politics and War*, p. 88.
24. Prosecutor vs. Tadić, 'Opinion and Judgment', p. 35.
25. Bosnian Serb Assembly, *Ustav Republike Srpske, sedmi deo*, Službeni glasnik (16 March 1992).
26. Gow, *The Serbian Project and Its Adversaries*, p. 129.
27. Colm Doyle, *Witness to War Crimes: Memoirs of a Peacekeeper in Bosnia* (Barnsley, 2018), p. 123.
28. Radovan Karadžić, 'Interview for *The Death of Yugoslavia* by the BBC', p. 3.
29. Morrison, *Sarajevo's Holiday Inn on the Frontline of Politics and War*, pp. 107–8.
30. *Balkan Battlegrounds*, p. 129.
31. Marko Attila Hoare, *How Bosnia Armed* (London, 2004), p. 40; Gow, *The Serbian Project and Its Adversaries*, p. 60.
32. The VRS would retain the institution 'Headquarters' (*Glavni Štab*) until 1996, when it was replaced with the more conventional 'General Staff' (*Đeneralštab*). Manojlo Milovanović, 'Stvaranje i razvoj vojne Republike Srpske u toku odbrambeno otadžbinskog rata u BiH, 1992. do 1995. God', in Vlada Republike Srpske, *Vojska Republike Srpske u odbrambeno-otadžbinskom ratu: Aspekti, organizacija, operacije* (Banja Luka, 2011), p. 28.
33. Milovanović, 'Stvaranje i razvoj vojne Republike Srpske', p. 28.
34. Ibid.
35. Ibid.
36. Ibid.
37. Ibid.
38. Bosnian Serb Assembly, *Odluka o formiranju vojske Srpske Republike Bosne i Herzegovine* (Banja Luka, 1992).
39. Gow, *The Serbian Project and Its Adversaries*, p. 62.
40. *Balkan Battlegrounds*, p. 130.
41. Gow, *The Serbian Project and Its Adversaries*, p. 77.
42. *Balkan Battlegrounds*, p. 130; Gow, *The Serbian Project and Its Adversaries*, p. 77.
43. Gow, *The Serbian Project and Its Adversaries*, p. 91.
44. Ibid., p. 182.
45. *Balkan Battlegrounds*, p. 130; Gow, *The Serbian Project and Its Adversaries*, p. 163.
46. Gow, *The Serbian Project and Its Adversaries*, p. 77.
47. The SVK was formally established on 19 March 1992.
48. Hoare, *How Bosnia Armed*, p. 69.
49. Bojan Dimitrijević, interview with the author (15 October 2017).
50. Doyle, *Witness to War Crimes*, pp. 27–8.
51. Milutin Kukanjac, 'Interview for *The Death of Yugoslavia* by the BBC', Liddell Hart Centre for Military Archives (1994), p. 18.
52. Bojan Dimitrijević, interview with the author (15 October 2017).
53. *Balkan Battlegrounds*, p. 130; Jovan Divjak, 'The First Phase, 1992–1993: Struggle for Survival and Genesis of the Army of Bosnia-Herzegovina', in Branka Magaš & Ivo Zanić, eds, *The War in Croatia and Bosnia-Herzegovina 1991–1995* (London, 2013), p. 143.
54. Prosecutor vs. Tadić, 'Opinion and Judgment', p. 32.
55. *Balkan Battlegrounds*, p. 130.
56. Ibid., p. 128.

57. Doyle, *Witness to War Crimes*, p. 52.
58. Prosecutor vs. Slobodan, 'Mustafa Candić, Testimony before the Court', pp. 12780–4.
59. Ibid., p. 12779.
60. Doyle, *Witness to War Crimes*, p. 41.
61. Ibid., p. 161.
62. *Balkan Battlegrounds*, p. 146.
63. Ibid., p. 145.
64. Ibid., p. 147.
65. Ibid., p. 140.
66. Divjak, 'The First Phase, 1992–1993', p. 160.
67. *Balkan Battlegrounds*, p. 149.
68. Prosecutor vs. Zdravko Tolimir et al., 'Second Consolidated Amended Indictment', *IT-05-88-PT* (ICTY, 2005), p. 5.
69. *Balkan Battlegrounds*, p. 142.
70. Milovanović, 'Stvaranje i razvoj vojne Republike Srpske', p. 32.
71. *Balkan Battlegrounds*, p. 141.
72. Radovan Karadžić, 'Interview for *The Death of Yugoslavia* by the BBC', p. 16.
73. The Sarajevo–Romanija Corps was formed from the JNA IV Corps, which included five tank battalions and an artillery regiment, supplemented by six brigades of light infantry raised from the local TO. *Balkan Battlegrounds*, p. 153.
74. Such comments may, of course, have constituted part of a campaign of disinformation. Života Panić, 'Interview for *The Death of Yugoslavia* by the BBC', Liddell Hart Centre for Military Archives (1995), pp. 39–40.
75. United Nations Security Council Resolution 757 (30 May 1992).
76. Milovanović, 'Stvaranje i razvoj vojne Republike Srpske', p. 31.
77. The corps were as follows: VRS Headquarters, I Krajina, II Krajina, Eastern Bosnia, Sarajevo-Romanija, Herzegovina. International Institute of Strategic Studies, *The Military Balance, 1993* (London, 1993), p. 74.
78. Jovo Blažanović, *Generali Vojske Republike Srpske* (Banja Luka, 2005), pp. 71–9.
79. Milovanović, 'Stvaranje i razvoj vojne Republike Srpske', p. 34.
80. Vladimir Petrović, 'Serbian Political Elites and the Vance–Owen Peace Plan', in Florian Bieber, Armina Galijaš, & Rory Archer, eds, *Debating the End of Yugoslavia* (London, 2014), p. 194.
81. Nina Caspersen, *Contested Nationalism: Serb Elite Rivalry in Croatia and Bosnia in the 1990s* (New York, 2010), p. 138.
82. Ibid.
83. Prosecutor vs. Slobodan Milošević, 'David Owen, Testimony before the Court', *IT-02-54* (ICTY, 2003), p. 28562.
84. Petrović, 'Serbian Political Elites and the Vance-Owen Peace Plan', p. 199.
85. Brendan O'Shea, *Bosnia's Forgotten Battlefield: Bihać* (Stroud, 2012), pp. 15–28.
86. Hoare, *How Bosnia Armed*, p. 114.
87. O'Shea, *Bosnia's Forgotten Battlefield*, pp. 22–3; *Balkan Battlegrounds*, p. 189.
88. *Balkan Battlegrounds*, p. 189.
89. International Institute of Strategic Studies, *The Military Balance, 1994* (London, 1994), p. 84.
90. This practice effectively came to an end following the January 1994 Washington Agreement.
91. Aziz Tafro, *Ruski i Grčki plaćenici u ratu u Bosni i Herzegovini* (Sarajevo, 2014), p. 32.

92. Tobias Pietz, 'Overcoming the Failings of Dayton: Defense Reform in Bosnia and Herzegovina', in Michael Innes, ed., *Bosnian Security after Dayton: New Perspectives* (London, 2006), pp. 157, 32.
93. Danijel Kovačević, 'Bosnian Serbs Unveil Monument to Russian War Volunteers', *Balkan Insight* (12 April 2017).
94. Takis Michas, *Unholy Alliance: Greece and Milošević's Serbia* (College Station, 2002), p. 18.
95. See Chapter 4 in this book.
96. *Balkan Battlegrounds*, p. 220.
97. Blažanović, *Generali Vojske Republike Srpske*, p. 84; Dušan Kovačevič, 'Vojsku mora financirati država', *Srpska vojska*, No. 16 (January 1994), p. 6.
98. *Balkan Battlegrounds*, p. 220.
99. Mike Redman, 'Joint ABiH–HVO Operations 1994: A Preliminary Analysis of the Battle of Kupres', *Journal of Slavic Military Studies*, No. 16, Vol. 4 (2007), p. 10.
100. Filip Švarm, 'Civilian–Military Games', *Vreme* (24 April 1995).
101. The Owen–Stoltenburg process took place in July and August 1993. For most of 1994, the Contact Group took the lead, and also failed.
102. Emma Daly, 'Serbs Keep Answer to Peace Plan a Secret', *The Independent* (20 July 1994).
103. The SDS dominated every major institution in RS aside from the VRS, including the parliament, the police, Ministry of Defence and industries, so sanctioning RS served to punish the SDS. *Balkan Battlegrounds*, p. 288.
104. Ibid., p. 222.
105. Blažanović, *Generali Vojske Republike Srpske*, p. 84.
106. Raymond Whitaker, 'Looking for Radovan', *The Independent* (21 July 2000).
107. O'Shea, *Bosnia's Forgotten Battlefield*, p. 129.
108. Ibid, p. 117.
109. John Pomfret, 'NATO Jets Bomb Serb Airfield', *Washington Post* (22 November 1994).
110. Emma Daly & Andrew Marshall, 'Bihać Fears Massacre', *The Independent* (27 November 1994); O'Shea, *Bosnia's Forgotten Battlefield*, p. 129.
111. O'Shea, *Bosnia's Forgotten Battlefield*, p. 134.
112. *Balkan Battlegrounds*, p. 222.
113. Ibid.
114. Milovan Milutinović, 'Jedinstvena uz srpski narod', *Srpska vojska*, No. 26 (January 1995), p. 16.
115. Ibid.
116. Milovanović, 'Stvaranje i razvoj vojne Republike Srpske', pp. 38–9.
117. Švarm, 'Civilian–Military Games'.
118. Ibid.
119. *Balkan Battlegrounds*, p. 301.
120. Ibid., p. 304.
121. Milovan Milutinović, 'Stasala uz narod', *Srpska vojska*, No. 30 (June 1995), p. 5.
122. Presiding Judge Almiro Rodrigues, 'Radislav Krstic Becomes the First Person to Be Convicted of Genocide at the ICTY and Is Sentenced to 46 Years Imprisonment', *ICTY Press Release* (ICTY, 2001).
123. Michas, *Unholy Alliance*, p. 1.
124. *Balkan Battlegrounds*, p. 370.
125. Gow, *The Serbian Project and Its Adversaries*, p. 192.

126. Ibid.

127. Caspersen, *Contested Nationalism*, p. 139.

128. Milan Martić's order to evacuate civilians from areas of 'Republic of Serb Krajina', Scan (ICTY, August 1995), available at: http://icr.icty.org/LegalRef/CMSDocStore/Public/BCS/Exhibit/Indexable/IT-06-90/ACE80815R0000319913.tif (accessed 31 October 2018).

129. Emma Daly, 'Bosnian Serbs Fall Out as Knin Is Lost', *The Independent* (6 August 1995).

130. Gow, *The Serbian Project and Its Adversaries*, p. 193.

131. Daly, 'Bosnian Serbs Fall Out as Knin Is Lost'.

132. Švarm, 'Civilian–Military Games'.

133. The HV could call upon an additional 220,000 reservists. International Institute of Strategic Studies, *The Military Balance, 1996* (London, 1996), p. 83.

134. Ryan Hendrickson, 'History: Crossing the Rubicon', *NATO Review* (NATO, 2005).

135. Ibid.

136. Michael Rose, *Fighting for Peace: Lessons from Bosnia* (New York, 1999), p. 349.

137. Gow, *The Serbian Project and Its Adversaries*, p. 198.

138. Ibid., p. 197.

139. Emma Daly, 'Thousands Flee as Bosnian Rebel Crushed: Muslim Troops Take Control of Bihac Fiefdom Run by "Daddy" Abdic', *The Independent* (10 August 1994).

140. O'Shea, *Bosnia's Forgotten Battlefield*, pp. 225–7.

141. *Balkan Battlegrounds*, p. 376.

142. Trevor Minter, interview with the author (10 September 2018).

143. Daniel Williams, 'NATO Continues Extensive Bombing across Bosnia', *Washington Post* (31 August 1995).

144. Gow, *The Serbian Project and Its Adversaries*, p. 197.

145. Ibid., p. 198.

146. Fiona Watson, 'Not Peace, but a Big Step Forward', *House of Commons Library, Research Paper 95/102* (October 1995), p. 20.

## 4 The Army of the Republic of Bosnia and Herzegovina and the Croat Defence Council

1. Jovan Divjak, 'The First Phase, 1992–1993: Struggle for Survival and Genesis of the Army of Bosnia-Herzegovina', in Branka Magaš & Ivo Žanić, eds, *The War in Croatia and Bosnia-Herzegovina 1991–1995* (London, 2013), p. 174; Central Intelligence Agency, Office of Russian and European Analysis, *Balkan Battlegrounds: A Military History of the Yugoslav Conflict, 1990–1995* (Washington, DC, 2002), p. 160.

2. CIA, *Balkan Battlegrounds* (Washington, DC, 2002), pp. 223–4.

3. James Gow, *The Serbian Project and Its Adversaries: A Strategy of War Crimes* (London, 2003), p. 256.

4. Quoted in Marko Attila Hoare, *How Bosnia Armed* (London, 2004), p. 119.

5. A detailed account of the civil war between the ARBiH III Corps and HVO troops in Operative Zone Central Bosnia is offered by Charles Shrader in *The Muslim–Croat Civil War in Central Bosnia: A Military History, 1992–1994* (College Station, 2003).

6. These divisions are outlined in more detail in the current chapter on pages 96–100.
7. A detailed account of the development and introduction of the Total National Defence policy which led to the formation of TO forces in each Yugoslav Republic and Autonomous Province can be found in Chapter 2 in this book.
8. Some command functions were re-centralised in 1981, but the republics maintained a key role in defence planning. James Horncastle. 'A House of Cards: The Yugoslav Concept of Total National Defence and Its Critical Weakness', *Macedonian Historical Review*, Vol. 2, No. 1 (2012), pp. 292–3.
9. Yugoslav Socialist Patriotism is discussed in Chapter 2 in this book.
10. Dieter Nohlen & Philip Stöver, *Elections in Europe: A Data Handbook* (Sinzheim, 2010), pp. 329–31.
11. Marko Attila Hoare, 'Civil–Military Relations in Bosnia-Herzegovina 1992–1995', in Branka Magaš & Ivo Zanić, eds, *The War in Croatia and Bosnia-Herzegovina 1991–1995* (London, 2013), p. 181.
12. Rasim Delić, *Armija Republike Bosne i Herzegovine: Nastanak, razvoj i odbrana zemlje, knjiga prva* (Sarajevo, 2007), p. 141.
13. Hoare, 'Civil–Military Relations in Bosnia-Herzegovina 1992–1995', p. 180.
14. Divjak, 'The First Phase', p. 158.
15. Vinko Pandurević, *Srbi u Bosni i Herzegovini: od deklaracije do konstitucije* (Belgrade, 2012), pp. 34–6.
16. Ibid., p. 44.
17. Stjepan Šiber, *Prevare zablude istina: Ratni dnevnik 1992* (Sarajevo, 2000), p. 15.
18. Rasim Delić notes that in 1991, only two of fourteen TO brigade commanders were Bosnian Muslim. Delić, *Armija Republike Bosne i Herzegovine, knjiga prva*, p. 141.
19. Hoare, *How Bosnia Armed*, p. 23.
20. Chuck Sudetic, 'Bosnia Asking U.N. for Peace Forces', *New York Times* (28 March 1992).
21. Alija Izetbegović, *Inescapable Questions: Autobiographical Notes* (Leicester, 2003), p. 116.
22. Steven Burg & Paul Shoup, *The War in Bosnia-Herzegovina: Ethnic Conflict and International Intervention* (New York, 2000), p. 64.
23. James Gow, *The Serbian Project and Its Adversaries: A Strategy of War Crimes* (London, 2003), p. 173.
24. Hoare, *How Bosnia Armed*, p. 52.
25. Divjak, 'The First Phase', p. 158; *Balkan Battlegrounds*, p. 143.
26. Mahmoud Cherif Bassiouni, *Final Report of the United Nations Commission of Experts Established Pursuant to Security Council Resolution 780 (1992): Annex III; The Military Structure, Strategy and Tactics of the Warring Factions* (UN, 1994), pp. 16–17.
27. Of 109 municipal TO staffs, 36 refused to recognize the government of BiH. Divjak, 'The First Phase', p. 183.
28. Most Bosnian Serb officials had left the BiH administration by April 1992; Hoare suggests that a member of the BiH presidency, Fikret Abdić, and the Minister of Interior Alija Delimustafić were working for Yugoslav military intelligence in 1992. Hoare, 'Civil–Military Relations in Bosnia-Herzegovina 1992–1995', p. 181; Major-General Aleksandar Vasilijević, a senior JNA commander, also contends that the KOS had two agents at the very top of the SDA leadership. *Balkan Battlegrounds*, p. 130.
29. Hoare, 'Civil–Military Relations in Bosnia-Herzegovina 1992–1995', p. 180.
30. Rasim Delić, *Armija Republike Bosne i Herzegovine: Nastanak, razvoj I odbrana zemlje, knjiga druga* (Sarajevo, 2007), p. 326.

31. Ibid., p. 328.
32. Delić, *Armija Republike Bosne i Herzegovine, knjiga prva*, p. 157.
33. Sefer Halilović, 'Interview for *The Death of Yugoslavia* by the BBC', Liddell Hart Centre for Military Archives (1995), p. 5.
34. Quoted in CIA, *Balkan Battlegrounds*, p. 130.
35. Alija Izetbegović, 'Speech to the Second Congress of the SDA', *Dnevni avaz* (September 1997), p. 2.
36. CIA, *Balkan Battlegrounds*, p. 132.
37. Halilović, 'Interview for *The Death of Yugoslavia* by the BBC', p. 3; CIA, *Balkan Battlegrounds*, p. 132.
38. CIA, *Balkan Battlegrounds*, p. 132; Kenneth Morrison & Elizabeth Roberts, *The Sandžak: A History* (London, 2013), p. 154.
39. Haris Halilović, 'Efikasnijim komandovanjem do slobode', *Prva linija*, No. 20 (January 1995), p. 4.
40. Divjak, 'The First Phase', p. 160.
41. Burg & Shoup, *The War in Bosnia-Herzegovina*, p. 129.
42. CIA, *Balkan Battlegrounds*, p. 152.
43. CIA, *Balkan Battlegrounds*, p. 152; Hoare, *How Bosnia Armed*, p. 46.
44. Colm Doyle, *Witness to War Crimes: The Memoirs of a Peacekeeper in Bosnia* (Barnsley, 2018), p. 129.
45. Divjak, 'The First Phase', p. 160.
46. Charles Shrader, *The Muslim–Croat Civil War in Central Bosnia, 1992–1994* (College Station, 2003), p. 34.
47. Hoare, *How Bosnia Armed*, p. 52.
48. Doyle, *Witness to War Crimes*, p. 129.
49. Laura Silber & Allan Little, *The Death of Yugoslavia* (London, 1996), p. 293.
50. Ibid.
51. Ibid.
52. Sabrina Ramet, *The Three Yugoslavias: State-Building and Legitimation, 1918–2005* (Indiana, 2006).
53. Jure Krišto, 'Deconstructing the Myth: Franjo Tuđman and Bosnia and Herzegovina', *Review of Croatian History*, Vol. 6, No. 1 (2011), p. 44.
54. Ibid.
55. Ivo Komšić, 'Interview for *The Death of Yugoslavia* by the BBC', Liddell Hart Centre for Military Archives (1995), pp. 5–6.
56. Ibid.
57. Prosecutor vs. Jadranko Prlić et al., 'Indictment', *IT-04-74* (ICTY, 2009), p. 7.
58. Krišto, 'Deconstructing the Myth', pp. 44–5.
59. Prosecutor vs. Jadranko Prlić et al., 'Indictment', p. 1.
60. Shrader, *The Muslim–Croat Civil War in Central Bosnia*, p. 29.
61. CIA, *Balkan Battlegrounds*, p. 134.
62. Prosecutor vs. Jadranko Prlić et al., 'Indictment', p. 3.
63. Ibid., pp. 2–3.
64. CIA, *Balkan Battlegrounds*, p. 134.
65. International Institute of Strategic Studies, *The Military Balance, 1993* (London, 1993), p. 74.
66. Ibid.; Klejda Mulaj, *Politics of Ethnic Cleansing: Nation-State Building and Provision of In/Security in Twentieth Century Balkans* (Lexington, 2010), p. 53; Shrader, *The Muslim–Croat Civil War in Central Bosnia*, p. 62.

67. CIA, *Balkan Battlegrounds*, p. 225.
68. Mulaj, *Politics of Ethnic Cleansing*, p. 53.
69. CIA, *Balkan Battlegrounds*, p. 133.
70. Burg & Shoup, *The War in Bosnia-Herzegovina*, p. 198.
71. CIA, *Balkan Battlegrounds*, p. 133.
72. Shrader, *The Muslim–Croat Civil War in Central Bosnia*, p. 46.
73. Krišto, 'Deconstructing the Myth', p. 46.
74. Hoare, *How Bosnia Armed*, p. 52.
75. Ibid.
76. Hasan Efendić, *Ko je branio Bosnu* (Sarajevo, 1998), p. 143.
77. According to the 1991 Census, Bosnian Serbs constituted 31.21 per cent of the population; 36.3 per cent of municipal TO Commands refused to side with the Bosnian government.
78. Efendić, *Ko je branio Bosnu*, p. 116.
79. Divjak, 'The First Phase', pp. 172–3.
80. Delić, *Armija, knjiga druga*, pp. 332–3.
81. Rasim Hodžić & Šefik Sabljica, eds, *Zbirka propisa iz odbrane* (Sarajevo, 1995), pp. 51–64.
82. Izetbegović, *Inescapable Questions*, p. 138.
83. Omer Karabeg, 'What Really Happened during the Dobrovoljacka Attack? (Interview with Jovan Divjak)', *Radio Free Europe* (8 March 2010).
84. Halilović, 'Interview for *The Death of Yugoslavia* by the BBC', p. 1.
85. Prosecutor vs. Sefer Halilovic, 'Indictment', *IT-01-48-I* (ICTY, 2001), p. 1.
86. Hoare, *How Bosnia Armed*, p. 78.
87. Ibid., p. 79.
88. UN Security Council, Resolution 713 (September 1991).
89. CIA, *Balkan Battlegrounds*, p. 139.
90. Hoare, 'Civil–Military Relations in Bosnia-Herzegovina 1992–1995', p. 184.
91. Divjak, 'The First Phase', p. 163.
92. Izetbegović, *Inescapable Questions*, p. 128.
93. Divjak, 'The First Phase', p. 165.
94. Ibid.
95. These brigades were as follows: I Tuzla, II Tuzla, I Zenica, I Podrina, I Lukavac, CVIII Brčko, I Bihaćka Krajina, the 'King Tomislav' Brigade, and four Sarajevo brigades; Hoare, *How Bosnia Armed*, p. 77.
96. Divjak, 'The First Phase', p. 161.
97. Shrader, *The Muslim–Croat Civil War in Central Bosnia*, p. 29.
98. Divjak, 'The First Phase', pp. 160–1.
99. Ibid.
100. Ibid.
101. Morrison & Roberts, *The Sandžak*, p. 154.
102. Hoare, 'Civil–Military Relations in Bosnia-Herzegovina 1992–1995', p. 188.
103. Shrader, *The Muslim–Croat Civil War in Central Bosnia*, p. 34.
104. Gow, *The Serbian Project and Its Adversaries*, p. 245.
105. Shrader, *The Muslim–Croat Civil War in Central Bosnia*, p. 35.
106. Ibid.
107. Sefer Halilović, *Lukava strategija* (Matica, Sarajevo, 1998), p. 151.
108. Shrader, *The Muslim–Croat Civil War in Central Bosnia*, p. 4.

109. Ajnija Omanić, Mevlida Serdarević, Amer Ovčina, Hajrunisa Omanić, and Jasna Omanić, 'Participation of Women in the 1992–1995 War in Bosnia and Herzegovina', *Acta med-hist Adriat*, Vol. 8, No. 1 (2010), p. 136.
110. Izetbegović, *Inescapable Questions*, p. 140.
111. Mirza Mukić, 'Divizion zemaljskih gromova', *Armija ljiljana*, No. 19 (December 1992), p. 1.
112. Ibid.
113. Anna Calori, 'Salt and Socialism: A Deconstruction of Tuzla's Political Identity in the Context of the Bosnian Conflict', *Ethnopolitics Papers*, No. 35 (2015), pp. 15–18.
114. Ibid.
115. Calori, 'Salt and Socialism', pp. 15–18.
116. Shrader, *The Muslim-Croat Civil War in Central Bosnia*, p. 46.
117. Gow, *The Serbian Project and Its Adversaries*, p. 236.
118. Slobodan Praljak, *Handbook: With Instruction on How to Think (mens rea) and How to Act (actus reas) in Order to Be Declared a Member of the Joint Criminal Enterprise at the International Criminal Tribunal in the Hague, How to Become a Joint Criminal?: Facts* (Zagreb, 2017), p. 174.
119. Ibid.
120. CIA, *Balkan Battlegrounds*, p. 225.
121. Divjak, 'The First Phase', p. 173.
122. Bohdana Dimitrovova, 'Bosniak or Muslim? Dilemma of One Nation with Two Names', *Southeast European Politics*, Vol. 2, No. 2 (2001), pp. 97–8.
123. Divjak, 'The First Phase', p. 162.
124. Šiber, *Prevare labude istina*, p. 218.
125. Halilović, *Lukava Strategija*, p. 151.
126. Divjak, 'The First Phase', p. 162; IISS, *The Military Balance, 1993*, p. 74.
127. Shrader, *The Muslim-Croat Civil War in Central Bosnia*, pp. 22–3.
128. Izetbegović, *Inescapable Questions*, p. 126.
129. CIA, *Balkan Battlegrounds*, p. 207.
130. Silber & Little, *The Death of Yugoslavia*, p. 295.
131. Ibid., p. 181; Shrader. *The Muslim-Croat Civil War in Central Bosnia*, p. 59.
132. Ibid., p. 43.
133. CIA, *Balkan Battlegrounds*, p. 196.
134. Ibid.
135. Ibid., p. 207.
136. Slobodan Praljak, *Development of Political and Military Preparations Regarding the Attacks of ABiH on HVO in Central Bosnia and the Valley of the Neretva River in the Period from 1992–1994: Mostar, ABiH Offensive against HVO 'Neretva 93,' Volunteers from Croatia (HV) in ABiH and HVO, and other Truths: Facts.* (Zagreb, 2014), p. 210.
137. Ibid.
138. CIA, *Balkan Battlegrounds*, p. 180.
139. Ibid., p. 198.
140. Ibid., p. 50.
141. Hoare, *How Bosnia Armed*, p. 91.
142. Ibid.
143. Izetbegović, *Inescapable Questions*, p. 166.
144. Statement of the Executive Board of the SDA (23 October 1993), quoted in Izetbegović, *Inescapable Questions*, pp. 167–8.

145. The Black Swans were one of the ARBiH's most elite units, and would later form the personal guard of Izetbegović whenever he left Sarajevo. Chuck Sudetic, 'Bosnia's Elite Force: Fed, Fit, Muslim', *New York Times* (16 June 1995); Izetbegović, *Inescapable Questions*, p. 167.
146. *Balkan Battlegrounds*, p. 201.
147. Ibid.
148. Ibid.; Hoare, 'Civil–Military Relations in Bosnia-Herzegovina 1992–1995', p. 191.
149. Izetbegović, *Inescapable Questions*, p. 177.
150. Burg & Shoup, *The War in Bosnia-Herzegovina*, p. 293.
151. United States Institute of Peace, *Washington Agreement* (1 March 1994).
152. Divjak, 'The First Phase', p. 165.
153. Haris Halilović, 'Efikasnijim komandovanjem do slobode', *Prva linija*, No. 20 (January 1995), p. 4.
154. CIA, *Balkan Battlegrounds*, p. 287.
155. Delić, *Armija, knjiga druga*, p. 342.
156. CIA, *Balkan Battlegrounds*, pp. 223–4.
157. Ibid.
158. Ibid.
159. Ibid., pp. 233–5.
160. Nermin Butković, 'Napokon bijelim figurama', *Prva linija*, No. 25 (June 1995), p. 4.
161. Izetbegović, *Inescapable Questions*, p. 182.
162. Ibid., p. 187.
163. Ibid., p. 210.
164. Ramet, *The Three Yugoslavias*, p. 389.
165. Faruk Kruševljanin, 'Nova misija velikog ratnika', *Armija ljiljana*, No. 57 (December 1994), p. 3.
166. Hoare, *How Bosnia Armed*, p. 109.
167. Quoted in Hoare, *How Bosnia Armed*, p. 110.
168. Divjak, 'The First Phase', p. 194.
169. 'Dan šehida oživio sjećanja na najbolje sinove BiH', *Klix.ba* (August 2012).
170. Trevor Minter, interview with the author (10 September 2018).
171. Izetbegović, *Inescapable Questions*, pp. 190, 204.
172. Delić, *Armija, knjiga druga*, p. 360.
173. Haris Halilović, 'Efikasnijim komandovanjem do slobode', *Prva linija*, No. 20 (January 1995), p. 4.
174. International Institute for Strategic Studies, *Military Balance, 1995* (London, 1993), pp. 79–80.
175. Ibid.
176. CIA, *Balkan Battlegrounds*, p. 284.
177. Misha Glenny, *The Fall of Yugoslavia*, 3rd edn (London, 1996), p. 265.
178. Ibid.
179. CIA, *Balkan Battlegrounds*, p. 309.
180. Ibid., p. 388.
181. Delić, *Armija, knjiga druga*, pp. 370–1.
182. Ceasefire Agreement for Bosnia and Herzegovina, *Annex II* (5 October 1995).
183. Minter, interview with the author (10 September 2018).
184. Ibid.
185. Delić, *Armija, knjiga druga*, p. 370.
186. CIA, *Balkan Battlegrounds*, p. 134.

187. Hoare, 'Civil–Military Relations in Bosnia-Herzegovina 1992–1995', p. 198.
188. Izetbegović, *Inescapable Questions*, p. 355.

# 5 The entity armies, 1995–2002

1. International Institute of Strategic Studies, *The Military Balance, 1996* (London, 1996), p. 81; Tobias Pietz, 'Defense Reform and the Failings of Dayton', in Michael A. Innes, ed. *Bosnian Security after Dayton: New Perspectives* (London, 2006), p. 156.
2. General Framework Agreement for Peace in Bosnia and Herzegovina (Dayton, 1995).
3. Ibid., Annex 1-A (Dayton, 1995).
4. Richard Holbrooke, *To End a War* (New York, 1998), p. 363.
5. General Framework Agreement for Peace in Bosnia and Herzegovina.
6. Ibid.
7. The PIC is composed of 55 countries and agencies that continue to support the peace process in BiH.
8. OHR, 'The Mandate of the OHR', *OHR Press Office* (16 February 2012).
9. Ibid.
10. Election results and detailed information on the electoral process are publicly available from the Organisation for Security and Cooperation in Europe Office for Democratic Institutions and Human Rights.
11. Such figures include professional soldiers, conscripts, and reservists. World Bank, *Technical Annex to Bosnia and Herzegovina for an Emergency Demobilization and Reintegration Project* (Washington, 1996), p. 1.
12. Pietz, 'Defense Reform and the Failings of Dayton', p. 157.
13. See Chapter 1 for more on using the military as a social agent or 'school of the nation'.
14. Rohan Maxwell, 'Bosnia-Herzegovina: From Three Armies to One', in Roy Licklider, ed., *New Armies from Old: Merging Competing Military Forces after Civil Wars* (Washington, DC, 2014), p. 183.
15. Holbrooke, *To End a War*, p. 363.
16. Carl Bildt, *Peace Journey: The Struggle for Peace in Bosnia* (London, 1998), p. 135.
17. General Framework Agreement for Peace in Bosnia and Herzegovina, Annex 4 (Dayton, 1995).
18. General Framework Agreement for Peace in Bosnia and Herzegovina.
19. General Framework Agreement for Peace in Bosnia and Herzegovina, Article 4 (Florence, 1996); General Framework Agreement for Peace in Bosnia and Herzegovina, Article 2 (Vienna, 1996).
20. The fourth army was SFOR; Rupert Wolfe Murray, ed., *IFOR on IFOR: NATO Peacekeepers in Bosnia-Herzegovina* (Edinburgh, 1996), p. 4.
21. OHR, Department for Legal Affairs, *Constitution of Republika Srpska* (Official Gazette of RS, 2000), Article 70.
22. Matthew Morton, 'Three Hearts in the Chest of One State: The Armed Forces of Bosnia and Herzegovina', *Journal of Slavic Military Studies*, Vol. 25, No. 4 (2012), p. 517.
23. Florence Gaub, *Military Integration after Civil Wars: Multiethnic Armies, Identity and Post-conflict Reconstruction* (London, 2011), p. 94.
24. Cody Phillips, *Bosnia-Herzegovina: The U.S. Army's Role in Peace Enforcement Operations 1995-2004*, US Army Center of Military History (Pub 70-97-1, 2005),

p. 15; Mike O'Conner, 'NATO Plans to Disarm Paramilitary Forces in Bosnia', *New York Times* (9 August 1997).

25. Murray, *IFOR on IFOR*, p. 43.
26. United States Institute of Peace, *Washington Agreement* (1 March 1994).
27. See Chapter 4 in this book.
28. Ibid.
29. United States Institute of Peace, *Washington Agreement*.
30. Jane Perlez, 'Muslim and Croatian Leaders Approve Federation for Bosnia', *New York Times* (15 August 1996).
31. Alija Izetbegović, *Inescapable Questions: Autobiographical Notes* (Leicester, 2003), p. 512.
32. Ibid., p. 440.
33. Taib Terović, 'U nove pobjede', *Prva linija*, No. 41 (April 1996), p. 6.
34. Rasim Delić, 'Svi moramo biti armija', *Prva linija*, No. 50 (April 1997), p. 4.
35. See Chapter 4 in this book.
36. Sergeant Peter Fitzgerald, 'The Armed Forces in Bosnia and Herzegovina', *SFOR Informer*, Vol. 127 (SFOR, 2001), p. 1; Charles Perry & Dimitris Keridis, *Defense Reform, Modernization, and Military Cooperation in Southeastern Europe* (Dulles, 2004), p. 262.
37. DRC Team 8, *Concept Paper on Parallelism* (Sarajevo, 2005).
38. International Crisis Group, 'Is Dayton Failing?: Bosnia Four Years after the Peace Agreement', *Balkans Report*, No. 80 (1999), p. 9.
39. General Framework Agreement for Peace in Bosnia and Herzegovina, Annex 1-A (Dayton, 1995).
40. The November 2000 elections were accompanied by a referendum, deemed illegal by the OSCE, on Croat autonomy in BiH. This was followed by a series of boycotts of federal institutions, the formation of parallel governance structures, and widespread protests. Thierry Domin, 'Political Situation in Bosnia and Herzegovina', *SFOR Informer*, Vol. 126 (14 November 2001).
41. Outi Keränen, 'International Statebuilding as Contentious Politics: The Case of Post-conflict Bosnia and Herzegovina', *Journal of Nationalism and Ethnicity*, Vol. 31, No. 3 (2013), p. 362.
42. OHR, *Chronology/Monthly Tracker 2001* (2001).
43. Fitzgerald, 'The Armed Forces in Bosnia and Herzegovina', p. 1.
44. Paul Williams, 'Promise Them Anything', *Weekly Standard* (18 December 1995).
45. Jane Sharp, 'Dayton Report Card', *International Security*, Vol. 22, No. 3 (1997), p. 116.
46. Peter Singer, *Corporate Warriors: The Rise of the Privatised Military Industry* (New York, 2003), p. 128.
47. Raffi Gregorian, interview with the author (18 July 2017).
48. Christopher Lamb, 'The Bosnian Train and Equip Programme: A Lesson in Inter-Agency Integration of Hard and Soft Power', *Institute for National Strategic Studies Strategic Perspectives*, No. 15 (2014), p. 11.
49. Editorial, 'Profesionalci dolaze!' *Prva linija*, No. 42 (May 1996), p. 1.
50. Ibid., p. 3.
51. Stockholm International Peace Research Institute, *Transfers of Major Conventional Weapons: Sorted by Supplier. Deals with Deliveries or Orders Made for Year Range 1996 to 2015*.
52. 'Temelj vojne organizacije Vojske Federacije BiH', *Prva linija*, No. 57 (December 1997), p. 9; Singer, *Corporate Warriors*, p. 129; Rohan Maxwell, interview with the author (20 October 2016).

53. Rohan Maxwell, interview with the author (20 October 2016).
54. Lamb, 'The Bosnian Train and Equip Programme: A Lesson in Inter-Agency Integration of Hard and Soft Power', p. 11.
55. Raffi Gregorian, interview with the author (18 July 2017).
56. Vinko Pandurević, *Oslovi doctrine odbrane republike srpske* (Belgrade, 1999), p. 107.
57. Graeme Herd & Tom Tracey, 'Democratic Civil Military Relations in Bosnia and Herzegovina: A New Paradigm for Protectorates?' *Conflict Studies Research Centre: Balkan Series*, Vol. 5, No. 66 (November 2005), p. 8
58. S. Poskić, 'Obuka – Imperativ daljeg razvoja', *Prva linija*, No. 58 (January 1998), p. 5.
59. Ibid., pp. 4–5.
60. Braco Kalaba, 'Obuka po svjetskim standardima', *Prva linija*, No. 49 (March 1997), p. 1; Braco Kalaba, 'Oružane snage za 21. stoljeće', *Prva linija*, No. 48 (February 1997), p. 1.
61. Ratko Mladić, 'Novogodišnja i božićna poruka glavnog štaba vojske Republike Srpske', *Srpska vojska*, No. 34 (December 1995), p. 4.
62. Ibid.
63. Ibid.
64. Ibid.
65. Raymond Whitaker, 'Looking for Radovan', *The Independent* (21 July 2000).
66. Prosecutor vs. Ratko Mladić, 'Amended Indictment', *IT-95–5/18-I* (ICTY, 2002), p. 1.
67. Julian Borger, *The Butcher's Trail: How the Search for Balkan War Criminals Became the Most Successful Manhunt in History* (New York, 2016), p. 206.
68. Tony Barber, 'Breakthrough as Karadžić Steps Down', *The Independent* (20 July 1996).
69. BBC, '"War Criminal" Karadžić Resigns', *BBC* (19 July 1996).
70. Prosector vs. Slobodan Milošević, Vojslav Šešelj, Testimony before the Court', *IT-02-54* (ICTY, 2005), p. 43368.
71. Ibid.
72. Ibid., pp. 43371–3.
73. Manojlo Milovanović, 'Stvaranje i razvoj vojne Republike Srpske u toku odbrambeno otadžbinskog rata u BiH, 1992. do 1995. God.' in Vlada Republike Srpske, *Vojska Republuke Srpske u odbrambeno-otadžbinskom ratu: Aspekti, organizacija, operacije* (Banja Luka, 2011), p. 35.
74. James Gow & Ivan Zverzhanovski, *Security, Democracy and War Crimes: Security Sector Transformation in Serbia* (Basingstoke, 2013), p. 124.
75. Ibid.
76. Vašić, 'The Yugoslav Army and the Post-Yugoslav Armies', p. 133.
77. Ibid.
78. Perry & Keridis, *Defense Reform, Modernization, and Military Cooperation in Southeastern Europe*, p. 266.
79. International Crisis Group, 'Is Dayton Failing?' p. 9.
80. Borislav Đurđević, 'Stvorena u borbi', *Srpska vojska*, No. 38 (June 1996), p. 10; see Chapter 3 in this book.
81. Gulner Aybet, 'NATO Conditionality in Bosnia and Herzegovina: Defense Reform and State-Building', *Problems of Post-Communism*, Vol. 57, No. 5 (September 2010), p. 26.
82. Rohan Maxwell & John Andreas Olsen, *Destination NATO: Defence Reform in Bosnia-Herzegovina, 2003–13* (London, 2013), p. 24; SIPRI, *Transfers of Major Conventional Weapons: Sorted by Supplier. Deals with Deliveries or Orders Made for Year Range 1996 to 2015.*

83. Rohan Maxwell, interview with the author (20 October 2016).
84. Borislav Đurđević, 'Odbrana je najvažniji posao države' (Interview with President of RS Biljana Plavšić), *Srpska vojska*, No. 43 (May 1997), p. 6.
85. Herd & Tracey, 'Democratic Civil Military Relations in Bosnia and Herzegovina', p. 8.
86. James Gow, *Legitimacy and the Military: The Yugoslav Crisis* (London, 1992), p. 31.
87. Đurđević, 'Stvorena u borbi', p. 9.
88. Đurđević, 'Odbrana je najvažniji posao države', p. 9.
89. Since unification it has also been celebrated as the Day of the 3rd Infantry (Republika Srpska) Regiment of the OSBiH.
90. Đurđević, 'Odbrana je najvažniji posao države', p. 6; M. Dizdar, 'Vojska je stub jedinstva Republike Srpske', *Srpska vojska*, No. 50 (May 1998), p. 8.
91. Borislav Đurđević, 'Vojska je stub jedinstva republike srpske', *Srpska Vojska*, No. 50 (May 1998), p. 1.
92. Borislav Đurđević, 'Neka sećanje na žrtve bude merilo naše ljubavi za republiku srpsku', *Srpska Vojska*, No. 50 (May 1998), p. 9.
93. PIC, *PIC Declaration*, PIC Main Meeting (Madrid, 16 December 1998), Military Issues Annex.
94. Ibid.
95. David Lightburn, 'Seeking Security Solutions', *NATO Review* (1 December 2000), p. 1.
96. PIC, *PIC Declaration*, Military Issues Annex.
97. Ibid.
98. Government Accountability Office, *Bosnia: Crime and Corruption Threaten Successful Implementation of the Dayton Peace Agreement* (Washington, DC, 2000), p. 2.
99. Christopher Bennett, *Bosnia's Paralysed Peace* (London, 2016), p. 114.
100. Bennett, *Bosnia's Paralysed Peace*, pp. 147–8; Paddy Ashdown, *Swords and Ploughshares: Bringing Peace to the 21st Century* (London, 2007), p. 245.
101. Perry & Keridis, *Defense Reform, Modernization, and Military Cooperation in Southeastern Europe*, p. 255.
102. Timothy Edwards, *Defence Reform in Croatia and Serbia-Montenegro* (Oxford, 2003), p. 38.
103. PIC, *PIC Declaration*, PIC Main Meeting (Brussels, 24 May 2000), Military Issues Annex.
104. Major General (retd) John Drewienkiewicz, 'Budgets as Arms Control – the Bosnian Experience', *RUSI Journal*, Vol. 148, No. 2 (2003), p. 32.
105. Herd & Tracey, 'Democratic Civil Military Relations in Bosnia and Herzegovina', p. 7.
106. Fitzgerald, 'The Armed Forces in Bosnia and Herzegovina', p. 1.
107. Ibid.
108. Herd & Tracey, 'Democratic Civil Military Relations in Bosnia and Herzegovina', p. 7.
109. Perry & Keridis, *Defense Reform, Modernization, and Military Cooperation in Southeastern Europe*, p. 257.
110. International Crisis Group, 'Bosnia's Alliance for (Smallish) Change', *Balkans Report No. 132* (2002), p. 1.
111. Julian Borger, '14 Years a Fugitive: The Hunt for Ratko Mladić, the Butcher of Bosnia', *The Guardian* (21 January 2016).
112. Edwards, *Defence Reform in Croatia and Serbia-Montenegro*, p. 65.
113. Aybet, 'NATO Conditionality in Bosnia and Herzegovina', p. 26.
114. NATO Secretary General Lord George Robertson, *Joint Press Conference* (Sarajevo, 13 July 2001).

115. 'Running Bosnia: The Viceroy Rules, OK? Not Everyone Thinks So', *The Economist* (24 July 2003).
116. Paddy Ashdown, *Inaugural Speech to BiH Parliament* (Sarajevo, 27 May 2002).
117. Paddy Ashdown, interview with the author (22 March 2016).
118. Ibid.
119. Ibid.
120. Drewienkiewicz, 'Budgets as Arms Control – the Bosnian Experience', p. 30.
121. Herd & Tracey, 'Democratic Civil Military Relations in Bosnia and Herzegovina', p. 8; Ashdown, *Swords and Ploughshares*, p. 235.
122. N. Zelenović, 'Ostaju dvije vojske', *Glas srpski* (21 September 2002), p. 3.
123. Ibid.
124. Paddy Ashdown, *Swords and Ploughshares*, p. 246.
125. Outi Keränen, *The Contentious Politics of Statebuilding: Strategies and Dynamics* (London, 2017), p. 70.
126. Ashdown, *Swords and Ploughshares*, p. 246.
127. Louis-Alexandre Berg, 'From Weakness to Strength: The Political Roots of Security Sector Reform in Bosnia and Herzegovina', *International Peacekeeping*, Vol. 21, No. 2 (2014), p. 155.
128. Lightburn, 'Seeking Security Solutions', p. 5.
129. Johan Galtung, 'Violence, Peace, and Peace Research', *Journal of Peace Research*, Vol. 6, No. 3 (1969), p. 183.
130. Anders Themnér & Thomas Ohlson, 'Legitimate Peace in Post-Civil War States: Towards Attaining the Unattainable', *Conflict, Security & Development*, Vol. 14, No. 1 (2014), p. 63.
131. Braco Kalaba, 'Reforma odbrambenog sistema Bosne i Hercegovine', *Prva linija*, No. 108 (June 2003), p. 8.

# 6 The Orao Affair and military unification

1. PIC, *PIC Declaration* PIC Main Meeting (Madrid, 16 December 1998), Military Issues Annex
2. Raffi Gregorian, interview with the author (18 July 2017).
3. Braco Kalaba, 'Vojska federacije sa unificiranim oznakama', *Prva linija*, No. 59 (February 1998), p. 9.
4. Oliver Poole, 'Inside £50m Nuclear Bunker That Couldn't Save Saddam', *The Telegraph* (12 January 2006).
5. Fena, 'Ambasada SAD traži istragu o predaji oružja Iraku', *Oslobođenje* (10 September 2002), p. 3.
6. M. Cepina, '"Orao" nije kriv', *Glas srpski* (11 September 2002), p. 3.
7. S. Raven, 'Tužbe zbog lažnih optužbi', *Glas srpski* (12 September 2002), p. 3.
8. Ibid.
9. V. Živak, 'BiH nije prekršila zabranu naoružavanja Iraka!' *Oslobođenje* (15 September 2002), p. 6.
10. Ibid.
11. Antonio Prlenda, 'Dvogodišnji let iznad Sadamovog gnijezda', *Oslobođenje* (8 October 2002), p. 7.
12. Ibid.

13. Ibid.
14. Onasa, 'Zavod "Orao" i dalje pod blokadom', *Oslobođenje* (13 October 2002), p. 4.
15. Onasa, 'SFOR ponovo u "Orlovim" sefovima', *Oslobođenje* (14 October 2002), p. 3.
16. Ibid.
17. Antonio Prlenda, 'Bijelinski "Orao" donosi sankcije za BiH?' *Oslobođenje*. (22 October 2002), p. 5.
18. Ibid.
19. Ibid.
20. Antonio Prlenda, 'BiH ima 24 sata da izbjegne sankcije', *Oslobođenje* (25 October 2002), p. 1.
21. Economics Institute of Sarajevo, *United Nations Development Programme Human Development Report* (Sarajevo, 2002), pp. 20–37.
22. Paddy Ashdown, *Swords and Ploughshares: Bringing Peace to the Twentieth Century* (London, 2007), p. 248.
23. Ibid.
24. OHR, 'High Representative Outlines Required Action Following "Orao" Scandal', *OHR Press Office* (28 October 2002).
25. A. Kalamujić, 'Država preuzima kontrolu nad kompletnim naoružanjem', *Oslobođenje* (26 October 2002), p. 4.
26. OHR, 'High Representative Outlines Required Action Following "Orao" Scandal'.
27. Ibid.
28. OHR, 'OHR BiH Media Round-up', *OHR Press Office* (28 October 2002), p. 3.
29. Prlenda, 'BiH ima 24 sata da izbjegne sankcije', p. 3.
30. Ibid.
31. Onasa, 'Demanti smijenjenog direktora "Orao" nikada nije prodavao oružje', *Oslobođenje* (26 October 2002), p. 5.
32. G. Dakić, ' "Orao" slomljenih krila', *Glas srpski* (25 October 2002), p. 3.
33. Aldijana Omeragić, 'Bond traži nove smjene dužnosnika RS', *Oslobođenje* (26 October 2002), p. 4.
34. Ibid.
35. Ibid.
36. Fena, 'Ako vi ne djelujete, djelovaće međunarodna zajednica', *Oslobođenje* (26 October 2002), p. 5.
37. Ibid.
38. Ibid.
39. Omeragić, 'Bond traži nove smjene dužnosnika RS', p. 4.
40. Aldijana Omeragić, 'Orlovo gnijezdo', *Oslobođenje* (26 October 2002), p. 2.
41. Ibid.
42. Zija Dizdarević, 'RS snaži BiH', *Oslobođenje* (29 October 2002), p. 2.
43. Ibid.
44. Fena, 'SFOR pronašao vezu između "Orla" i Iraka', *Oslobođenje* (27 October 2002), p. 7.
45. George W. Bush, 'President Bush's address to the United Nations', *CNN* (12 September 2002).
46. Richard Norton-Taylor, 'Britain and US Step Up Bombing Campaign in Iraq', *The Guardian* (4 December 2002).
47. Michael Gordon, 'After the War: Preliminaries; US Air Raids in '02 Prepared for War in Iraq', *New York Times* (20 July 2003).

48. V. Živak, 'Odgovornost vlasti RS utvrdiće se tek po okončanju istrage!' *Oslobođenje* (28 October 2002), p. 4.
49. Ibid.
50. BBC, 'Bosnian Officials Quit over Iraq Sales', *BBC News* (29 October 2002).
51. Sense, 'Bosna pred najtežom krizom od završetka rata', *Oslobođenje* (31 October 2002), p. 7.
52. Ashdown, *Swords and Ploughshares*, p. 250.
53. Ibid.
54. Dizdarević, 'RS snaži BiH', p. 2.
55. Sense, 'Bosna pred najtežom krizom od završetka rata', p. 7.
56. Ashdown, *Swords and Ploughshares*, p. 262.
57. Ibid.
58. Ibid., p. 251.
59. Ian Traynor, 'Bosnia's Arms to Iraq Scandal Claims Top Political Scalp', *The Guardian* (3 April 2003).
60. Jolyjon Naegele, 'Bosnia: Political Stability in Question Amid Scandals, Espionage Charges', *Radio Free Europe* (3 April 2003).
61. Ibid.
62. Ashdown, *Swords and Ploughshares*, pp. 279–80.
63. Ibid.
64. Traynor, 'Bosnia's Arms to Iraq Scandal Claims Top Political Scalp'.
65. Paddy Ashdown, interview with the author (22 March 2016).
66. Traynor, 'Bosnia's Arms to Iraq Scandal Claims Top Political Scalp'.
67. N. Z., 'Ostavka mirka Šarovića', *Glas srpski* (3 April 2003), p. 1.
68. BBC, 'Ashdown Clips Bosnian Serb Wings', *BBC News* (2 April 2003).
69. OHR, 'High Representative Comments on Resignation of Mirko Sarovic from BiH Presidency', *OHR Press Office* (2 April 2003).
70. OHR, 'High Representative Acts to Ensure That Military in BiH Are under Effective Civilian Control', *OHR Press Office* (2 April 2003).
71. OHR, 'High Representative Comments on Resignation of Mirko Sarovic from BiH Presidency'.
72. OHR, 'High Representative Acts to Ensure That Military in BiH Are under Effective Civilian Control'.
73. Ibid.
74. Gregorian, interview with the author.
75. Ibid.
76. OHR, 'High Representative Appoints Defence Reform Commission', *OHR Press Office* (08 May 2003).
77. Defence Reform Commission, *The Path to Partnership for Peace: Report of the Defence Reform Commission* (Sarajevo, 2003), p. i.
78. Ibid., p. iii.
79. Government Publishing Office, *Executive Order 13304 – Termination of Emergencies with Respect to Yugoslavia and Modification of Executive Order 13219 of June 26, 2001* (29 May 2003).
80. Amra Kebo, 'Regional Report: US Sanctions Alarm Bosnians', *Institute for War & Peace Reporting* (01 May 2005).
81. Defence Reform Commission, *The Path to Partnership for Peace* (Sarajevo, 2003).
82. Ibid., p. 2.
83. Ibid., pp. 2–3.

84. Ibid., p. 5.
85. OHR, 'The Eyes of Europe and the World Are on BiH', *OHR Press Office* (24 September 2003).
86. Ibid.
87. OHR, 'High Representative Welcomes NATO Ministers' Positive Response to BiH', *OHR Press Office* (04 December 2003).
88. OSBiH Public Affairs Office, *Brochure of the Ministry of Defense and the Armed Forces of Bosnia and Herzegovina* (Sarajevo, 2011), p. 4.
89. Gregorian, interview with the author.
90. OSBiH Public Affairs Office, *Brochure of the Ministry of Defense and the Armed Forces of Bosnia and Herzegovina*, p. 4.
91. OHR, 'High Representative Extends DRC Mandate', *OHR Press Office* (31 December 2004).
92. Defence Reform Commission, *AFBiH: A Single Military Force for the 21st Century* (Sarajevo, 2005), p. iv.
93. Gregorian, interview with the author.
94. Ibid.
95. Gregorian, interview with the author.
96. Ibid.
97. DRC, *AFBiH*, p. 1.
98. Gregorian, interview with the author.
99. Ibid.
100. DRC, *AFBiH*, p. 1.
101. Ibid., p. 21.
102. Rohan Maxwell & John Andreas Olsen, *Destination NATO: Defence Reform in Bosnia and Herzegovina, 2003–2013* (London, 2013), p. 75.
103. The British Army, Canadian Army, and the Belgian Armed Forces all employ ethnic identification.
104. DRC, *AFBiH*, p. ii.
105. Gregorian, interview with the author.
106. See Chapter 2.
107. Gregorian, interview with the author.
108. See Chapter 2 for a case study on the Lebanese Army.
109. DRC, *AFBiH*, p. 21.
110. James Gow, *Legitimacy and the Military: The Yugoslav Crisis* (London, 1992), p. 107.
111. OSBiH Public Affairs Office, *Brochure of the Ministry of Defense and the Armed Forces of Bosnia and Herzegovina*, p. 21.
112. DRC, *AFBiH*, p. 9.
113. Ibid., p. 25.
114. Ibid.
115. Ibid.
116. Gregorian notes that at the time, it was hoped that incentives for promotion and pay associated with a duty station in another location would attract people to move across the Inter-Entity Boundary Line. He suggests that in the first few years after the formation of the AFBiH, such incentives were successful. Gregorian, interview with the author.
117. DRC, *AFBiH*, p. 26.
118. DRC, *AFBiH*, pp. 6–7.
119. Maxwell & Olsen, *Destination NATO*, p. 76.

120. Ibid., pp. 76–7.
121. Ibid., p. 75.
122. OHR, 'SDR Ney Congratulates DRC on Achievements', OHR Press Office (16 December 2005).
123. OSBIH Public Affairs Office, *Brochure of the Ministry of Defense and the Armed Forces of Bosnia and Herzegovina*, pp. 23–4.
124. Ashdown, interview with the author.
125. Ibid.
126. Ibid.
127. Gregorian, interview with the author.
128. Johan Galtung, 'Violence, Peace, and Peace Research', *Journal of Peace Research*, Vol. 6, No. 3 (1969), p. 183; Anders Themnér & Thomas Ohlson, 'Legitimate Peace in Post–Civil War States: Towards Attaining the Unattainable', *Conflict, Security & Development*, Vol. 14, No. 1 (2014), p. 63.
129. Ashdown, interview with the author.
130. Ibid.
131. Gregorian, interview with the author; Ashdown, interview with the author.

## 7 The Armed Forces of Bosnia and Herzegovina

1. Law on Defence of Bosnia and Herzegovina, *Official Gazette of Bosnia and Herzegovina*, Vol. 88, No. 5 (2005).
2. Ibid.
3. Selmo Cikotić, interview with *Bilten*, in BiH Ministry of Defence, 'Prva rotacija Pješadijske jedinice OS BiH u misiji ISAF', *Bilten*, No. 4 (2010), p. 4.
4. UN Peacekeeping, *United Nations Mission in Bosnia and Herzegovina: Background* (New York, 2003), available at: https://peacekeeping.un.org/fr/mission/past/unmibh/background.html (accessed 1 February 2021).
5. Ibid.
6. United Nations Secretary-General Kofi Annan, *Report of the Secretary-General on the United Nations Mission in Bosnia and Herzegovina: S/2002/1314* (New York, 2002), p. 6.
7. BiH Ministry of Defence, 'Informacija o učešću jedinica OS BiH u operaciji „Iračka Sloboda" u Iraku', *Mirovne misije* (2009), available at: http://mod.gov.ba/OS_BIH/Aktivnosti/mirovne_misije/default.aspx?id=20168 (accessed 1 February 2021).
8. BiH Ministry of Defence, 'Iskustva iz misije u Iraku: Rijetka prilika vojnicima i podoficirima za sticanje iskustva', *Bilten*, No. 5 (2010), p. 12.
9. Samir Huseinović, 'Vojnici iz BiH odlaze u Irak u borbenu misiju', *Deutsche Welle* (18 August 2008), available at: https://www.dw.com/sr/vojnici-iz-bih-odlaze-u-irak-u-borbenu-misiju/a-3575047 (accessed 1 February 2021).
10. BiH Ministry of Defence, 'Informacija o učešću jedinica OS BiH u operaciji „Iračka Sloboda" u Iraku'.
11. Rohan Maxwell, interview with the author (11 February 2021).
12. Law on the Participation of the Members of the AF BiH, Police Officers, Civil Servants and Other Employees in Peacekeeping Operations and Other Activities Abroad (Official Gazette of BiH, No. 14/2005); Rohan Maxwell, interview with the author (11 February 2021).
13. BiH Ministry of Defence, 'BiH postala članica misije ISAF-a', *Bilten*, No. 1 (2009), p. 2.

14. BiH Ministry of Defence, 'Osposobljenost, visoka motiviranost i discipliniranost pripadnika OS BiH', *Bilten*, No. 5 (2010), p. 5.

15. BiH Ministry of Defence and Armed Forces of Bosnia and Herzegovina, *Brochure* (Sarajevo, 2011), pp. 24–5.

16. BiH Ministry of Defence, 'Instruktori vojne policije OS BiH u misiji ISAF', *Mirovne misijie* (2012), available at: http://www.mod.gov.ba/OS_BIH/Aktivnosti/mirovne_mis ije/?id=20124 (accessed 1 February 2021).

17. BiH Ministry of Defence, 'Ispraćaj 45 pripadnika iz sastava 6. Pješadijske brigade OS BiH u misiju podrške miru u Afghanistan', *Mirovne misije* (2016), available at: https:// www.mod.gov.ba/OS_BIH/Aktivnosti/mirovne_misije/?id=52923 (accessed 1 February 2021).

18. BiH Ministry of Defence, 'Ceremonija ispraćaja Pješadijske jedinice iz sastava 4. pbr OS BiH i jedinice Vojne policije OS BiH u misiju podrške miru u IR Afganistan', *Mirovne misije* (2019), available at: http://www.mod.gov.ba/OS_BIH/Aktivnosti/ mirovne_misije/?id=72392 (accessed 1 February 2021); NATO, *Resolute Support Mission(RSM): Key Facts and Figures* (2020), p. 2.

19. US Embassy in Bosnia and Herzegovina, 'Soldiers of the Armed Forces of BiH Receive Awards and Recognition', *News & Events* (2015), available at: https:// ba.usembassy.gov/soldiers-armed-forces-bih-receive-awards-recognition/ (accessed 1 February 2021).

20. US Department of Defense, 'Defense Official Welcomes Bosnia-Herzegovina's President to Pentagon', *News* (26 November 2019), available at: https://www.defense. gov/Explore/Features/story/Article/2026739/defense-official-welcomes-bosnia-herze govinas-president-to-pentagon/source/GovDelivery/ (accessed 1 February 2021).

21. Monthly records of personnel contributions to UN peacekeeping operations are available at: https://peacekeeping.un.org/en/troop-and-police-contributors (accessed 1 February 2021).

22. UN Peacekeeping, *MONUSCO Fact Sheet* (New York, 2021), available at: https://peace keeping.un.org/en/mission/monusco (accessed 1 February 2021).

23. BiH Ministry of Defence, 'Mirovna misija UN-a u Demokrtaskoj Republici Kongo. (MONUC)', *Bilten*, No. 2 (2009), p. 12; BiH Ministry of Defence, 'Iskustva iz UN misije – Kongo: Vojni posmatrač mora biti psihički jak i prilagodljiv', *Bilten*, No. 5 (2010), p. 11.

24. BiH Ministry of Defence, *Armed Forces of Bosnia and Herzegovina* (Sarajevo, 2015), p. 14.

25. BiH Ministry of Defence, 'Iskustva iz misije u Etiopiji i Eritreji – UNMEE: Obaveza je vojnika služiti u cilju globalne sigurnosti', *Bilten*, No. 5 (2010), p. 10.

26. UN Peacekeeping, *United Nations Multidimensional Integrated Stabilization Mission in Mali: Personnel* (New York, 2021), available at: https://minusma.unmissions.org/en/ personnel (accessed 1 February 2021).

27. BiH Ministry of Defence, 'Prijem za oficire koji odlaze u misiju EU u Centralnoafričku Republiku', *Mirovne misije* (2017), available at: http://www.mod. gov.ba/aktuelnosti/vijesti/?id=57111 (accessed 1 February 2021); European Council, 'Central African Republic: Military Training Mission Expanded and Extended', *Press Releases* (2018), available at: https://www.consilium.europa.eu/en/press/press-relea ses/2018/07/30/central-african-republic-training-mission-prolonged-with-enlarged-mandate/ (accessed 1 February 2021); BiH Ministry of Defence, 'EUTM RCA', *Bilten*, No. 18 (2019), p. 31.

28. BiH Ministry of Defence, 'Mirovne misije – Iskustva: Mirovna misija Europske unije', *Bilten*, No. 17 (2018), p. 27.
29. BiH Ministry of Defence, 'Iskustva iz misije u Afganistanu: Misija – prilika da vojnik naučeno primijeni u realnim ratnim uslovima', *Bilten*, No. 5 (2010), p. 7.
30. BiH Ministry of Defence, 'Iskustva iz misije u Etiopiji i Eritreji – UNMEE'.
31. BiH Ministry of Defence, 'Iskustva iz misije u Afganistanu: Misija – prilika da vojnik naučeno primijeni u realnim ratnim uslovima', *Bilten*, No. 5 (2010), p. 7.
32. Selmo Cikotić, interview with *Bilten* in BiH Ministry of Defence, 'Prva rotacija Pješadijske jedinice OS BiH u misiji ISAF', p. 4.
33. BiH Ministry of Defence, 'Intervju – komandant NATO štaba u Sarajevu brigadni general David Enyeart: Pripadnici Oružanih snaga BiH na najbolji način će predstaviti svoju zemlju', *Bilten*, No. 5 (2010), p. 8.
34. In Burundi, e.g., lucrative postings to African Union and UN peacekeeping missions remain largely the preserve of predominantly Hutu former National Council for the Defense of Democracy – Forces for the Defense of Democracy (*Conseil National Pour la Défense de la Démocratie – Forces pour la Défense de la Démocratie*, CNDD–FDD) combatants. See Short, 'Assessing International Statebuilding Initiative Effectiveness at Preventing Armed Conflict Recurrence'.
35. Maxwell, interview with the author (11 February 2021).
36. BiH Ministry of Defence, 'Iskustva iz misije u Iraku: Multinacionalno okruženje – prilika za promociju i unapređenje', p. 13.
37. Alan Crosby & Aida Djugum, ' "The Killer Is Still Waiting": Two Decades On, Land Mines Still Wreaking Havoc in Bosnia', *Radio Free Europe/Radio Liberty* (4 October 2017), available at: https://www.rferl.org/a/bosnia-land-mines-deminers-maim-kill-funding-princess-diana/28773102.html (accessed 10 February 2021).
38. Mine Action Review, *Clearing the Mines 2020* (2020), p. 49.
39. Ibid.
40. Norwegian People's Aid, *Bosnia and Herzegovina: Mine Action and Disarmament* (NPA, 2020), available at: https://www.npaid.org/mine-action-and-disarmament/where-we-work/bosnia-and-herzegovina (accessed 10 February 2021); Mine Action Review, *Clearing the Mines 2020*, p. 49.
41. Mine Action Review, *Clearing Cluster Munition Remnants 2020* (2020), p. 27; Maxwell, interview with the author (11 February 2021).
42. Mine Action Review, *Clearing the Mines 2020*, p. 52.
43. Ibid., p. 49.
44. European Union Force in BiH Operation Althea, 'Joint Press Statement: Lower demining capacity is a safety threat to BiH citizens', *Press Statements*. (10 March 2020), available at: http://www.euforbih.org/index.php/press-corner/press-stateme nts/2696-lower-demining-capacity-is-a-safety-threat-to-bih-citizens (accessed 10 February 2021).
45. BiH Ministry of Defence, *Brochure* (2015), p. 52.
46. Ibid., p. 54.
47. BiH Ministry of Defence, 'Oružane snage BiH su nezamjenljiv faktor u afirmaciji Bosne i Hercegovine', Vijesti (28 November 2014), available at: http://www.mod.gov.ba/aktuelnosti/vijesti/?id=37361 (accessed 10 February 2021).
48. US National Guard, *State Partnership Program* (US National Guard, 2021), available at: https://www.nationalguard.mil/leadership/joint-staff/j-5/international-affairs-divis ion/state-partnership-program/ (accessed 10 February 2021).

49. US Government Accountability Office, *State Partnership Program: Improved Oversight, Guidance, and Training Needed for National Guard's Efforts with Foreign Partners (GAO-12-548)* (Washington, DC, 2012), p. 10.

50. Specialist Thaddeus Harrington, 'State Partnership Program', *Maryland Line (State Partnership Edition)* (2013), pp. 26–7.

51. BiH Ministry of Defence, 'Pripadnici OS BiH na testiranju za Značku eksperta pješadije u SAD-u', *Vijesti* (07 June 2015), available at: http://www.mod.gov.ba/aktu elnosti/vijesti/?id=41236 (accessed 10 February 2021).

52. BiH Ministry of Defence, 'Pripadnici OS BiH najbolji strani vojnici na natjecanju u Marylandu', *Bilten*, No. 20 (2020), p. 27.

53. BiH Ministry of Defence, 'Svečanost u povodu obilježavanja 15 godina Državnog partnerskog programa između Bosne i Hercegovine i američke savezne države Maryland', *Vijesti* (27 November 2018), available at: http://www.mod.gov.ba/aktuelno sti/vijesti/?id=68523 (accessed 10 February 2021).

54. Major Kurt Rauschenberg, 'Maryland Guard Celebrates Unity with Bosnia-Herzegovina', *National Guard State Partnership Program News* (3 December 2018), available at: https://www.nationalguard.mil/News/State-Partnership-Program/Arti cle/1703991/maryland-guard-celebrates-unity-with-bosnia-herzegovina/ (accessed 10 February 2021).

55. Deputy Assistant Secretary Evelyn Farkas of Defense for Russian, Ukrainian and Eurasian Affairs. Quoted in Amaani Lyle, 'Maryland Guard Partners with Bosnia and Herzegovina for Peace, Security', *Maryland Line* (2013), p. 4.

56. Ibid.

57. NATO, *Partnership for Peace Programme* (Brussels, 2021), available at: https://www. nato.int/cps/en/natohq/topics_50349.htm (accessed 10 February 2021).

58. NATO, *Partnership for Peace Planning and Review Process* (Brussels, 2021), available at: https://www.nato.int/cps/su/natohq/topics_68277.htm (accessed 10 February 2021).

59. NATO, *Individual Partnership Action Plans* (Brussels, 2017), available at: https://www. nato.int/cps/en/natohq/topics_49290.htm (accessed 25 February 2021).

60. BiH Ministry of Defence, 'Početak nove faze za BiH na putu ka punopravnom članstvu u NATO-u', *Bilten*, No. 2 (2009), p. 2.

61. NATO, *Partnership Interoperability Initiative* (Brussels, 2021), available at: https:// www.nato.int/cps/en/natohq/topics_132726.htm (accessed 10 February 2021).

62. BiH Ministry of Defence, 'Pripadnici OS BiH na međunarodnoj vježbi "Immediate Response 19" u Republici Hrvatskoj', *Vijesti* (23 May 2019), available at: http://www. mod.gov.ba/aktuelnosti/vijesti/?id=71925 (accessed 10 February 2021); US European Command, 'U.S. Air Force Partners with Armed Forces in Bosnia and Herzegovina for Air-Ground Integration Bilateral Exercise', *News* (20 November 2020), available at: https://www.eucom.mil/article/40888/us-air-force-partners-with-armed-forces-in-bosnia-and-herzegovina-for-air-ground-integrati (20 November 2020).

63. BiH Ministry of Defence, 'Ispunjavanje partnerskih ciljeva – na Manjači SEL-1: Ocjenjivanje bataljonske grupe lake pješadije', *Bilten*, No. 19 (2019), pp. 3–4; NATO Joint Forces Command Naples, 'JFC Naples Supports Light Infantry Evaluation', *News* (27 September 2019), available at: https://jfcnaples.nato.int/newsroom/news/2019/jfc-naples-supports-light-infantry-evaluation (accessed 10 February 2021).

64. BiH Ministry of Defence, 'Završena vježba Bataljonske grupe lake pješadije Oružanih snaga BiH na vojnom poligonu „Manjača"', *Vijesti* (25 September 2020), available at: http://www.mod.gov.ba/aktuelnosti/vijesti/?id=81557 (accessed 10 February 2021).

65. Maxwell, interview with the author (11 February 2021).

66. Ibid.

67. Heinz Vetschera, 'Politics and Higher Military Education in Bosnia and Herzegovina: A Missed Opportunity', *Connections*, Vol. 11, No. 4 (2012), pp. 123–4.

68. PSOTC, *History* (Sarajevo, 2021), available at: http://www.psotc.org/Content/Read/history (accessed 10 February 2021).

69. British Embassy Sarajevo, 'Best and Brightest Required to Lead the Armed Forces of Bosnia and Herzegovina', *News* (2 October 2013).

70. BiH Ministry of Defence, *Brochure*, p. 15.

71. BiH Ministry of Defence, 'Kadet Mlakić najbolji na Kraljevskoj vojnoj akademiji', *Bilten*, No. 17 (2018), p. 41.

72. BiH Ministry of Defence, 'Veliki uspjeh naših vojnika u Velikoj Britaniji i Estoniji', *Bilten*, No. 18 (2019), pp. 14–15.

73. BiH Ministry of Defence, 'Školovanje personala u inostranstvu', *Bilten*, No. 19 (2019), p. 38.

74. BiH Ministry of Defence, 'Pristup žena oružanim snagama značajan je segment demokratizacije vojnog okruženja', *Vijesti* (29 October 2013), available at: http://www.mod.gov.ba/aktuelnosti/vijesti/?id=28236 (accessed 10 February 2021).

75. UN Security Council, *Resolution 1325* (New York, 2000).

76. UN Peacekeeping, *Women in Peacekeeping* (New York, 2020), available at: https://peacekeeping.un.org/en/women-peacekeeping (accessed 10 February 2021); Alexandra Ivanovic, 'Why the United Nations Needs More Female Peacekeepers', *United Nations University Publications* (09 July 2014), available at: https://unu.edu/publications/articles/why-un-needs-more-female-peacekeepers.html (accessed 10 February 2021).

77. Bojana Balon, ed., *The Position of Women in the Armed Forces in the Western Balkans* (UNDP, 2014), p. 14; BiH Ministry of Defence, 'Svečano obilježena 20. godišnjica Rezolucije Vijeća sigurnosti UN 1325 „Žene, mir i sigurnost"', *Vijesti* (30 October 2020), available at: http://www.mod.gov.ba/aktuelnosti/vijesti/?id=82260 (accessed 10 February 2021).

78. BiH Ministry of Human Rights and Refugees, *Akcioni plan za implementaciju UNSCR 1325 „Žene, mir i sigurnost" u Bosni i Hercegovini za period 2018–2022. godine* (Sarajevo, 2017), pp. 9–10.

79. Eva Galindo Soriano, 'Bosnia and Herzegovina Is Looking for More "Warrior-Diplomats"', *OSCE Stories* (27 April 2012), available at: https://www.osce.org/bih/119928 (accessed 10 February 2021); Anadolu Agency, 'Opening Doors: Bosnia's Trailblazing Female Brigadier', *AA World* (10 March 2015), available at: https://www.aa.com.tr/en/world/opening-doors-bosnias-trailblazing-female-brigadier/68327 (accessed 10 February 2021).

80. BiH Ministry of Human Rights and Refugees, *Akcioni plan za implementaciju UNSCR 1325*, p.11

81. Centre for Security Studies, Sarajevo, *Bosnia and Herzegovina in Peace Missions: Contribution to Maintaining Peace in the World* (Sarajevo, 2018), p. 11.

82. Ibid., p. 12.

83. Stockholm International Peace Research Institute, *Yearbook: Armaments, Disarmament and International Security* (Stockholm, 2020), available at: https://data.worldbank.org/indicator/MS.MIL.XPND.GD.ZS?locations=BA (accessed 10 February 2021).

84. Ibid.

85. Aida Đugum, 'Zašto se osipaju Oružane snage BiH?' *Radio Slobodna Evropa* (8 March 2018), available at: https://www.slobodnaevropa.org/a/oruzane-snage-bih-zar ade-izbori/29087099.html (accessed 10 February 2021).

86. Klix, 'Koliko BiH zaostaje u naoružanju i vojnoj opremi za susjedima: U potpunosti zavisimo od donacija', *Klix.ba* (31 August 2019), available at: https://www.klix.ba/vije sti/bih/koliko-bih-zaostaje-u-naoruzanju-i-vojnoj-opremi-za-susjedima-u-potpuno sti-zavisimo-od-donacija/190831075 (accessed 10 February 2021).

87. Mine Action Review, *Clearing Cluster Munition Remnants 2020*, p. 27.

88. Klix, 'Koliko BiH zaostaje u naoružanju i vojnoj opremi za susjedima'.

89. US Embassy in Bosnia and Herzegovina, 'Remarks at UH 2-LOA Signing Ceremony', *News & Events* (13 December 2019), available at: https://ba.usembassy.gov/ambassa dor-nelsons-remarks-at-uh-2-loa-signing-ceremony/ (accessed 10 February 2021).

90. Samir Huseinović, 'Vojna inferiornost BiH u odnosu na susjede', *Deutsche Welle* (18 October 2020), available at: https://www.dw.com/hr/vojna-inferiornost-bih-u-odnosu-na-susjede/a-55315359 (accessed 10 February 2021); BiH Ministry of Defence, 'Vlada SAD u 2019. donirala 20 vozila Humvee', *Bilten*, No. 19 (2019), p. 12; BiH Ministry of Defence, 'Donacija Vlade SAD za deminerske jedinice OS BiH', *Vijesti* (23 September 2011), available at: http://www.mod.gov.ba/aktuelnosti/vije sti/?id=763 (accessed 10 February 2021); BiH Ministry of Defence, 'Donacija jezičkih laboratorija od strane Vlade SAD-a', *Vijesti* (17 February 2014), available at: http:// www.mod.gov.ba/OS_BIH/struktura/Komanda_za_podrsku/?id=30654 (accessed 10 February 2021); BiH Ministry of Defence, 'Današnja donacija obavezuje da dodjeljene zadatke izvršavamo još profesionalnije, odgovornije i kvalitetnije', *Vijesti* (22 January 2014), available at: http://www.mod.gov.ba/aktuelnosti/vijesti/?id=30219 (accessed 10 February 2021)

91. BiH Ministry of Defence, 'Kineska vojna pomoć', *Bilten*, No. 19 (2019), p. 25; BiH Ministry of Defence, 'Ministarstvo odbrane SR Njemačke doniralo 15 dizalica za helikoptere UH-1H', *Vijesti* (21 March 2017), available at: http://www.mod.gov.ba/ aktuelnosti/vijesti/?id=54530 (accessed 10 February 2021); BiH Ministry of Defence, 'Nastavak podrške Kraljevine Saudijske Arabije Ministarstvu odbrane BiH – donacija finansijskih sredstava Oružanim snagama BiH za unapređenje skladišta naoružanja i municije', *Vijesti* (05 July 2018), available at: http://www.mod.gov.ba/aktuelnosti/ vijesti/?id=64579 (accessed 10 February 2021); BiH Ministry of Defence, 'Donacija Oružanih snaga Švajcarske MO BiH i OS BiH', *Vijesti* (13 July 2012), available at: http://www.mod.gov.ba/aktuelnosti/vijesti/?id=1445 (accessed 10 February 2021); Huseinović, 'Vojna inferiornost BiH u odnosu na susjede'.

92. BiH Ministry of Defence, 'Pripadnici OS BiH na međunarodnoj vježbi "Immediate Response 19" u Republici Hrvatskoj'.

93. Maja Beker, 'Dodik: Oružane snage nisu snage BiH već strane sile, žali Bože troška', *N1 BiH* (20 November 2020), available at: https://ba.n1info.com/vijesti/a491 200-dodik-oruzane-snage-nisu-snage-bih-vec-strane-sile-zali-boze-troska/ (accessed 10 February 2021).

94. Ibid.

95. European Commission for Democracy through Law, *Opinion on the Constitutional Situation in Bosnia and Herzegovina and the Powers of the High Representative, CDL-AD (2005) 004* (Venice, 2005), p. 5; Edin Barimac, 'Zajednička vježba OS BiH i Vojske Srbije po NATO standardima', *Nezavisne novine* (19 December 2020), available at: https://www.nezavisne.com/novosti/bih/Zajednicka-vjezba-OS-BiH-i-Vojske-Srbije-po-NATO-standardima/637223 (accessed 10 February 2021).

96. SIPRI, *Military Expenditure by Country as Percentage of Gross Domestic Product, 1988–2019* (Stockholm, 2020), available at: https://www.sipri.org/databases/milex (accessed 10 February 2021).
97. Maxwell, interview with the author (11 February 2021).
98. DW Komentar, '(De) militarizacija najuspješnijeg projekta u BiH', *Deutsche Welle* (1 December 2012), available at: https://www.dw.com/bs/de-militarizacija-najus pje%C5%A1nijeg-projekta-u-bih/a-16421618 (accessed 10 February 2021).
99. Darko Momić, 'MUP RS tajno prodao više od 10 hiljada pušaka i pištolja!' *CAPITAL.ba* (16 April 2018), available at: https://www.capital.ba/mup-rs-tajno-prodao-vise-od-10-hiljada-pusaka-i-pistolja/ (accessed 10 February 2021); Julian Borger, 'Arms Shipment to Bosnian Serbs Stokes EU Fears', *The Guardian* (13 February 2018), available at: https://www.theguardian.com/world/2018/feb/13/bosn ian-serb-police-arms-purchase-stokes-eu-fears (accessed 10 February 2021); Dragan Maksimović, "Žandarmerija – osniva li Republika Srpska svoju vojsku?' *Deutsche Welle* (26 September 2019), available at: https://www.dw.com/hr/%C5%BEanda rmerija-osniva-li-republika-srpska-svoju-vojsku/a-50584619 (accessed 10 February 2021).
100. Nevena Stanojević, 'Žandarmerija – Elitna jedinica MUP-a garant bezbjednosti Republike Srpske', *banjaluka.net* (11 March 2020), available at: https://banjaluka. net/zandarmerija-elitna-jedinica-mup-a-garant-bezbjednosti-republike-srpske/ (accessed 10 February 2021).
101. International Foundation for Electoral Systems, *Bosnia and Herzegovina* (Arlington, 2021), available at: https://www.electionguide.org/countries/id/28/ (accessed 10 February 2021).
102. Ashdown, interview with the author (22 March 2016).
103. Branka Topić-Pavković, 'Characteristics of Value Added Tax in Bosnia and Herzegovina', *Mediterranean Journal of Social Sciences*, Vol. 6, No. 2 (2015), p. 79.
104. NATO, 'Joint Press Conference with NATO Secretary General Jens Stoltenberg and the Chairman of the Tri-Presidency of Bosnia and Herzegovina, Mladen Ivanić', *Speeches & Transcripts* (2 February 2017), available at: https://www. nato.int/cps/en/natohq/opinions_140549.htm?selectedLocale=en (accessed 10 February 2021).
105. Danas Online, 'Dodik: SZP predložio formiranje obaveštajne službe u OS BiH', *Danas* (23 October 2016), available at: https://www.danas.rs/svet/dodik-szp-predlo zio-formiranje-obavestajne-sluzbe-u-os-bih/ (accessed 10 February 2021).
106. Ipsos, *Bosnia and Herzegovina: Understanding Perceptions of Violent Extremism and Foreign Influence, March 29, 2018 – April 12, 2018* (Washington, DC, 2018), p. 40.
107. Center for Euro-Atlantic Studies & Center for Free Elections and Democracy, *Serbia and West: This Is US* (Belgrade, 2020), p. 5.
108. Human Rights Watch, 'Civilian Deaths in the NATO Air Campaign', *Human Rights Watch Report*, Vol. 12, No. 1 (2000), p. 2.
109. Ipsos, *Bosnia and Herzegovina*, p. 43; Center for Euro-Atlantic Studies & Center for Free Elections and Democracy, *Serbia and West*, p. 6.
110. Samir Huseinović, '„Vojno neutralna" Republika Srpska?' *Deutsche Welle* (18 October 2017), available at: https://www.dw.com/sr/vojno-neutralna-republika-srpska/a-41009080 (accessed 10 February 2021).
111. Đorđe Latinović, 'Srbi, NATO i realpolitika', *Nezavisne novine* (14 May 2019), available at: https://www.nezavisne.com/novosti/kolumne/Srbi-NATO-i-realpolit ika/538204 (accessed 10 February 2021).

112. N1 BiH, 'Donijet ćemo odluku o članstvu u NATO-u, a Dodik će ponovo u tome učestvovati', *N1 BiH* (04 July 2020), available at: https://ba.n1info.com/vijesti/a445 225-komsic-i-dodik-o-nato-u/ (accessed 10 February 2021).

113. Beta, 'SDS: Dodik prevarom isključio institucije i građane RS iz odlučivanja o ulasku BiH u NATO', *Danas* (24 December 2019), available at: https://www.danas. rs/svet/sds-dodik-prevarom-iskljucio-institucije-i-gradjane-rs-iz-odlucivanja-o-ula sku-bih-u-nato/ (accessed 10 February 2021).

114. NATO, 'Joint Press Conference with NATO Secretary General Jens Stoltenberg and the Chairman of the Tri-Presidency of Bosnia and Herzegovina, Mladen Ivanić'.

115. Latinović, 'Srbi, NATO i realpolitika'.

116. Maxwell, interview with the author (11 February 2021).

117. H.J.I., 'Oružane snage BiH obilježavaju 15 godina postojanja', *Dnevni avaz.* (30 November 2020), available at: https://avaz.ba/vijesti/bih/612837/oruzane-snage-bih-obiljezavaju-15-godina-postojanja (accessed 21 February 2021).

118. Eleanor Rose, 'Defiant Bosnian Serbs Celebrate Banned "National Day"', *Balkan Insight* (09 January 2017), available at: https://balkaninsight.com/2017/01/10/invest igation-promised-into-army-participation-in-banned-holiday-01-10-2017/ (accessed 21 February 2021).

119. Politika, 'Hrvati neće u vojsku BiH, Srbi zainteresovaniji od Bošnjaka', *Politika* (27 July 2020), available at: http://www.politika.rs/sr/clanak/459218/Hrvati-nece-u-voj sku-BiH-Srbi-zainteresovaniji-od-Bosnjaka# (accessed 21 February 2021).

120. BiH Ministry of Defence, 'Svečano obilježen Dan 3. pješadijskog (Republika Srpska) puka Oružanih snaga BiH i Dan Vojske Republike Srpske', *Vijesti* (13 May 2019), available at: http://mod.gov.ba/aktuelnosti/vijesti/?id=71553 (accessed 21 February 2021).

# Conclusion

1. Ashdown, interview with the author (22 April 2016).

2. Ibid.

3. US Embassy in Bosnia and Herzegovina, 'Remarks at UH 2-LOA Signing Ceremony', *News & Events* (2019), available at: https://ba.usembassy.gov/ambassador-nelsons-remarks-at-uh-2-loa-signing-ceremony/ (accessed 23 February 2021).

4. Maxwell, interview with the author (11 February 2021).

5. Ibid.

6. Ibid.

7. Ashdown, interview with the author (22 April 2016).

8. Ibid.

# Bibliography

## Documents

Annan, Kofi. *'We The Peoples': The Role of the United Nations in the 21st Century* (New York, 2000).

*Armija ljiljana*. No. 19 (December 1992).

*Armija ljiljana*. No. 57 (December 1994).

Ashdown, Paddy. *Inaugural Speech to BiH Parliament* (Sarajevo, 27 May 2002).

Ashdown, Paddy. 'Appendix'. *Swords and Ploughshares* (London, 2007).

AVNOJ. *The Declaration from the Second Session of the Anti-Fascist Council of National Liberation of Yugoslavia* (Jajce, 1943).

Bassiouni, Mahmoud Cherif. *Final Report of the United Nations Commission of Experts Established Pursuant to Security Council Resolution 780 (1992), Annex III: The Military Structure, Strategy and Tactics of the Warring Factions* (UN, 1994).

BiH Ministry of Defence. *Armed Forces of Bosnia and Herzegovina* (Sarajevo, 2015).

BiH Ministry of Defence. 'Ceremonija ispraćaja Pješadijske jedinice iz sastava 4. pbr OS BiH i jedinice Vojne policije OS BiH u misiju podrške miru u IR Afganistan'. *Mirovne misije* (2019).

BiH Ministry of Defence. 'Današnja donacija obavezuje da dodjeljene zadatke izvršavamo još profesionalnije, odgovornije i kvalitetnije'. *Vijesti* (22 January 2014).

BiH Ministry of Defence. 'Donacija jezičkih laboratorija od strane Vlade SAD-a'. *Vijesti* (17 February 2014).

BiH Ministry of Defence. 'Donacija Oružanih snaga Švajcarske MO BiH i OS BiH'. *Vijesti* (13 July 2012).

BiH Ministry of Defence. 'Donacija Vlade SAD za deminerske jedinice OS BiH'. *Vijesti* (23 September 2011).

BiH Ministry of Defence. 'Informacija o učešću jedinica OS BiH u operaciji „Iračka Sloboda" u Iraku'. *Mirovne misije* (2009).

BiH Ministry of Defence. 'Instruktori vojne policije OS BiH u misiji ISAF'. *Mirovne misijie* (2012).

BiH Ministry of Defence. 'Ispraćaj 45 pripadnika iz sastava 6. Pješadijske brigade OS BiH u misiju podrške miru u Afghanistan'. *Mirovne misije* (2016).

BiH Ministry of Defence. 'Ministarstvo odbrane SR Njemačke doniralo 15 dizalica za helikoptere UH-1H'. *Vijesti* (21 March 2017).

BiH Ministry of Defence. 'Nastavak podrške Kraljevine Saudijske Arabije Ministarstvu odbrane BiH – donacija finansijskih sredstava Oružanim snagama BiH za unapređenje skladišta naoružanja i municije'. *Vijesti* (5 July 2018).

BiH Ministry of Defence. 'Oružane snage BiH su nezamjenljiv faktor u afirmaciji Bosne i Hercegovine'. *Vijesti* (28 November 2014).

BiH Ministry of Defence. 'Prijem za oficire koji odlaze u misiju EU u Centralnoafričku Republiku'. *Mirovne misije* (2017).

BiH Ministry of Defence. 'Pripadnici OS BiH na međunarodnoj vježbi "Immediate Response 19" u Republici Hrvatskoj'. *Vijesti* (23 May 2019).

BiH Ministry of Defence. 'Pripadnici OS BiH na testiranju za Značku eksperta pješadije u SAD-u'. *Vijesti* (7 June 2015).

BiH Ministry of Defence. 'Pristup žena oružanim snagama značajan je segment demokratizacije vojnog okruženja'. *Vijesti* (29 October 2013).

BiH Ministry of Defence. 'Svečano obilježena 20. godišnjica Rezolucije Vijeća sigurnosti UN 1325, Žene, mir i sigurnost'. *Vijesti* (30 October 2020).

BiH Ministry of Defence. 'Svečano obilježen Dan 3. pješadijskog (Republika Srpska) puka Oružanih snaga BiH i Dan Vojske Republike Srpske'. *Vijesti* (13 May 2019).

BiH Ministry of Defence. 'Svečanost u povodu obilježavanja 15 godina Državnog partnerskog programa između Bosne i Hercegovine i američke savezne države Maryland'. *Vijesti* (27 November 2018).

BiH Ministry of Defence. 'Završena vježba Bataljonske grupe lake pješadije Oružanih snaga BiH na vojnom poligonu, Manjača'. *Vijesti* (25 September 2020).

BiH Ministry of Defence and Armed Forces of Bosnia and Herzegovina. *Brochure* (Sarajevo, 2011).

BiH Ministry of Human Rights and Refugees. *Akcioni plan za implementaciju UNSCR 1325, Žene, mir i sigurnost" u Bosni i Hercegovini za period 2018–2022. godine* (Sarajevo, 2017).

*Bilten*, No. 1 (2009).

*Bilten*, No. 2 (2009).

*Bilten*, No. 4 (2010).

*Bilten*, No. 5 (2010).

*Bilten*, No. 17 (2018).

*Bilten*, No. 18 (2019).

*Bilten*, No. 19 (2019).

*Bilten*, No. 20 (2020).

Bosnian Serb Assembly. *Odluka o formiranju vojske Srpske Republike Bosne i Hercegovine* (Banja Luka, 1992).

Bosnian Serb Assembly. *Ustav Republike Srpske, sedmi deo* (Banja Luka, 1992).

British Embassy Sarajevo. 'Best and Brightest Required to Lead the Armed Forces of Bosnia and Herzegovina'. *UK Government Announcements* (2 October 2013).

Bush, George W. 'President Bush's address to the United Nations'. *CNN* (12 September 2002).

Ceasefire Agreement for Bosnia and Herzegovina. *Annex II* (5 October 1995).

Constituent Assembly of the Federative People's Republic of Yugoslavia. *Constitution of the Federal People's Republic of Yugoslavia* (Belgrade, 1946).

Constituent Assembly of the Federative People's Republic of Yugoslavia. *Constitution of the Federal People's Republic of Yugoslavia* (Belgrade, 1974).

Defence Reform Commission. *AFBiH: A Single Military Force for the 21st Century* (Sarajevo, 2005).

Defence Reform Commission. *The Path to Partnership for Peace: Report of the Defence Reform Commission* (Sarajevo, 2003).

Defence Reform Commission Team 8. *Concept Paper on Parallelism* (Sarajevo, 2005).

Economics Institute of Sarajevo. *United Nations Development Programme Human Development Report* (Sarajevo, 2002).

European Commission for Democracy Through Law. *Opinion on the Constitutional Situation in Bosnia and Herzegovina and the Powers of the High Representative, CDL-AD (2005) 004* (Venice, 2005).

European Council. 'Central African Republic: military training mission expanded and extended'. *Press Releases* (2018).

European Union Force in BiH Operation Althea. 'Joint Press Statement: Lower Demining Capacity Is a Safety Threat to BiH Citizens'. *Press Statements* (10 March 2020).

General Framework Agreement for Peace in Bosnia and Herzegovina (Dayton, 1995).

Harrington, Specialist Thaddeus. 'State Partnership Program'. *The Maryland Line (State Partnership Edition)* (2013).

Hodžić, Rasim & Šefik Sabljica, eds. *Zbirka propisa iz odbrane* (Sarajevo, 1995).

ICTY. *About the ICTY* (The Hague, 2020). Available at: https://www.icty.org/en/about (accessed 27 October 2020).

International Commission on Intervention and State Sovereignty. *The Responsibility to Protect* (Ottawa, 2001).

International Crisis Group. 'Is Dayton Failing?: Bosnia Four Years after the Peace Agreement'. *Balkans Report*, No. 80 (1999).

International Foundation for Electoral Systems. *Bosnia and Herzegovina* (Arlington, 2021).

International Crisis Group. 'Bosnia's Alliance for (Smallish) Change'. *Balkans Report No. 132* (2002).

International Institute of Strategic Studies. *The Military Balance, 1993* (London, 1993).

International Institute of Strategic Studies. *The Military Balance, 1994* (London, 1994).

International Institute of Strategic Studies. *The Military Balance, 1996* (London, 1996).

Ipsos. *Bosnia and Herzegovina: Understanding Perceptions of Violent Extremism and Foreign Influence, March 29, 2018 – April 12, 2018* (Washington, DC, 2018).

Law on Defence of Bosnia and Herzegovina. *Official Gazette of Bosnia and Herzegovina*, Vol. 88, No. 5 (2005).

Law on the Participation of the Members of the AF BiH, Police Officers, Civil Servants and Other Employees in Peacekeeping Operations and Other Activities Abroad. *Official Gazette of BiH*, No. 14 (2005).

Lightburn, David. 'Seeking Security Solutions'. *NATO Review* (1 December 2000).

Lyle, Amaani. 'Maryland Guard Partners with Bosnia and Herzegovina for Peace, Security'. *The Maryland Line* (2013).

Mine Action Review. *Clearing Cluster Munition Remnants 2020* (2020).

Mine Action Review. *Clearing the Mines 2020* (2020).

NATO. *Individual Partnership Action Plans* (Brussels, 2017).

NATO. 'Joint Press Conference with NATO Secretary General Jens Stoltenberg and the Chairman of the Tri-Presidency of Bosnia and Herzegovina, Mladen Ivanić'. *Speeches & Transcripts* (2 February 2017).

NATO. *Partnership for Peace Planning and Review Process* (Brussels, 2021).

NATO. *Partnership for Peace Programme* (Brussels, 2021).

NATO. *Partnership Interoperability Initiative* (Brussels, 2021).

NATO. *Resolute Support Mission (RSM): Key Facts and Figures* (2020).

NATO Joint Forces Command Naples. 'JFC Naples Supports Light Infantry Evaluation'. *News* (27 September 2019).

Norwegian People's Aid. *Bosnia and Herzegovina: Mine Action and Disarmament* (NPA, 2020).

OHR. *Chronology/Monthly Tracker 2001* (2001).

OHR. 'High Representative Acts to Ensure that Military in BiH Are under Effective Civilian Control'. *OHR Press Office* (2 April 2003).

OHR. 'High Representative Appoints Defence Reform Commission'. *OHR Press Office* (8 May 2003).

OHR. 'High Representative Comments on Resignation of Mirko Sarovic from BiH Presidency'. *OHR Press Office* (2 April 2003).

OHR. 'High Representative Extends DRC Mandate'. *OHR Press Office* (31 December 2004).

OHR. 'High Representative Outlines Required Action Following "Orao" Scandal'. *OHR Press Office* (28 October 2002).

OHR. 'High Representative Welcomes NATO Ministers' Positive Response to BiH'. *OHR Press Office* (4 December 2003).

OHR. 'OHR BiH Media Round-up'. *OHR Press Office* (28 October 2002).

OHR. 'SDR Ney Congratulates DRC on Achievements'. *OHR Press Office* (16 December 2005).

OHR. 'The Eyes of Europe and the World Are on BiH'. *OHR Press Office* (24 September 2003).

OHR. 'The Mandate of the OHR'. *OHR Press Office* (16 February 2012).

OHR, Department for Legal Affairs. *Constitution of Republika Srpska* (Official Gazette of RS, 2000).

Oružane snage Bosne i Hercegovine Public Affairs Office. *Brochure of the Ministry of Defense and the Armed Forces of Bosnia and Herzegovina* (Sarajevo, 2011).

Phillips, Cody. *Bosnia-Herzegovina: The U.S. Army's Role in Peace Enforcement Operations 1995-2004* (Pub 70-97-1) (US Army Center of Military History, 2005).

PIC. *PIC Declaration* (PIC Main Meeting, Madrid, 16 December 1998). Military Issues Annex.

PIC. *PIC Declaration* (PIC Main Meeting, Brussels, 24 May 2000). Military Issues Annex.

Presiding Judge Almiro Rodrigues. 'Radislav Krstic Becomes the First Person to be Convicted of Genocide at the ICTY and Is Sentenced to 46 Years Imprisonment'. *ICTY Press Release* (ICTY, 2001).

Prosecutor vs. Halilović, Sefer. 'Indictment'. *IT-01-48-I* (ICTY, 2001).

Prosecutor vs. Milošević, Slobodan. 'David Owen, Testimony before the Court'. *IT-02-54* (ICTY, 2003).

Prosecutor vs. Milošević, Slobodan. 'Mustafa Candić, Testimony before the Court'. *IT-02-54* (ICTY, 2002).

Prosector vs. Milošević, Slobodan. 'Vojslav Šešelj, Testimony before the Court'. *IT-02-54* (ICTY, 2005).

Prosecutor vs. Mladić, Ratko. 'Amended Indictment'. *IT-95-5/18-I* (ICTY, 2002).

Prosecutor vs. Mladić, Ratko. 'Fourth Amended Indictment'. *IT-09-92-PT* (ICTY, 2011).

Prosecutor vs. Prlić, Jadranko, et al. 'Indictment'. *IT-04-74* (ICTY, 2009).

Prosecutor vs. Tadić, Duško. 'James Gow, Testimony before the Court'. *IT-94-1-T* (ICTY, 1996).

Prosecutor vs. Tadić, Duško. 'Opinion and Judgment'. *IT-94-1-T* (ICTY, 1997).

Prosecutor vs. Tolimir, Zdravko, et al. 'Second Consolidated Amended Indictment'. *IT-05-88-PT* (ICTY, 2005).

*Prva linija*, No. 20 (January 1995).

*Prva linija*, No. 25 (June 1995).

*Prva linija*, No. 41 (April 1996).

*Prva linija*, No. 42 (May 1996).

*Prva linija*, No. 48 (February 1997).

*Prva linija*, No. 49 (March 1997).

*Prva linija*, No. 50 (April 1997).

*Prva linija*, No. 58 (January 1998).

*Prva linija*, No. 59 (February 1998).

*Prva linija*, No. 108 (June 2003).

PSOTC. *History* (Sarajevo, 2021).

Rauschenberg, Major Kurt. 'Bosnia and Herzegovina Armed Forces Celebrate Armed Forces Day, Marking 13 Years of Unified Military'. *U.S. Army News* (1 December 2018).

Rauschenberg, Major Kurt. 'Maryland Guard Celebrates Unity with Bosnia-Herzegovina'. *National Guard State Partnership Program News* (3 December 2018).

Robertson, NATO Secretary General Lord George. *Joint Press Conference* (Sarajevo, 13 July 2001).

Roosevelt, Franklin. *Executive Order 8802* (25 June 1941).

Scher, Major Adam. 'The Collapse of the Iraqi Army's Will to Fight: A Lack of Motivation, Training, or Force Generation'. *Military Review* (2016).

Soriano, Eva Galindo. 'Bosnia and Herzegovina Is Looking for More "Warrior-Diplomats"'. *OSCE Stories* (27 April 2012).

*Srpska vojska*, No. 16 (January 1994).

*Srpska vojska*, No. 26 (January 1995).

*Srpska vojska*, No. 30 (June 1995).

*Srpska vojska*, No. 34 (December 1995).

*Srpska vojska*, No. 38 (June 1996).

*Srpska vojska*, No. 43 (May 1997).

*Srpska vojska*, No. 50 (May 1998).

Stockholm International Peace Research Institute. *Transfers of Major Conventional Weapons: Sorted by Supplier. Deals with Deliveries or Orders Made for Year Range 1996 to 2015* (Stockholm, 2016).

Truman, Harry. *Executive Order 9981* (26 July 1948).

UN Peacekeeping. *MONUSCO Fact Sheet* (New York, 2021).

UN Peacekeeping. *United Nations Mission in Bosnia and Herzegovina: Background* (New York, 2003).

UN Peacekeeping. *United Nations Multidimensional Integrated Stabilization Mission in Mali: Personnel* (New York, 2021).

UN Peacekeeping. *Women in Peacekeeping* (New York, 2020).

United Nations Secretary-General Kofi Annan. *Report of the Secretary-General on the United Nations Mission in Bosnia and Herzegovina: S/2002/1314* (New York, 2002).

UN Security Council. *Resolution 713* (September 1991).

UN Security Council. *Resolution 757* (May 1992).

UN Security Council. *Resolution 1325* (New York, 2000).

US Department of Defense. *Bosnia Country Handbook: Peace Implementation Force* (Washington, DC, 1995).

US Department of Defense. 'Defense Official Welcomes Bosnia-Herzegovina's President to Pentagon'. *News* (26 November 2019).

US Embassy in Bosnia and Herzegovina. 'Remarks at UH 2-LOA Signing Ceremony'. *News & Events* (13 December 2019).

US Embassy in Bosnia and Herzegovina. 'Soldiers of the Armed Forces of BiH Receive Awards and Recognition'. *News & Events* (2015).

US European Command. 'U.S. Air Force Partners with Armed Forces in Bosnia and Herzegovina for Air-Ground Integration Bilateral Exercise'. *News* (20 November 2020).

US National Guard. *State Partnership Program* (US National Guard, 2021).

United States Institute of Peace. *Washington Agreement* (1 March 1994).

United States Government Accountability Office. *Bosnia: Crime and Corruption Threaten Successful Implementation of the Dayton Peace Agreement* (Washington, DC, 2000).

US Government Accountability Office. *State Partnership Program: Improved Oversight, Guidance, and Training Needed for National Guard's Efforts with Foreign Partners (GAO-12-548)* (Washington, DC, 2012).

United States Government Publishing Office. *Executive Order 13304 – Termination of Emergencies with Respect to Yugoslavia and Modification of Executive Order 13219 of June 26, 2001* (29 May 2003).

Williams, Paul. 'Promise Them Anything'. *Weekly Standard* (18 December 1995).

World Bank. *Technical Annex to Bosnia and Herzegovina for an Emergency Demobilization and Reintegration Project* (Washington, 1996).

## Interviews with the author

Ashdown, Paddy (22 March 2016).

Dimitrijević, Bojan (15 October 2017).

Gregorian, Raffi (18 July 2017).

Hadžović, Denis (14 September 2016).

Hebib, Avdo (27 August 2017).

Maxwell, Rohan (20 October 2016).

Maxwell, Rohan (11 February 2021).

Minter, Trevor (10 September 2018).

OSCE Security Team Led by Paul Martin (11 October 2016).

Steubner, Bill (22 July 2017).

Turčalo, Sead (21 October 2016).

## Other interviews

Ganić, Ejup. 'Interview for *The Death of Yugoslavia* by the BBC' (Liddell Hart Centre for Military Archives, 1995).

Halilović, Sefer. 'Interview for *The Death of Yugoslavia* by the BBC' (Liddell Hart Centre for Military Archives, 1995).

Karadžić, Radovan. 'Interview for *The Death of Yugoslavia* by the BBC' (Liddell Hart Centre for Military Archives, 1995).

Komšić, Ivo. 'Interview for *The Death of Yugoslavia* by the BBC' (Liddell Hart Centre for Military Archives, 1993).

Kukanjac, Milutin. 'Interview for *The Death of Yugoslavia* by the BBC' (Liddell Hart Centre for Military Archives, 1994).

Panić, Života. 'Interview for *The Death of Yugoslavia* by the BBC' (Liddell Hart Centre for Military Archives, 1995).

## Publications by participants

Ashdown, Paddy. *A Fortunate Life* (London, 2009).

Ashdown, Paddy. *Swords and Ploughshares: Bringing Peace to the 21st Century* (London, 2007).

Bildt, Carl. *Peace Journey: The Struggle for Peace in Bosnia* (London, 1998).

Dedijer, Vladimir. *Tito Speaks: His Self-Portrait and Struggle with Stalin* (Norwich, 1953).

Delić, Rasim. *Armija Republike Bosne i Herzegovine: Nastanak, razvoj i odbrana zemlje, knjiga prva* (Sarajevo, 2007).

Delić, Rasim. *Armija Republike Bosne i Herzegovine: Nastanak, razvoj I odbrana zemlje, knjiga druga* (Sarajevo, 2007).

Doyle, Colm. *Witness to War Crimes: Memoirs of a Peacekeeper in Bosnia* (Barnsley, 2018).

Divjak, Jovan. 'The First Phase, 1992–1993: Struggle for Survival and Genesis of the Army of Bosnia-Herzegovina'. In Branka Magaš & Ivo Zanić, eds. *The War in Croatia and Bosnia-Herzegovina 1991–1995* (London, 2013).

Domin, Thierry. 'Political Situation in Bosnia and Herzegovina'. *SFOR Informer*, Vol. 126 (14 November 2001).

Drewienkiewicz, Major General (retd) John. 'Budgets as Arms Control – the Bosnian Experience'. *RUSI Journal*, Vol. 148, No. 2 (2003).

Efendić, Hasan. *Ko je branio Bosnu* (Sarajevo, 1998).

Fitzgerald, Sergeant Peter. 'The Armed Forces in Bosnia and Herzegovina'. *SFOR Informer*, Vol. 127 (SFOR, 2001).

Halilović, Sefer. *Lukava strategija* (Sarajevo, 1998).

Holbrooke, Richard. *To End a War* (New York, 1998).

Izetbegović, Alija. *Inescapable Questions: Autobiographical Notes* (Leicester, 2003).

Izetbegović, Alija. 'Speech to the Second Congress of the SDA'. *Dnevni avaz* (September 1997), p. 2.

Jović, Borisav. *Poslednji dani SFRJ: Dnevne zabeleške iz perioda 15. V 1989–8. VII 1992* (Belgrade, 2000).

Lamb, Christopher. 'The Bosnian Train and Equip Programme: A Lesson in Inter-Agency Integration of Hard and Soft Power'. *Institute for National Strategic Studies Strategic Perspectives*, No. 15 (2014).

Ljubičić, Nikola. *Total National Defence – Strategy of Peace* (Belgrade, 1977).

Loyd, Anthony. *My War Gone By, I Miss It So* (London, 2000).

Mamula, Branko. *Small Countries' Defence* (Belgrade, 1988).

Mladenović, Olga, ed. *The Yugoslav Concept of General People's Defense* (Belgrade, 1970).

Murray, Rupert Wolfe, ed. *IFOR on IFOR: NATO Peacekeepers in Bosnia-Herzegovina* (Edinburgh, 1996).

Pandurević, Vinko. *Oslovi doctrine odbrane republike srpske* (Belgrade, 1999).

Pandurević, Vinko. *Srbi u Bosni i Hercegovini: od deklaracije do konstitucije* (Belgrade, 2012).

Praljak, Slobodan. *Development of Political and Military Preparations Regarding the Attacks of ABiH on HVO in Central Bosnia and the Valley of the Neretva River in the Period from 1992–1994: Mostar, ABiH Offensive against HVO 'Neretva 93,' Volunteers from Croatia (HV) in ABiH and HVO, and Other Truths: Facts* (Zagreb, 2014).

Praljak, Slobodan. *Handbook: With Instruction on How to Think (mens rea) and How to Act (actus reas) in Order to Be Declared a Member of the Joint Criminal Enterprise at the*

*International Criminal Tribunal in the Hague, How to Become a Joint Criminal?: Facts* (Zagreb, 2017).

Rose, Michael. *Fighting for Peace: Lessons from Bosnia* (New York, 1999).

Seferović, Mensur, ed. *Armed Forces of the SFRY: On Guard of the Peace and Freedom* (Belgrade, 1977).

Šiber, Stjepan. *Prevare zablude istina: Ratni dnevnik 1992* (Sarajevo, 2000).

Tito, Josip Broz. *The Selected Works of Josip Broz Tito* (New York, 2013).

Vlada Republike Srpske. *Vojska Republike Srpske u odbrambeno-otadžbinskom ratu: Aspekti, organizacija, operacije* (Banja Luka, 2011).

Váchal, Josef. *Malíř na frontě. Soca a Italie 1917–18* (Prague, 1929).

# Newspaper and media articles

Anadolu Agency. 'Opening Doors: Bosnia's Trailblazing Female Brigadier'. *AA World* (10 March 2015).

Antic, Zdenko. 'National Structure of the Yugoslav Army Leadership'. *Radio Free Europe* (1972).

Antic, Zdenko. 'Yugoslav Army Influence to Be Strengthened'. *Radio Free Europe* (1974).

Barber, Tony. 'Breakthrough as Karadžić Steps Down'. *The Independent* (20 July 1996).

Barimac, Edin. 'Zajednička vježba OS BiH i Vojske Srbije po NATO standardima'. *Nezavisne novine* (19 December 2020).

BBC. 'Ashdown Clips Bosnian Serb Wings'. *BBC News* (2 April 2003).

BBC. 'Bosnian Officials Quit over Iraq Sales'. *BBC News* (29 October 2002).

BBC. '"War Criminal" Karadžić Resigns'. *BBC News* (19 July 1996).

Beker, Maja. 'Dodik: Oružane snage nisu snage BiH već strane sile, žali Bože troška'. *N1 BiH* (20 November 2020).

Beta. 'SDS: Dodik prevarom isključio institucije i građane RS iz odlučivanja o ulasku BiH u NATO'. *Danas* (24 December 2019).

Bičakčić, Almir. 'Tegeltija je zakočio MAP'. *Oslobođenje* (2021).

Borger, Julian. '14 Years a Fugitive: The Hunt for Ratko Mladić, the Butcher of Bosnia'. *The Guardian* (21 January 2016).

Borger, Julian. 'Arms Shipment to Bosnian Serbs Stokes EU Fears'. *The Guardian* (13 February 2018).

Borger, Julian. 'Brutal Cog in Serb Machine'. *The Guardian* (17 January 2000).

Byrne, Andrew. 'Bosnian Serb Forces Take Part in Illegal "Statehood Day" Parade'. *Financial Times* (9 January 2017).

Cepina, M. '"Orao" nije kriv'. *Glas srpski* (11 September 2002).

Crosby, Alan. 'Bosnian Serb Leader's Call for Wartime Uniforms Tugs at Bosnia's Nationalist Threads'. *Radio Free Europe* (13 May 2019).

Crosby, Alan & Aida Djugum. '"The Killer Is Still Waiting": Two Decades on, Land Mines Still Wreaking Havoc in Bosnia'. *Radio Free Europe/Radio Liberty* (4 October 2017).

Dakić, G. 'Orao' slomljenih krila'. *Glas srpski* (25 October 2002).

Daly, Emma. 'Bosnian Serbs Fall Out as Knin Is Lost'. *The Independent* (6 August 1995).

Daly, Emma. 'Serbs Keep Answer to Peace Plan a Secret'. *The Independent* (20 July 1994).

Daly, Emma. 'Thousands Flee as Bosnian Rebel Crushed: Muslim Troops Take Control of Bihac Fiefdom Run by "Daddy" Abdic'. *The Independent* (10 August 1994).

Daly, Emma & Andrew Marshall. 'Bihać Fears Massacre'. *The Independent*
(27 November 1994).

'Dan šehida oživio sjećanja na najbolje sinove BiH'. *Klix.ba* (August 2012).

Danas Online. 'Dodik: SZP predložio formiranje obaveštajne službe u OS BiH'. *Danas*
(23 October 2016).

Dizdarević, Zija. 'RS snaži BiH'. *Oslobođenje* (29 October 2002).

Đugum, Aida. 'Zašto se osipaju Oružane snage BiH?' *Radio Slobodna Evropa*
(8 March 2018).

DW Komentar. '(De) militarizacija najuspješnijeg projekta u BiH'. *Deutsche Welle*
(1 December 2012).

Fena. 'Ako vi ne djelujete, djelovaće međunarodna zajednica'. *Oslobođenje*
(26 October 2002).

Fena. 'Ambasada SAD traži istragu o predaji oružja Iraku'. *Oslobođenje*
(10 September 2002).

Fena. 'SFOR pronašao vezu između "Orla" i Iraka'. *Oslobođenje* (27 October 2002).

Fisk, Robert. 'Opposition Demonstrations Turn Beirut into a Violent Sectarian
Battleground'. *The Independent* (24 January 1990).

Gordon, Michael. 'After the War: Preliminaries; US Air Raids in '02 Prepared for War in
Iraq'. *New York Times* (20 July 2003).

H.J.I. 'Oružane snage BiH obilježavaju 15 godina postojanja'. *Dnevni avaz*
(30 November 2020).

Huseinović, Samir. 'Vojna inferiornost BiH u odnosu na susjede'. *Deutsche Welle*
(18 October 2020).

Huseinović, Samir. 'Vojnici iz BiH odlaze u Irak u borbenu misiju'. *Deutsche Welle*
(18 August 2008).

Huseinović, Samir. '„Vojno neutralna' Republika Srpska?' *Deutsche Welle*
(18 October 2017).

Kalamujić, A. 'Država preuzima kontrolu nad kompletnim naoružanjem'. *Oslobođenje*
(26 October 2002).

Karabeg, Omer. 'What Really Happened During the Dobrovoljacka Attack? (Interview
with Jovan Divjak)'. *Radio Free Europe* (8 March 2010).

Kebo, Amra. 'Regional Report: US Sanctions Alarm Bosnians'. *Institute for War & Peace
Reporting* (1 May 2005).

Klix. 'Koliko BiH zaostaje u naoružanju i vojnoj opremi za susjedima: U potpunosti
zavisimo od donacija'. *Klix.ba* (31 August 2019).

Kovačević, Danijel. 'Bosnian Serbs Unveil Monument to Russian War Volunteers'. *Balkan
Insight* (12 April 2017).

Latinović, Đorđe. 'Srbi, NATO i realpolitika'. *Nezavisne novine* (14 May 2019).

Maksimović, Dragan. 'Žandarmerija – osniva li Republika Srpska svoju vojsku?' *Deutsche
Welle* (26 September 2019).

Momić, Darko. 'MUP RS tajno prodao više od 10 hiljada pušaka i pištolja!' *CAPITAL.ba*
(16 April 2018).

N1 BiH. 'Donijet ćemo odluku o članstvu u NATO-u, a Dodik će ponovo u tome
učestvovati'. *N1 BiH* (4 July 2020).

Naegele, Jolyjon. 'Bosnia: Political Stability in Question Amid Scandals, Espionage
Charges'. *Radio Free Europe* (3 April 2003).

Norton-Taylor, Richard. 'Britain and US Step Up Bombing Campaign in Iraq'. *The
Guardian* (4 December 2002).

Numanović, Emir. 'Muslimani – pouzdani vojnici Austro-Ugarske Monarhije'. *Deutsche Welle* (25 June 2014).

N.Z. 'Ostavka mirka Šarovića'. *Glas srpski* (3 April 2003).

Omeragić, Aldijana. 'Bond traži nove smjene dužnosnika RS'. *Oslobođenje* (26 October 2002).

Omeragić, Aldijana. 'Orlovo gnijezdo'. *Oslobođenje* (26 October 2002).

O'Conner, Mike. 'NATO Plans to Disarm Paramilitary Forces in Bosnia'. *New York Times* (9 August 1997).

Onasa. 'Demanti smijenjenog direktora 'Orao' nikada nije prodavao oružjc'. *Oslobođenje* (26 October 2002).

Onasa. 'SFOR ponovo u "Orlovim" sefovima'. *Oslobođenje* (14 October 2002).

Onasa. 'Zavod "Orao" i dalje pod blokadom'. *Oslobođenje* (13 October 2002).

Perlez, Jane. 'Muslim and Croatian Leaders Approve Federation for Bosnia'. *New York Times* (15 August 1996).

Perraudin, Frances. 'Iraqi Army Lacks "Moral Cohesion" to Fight Isis, Says UK Military Chief'. *The Guardian* (25 May 2015).

Politika. 'Hrvati neće u vojsku BiH, Srbi zainteresovaniji od Bošnjaka'. *Politika* (27 July 2020).

Pomfret, John. 'NATO Jets Bomb Serb Airfield'. *Washington Post* (22 November 1994).

Poole, Oliver. 'Inside £50m Nuclear Bunker that Couldn't Save Saddam'. *The Telegraph* (12 January 2006).

Prlenda, Antonio. 'BiH ima 24 sata da izbjegne sankcije'. *Oslobođenje* (25 October 2002).

Prlenda, Antonio. 'Bijelinski "Orao" donosi sankcije za BiH?' *Oslobođenje* (22 October 2002).

Prlenda, Antonio. 'Dvogodišnji let iznad Sadamovog gnijezda'. *Oslobođenje* (8 October 2002).

Raven, S. 'Tužbe zbog lažnih optužbi'. *Glas srpski* (12 September 2002).

RFE/RL Balkan Service. 'Bosnian Parliament Breaks 14-Month Impasse, OKs Government'. *Radio Free Europe/Radio Liberty* (23 December 2019).

Rose, Eleanor. 'Defiant Bosnian Serbs Celebrate Banned "National Day"'. *Balkan Insight* (9 January 2017).

'Running Bosnia: The Viceroy Rules, OK? Not Everyone Thinks So'. *The Economist* (24 July 2003).

Salkić, Jakub. 'Dova za domovinu na bedme Bosne'. *Stav arhiv* (14 August 2019).

Sense. 'Bosna pred najtežom krizom od završetka rata'. *Oslobođenje* (31 October 2002).

Short, Elliot. 'Think the Bosnia Conflict Was a Civil War?' *War Is Boring* (2018).

Stankovic, Slobodan. 'Aleksandar Rankovic – Political Profile of a Yugoslav "Stalinist."' *Radio Free Europe* (1983).

Stankovic, Slobodan. 'Tito Praises Yugoslav Army'. *Radio Free Europe* (1971).

Stankovic, Slobodan. 'What Does the Yugoslav Army Think?' *Radio Free Europe* (1971).

Stankovic, Slobodan. 'Yugoslav Defense Minister Calls the Army the "Backbone of the System"'. *Radio Free Europe* (1983).

Stanojević, Nevena. 'Žandarmerija – Elitna jedinica MUP-a garant bezbjednosti Republike Srpske'. *banjaluka.net* (11 March 2020).

Sudetic, Chuck. 'Bosnia Asking U.N. for Peace Forces'. *New York Times* (28 March 1992).

Sudetic, Chuck. 'Bosnia's Elite Force: Fed, Fit, Muslim'. *New York Times* (16 June 1995).

Švarm, Filip. 'Civilian-Military Games'. *Vreme* (24 April 1995).

Traynor, Ian. 'Bosnia's Arms to Iraq Scandal Claims Top Political Scalp'. *The Guardian* (3 April 2003).

George Frederick Willcoxon. 'Why Do Countries Relapse into War? Here Are Three Good Predictors'. *Washington Post* (29 March 2017).

Williams, Daniel. 'NATO Continues Extensive Bombing Across Bosnia'. *Washington Post* (31 August 1995).

Williams, Vanessa. 'Defense Secretary Carter: Iraq's Forces Showed "no will to fight" Islamic State'. *Washington Post* (24 May 2015).

Whitaker, Raymond. 'Looking for Radovan'. *The Independent* (21 July 2000).

Zelenović, N. 'Ostaju dvije vojske'. *Glas srpski* (21 September 2002).

Živak, V. 'BiH nije prekršila zabranu naoružavanja Iraka!' *Oslobođenje* (15 September 2002).

Živak, V. 'Odgovornost vlasti RS utvrdiće se tek po okončanju istrage!' *Oslobođenje* (28 October 2002).

## Secondary literature

Aitchison, Andy. 'Police Reform in Bosnia and Herzegovina: State, Democracy and International Assistance'. *Policing and Society*, Vol. 17, No. 4 (2007), pp. 321–43.

Allandsson, Marie, Erik Melander, & Lotta Themner. 'Organised Violence, 1989–2016'. *Journal of Peace Research*, Vol. 54, No. 4 (2017), pp. 574–87.

Alexander, Leslie & Walter Rucker, eds. *Encyclopedia of African American History* (Santa Barbara, 2010).

Anderson, Benedict. *Imagined Communities: Reflections on the Origin and Spread of Nationalism* (London, 2016).

Aybet, Gülner. 'NATO Conditionality in Bosnia and Herzegovina: Defense Reform and State-Building.' *Problems of Post-Communism*, Vol. 57, No. 5 (2010) pp. 20–34.

Aybet, Gülner & Florian Bieber. 'From Dayton to Brussels: The Impact of EU and NATO Conditionality on State Building in Bosnia & Hercegovina'. *Europe-Asia Studies*, Vol. 63, No. 10 (2011), pp. 1911–37.

Azar, Edward, ed. *The Emergence of a New Lebanon: Fantasy or Reality?* (Santa Barbara, 1984).

Bajrović, Rauf, Richard Kraemer, & Emir Suljagić. *Bosnia on the Chopping Block: The Potential for Violence and Steps to Prevent It* (Philadelphia, 2018).

Baker, Catherine. *The Yugoslav Wars of the 1990s* (London, 2015).

Balon, Bojana, ed. *The Position of Women in the Armed Forces in the Western Balkans* (UNDP, 2014).

Barak, Oren. 'Commemorating Malikiyya: Political Myth, Multiethnic Identity and the Making of the Lebanese Army'. *History and Memory*, Vol. 13, No. 1 (2001), pp. 60–84.

Barak, Oren. *The Lebanese Army: A National Institution in a Divided Society* (New York, 2009).

Barany, Zoltan. *The Future of NATO Expansion: Four Case Studies* (Cambridge, 2003).

Barany, Zoltan. *The Solider and the Changing State: Building Democratic Armies in Africa, Asia, Europe and the Americas* (Princeton, 2012).

Bassett, Richard. *For God and Kaiser: The Imperial Austrian Army* (New Haven, 2016).

Batinić, Jelena. *Women and Yugoslav Partisans: A History of World War II Resistance* (Cambridge, 2015).

Beamer, Glen. 'Elite Interviews and State Politics Research'. *State Politics and Policy Quarterly*, Vol. 2, No. 1 (2002), pp. 86–96.

Bebler, Anton, ed. *Civil–Military Relations in Post-Communist States: Central and Eastern Europe in Transition* (Santa Barbara, 1997).

Bellamy, Christopher. 'Reflections on the Civil War in Bosnia and Foreign Intervention 1992–98'. *Civil Wars*, Vol. 1, No. 2 (1998), pp. 1–25.

Belloni, Roberto. 'Bosnia: Dayton Is Dead! Long Live Dayton!' *Nationalism and Ethnic Politics*, Vol. 15, No. 3 (2009), pp. 355–75.

Bennett, Christopher. *Bosnia's Paralysed Peace* (London, 2016).

Berg, Louis-Alexandre. 'From Weakness to Strength: The Political Roots of Security Sector Reform in Bosnia and Herzegovina'. *International Peacekeeping*, Vol. 21, No. 2 (2014), pp. 149–64.

Bieber, Florian. 'After Dayton, Dayton? The Evolution of an Unpopular Peace'. *Ethnopolitics*, Vol. 5, No. 1 (2006), pp. 15–31.

Bieber, Florian. 'Bosnia-Herzegovina: Slow Progress towards a Functional State'. *Southeast European and Black Sea Studies*, Vol. 6, No. 1 (2007), pp. 43–64.

Bieber, Florian. 'Building Impossible States? State-Building Strategies and EU Membership in the Western Balkans'. *Europe-Asia Studies*, Vol. 63, No. 10 (2011), pp. 1783–802.

Bieber, Florian. *Post-war Bosnia: Ethnic Structure, Inequality and Governance of the Public Sector* (London, 2006).

Bieber, Florian, Armina Galijaš, & Rory Archer. *Debating the End of Yugoslavia* (London, 2014).

Bjelajac, Mile. *Jugoslovensko iskustvo sa multietničkom armijom 1918–1991* (Belgrade, 1999).

Bjelakovic, Nebojsa & Francesco Strazzari. 'The Sack of Mostar, 1992–1994: The Politico-military Connection'. *European Security*, Vol. 8, No. 2 (1999), pp. 73–102.

Blažanvoić, Jovo. *Generali Vojske Republike Srpske* (Banja Luka, 2005).

Borger, Julian. *The Butcher's Trail: How the Search for Balkan War Criminals Became the Most Successful Manhunt in History* (New York, 2016).

Bose, Sumantra. *Bosnia after Dayton: Nationalist Partition and International Intervention* (Oxford, 2007).

Bose, Sumantra. 'The Bosnian State a Decade after Dayton'. *International Peacekeeping*, Vol. 12, No. 3 (2005), pp. 322–35.

Bowen, Desmond & Jean Bowen. *Heroic Option: The Irish in the British Army* (Barnsley, 2005).

Brockliss, Laurence & David Eastwood, eds. *A Union of Multiple Identities: The British Isles, c.1750 – c.1850* (Manchester, 1997).

Bruneau, Thomas & Scott Tollefson, eds. *Who Guards the Guardians and How: Democratic Civil–Military Relations* (College Station, 2006).

Burg, Steven & Paul Shoup. *The War in Bosnia-Herzegovina: Ethnic Conflict and International Intervention* (New York, 2000).

Busterud, Ingrid Olstad. 'Defense Sector Reform in the Western Balkans – Different Approaches and Different Tools'. *European Security*, Vol. 24, No. 2 (2015), pp. 335–52.

Caddick-Adams, Peter. 'Civil Affairs Operations by IFOR and SFOR in Bosnia, 1995-97'. *International Peacekeeping*, Vol. 5, No. 3 (1998), pp. 142–54.

Call, Charles T. & Vanessa Wyeth, eds. *Building States to Build Peace* (Boulder, 2008).

Calori, Anna. 'Salt and Socialism: A Deconstruction of Tuzla's Political Identity in the Context of the Bosnian Conflict'. *Ethnopolitics Papers*, No. 35 (2015), pp. 1–29.

Carmichael, Cathie. *A Concise History of Bosnia* (Cambridge, 2015).

Casperson, Nina. *Contested Nationalism: Serb Elite Rivalry in Croatia and Bosnia in the 1990s* (New York, 2010).

Caplan, Richard. 'Assessing the Dayton Accord: The Structural Weaknesses of the General Framework Agreement for Peace in Bosnia and Herzegovina'. *Diplomacy & Statecraft*, Vol. 11, No. 2 (2000), pp. 213–32.

Čapo, Hrvoje. 'Former Austro-Hungarian Officers in the Army of the Kingdom of Serbs, Croats and Slovenes/Yugoslavia'. *Review of Croatian History*, Vol. 5, No. 1 (2009), pp. 113–36.

Center for Euro-Atlantic Studies & Center for Free Elections and Democracy. *Serbia and West: This Is US* (Belgrade, 2020).

Central Intelligence Agency, Office of Russian and European Analysis. *Balkan Battlegrounds: A Military History of the Yugoslav Conflict, 1990–1995* (Washington, DC, 2002).

Centre for Security Studies – BiH. *Bosnia and Herzegovina in Peace Missions: Contribution to Maintaining Peace in the World* (Sarajevo, 2018).

Clausewitz, Carl von. *On War*. Trans. J. J. Graham and F. N Maude (Ware, 1997).

Cohen, Lenard & Jasna Dragović-Soso, eds. *State Collapse in South-Eastern Europe: New Perspectives on Yugoslavia's Disintegration* (West Lafayette, 2008).

Conway, Stephen. 'War and National Identity in the Mid-Eighteenth-Century British Isles'. *English Historical Review*, Vol. 116, No. 468 (2001), pp. 863–93.

Cookson, John. *The British Armed Nation, 1793–1815* (Oxford, 1997).

Cox, John. *The History of Serbia* (Greenwood, 2002).

Danopoulos, Constantine & Daniel Zirker, eds. *Civil–Military Relations in the Soviet and Yugoslav Successor States* (Boulder, 1996).

Davis, Diane & Anthony Pereira, eds. *Irregular Armed Forces and Their Role in Politics and State Formation* (Cambridge, 2003).

Deák, István. *Beyond Nationalism: A Social and Political History of the Habsburg Officer Corps, 1848–1918* (Oxford, 1989).

Deakin, William. *The Embattled Mountain* (Oxford, 1971).

Dennis, Peter & Jeffrey Grey, eds. *Raise, Train and Sustain: Delivering Land Combat Power* (Canberra, 2010).

Dimitrovova, Bohdana. 'Bosniak or Muslim? Dilemma of One Nation with Two Names'. *Southeast European Politics*, Vol. 2, No. 2 (2001), pp. 94–108.

Djokić, Dejan. *Elusive Compromise: A History of Interwar Yugoslavia* (New York, 2007).

Djokić, Dejan, ed. *Yugoslavism: Histories of a Failed Idea, 1918–1992* (London, 2003).

Djokić, Dejan & James Ker-Lindsay, eds. *New Perspectives on Yugoslavia: Key Issues and Controversies* (Abingdon, 2010).

Dreisziger, Nándor, ed. *Ethnic Armies: Polyethnic Armed Forces from the Time of the Hapsburgs to the Age of the Superpowers* (Ontario, 1990).

Dudley, Danijela. 'Civil–Military Relations in Bosnia and Herzegovina: State Legitimacy and Defense Institutions'. *Armed Forces & Society*, Vol. 42, No. 1 (2015), pp. 119–44.

Dulić, Tomislav & Roland Kostić. 'Yugoslavs in Arms: Guerrilla Tradition, Total Defence and the Ethnic Security Dilemma'. *Europe-Asia Studies*, Vol. 62, No. 7 (2010), pp. 1051–72.

Dyker, David & Ivan Vejvoda, eds. *Yugoslavia and After: A Study in Fragmentation, Despair and Rebirth* (Harlow, 1996).

Edwards, Timothy. *Defence Reform in Croatia and Serbia-Montenegro* (Oxford, 2003).

Enloe, Cynthia. *Ethnic Soldiers: State Security in a Divided Society* (London, 1980).

Finer, Samuel. *The Man on Horseback: The Role of the Military in Politics* (London, 1962).

Forster, Anthony, Timothy Edmunds, & Andrew Cottey, eds. *The Challenge of Military Reform in Postcommunist Europe: Building Professional Armed Forces* (Basingstoke, 2002).

French, David. *Military Identities: The Regimental System, the British Army, and the British People, c.1870-2000* (Oxford, 2007).

Fukuyama, Francis. *Statebuilding: Governance and World Order in the Twenty-First Century* (London, 2004).

Fukuyama, Francis. 'The Imperative of State-Building'. *Journal of Democracy*, Vol. 15, No. 2 (2004), pp. 17–31.

Galtung, Johan. 'Violence, Peace, and Peace Research'. *Journal of Peace Research*, Vol. 6, No. 3 (1969), pp. 167–91.

Gates, Scott, Håvard Mokleiv Nygård, & Esther Trappeniers. 'Conflict Recurrence'. *PRIO Conflict Trends*, No. 2 (2016).

Gaub, Florence. *Military Integration after Civil Wars: Multiethnic Armies, Identity and Post-Conflict Reconstruction* (London, 2011).

Gaub, Florence. 'Multi-Ethnic Armies in the Aftermath of Civil War: Lessons Learned from Lebanon'. *Defence Studies*, Vol. 7, No. 1 (2007), pp. 5–20.

Gilbert, Andrew. 'Dayton at Twenty: Towards New Politics in Bosnia-Herzegovina'. *Southeast European and Black Sea Studies*, Vol. 15, No. 4 (2015), pp. 605–10.

Glenny, Misha. *The Fall of Yugoslavia* (London, 1996).

Goetze, Catherine & Dejan Guzina. 'Peacebuilding, Statebuilding, Nationbuilding – Turtles All the Way Down?' *Civil Wars*, Vol. 10, No. 4 (2008), pp. 319–47.

Gow, James. *Legitimacy and the Military: The Yugoslav Crisis* (London, 1992).

Gow, James. *The Serbian Project and Its Adversaries* (London, 2003).

Gow, James. *Triumph of the Lack of Will: International Diplomacy and the Yugoslav War* (London, 1997).

Gow, James & Ivan Zverzhanovski. *Security, Democracy and War Crimes: Security Sector Transformation in Serbia* (Basingstoke, 2013).

Gyarmati, Istvan & Theodor Winkler, eds. *Post–Cold War Defense Reform: Lessons Learned in Europe and the United States* (Washington, DC, 2002).

Hadžić, Miroslav. *The Yugoslav People's Agony: The Role of the Yugoslav People's Agony* (Farnham, 2002).

Hall, Richard. *The Balkan Wars, 1912-1913: Prelude to the First World War* (Abingdon, 2000).

Hallenbeck, Ralph. *Military Force as an Instrument of U.S. Foreign Policy: Intervention in Lebanon, August 1982–February 1984* (Santa Barbara, 1991).

Harland, David. 'Never Again: International Intervention in Bosnia and Herzegovina'. *UK Government Stabilisation Unit* (2017).

Hendrickson, Ryan. 'History: Crossing the Rubicon'. *NATO Review* (2005).

Herd, Graeme & Tom Tracey. 'Democratic Civil Military Relations in Bosnia and Herzegovina: A New Paradigm for Protectorates?' *Conflict Studies Research Centre: Balkan Series*, Vol. 5, No. 66 (2005), pp. 549–65.

Herodotus. *The Histories*. Trans. Aubrey De Selincourt (London, 2003).

Herrick, Richard. *The Yugoslav People's Army: Its Military and Political Mission* (Monterey, 1980).

Herspring, Dale & Ivan Volgyes, eds. *Civil–Military Relations in Communist Systems* (Boulder, 1978).

Hoare, Marko Attila. *Genocide and Resistance in Hitler's Bosnia: The Partisans and the Chetniks, 1941–1943* (London, 2006).

Hoare, Marko Attila. *How Bosnia Armed* (London, 2004).

Hoare, Marko Attila. 'The Bosnian War's Forgotten Turning Point: The Bihać Crisis of Autumn 1994'. *Journal of Slavic Military Studies*, Vol. 24, No. 1 (2011), pp. 88–114.

Hoare, Marko Attila. *The History of Bosnia: From the Middle Ages to the Present Day* (London, 2006).

Hoare, Marko Attila. 'Whose Is the Partisan Movement? Serbs, Croats and the Legacy of a Shared Resistance'. *The Journal of Slavic Military Studies*, Vol. 15, No. 4 (2002), pp. 24–41.

Hobsbawm, Eric. *Nations and Nationalism since 1780: Programme, Myth, Reality* (Cambridge, 1992).

Hobsbawm, Eric & Terence Ranger, eds. *The Invention of Tradition* (Cambridge, 2010).

Hoffman, Frank. 'Hybrid Warfare and Challenges'. *Small Wars Journal*, Vol. 52, No. 1 (2009), pp. 34–9.

Holmberg, Arita. 'The Changing Role of NATO: Exploring the Implications for Security Governance and Legitimacy'. *European Security*, Vol. 20, No. 4 (2011), pp. 529–46.

Holsti, Kalevi. *The State, War, and the State of War* (Cambridge, 1996).

Horncastle, James. 'A House of Cards: The Yugoslav Concept of Total National Defence and Its Critical Weakness'. *Macedonian Historical Review*, Vol. 2, No. 1 (2012), pp. 285–302.

Horncastle, James. 'Croatia's Bitter Harvest – Total National Defence's Role in the Croatian War of Independence'. *Small Wars & Insurgencies*, Vol. 26, No. 1 (2015), pp. 744–63.

Horncastle, James. 'Reaping the Whirlwind: Total National Defense's Role in Slovenia's Bid for Secession'. *Journal of Slavic Military Studies*, Vol. 26, No. 3 (2013), pp. 528–50.

Human Rights Watch. 'Civilian Deaths in the NATO Air Campaign'. *Human Rights Watch Report*, Vol. 12, No. 1 (2000).

Huntington, Samuel. *Political Order in Changing Societies* (Yale, 1968).

Huntington, Samuel. *The Soldier and the Changing State* (Oxford, 1970).

Hutečka, Jiří. *Men under Fire: Motivation, Morale, and Masculinity among Czech Soldiers in the Great War, 1914–1918* (Oxford, 2019).

Innes, Michael. *Bosnian Security after Dayton: New Perspectives* (London, 2006).

Irwin, Lieutenant General Sir Alistair. 'What Is Best in the Regimental System?' *The RUSI Journal*, Vol. 149, No. 5 (2008), pp. 32–6.

Ivanovic, Alexandra. 'Why the United Nations Needs More Female Peacekeepers'. United Nations University Publications (2014).

Jelavich, Charles & Barbara Jelavich. *The Establishment of the Balkan National States, 1804–1920* (Seattle, 1993).

Johnson, A. Ross. *Total National Defence in Yugoslavia* (Santa Monica, 1971).

Jones, Chris. 'François Mitterrand's Visit to Sarajevo, 28 June 1992'. *Diplomacy & Statecraft*, Vol. 28, No. 2 (2017), pp. 296–319.

Juvenal. *Thirteen Satires of Juvenal, Volume 1*. Trans. John Mayor (Cambridge, 2010).

Karsten, Peter. 'Irish Soldiers in the British Army, 1792–1922: Suborned or Subordinate'. *Journal of Social History*, Vol. 17, No. 1 (1993), pp. 31–64.

Kartsonaki, Argyro. 'Twenty Years after Dayton: Bosnia-Herzegovina (Still) Stable and Explosive'. *Civil Wars*, Vol. 18, No. 4 (2017), pp. 488–516.

Kennedy, Catriona & Matthew McCormack, eds. *Soldiering in Britain and Ireland, 1750–1850* (Basingstoke, 2013).

Keränen, Outi. 'International Statebuilding as Contentious Politics: The Case of Post Conflict Bosnia and Herzegovina'. *Journal of Nationalism and Ethnicity*, Vol. 31, No. 3 (2013), pp. 354–70.

Keränen, Outi. *The Contentious Politics of Statebuilding: Strategies and Dynamics* (London, 2017).

Kerr, Rachel. 'The Road from Dayton to Brussels? The International Criminal Tribunal for the Former Yugoslavia and the Politics of War Crimes in Bosnia'. *European Security*, Vol. 14, No. 3 (2005), pp. 319–37.

Kleinfeld, Gerald & Lewis Tambs. *Hitler's Spanish Legion: The Blue Division in Russia in WWII* (Mechanicsburg, 2014).

Kolkowicz, Roman & Andrzej Korbonski, eds. *Soldiers, Peasants, and Bureacrats: Civil–Military Relations in Communist and Modernizing Societies* (London, 1982).

Kolstø, Pål & Davor Paukovic. 'The Short and Brutish Life of Republika Srpska Krajina: Failure of a De Facto State'. *Ethnopolitics*, Vol. 13, No. 4 (2014), pp. 309–27.

Koonings, Kees &, Dirk Krujt, eds. *Political Armies: The Military and Nation Building in the Age of Democracy* (London, 2002).

Krebs, Ronald. 'A School for the Nation? How Military Service Does Not Build Nations, and How It Might'. *International Security*, Vol. 28, No. 4 (2004), pp. 85–124.

Krebs, Ronald. 'One Nation under Arms? Military Participation Policy and the Politics of Identity'. *Security Studies*, Vol. 14, No. 3 (2005), pp. 529–64.

Krebs, Ronald & Roy Licklider. 'United They Fall: Why the International Community Should Not Promote Military Integration after Civil War'. *International Security*, Vol. 40, No. 3 (2015), pp. 93–138.

Krišto, Jure. 'Deconstructing a Myth: Franjo Tuđman and Bosnia and Herzegovina'. *Review of Croatian History*, Vol. 6, No. 1 (2011), pp. 37–66.

Lane, Ann. *Yugoslavia: When Ideas Collide* (London, 2004).

Lasswell, Harold. 'The Garrison State'. *American Journal of Sociology*, Vol. 46, No. 4 (1941), pp. 455–68.

Leoussi, Athena & Steven Grosby, eds. *Nationalism and Ethnosymbolism: History, Culture and Ethnicity in the Formation of Nations* (Edinburgh, 2006).

Licklider, Roy, ed. *New Armies from Old: Merging Competing Military Forces after Civil Wars* (Washington, DC, 2014).

Ljiphart, Arend. 'Constitutional Design for Divided Societies'. *Journal of Democracy*, Vol. 15, No. 2 (2004), pp. 96–109.

Lovrenović, Ivan. *Bosnia: A Cultural History* (London, 2001).

Lucas, James. *Fighting Troops of the Austro-Hungarian Army, 1868–1914* (Cheltenham, 1987).

Lucander, David. *Winning the War for Democracy: The March on Washington Movement, 1941-1946* (Chicago, 2014).

Lurås, Helge. 'Democratic Oversight in Fragile States: The Case of Intelligence Reform in Bosnia and Herzegovina'. *Intelligence & National Security*, Vol. 29, No. 4 (2014), pp. 600–18.

Luthar, Breda & Maruša Pušnik, eds. *Remembering Utopia: The Culture of Everyday Life in Socialist Yugoslavia* (Washington, DC, 2010).

Machiavelli, Niccolo. *The Art of War*. Trans. P. Bondanella and M. Musa (London, 1995).

Maktabi, Rania. 'The Lebanese Census of 1932 Revisited. Who Are the Lebanese?' *British Journal of Middle Eastern Studies*, Vol. 26, No. 2 (1999), pp. 219–41.

Malcom, Noel. *Bosnia: A Short History* (London, 1996).

Malešević, Siniša. 'The Mirage of Balkan Piedmont: State Formation and Serbian Nationalisms in the Nineteenth and Early Twentieth Centuries'. *Nations and Nationalism*, Vol. 23, No. 1 (2017), pp. 129–50.

Mallinson, Allan. *The Making of the British Army: From the English Civil War to the War on Terror* (London, 2009).

Marvin, Carolyn & David Ingle. 'Blood Sacrifice and the Nation: Revisiting Civil Religion'. *Journal of the American Academy of Religion*, Vol. 64, No. 4 (1996), pp. 767–80.

Matthew, Christopher Anthony. *On the Wings of Eagles: The Reforms of Gaius Marius and the Creation of Rome's First Professional Soldiers* (Newcastle, 2010).

Maxwell, Rohan & John Andreas Olsen. *Destination NATO: Defence Reform in Bosnia-Herzegovina, 2003–13* (London, 2013).

Meuhlmann, Thomas. 'International Policing in Bosnia and Herzegovina. The Issue of Behavioural Reforms Lagging behind Structural Reforms, Including the Issue of Reengaging the Political Elite in a New System'. *European Security*, Vol. 16, No. 3 (2007), pp. 375–96.

Meuhlmann, Thomas. 'Police Restructuring in Bosnia-Herzegovina: Problems of Internationally-led Security Sector Reform'. *Journal of Intervention and Statebuilding*, Vol. 2, No. 1 (2008), pp. 1–22.

Michas, Takis. *Unholy Alliance: Greece and Milošević's Serbia* (College Station, 2002).

Milivojević, Marko, John Allcock, & Pierre Maurer. *Yugoslavia's Security Dilemmas: Armed Forces, National Defence and Foreign Policy* (Braford, 1988).

Miller, Lohr. 'Politics, the Nationality Problem, and the Habsburg Army, 1848–1914 (Volumes I and II)'. *LSU Historical Dissertations and Theses*, No. 5336 (1992).

Mills, Richard. *The Politics of Football in Yugoslavia: Sport, Nationalism, and the State* (London, 2018).

Morrison, Kenneth & Elizabeth Roberts. *The Sandžak: A History* (London, 2013).

Morrison, Kenneth. *Sarajevo's Holiday Inn on the Frontline of Politics and War* (London, 2018).

Morton, Matthew. 'Three Hearts in the Chest of One State: The Armed Forces of Bosnia and Herzegovina'. *Journal of Slavic Military Studies*, Vol. 25, No. 4 (2012), pp. 512–32.

Mulaj, Klejda. *Politics of Ethnic Cleansing: Nation-State Building and Provision of In/Security in Twentieth Century Balkans* (Lexington, 2010).

Murphey, Rhoads. *Ottoman Warfare, 1500-1700* (New Brunswick, 1999).

Murray, Archibald. *History of the Scottish Regiments of the British Army* (Glasgow, 1862).

Neumayer, Christoph & Erwin Schmidl, eds. *The Emperor's Bosniaks: The Bosnian-Herzegovinian Troops in the k.u.k. Army, History and Uniforms from 1878 to 1918* (Vienna, 2008).

Newman, John Paul. *Yugoslavia in the Shadow of War: Veterans and the Limits of State Building, 1903–1945* (Cambridge, 2015).

Niebuhr, Robert. 'Enlarging Yugoslavia: Tito's Quest for Expansion, 1945–1948'. *European History Quarterly*, Vol. 47, No. 2 (2017), pp. 284–310.

Nohlen, Dieter & Philip Stöver. *Elections in Europe: A Data Handbook* (Sinzheim, 2010).

Nordlinger, Eric. *Soldiers in Politics: Military Coups and Governments* (Upper Saddle River, 1977).

Ognjenović, Gorana & Jasna Jozelić, eds. *Titoism, Self-Determination, Nationalism, Cultural Memory: Volume Two, Tito's Yugoslavia, Stories Untold* (New York, 2016).

Omanić, Ajnija, Mevlida Serdarević, Amer Ovčina, Hajrunisa Omanić, & Jasna Omanić. 'Participation of Women in the 1992–1995 War in Bosnia and Herzegovina'. *Acta med-hist Adriat*, Vol. 8, No. 1 (2010), pp. 135–44.

O'Shea, Brendan. *Bosnia's Forgotten Battlefield: Bihać* (Stroud, 2012).

Ottaway, Marina. 'Rebuilding State Institutions in Collapsed States'. *Development and Change*, Vol. 33, No. 5 (2002), pp. 1001–23.

Pantelić, Ivana. 'Yugoslav Female Partisans in World War II'. *Cahiers balkanique*, Vol. 43, No. 1 (2013), pp. 1–11.

Paris, Roland & Timothy Sisk. *The Dilemmas of Statebuilding: Confronting the Contradictions of Postwar Peace Operations* (London, 2009).

Pavlowitch, Steven. *Hitler's New Disorder: The Second World War in Yugoslavia* (London, 2008).

Pettersson, Thérése & Magnus Öberg. 'Organized Violence, 1989–2019'. *Journal of Peace Research*, Vol. 57, No. 4 (2020), pp. 597–613.

Peled, Alon. *A Question of Loyalty: Military Manpower Policy in Multiethnic States* (New York, 1998).

Perović, Jeronim. 'The Tito–Stalin Split: A Reassessment in Light of New Evidence'. *Journal of Cold War Studies*, Vol. 9, No. 2 (2007), pp. 32–63.

Perry, Charles & Dimitris Keridis. *Defense Reform, Modernization, and Military Cooperation in Southeastern Europe* (Dulles, 2004).

Perry, Valery & Soeren Keil. 'The OSCE Mission in Bosnia and Herzegovina: Testing the Limits of Ownership'. *Nationalities Papers*, Vol. 41, No. 3 (2013), pp. 371–94.

Perry, Valery & Soeren Keil, eds. *State-Building and Democratization in Bosnia and Herzegovina* (Aldershot, 2015).

Pettifer, James & Tom Buchanan, eds. *War in the Balkans: Conflict and Diplomacy Since World War I* (London, 2020).

Prauser, Steffan & Arfon Rees, eds. *The Expulsion of the 'German' Communities from Eastern Europe at the End of the Second World War*. EUI Working Paper HEC (Florence, 2004).

Putnik, Vladana. 'Second World War Monuments in Yugoslavia as Witnesses of the Past and the Future'. *Journal of Tourism and Cultural Change*, Vol. 14, No. 3 (2016), pp. 206–21.

Ramet, Sabrina. *Nationalism and Federalism in Yugoslavia, 1962–1991* (Bloomington, 1992).

Ramet, Sabrina. *The Three Yugoslavias: State-Building and Legitimation, 1918–2004* (Bloomington, 2006).

Ramet, Sabrina. *Thinking about Yugoslavia: Scholarly Debates about the Yugoslav Breakup and the Wars in Bosnia and Kosovo* (Cambridge, 2005).

Redman, Mike. 'Joint ABiH–HVO Operations 1994: A Preliminary Analysis of the Battle of Kupres'. *Journal of Slavic Military Studies*, Vol. 4, No. 16 (2007), pp. 1–11.

Roberts, Adam. *Nations in Arms: The Theory & Practice of Territorial Defence* (London, 1976).

Rothenberg, Gunther E. *The Army of Francis Joseph* (West Lafayette, 1976).

Rothenberg, Gunther E. *The Military Border in Croatia, 1740–1881* (Chicago, 1966).

Ruthner, Clemens, et al., eds. *WechselWirkungen: Austria-Hungary, Bosnia-Herzegovina, and the Western Balkans* (New York, 2015).

Schindler, John. 'Defeating Balkan Insurgency: The Austro-Hungarian Army in Bosnia-Hercegovina, 1878–82'. *Journal of Strategic Studies*, Vol. 27, No. 3 (2004), pp. 528–52.

Schindler, John. *Fall of the Double Eagle: The Battle for Galicia and the Demise of Austria-Hungary* (Nebraska, 2015).

Sebastián, Sofia. 'Statebuilding in Divided Societies: The Reform of Dayton in Bosnia and Herzegovina'. *Journal of Intervention and Statebuilding*, Vol. 4, No. 3 (2010), pp. 323–44.

Seroka, Jim & Vukasin Pavlovic, eds. *The Tragedy of Yugoslavia: The Failure of Democratic Transformation* (New York, 1992).

Sharp, Jane. 'Dayton Report Card'. *International Security*, Vol. 22, No. 3 (1997), pp. 101–37.

Short, Elliot. 'Assessing International Statebuilding Initiative Effectiveness at Preventing Armed Conflict Recurrence: The Cases of Burundi, Chad, Côte d'Ivoire, and Nepal'. The Better Evidence Project at George Mason *University* (2020).

Short, Elliot. *Stopping War: 101 Successful Efforts to Reduce Armed Conflict*. Lesswar.org (2020).

Short, Elliot. 'The Orao Affair: The Key to Military Integration in Post-Dayton Bosnia and Herzegovina'. *Journal of Slavic Military Studies*, Vol. 31, No. 1 (2018), pp. 37–64.

Short, Elliot. 'The Regimental System and the Armed Forces of Bosnia and Herzegovina'. Centre for Security Studies – BiH (2018).

Short, Elliot & Milt Lauenstein. *Peace and Conflict Since 1991: War, Intervention, and Peacebuilding Organizations* (New York, 2020).

Shrader, Charles. *The Muslim–Croat Civil War in Central Bosnia, 1992–1994* (College Station, 2003).

Silber, Laura & Allan Little. *The Death of Yugoslavia* (London, 1996).

Singer, Peter. *Corporate Warriors: The Rise of the Privatised Military Industry* (New York, 2003).

SIPRI. *Military Expenditure by Country as Percentage of Gross Domestic Product, 1988–2019* (Stockholm, 2020).

SIPRI. *Yearbook: Armaments, Disarmament and International Security* (Stockholm, 2020).

Sisk, Timothy. *Statebuilding* (Cambridge, 2013).

Smith, Anthony. *Ethno-symbolism and Nationalism* (London, 2009).

Smith, Anthony. *National Identity* (London, 1991).

Smith, Anthony. *Nationalism: Theory, Ideology, History* (Polity Press, 2010).

Smith, Anthony. 'When Is a Nation?' *Geopolitics*, Vol. 7, No. 2 (2002), pp. 5–32.

Staples, James. 'Defence Reform and PfP in Bosnia and Herzegovina'. *RUSI Journal*, Vol. 148, Vol. 4 (2008), pp. 34–9.

Strachan, Hew. 'Scotland's Military Identity'. *Scottish Historical Review*, Vol. 85, No. 2 (2008), pp. 315–32.

Strand, Håvard, Siri Aas Rustad, Håvard Mokleiv Nygård, & Håvard Hegre. 'Trends in Armed Conflict, 1946–2019'. *PRIO Conflict Trends*, No. 8 (2020).

Szayna, Thomas S., et al. *Conflict Rends and Conflict Drivers: An Empirical Assessment of Historical Conflict Patterns and Future Conflict Projections* (Santa Monica, 2017).

Tafro, Aziz. *Ruski i Grčki plaćenici u ratu u Bosni i Herzegovini* (Sarajevo, 2014).

Themnér, Anders & Thomas Ohlson. 'Legitimate Peace in Post-Civil War States: Towards Attaining the Unattainable'. *Conflict, Security & Development*, Vol. 14, No. 1 (2014), pp. 61–87.

Thompson, Mark. *A Paper House: The Ending of Yugoslavia* (London, 1992).

Tilly, Charles. *Coercion, Capital, and European States, AD 990–1990* (Blackwell, 1992).

Tomasevich, Jozo. *War and Revolution in Yugoslavia: 1941–1945* (Stanford, 2001).

Topić-Pavković, Branka. 'Characteristics of Value Added Tax in Bosnia and Herzegovina'. *Mediterranean Journal of Social Sciences*, Vol. 6, No. 2 (2015), p. 79.

Trošt, Tamara Pavasović. 'A Personality Cult Transformed: The Evolution of Tito's Image in Serbian and Croatian Textbooks, 1974–2010'. *Studies in Ethnicity and Nationalism*, Vol. 14, No. 1 (2014), pp. 146–70.

Tzu, Sun. *The Art of War*. Trans. Lionel Giles (Minneapolis, 2006).

Walter, Barbara. 'Conflict Relapse and the Sustainability of Post-Conflict Peace'. *World Development Report 2011: Background Paper* (2011).

Watson, Alexander. *Ring of Steel: Germany and Austria-Hungary at War, 1914–1918* (London, 2015).

Watson, Fiona. 'Not Peace, but a Big Step Forward'. *House of Commons Library Research Paper 95/102* (October 1995).

Weber, Max. *The Theory of Social and Economic Organisation.* Trans. A. M. Henderson and Talcott Parsons (Oxford, 1947).

Velikonja, Mitja. *Religious Separation and Political Intolerance in Bosnia-Herzegovina* (College Station, 2003).

Vetschera, Heinz. 'Politics and Higher Military Education in Bosnia and Herzegovina: A Missed Opportunity'. *Connections*, Vol. 11, No. 4 (2012), pp. 114–26.

Vulliamy, Ed. *The War Is Dead, Long Live the War* (The Bodley Head, 2012).

# Websites

'Milan Martić's Order to Evacuate Civilians from Areas of 'Republic of Serb Krajina' – Scan. http://icr.icty.org/LegalRef/CMSDocStore/Public/BCS/Exhibit/Indexable/IT-06-90/ACE80815R0000319913.tif (accessed 31 October 2018).

'Online Historical Population Reports'. http://histpop.org/ohpr/servlet/Show?page=Home (accessed 21 February 2018).

'Monthly Records of Personnel Contributions to UN Peacekeeping Operations'. https://peacekeeping.un.org/en/troop-and-police-contributors (accessed 01 February 2021).

# Index

CPSIA information can be obtained
at www.ICGtesting.com
Printed in the USA
LVHW080342220422
716943LV00004B/18

9 781350 190931